Praise f Giants

"Stunning . . . John Stauffer has given us the most insightful portrait of either Lincoln or Douglass in years."

—Richard S. Newman, author of *Freedom's Prophet: Bishop Richard Allen, the AME Church, and the Black Founding Fathers*

"John Stauffer's collective biography of Frederick Douglass and Abraham Lincoln stands apart from other biographies by focusing on how each man continually remade himself . . . [It] dissolves traditional conceptions of these two seminal figures . . . and tells the poignant story of how these preeminent self-made men helped transform the nation."

—Henry Louis Gates Jr., Harvard University, author of *America Behind the Color Line*

"GIANTS moves beyond biography to allow us to recover the inner lives of two utterly uncommon common men."

—Steve Mintz, author of *Moralists and Modernizers: America's Pre-Civil War Reformers*

GIANTS

the parallel lives of
Frederick Douglass & Abraham Lincoln

JOHN STAUFFER

TWELVE

LARGE PRINT

Twelve
Hachette Book Group
237 Park Avenue
New York, NY 10017

Visit our Web site at www.HachetteBookGroup.com.

Twelve is an imprint of Grand Central Publishing.
The Twelve name and logo are trademarks of Hachette Book Group, Inc.

Printed in the United States of America

First Edition: November 2008
10 9 8 7 6 5 4 3 2 1

Library of Congress Cataloging-in-Publication Data
Stauffer, John
    Giants : the parallel lives of Frederick Douglass and Abraham Lincoln / John Stauffer.—1st ed.
        p. cm.
    Includes bibliographical references.
    ISBN-13: 978-0-446-58009-0 (regular ed.)
    ISBN-13: 978-0-446-54122-0 (large print ed.)
    ISBN-10: 0-446-58009-0 (regular ed.)
    ISBN-10: 0-446-54122-2 (large print ed.)
    1. Douglass, Frederick, 1818–1895. 2. African American abolitionists—Biography. 3. Abolitionists—United States—Biography. 4. Lincoln, Abraham, 1809–1865. 5. Presidents—United States—Biography. I. Title.
    E449.D75S73 2008
    920.073—dc22
    [B]   2008010256

The Large Print edition published in accord with the standards of the N.A.V.H.

For Deb and Erik

Contents

I like to believe that for Lincoln, ... it was a matter of maintaining within himself the balance between two contradictory ideas— that we must talk and reach for common understandings, precisely because all of us are imperfect and can never act with the certainty that God is on our side; and yet at times we must act nonetheless, as if we are certain, protected from error only by providence.

The best I can do in the face of our history is remind myself that it has not always been the pragmatist, the voice of reason, or the force of compromise, that has created the conditions for liberty. The hard, cold facts remind me that it was ... men like Frederick Douglass who recognized that power would concede nothing without a fight.

—Barack Obama, *The Audacity of Hope: Thoughts on Reclaiming the American Dream* (2006)

Preface

FREDERICK DOUGLASS AND ABRAHAM LINCOLN are the two preeminent self-made men in American history. Lincoln was born dirt poor, had less than one year of formal schooling, and became one of the nation's greatest presidents. Douglass spent the first twenty years of his life as a slave, had no formal schooling, and became the most famous black man in the Western world and one of the nation's greatest writers.

In ways I never could have imagined before starting this project, they also led strikingly parallel lives. They learned to read and remake themselves from the same core set of books: the Bible; Shakespeare; Lord Byron; Robert Burns; *Aesop's Fables*; and *The Columbian Orator*, a popular anthology of speeches for boys.[1] They avoided tobacco and alcohol at a time when people regularly chewed and drank on the job.

They became dazzling orators when public speaking was one of the few forms of entertainment, equivalent to professional sports or popular music today. And they were strapping men, at least a half foot taller on average than their peers, when physical prowess could determine success or failure, even life or death.[2]

In explaining their destiny, Douglass and Lincoln both quoted the same line from Shakespeare's *Hamlet*: "There's a divinity that shapes our ends, / Rough-hew them how we will."[3] They exemplified the hope of America by pursuing their inalienable rights and continually remaking themselves. And they delved into the past to forge their way forward. They were reformers who believed that history is the activist's muse.[4]

In the process they muddied the racial divide, by turns becoming enemies and friends. More than once Douglass called Lincoln a representative racist and the greatest obstacle to freedom in America. He brilliantly exposed Lincoln's limitations as a champion of freedom, while Lincoln spent most of his life hoping to rid the nation of blacks (and slavery).

They were also pragmatists, able to put aside their vast differences and come together as friends. In 1860 Douglass helped elect Lincoln as president. At a time when most whites would not let a black man cross their threshold, Lincoln met Douglass three times at the White House. Their friendship was chiefly utilitarian: Lincoln needed Douglass to help him destroy the Confederacy; Douglass knew that Lincoln could help him end slavery. But they also genuinely liked and admired each other.

In placing their lives side by side, reflecting the one off the other, we gain a fuller picture of each man's career and character, and a better understanding of how friends, mentors, lovers, and rivals shaped them. We also acquire a richer sense of the nature of personal transformation and its limitations. Then too, relying primarily on their words and actions offers an on-the-ground perspective of how racial difference shaped the texture of their lives and times.

Rich ironies complicate our preconceived ideas about these men and self-made men generally. Douglass and Lincoln are among America's great intellectuals, yet both grew up in vicious worlds and referred to a fight as a turning point in their careers. They were wordsmiths who never learned a foreign language. Instead they evolved from speaking in dialect (almost a foreign tongue) to polite English. While most people today think of Lincoln as one of the nation's greatest orators, at the time Douglass was considered the art's exemplar. Both men early on recognized that public speaking could matter more than pedigree or connections as an entrée into public life. They overcame despair with the help of humor. And they married up, the women in their lives being partly responsible for their success.

Douglass and Lincoln championed the concept of self-made men even before the term was invented in 1832.[5] As they remade themselves they urged others to follow their lead. They cut people off after outgrowing them but reconnected when their paths again converged. For them, there was nothing static about friendship or the self.

One of Douglass's signature speeches was called "Self-Made Men," which he delivered over fifty times. He revised it as he evolved, much as he wrote three autobiographies. The heart of the speech described how men and women could better their condition through hard work and education. Lincoln too believed in these templates as the primary means to self-improvement. But the ultimate goal of such transformation was to improve society rather than to get rich. In remaking the self, you reformed society.[6]

The very existence of slavery, whether the "wage slavery" of poor whites or black chattel slavery, precluded the possibility of self-making. Being "fatally fixed for life" constituted a national tragedy, both men believed.[7] Long before he befriended Douglass, Lincoln included blacks in his dream of self-making: "I want every man to have the chance—and I believe a black man is entitled to it—in which he can better his condition."[8] But Lincoln also believed that blacks would need to leave the country in order to uplift themselves. Douglass helped him to alter this view.

Ultimately, Douglass and Lincoln understood that self-making was antithetical to racism. This was because the idea of "whiteness" (white skin) as a sign of superiority and justification for oppressing blacks *depended* on believing that the self was fixed and unchanging. Douglass and Lincoln moved beyond the traditional idea of "character" as fixed and based primarily on heredity and social status, and instead saw the self in a state of continual flux. Douglass captured the importance of such evolution in a eulogy of Lincoln: "the higher we go up in the gradations of humanity and moral greatness, the further we get from prejudices."[9] Stasis led to narrowness and pettiness.

Both men stood at the forefront of a major shift in cultural history, which rejected the status quo of fixed social stations and included blacks and whites, though rarely women, in the national ideals of freedom and equality. But this shift had limits. Douglass and Lincoln came of age during the heyday of self-made men, when rags-to-riches tales were also realities. Yet in the South slaveowning was the surest route to self-making.

Ironically, Douglass and Lincoln came together as friends during a war that transformed American society and in the process greatly restricted the possibility of self-making. The war abolished slavery and nominally gave suffrage to black men. But it also brought a surge of racism, a vicious backlash against blacks as a means of reuniting North and South, and enormous bureaucracies and disparities of wealth that impeded social mobility among the lower classes. In the Gilded Age, the self-made man became a public myth.[10] In this sense, Douglass and Lincoln rose from the dregs to the heights of society in ways scarcely imaginable fifty years later.

This collective biography opens a window on the transformation of American society by the Civil War.[11] The two men's personal conflicts often paralleled the nation's conflicts, their inner turmoil reflecting national turmoil. In fact, the two men's responses to each other provide a roadmap for the changing political landscape. Douglass repeatedly lost faith in Lincoln, only to find it again. His changing perspectives chart not only the political journeys of both men but also the nation's journey toward its Second Revolution. Their intertwined story, of change and self-making, alliances and conflicts, is also the nation's story.[12]

PROLOGUE

---

*Meeting the President
(August 10, 1863)*

FREDERICK DOUGLASS had dreamed of a better homecoming than this. On the muggy night of August 10, 1863, his train rolled into Baltimore, the city he had fled on the same tracks twenty-five years earlier. He had left in disguise on the Underground Railroad; he returned on the Baltimore and Ohio in a first-class sleeper. As his train approached Baltimore's President Street station, he anxiously looked through the ventilator at familiar streets, now empty, and the dark outlines of buildings. He hoped the stop would be brief. Slavery was still legal in Maryland, and he had read of planters kidnapping free blacks and putting them to work as slaves. He was only passing through to Washington, D.C., where Congress had abolished slavery a year earlier.[1] His destination was the White House.

The former slave hoped to meet with President Lincoln. Douglass had no appointment; in fact, his trip had been rather spontaneously planned. But he nevertheless sought to confront Lincoln and air his complaints about the administration's treatment of black soldiers. From the beginning of the war, he had been telling Lincoln in speeches and his newspaper to arm blacks; and for the past six months, after the government finally allowed blacks to serve, he had been recruiting, urging "men of color, to arms" as a way to vanquish the rebels and achieve black freedom and the rights of citizens.[2] He had helped fill the muster rolls of the Massachusetts Fifty-fourth Volunteers, the nation's first black regiment from a free state. Two of his sons had been among the first to enlist, and his older son had been wounded in the desperate charge on Fort Wagner.[3] But black soldiers received about half the pay of whites and were not being promoted for distinguished service. Worse still, black prisoners were being murdered or enslaved by Confederates. As a result of these injustices, Douglass had quit recruiting and decided to go to Washington to plead his case to the president. His "faith in Mr. Lincoln" as "a man of action rather than words" was "now nearly gone," he declared.[4] He hoped to recoup that faith in the man and the nation.

The long trip from Rochester would soon be over. Although Douglass was used to train travel, and while service had improved markedly since his first ride in Baltimore in 1838, it was anything but comfortable. Beds in the sleeper were essentially seats converted into narrow planks, and with the constant sway and bounce of the cars, the effect was "like trying to sleep on the back of a runaway horse." The jarring was so intense that it was virtually impossible to read or write. And throughout the trip, dust, cinders, and coal smoke poured in through the ventilators. As Douglass neared the end of his multiday ride, he was worn out with fatigue, his muscles ached from the confinement, and he was covered with a fine layer of black soot. His dark clothes and complexion helped hide the soot—it was one of the few instances in which having dark skin was an advantage. At the end of the trip, *everyone* looked "blacker than the Ethiop," as one contemporary put it; and there was no place to "bathe yourselves like Christians."[5]

As the train approached Washington, Douglass wondered whether or not he should have come. It was dangerous for a black man to travel alone into slave country. Then too, his sense of urgency and outrage had abated somewhat, for after he had quit recruiting, he learned that Lincoln had

signed an order aimed at preventing Confederates from murdering blacks. It stipulated that "for
every soldier killed in violation of the laws of
war a rebel soldier shall be executed." The order
should have been issued four months earlier, before hundreds of blacks had been murdered. It
"comes late, but it comes."[6]

It was almost dawn when Douglass disembarked at the B&O station on New Jersey Avenue and C Street, a few blocks from the Capitol.[7]
Yet the city was bustling. He could not help
but notice the large numbers of blacks, some
already working, a few sleeping in the open
air. In a little over a year, over eleven thousand
freedmen and -women, called "contraband of
war," had flocked to the city, and another three
thousand were housed nearby at Alexandria.[8]

Douglass looked nothing like these contrabands. Forty-five years old, he cut a striking
figure. Tall (just over six feet) and athletic, he was
formally dressed in a dark overcoat and a high-
collared white shirt. His hair, peppered with gray,
circled his head like a black globe (or afro, though
he combed it back); and above his right eye, a
streak of white shot out from his scalp, tinctur-
ing the symmetry until it diffused into gray at the
back of his head. A goatee, neatly trimmed and
coal black, added gravity to his countenance. Altogether, he looked "majestic in his wrath," as one

Figure 1.
Frederick
Douglass,
around the
time of the
Civil War.
*(Library of
Congress)*

observer noted (see figure 1).⁹ The contrabands, by contrast, were dressed in rags or ill-fitting clothes taken as they fled from their former masters. Some were naked, most were shoeless, and many looked sick. As Douglass knew, smallpox had broken out among the contrabands housed in an army barracks called Duff Green's Row, just east of the Capitol. So had measles, diphtheria, and scarlet and typhoid fever. On some days at Duff Green's, there were "as many as ten deaths reported in twenty-four hours."¹⁰ Compared to Douglass, these contrabands seemed almost a

different order of humanity. But Douglass knew
that most whites would link them with him simply because of his skin color.

Union soldiers were intermixed with the
contrabands on the streets. Some were on duty;
others were obviously wounded, with an arm
or leg missing, but still in uniform; still others
looked sick or hungover. The city was teem-
ing with hospitals, converted from churches,
colleges, and hotels, with larger complexes on
Armory and Judiciary squares. Even the Patent Office had been converted into a hospital.[11]
Between the contrabands and the hospitals, it
seemed like a city of the dead and dying.

Few whites with money were around. After
all, with the heat and humidity, and hundreds
of freed-men and -women flocking there every
day, the city was an incubator of disease. The
moneyed class had left for their summer homes.
"This town is as dismal now as a defaced tomb-
stone," John Hay, Lincoln's secretary, had written a friend three days before Douglass arrived.
"Everyone has gone." Everyone with means, that
is; everyone who had a place to go *to*, which
was a small percentage of Washington's seventy-five thousand people.[12]

As Douglass headed toward the White House,
he had no idea whether or not he would even
be granted an interview, and if so, what kind

of reception he would receive. All he had as an entrée were tenuous connections with a few antislavery congressmen; his fame as an abolitionist, author, and newspaperman; and a letter in his pocket from a radical Boston Brahmin named George Stearns, who had spearheaded Northern recruitment and was well-connected with official Washington. In his letter Stearns "authorized" Douglass to "go to Washington as my agent to transact business connected with the recruiting service." It wasn't much of a letter of introduction, for it was vague (Stearns did not know Lincoln) and patronizing.[13] As an admittance to the White House, Douglass hoped his own name would carry more weight than this Brahmin letter.

His luck suddenly turned when he ran into Samuel Pomeroy, the antislavery senator from Kansas. Born in Massachusetts and educated at Amherst College, Pomeroy was a mixture of New England gentility and Dodge City crudeness. He was "large and portly though not tall," with a big bald head save for a few thin strands that ran over his scalp and down the back, exploding into a ridge of curls around the ears.[14] A full beard almost hid his thin lips, which, when closed, looked like a slight smile or smirk, you couldn't tell which (see figure 2).

Pomeroy had first made a name for himself

Figure 2.
Kansas senator
Samuel C.
Pomeroy.
*(Library of
Congress)*

as the financial agent of the New England Emigrant Aid Company, disbursing over $100,000
to settlers who wanted to keep Kansas safe
from slavery. He had met Douglass in the 1850s
while trying to "save" Kansas from slavery.
They had shared a sense of purpose with John
Brown; but while Brown and Douglass were
close friends, there was no love lost between
Brown and Pomeroy. Brown had little patience
for men who were all talk, and he likened Pomeroy to a strutting rooster.[15]

As a senator, Pomeroy had a Janus-faced reputation. On the one hand, he was known as
a fierce opponent of slavery. Indeed, he had
introduced the bill that became the Confisca-

tion Act of July 17, 1862, which freed slaves who escaped from disloyal masters into Union lines; and he had encouraged Lincoln to issue the Emancipation Proclamation of January 1, 1863, which declared that slaves in the rebel states were "forever free."[16] On the other hand, his name had recently become associated with backroom deals, corruption, and bribery.[17] Whether or not Douglass knew of Pomeroy's unseemly side, he gladly accepted the senator's offer to accompany him on his mission.

They went first to the War Department, near the White House in President's Park, where Douglass called on Secretary of War Edwin Stanton.[18] Stanton had a reputation for conducting "very brisk, not to say brusk" interviews.[19] A brilliantly efficient and thorough bureaucrat, he looked like an eccentric professor and was easily recognizable by his thick muttonchops and long straight beard that dangled past his sternum (see figure 3). He knew of Douglass and granted him a thirty-minute interview, which Douglass considered "a special privilege."[20]

Throughout the meeting, Douglass found Stanton "cold and business-like" but "earnest." He explained to the secretary of war that in recruiting and utilizing blacks, the government needed to understand "that the negro was the victim of two extreme opinions."[21] In

Figure 3.
Secretary of War
Edwin Stanton.
(Library of Congress)

the positive stereotype, blacks outdid whites in their piety, benevolence, and self-sacrifice. They were Uncle Toms, in other words, Christlike, and thus a source of individual and national redemption. In the negative stereotype, blacks were the devil incarnate, and, if armed, would murder white men and rape white women. Both stereotypes tended to view blacks as lacking competence or courage as soldiers.[22]

It was thus unhelpful for Stanton to regard the black man "either as an angel or a demon," Douglass emphasized. "He is a man and should be dealt with purely as such." Black soldiers were just like white soldiers: some were brave, others cowardly; some were "ambitious and aspiring," others apathetic. In raising black troops, the government should thus conform to these "essential facts."[23]

Stanton suddenly interrupted. How do the present conditions of black troops conflict with your views? he asked. "In the unequal pay accorded them," Douglass calmly responded. They have no incentive, and "regulations confine them to the dead level of privates or non-commissioned officers."[24]

Stanton now found himself on the defensive. He explained the various "difficulties and prejudices to be surmounted" before equality could be achieved, and he described his efforts to give blacks the same pay, rations, uniforms, and equipment as whites.[25] Indeed, he claimed that he had personally drafted a congressional bill to this effect, which had passed the House but was defeated in the Senate. Here Stanton lied, for there is no such bill by him on record.[26]

Moreover, Stanton did not tell Douglass that in August 1862, he had authorized General Rufus Saxton in South Carolina to muster up to five thousand black soldiers, who were to "receive *the same pay and rations as*" whites. Apparently he had been nervous about issuing the order, for he attached a note to it, insisting, "This must never see daylight, because it is so much in advance of public opinion." As if heeding his own advice, Stanton had then retreated from his equal pay order, deferring instead to the Militia Act of July 1862, which discriminated against black recruits by paying them as laborers ($7 a month) and not as soldiers ($13 a month). Had he been forthright with Douglass, he would have told him what he had told his white critics: "that some white regiments had complained of being placed on an equality with negroes, and that [equal pay] interfered with recruiting white soldiers." Instead, he pretended that he was doing everything in his power to give blacks the same pay as whites.[27]

Douglass sensed that Stanton was equivocating and that the meeting might turn combative. If he was to accomplish his mission, he decided, he needed to conciliate; and so he told Stanton that in the long run pay was not of primary concern: black soldiers "had a cause quite independent of pay" or rank; they sought freedom for their race and recognition as U.S. citizens.[28]

Now Stanton was the one to conciliate. He truly wanted equal pay for black soldiers, he repeated, and he sought to make "merit the criterion of promotion," regardless of race.

He vowed to promote any black man recommended by his superior officer. Then, as if to show Douglass he was in earnest, he offered to employ him as a commissioned officer. He promised Douglass the position of assistant adjutant to help recruit freedmen in the South.[29]

Stanton assured Douglass he was needed and asked how soon he could be ready. "In two weeks," Douglass replied; and Stanton could send "my commission . . . to me at Rochester."[30]

Stanton then ordered Douglass to "report to General [Lorenzo] Thomas," who was organizing black troops in Vicksburg, Mississippi, and to "cooperate with him in raising said troops."[31] He also ordered him to see John Usher, the secretary of the interior, to obtain a pass that would allow him to travel freely throughout Union lines. With that, Stanton ended the interview.

Douglass was stunned. He had debated scores of accomplished men, but never someone so eminent as Stanton. Not once did Stanton compliment him, but the secretary of war had just asked him to become the first black assistant adjutant of the United States Army![32] It was the highest tribute Stanton could have given him. Gold bars would soon be set against a field of blue on a black man!

Douglass could hardly contain his excitement. Pomeroy, who had sat through the interview, was amazed at his performance. He had nowhere near Douglass's talent for public speaking, and in an age when great orators were analogous to star athletes, he likely took mental notes on how to improve his own rhetorical style.[33]

He led Douglass to Usher's office, still somewhat in awe of this black man. Usher, who had already been notified of Douglass's visit by an aide, saw them immediately and wrote the following note:

> Department of the Interior
> Washington D.C. Augt 10, 1863
>
> To Whom it may concern.
>
> The bearer of this, Frederick Douglass, is known to us as a loyal, free man, and is, hence, entitled to travel, unmolested.
>
> We trust he will be recognized everywhere, as a free man, and a gentleman.
>
> Respectfully,
>
> J. P. Usher, Secy.

Pomeroy, as if feeling left out, added his name to the pass, in rather large script.[34]

As they left the Interior Department they ran into the postmaster general, Montgomery Blair. Douglass explained that he had just received a commission and showed him his pass, and Blair added his name to the paper with a brief addendum: "Pass this bearer, Frederick Douglass, who is known to me to be a free man." Within an hour or so, Douglass had secured endorsements from three of the most powerful men in the nation.

He was now more determined than ever to meet the president, and he hurried to the White House, with Pomeroy puffing and sweating as he tried to keep up. Though it was still early morning, the stairway to Lincoln's office was already filled with patronage-seekers, all of them white men. They did not seem pleased to see a black man among them. Douglass sent up his card and sat down on the stairway.[35] He had just crossed a momentous hurdle; but this next one was on an altogether different scale. It would probably be a very long wait.

Lincoln left the White House during these hot August nights to spend evenings at the Soldiers' Home, an asylum for veterans in the wooded hills north of Boundary Street. Though only a few miles away, it offered a brief respite from the stench and sweat of the city and the never-ending lines of callers, some of whom waited through the night. He returned most mornings amid a company of cavalry, their "sabres drawn and held upright over their shoulders."[36]

Walt Whitman, who worked as a freelance nurse and lived on the route to the Soldiers' Home, watched this presidential procession "almost daily." To Whitman, Lincoln did not look presidential: dressed in a "plain black" coat, "somewhat rusty and dusty," and a "black stiff hat," he looked about "as ordinary in attire" as "the commonest man." Whitman meant it as a compliment, however; after all, he called himself "one of the roughs." Indeed, he seemed half in love with Lincoln, virtually stalking him and recording his sightings in his diary. His description of the president at times suggests infatuation: "a curious little white cloud, the only one in that part of the sky, appear'd like a hovering bird, right over him." Whitman pretended a certain degree of intimacy with Lincoln: "We have got so that we always exchange bows, and very cordial ones." But the poet and president never met.[37]

Lincoln probably didn't even recognize Whitman (though he had read him), and the cordial "bows" were possibly Lincoln's tendency to tilt or lean his head forward.[38] Just a day earlier (August 9), Lincoln had sat for his photograph at Alexander Gardner's studio, and had leaned his head on his hand, an effect that he liked

Figure 4.
Alexander
Gardner
photograph
of Abraham
Lincoln.
*(Lloyd
Ostendorf
Collection)*

very much (see figure 4).[39] This habit may have been the result of exhaustion. He slept only a few hours a night, and the war had worn him down. According to one longtime friend, the former "happy-faced" lawyer now looked "grizzled, his gait more stooping, his countenance sallow," and there was "a sunken, deathly look about the large, cavernous eyes."[40]

The last six weeks had been especially exasperating. Lincoln was still upset over General Meade's inaction after defeating Lee at Gettysburg on July 4. Letting Lee retreat back to Virginia was one of the great blunders of the war.

"He was within your easy grasp, and to have closed upon him would . . . have ended the war. As it is, the war will be prolonged indefinitely," Lincoln wrote in a letter to Meade that he never sent. He had expressed even greater frustration to his son Robert. "If I had gone up there, I could have whipped them myself." And to John Hay he said, "Our army held the war in the hollow of their hand and they would not close it."[41]

The other military success on July 4, Grant's taking of Vicksburg, had been more heartening. It was one of the most important victories of the war, for Grant secured the Mississippi River, cut the South in two, and forced the unconditional surrender of thirty thousand Confederate soldiers. Lincoln told Grant he had done an "almost inestimable service" for the country. And to Hay he said, "Grant is my man and I am his the rest of the war." In the immediate wake of these two victories, Lincoln had proclaimed a national day of Thanksgiving, in which he called on Americans to acknowledge God's role in the recent victories and to pray for those who had suffered and for a swift end to the war.[42]

His Thanksgiving proclamation had become something of a charade, however, for on the very day he issued it (July 15), working-class men in

New York City unleashed their rage against the government's conscription act by rioting and killing blacks. Consisting mostly of Irish Democrats, the mob complained that they were being drafted "to fight for the niggers" who would come north and take their jobs; and as draft officers began drawing names, they went on a four-day rampage, killing or maiming virtually every black they could get their hands on. Some they lynched from lampposts, one was "roasted alive in Madison Square," and they burned the Colored Orphan Asylum to the ground. Over one hundred people (disproportionately black) were killed before Union troops, fresh from Gettysburg, brought order to the city.[43]

Frederick Douglass had summed up the mood—"beat, shoot, hang, stab, kill, burn and destroy the Negro, was the cry of the crowd"— and he had urged government protection for blacks and prosecution against the perpetrators. But Lincoln had felt helpless to do anything about the worst riot in American history. So intense was the working-class opposition to the draft, and to a war that made blacks free, that he had decided not to declare martial law or prosecute the instigators. Such a move would be like touching "a match to a barrel of gunpowder," he said. And so he did nothing: "one rebellion at a time is about as much as we can conveniently handle."[44]

Things were much quieter now. Congress had adjourned, fewer people were badgering him, and he was in better spirits. When he went to Gardner's studio to have his picture taken, he told John Hay that "the rebel power is at last beginning to disintegrate" and "they will break to pieces if we will only stand firm." He was now beginning to focus more intensely on the role of blacks in the war and the nation. The fate of former slaves, he believed, was "the greatest question ever presented to practical statesmanship."[45]

After two and a half years of war, Lincoln finally appreciated the efficacy of blacks in Union blue. A week ago Grant had written to say that "arming the negro" and the Emancipation Proclamation together were "the heaviest blow yet given the Confederacy." Lincoln agreed; with the Mississippi River now opened, "I think at least a hundred thousand [black troops] can, and ought to be rapidly organized along its shores." Black soldiers, he added, represent "a resource which, if vigorously applied now, will soon close the contest" by "weakening the enemy and strengthening us."[46] It was an astonishing statement: blacks can win the war for us and assure their own freedom, he was saying.

Yet despite the great faith he now placed in blacks, Lincoln remained doubtful about their ability to live as free and equal citizens in the United States. For years he had championed colonization as the solution to the problems of slavery and race. Sending blacks to a distant land would free the nation of slavery and racial prejudice. He had obtained control over $600,000 for colonizing blacks, and he knew he could get a lot more money if he needed it. The problem was that most blacks didn't want to leave.[47]

In 1862 he had authorized a contract between the United States and a company called Chiriqui Improvement, in the hopes of sending blacks to the republic of Colombia. He had named Samuel Pomeroy as the principal agent for the plan, in part owing to Pomeroy's success in sending settlers to Kansas. Lincoln had given Pomeroy $25,000 to implement the plan, and by August 1862 Pomeroy had arranged to send up to five hundred blacks to the Isthmus of Chiriqui (now part of Panama).[48]

To promote his scheme Lincoln had invited a group of Washington blacks to the White House to encourage them to leave the United States to become coal miners in Chiriqui. "You and we are different races," he told them. "We have between us a broader difference than exists between almost any other two races. . . . Your race are suffering, in my judgment, the greatest wrong inflicted on any people. But even when you cease to be slaves, you are yet far removed from being placed on an equality with the white race. You are cut off from many of the advantages which the other race enjoy." The very presence of blacks in the country, Lincoln added, was the cause of the war, even though men on both sides "do not care for you one way or the other." He concluded, "It is better for us both to be separated."[49]

The speech had been widely circulated, as intended, but most blacks had scoffed at it. The harshest critique had come from Frederick Douglass, who penned a public rebuttal. In Central and South America "distinct races live peaceably together in the enjoyment of equal rights" without civil wars, he noted. He sneered at the notion that blacks were the cause of the war. A horse thief did not apologize for his theft by blaming the horse. "No, Mr. President, it is not the innocent horse that makes the horse thief, but the cruel and brutal cupidity of those who wish to possess horses, or money and Negroes, by means of theft, robbery, and rebellion." He called Lincoln "a genuine representative of American prejudice" who had few principles of "justice and humanity." And the form was as reprehensible as the content: "Mr. Lincoln in all his writings has manifested a decided awkwardness in the management of the English language."[50]

Lincoln had to abandon the project after the neighboring countries of Honduras, Nicaragua, and Costa Rica protested and threatened to send in troops to prevent settlement. And he never retrieved the $25,000 he had given Pomeroy to execute the project.[51] Nevertheless, he soon latched on to another site: Cow Island, off the southern peninsula of Haiti.[52] (He was so desperate to find a destination for blacks that he ignored the symbolism of shipping them to a place named for beasts of burden.) Some New York financiers offered to ship five hundred blacks to Cow Island and "guarantee" them homes, schools, medical care, and good farmland in return for a fee of $50 per émigré, or $25,000. Although most of his advisers opposed the plan, Lincoln agreed to it, and in mid-April 1863, 453 former slaves set sail on the *Ocean Ranger*.[53]

Everything went wrong. Over the past month, Lincoln had learned that smallpox had broken out on board the ship, and when the émigrés arrived, they were besieged with malarial fevers from the insects. On top of this, the financiers had duped Lincoln and the emigrants: there were no homes, schools, or medical care on the island; the soil was poor; and no approval had been obtained from the Haitian government.[54]

After hearing these reports from Cow Island, Lincoln abandoned the idea of colonization. In mid-July he had told John Eaton, a chaplain who organized freedmen, how the Cow Island émigrés "were suffering intensely from a pest of 'jiggers' from which there seemed to be no escape or protection." Lincoln's distress "was as keen as it was sincere," and Eaton considered it "an illustration of his kindness of heart." Indeed, he was struck by the "spectacle of the President of the United States" being "genuinely affected by the discomfort occasioned a little group of Negroes by an insect no bigger than a pinhead." Lincoln's guilt about the plight of the émigrés seemed almost palpable, and he ordered a transport to bring them home.[55]

Lincoln was trying to imagine a society in which blacks and whites lived together in freedom and equality. He had agreed with Eaton that colonization failed to solve the "Negro question"; and he had asked the chaplain numerous questions about the freedmen who came into Union lines: What was their object? How did they understand freedom? What could they do for themselves?[56] A few days earlier he had written Nathaniel Banks, commander of the Union-occupied area of Louisiana, to express his hopes that the state would "adopt some practical system by which the two races could gradually live themselves out of their *old* relation to each other, and both come out better prepared for the *new*. Education for young blacks should be included in the plan," including training for work under a contract rather than a lash. But aside from that, he was unsure what the new relationship between whites and blacks might look like. He believed that "negroes, like other people, act upon motives. Why should they do any thing for us, if we do nothing for them?"[57]

These issues may have been on Lincoln's mind when his doorman told him that Frederick Douglass had just sent up his card and that he and Samuel Pomeroy were downstairs waiting to see him. Lincoln told the doorkeeper to bring them up.

Douglass had heard of men waiting a week to see the president. Some of the applicants ahead of him in the line looked like they had been waiting that long; others "looked eager" and fresh. He fully expected "to have to wait at least half a day." But within two minutes of sending up his card, a messenger called for him.

As Douglass elbowed his way up the stairs, followed by Pomeroy, he heard someone remark, "Yes, damn it, I knew they would let the nigger through."[58]

When Douglass and Pomeroy entered Lincoln's office, the president was sitting informally in a chair that was much too small for his six-foot-four-inch frame. He was "taking it easy," his feet "in different parts of the room," as Douglass noted. Lincoln rose to greet him, reached out his hand, and said, "Mr. Douglass, I know you; I have read about you. . . . Sit down, I am glad to see you." He put Douglass "quite at ease at once"; but he virtually ignored Pomeroy, who remained silent through much of the meeting.[59]

Lincoln immediately went on the defensive. Knowing that Douglass had frequently criticized him, he sought to clarify his position. Although Lincoln did not bring up black colonization, or Douglass's critique of it, he referred to a speech Douglass had given in Boston in early 1862, widely published, in which Douglass had said that the "most disheartening feature" of the war was not the military disasters but "the tardy, hesitating, and vacillating policy of the President," especially Lincoln's policies on freeing and arming blacks.[60] Lincoln admitted that he had sometimes been slow to act, but he denied vacillating: "when I have once taken a position, I have never retreated from it."[61]

This gave Douglass confidence. He felt that "whoever else might abandon his antislavery policy, President Lincoln would stand firm to his." And he could not think of an instance in which Lincoln had reversed his position.[62]

He thanked the president for issuing the retaliatory order against the rebels who murdered or enslaved captured black soldiers, and then asked why it took him so long to do it.

Because "the country needed talking up to [on] that point," Lincoln replied.[63] Had he issued the order sooner, such was "the state of public popular prejudice that an outcry would have been raised." People would have said, "Ah! We thought it would come to this. White men [are] to be killed for negroes." Lincoln had waited until black soldiers "distinguished themselves for bravery and general good conduct." The thousands of captured blacks murdered and enslaved were thus "necessary" sacrifices, Lincoln said; they prepared the way for his retaliatory order.[64]

When Douglass raised the issue of unequal pay, Lincoln rationalized it by saying that black soldiers offended "popular prejudice," and so for the time being, unequal pay was a "necessary concession" for black enlistment. Moreover, blacks "had larger motives for being soldiers than white men" did, and "they ought to be willing to enter the service upon any condition."[65] Nevertheless, Lincoln assured Douglass that eventually black soldiers would receive the same pay as white soldiers. And he promised to sign any promotion for blacks that Stanton recommended.

Although Douglass was not wholly satisfied with Lincoln's views, he was struck by the president's honesty and sincerity. "I have never seen a more transparent countenance. There was not the slightest shadow of embarrassment after the first moment."[66] And Lincoln did not act superior simply because he was white: "I was never in any way reminded of my humble origin, or of my unpopular color," Douglass noted.[67] Lincoln's apparent lack of racism was remarkable, for he never considered himself an abolitionist or radical. Among Douglass's abolitionist white friends, by contrast, there were often awkward moments, especially during debates, that Douglass attributed to racial differences. Lincoln's eloquence also surprised him: he spoke "with an earnestness and fluency of which I had not suspected of him."[68]

The president seemed to feel genuinely comfortable around Douglass, and it put Douglass at ease. Indeed, at the end of the meeting, Douglass excitedly told Lincoln that Stanton had offered him a commission, and that he "intended to go South and help the recruiting" of freedmen.[69] Then he proudly showed the president his pass. Lincoln read it, turned it sideways, and wrote, "I concur. A. Lincoln. Aug. 10, 1863."[70] In the space of a morning, Douglass had received signatures from the president, two cabinet members, and a senator to travel through Union lines representing the United States military (see figure 5).

Douglass took the next train out of Washington. He didn't want to overstay his welcome and was eager to prepare for the move south. Almost as soon as he got home he received a letter from Stanton instructing him to proceed to Vicksburg and report to General Thomas. Douglass replied on August 14, asking for clarification of his commission and wanting to know what his specific rank, pay, and duties would be.[71]

Two days later he said farewell to the readers of his newspaper. For sixteen years he had devoted himself to his four-page weekly, which became a monthly in 1860.[72] Despite funding problems and an intensive lecture schedule, his paper had become one of the best-known abolitionist organs in the country. It was an emotional parting: "I shall never cease to regard

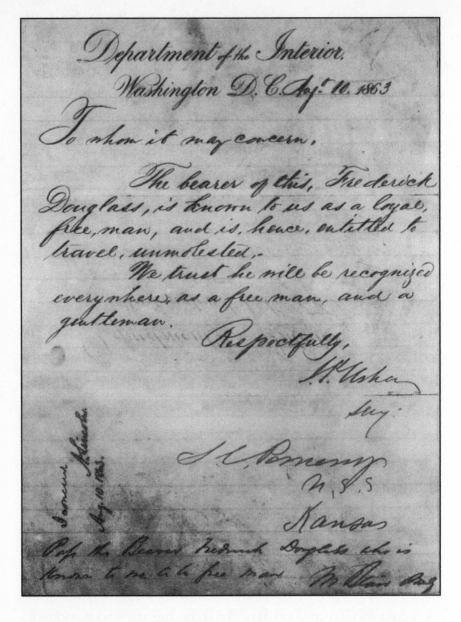

Figure 5. Douglass's safe-conduct pass, signed by President Lincoln, Senator Pomeroy, Secretary of the Interior John P. Usher, and Postmaster General Montgomery Blair. *(Library of Congress)*

these years of editorial toil on my part and of sympathy and support on your part as among the most cheerful and happy of my life," he told his readers in his "Valedictory," which he included as the last page of the August issue. Then he proudly explained why he was discontinuing his paper: "I am going South to assist Adjutant General Thomas in the organization of colored troops, who shall win for the millions in bondage the inestimable blessings of liberty and country."[73]

A few days later Douglass began to worry. Stanton had not responded to his request for information. In a letter to a friend, Douglass said Stanton was keeping him "in the dark on all essential points. He only commands me to go. Like King Lewis [in Shakespeare's *Henry VI*], he thinks a citizen is a person having duties but no rights. I shall obey, however, hoping that all will be well in the end."[74] A few days later he received the hoped-for letter. In terms of duties, Stanton told him "to aid General Thomas in any way that your influence with the colored race can be made available" in the recruiting effort. That was certainly vague. The letter said nothing about his commission or officer rank. And as for pay, Douglass was told that he would continue to receive it from George Stearns, who had been paying him from private donations for his recruitment of Northern blacks.[75] That was odd, for shouldn't his pay come directly from the War Department?

Douglass's commission never came. There was no word from the War Department, no word from the White House. As with so many bureaucracies, the rejection came in the form of silence. And so he decided not to go south, even though Stearns offered him a salary at $100 a month plus expenses, roughly the pay of a first lieutenant.[76] He was thrilled about the prospect, but given the increased danger, he refused to be a pawn of a government that had duped him. He would go only as a commissioned officer of the U.S. Army, not as a private recruiter. "I knew too much of camp life and the value of shoulder straps in the army to go into the service without some visible mark of my rank." Douglass concluded that Stanton had had a change of heart, deciding that "the time had not yet come for a step so radical." Stanton was a man "of an impulsive nature" who "made rash promises which he afterward revoked without regret or apology."[77]

Douglass never blamed Lincoln, however, even though the president knew about the commission and should have expected a letter from Stanton to approve. Indeed, at a December 1863 lecture, Douglass proudly referred to his meeting with Lincoln; but instead of criticizing him for "vacillating" about the commission or committing a lie of omission, he announced that he had "been down there to see the President" and considered the popular prefix to Lincoln's name to be appropriate: "he will go down to posterity, if the country is saved, as 'Honest Abraham.' "[78]

Suddenly, it was as though Douglass remembered what had actually happened to him in the maw of Washington, for in the next breath he said, "We are not to be saved by Abraham Lincoln, but by that power behind the throne"— meaning blacks and abolitionists. The Union as it was could not and should not be saved. "We do not want it. We have outlived the old Union." Douglass had outlived the old Union a long time ago, with its sanctioning of slavery and its horrible racial prejudice; he had long been "ashamed of it."[79]

It is nevertheless striking that Douglass should exonerate Lincoln and recall his meeting with fondness. Despite their considerable differences in strategy and opinion, and a broken promise, Douglass always felt extremely comfortable around Lincoln, more so than around most other white men, including abolitionists. Indeed, Douglass sensed a kindred spirit in Lincoln, and the affection was mutual:

"Mr. Douglass, never come to Washington without calling upon me," Lincoln told him after their August 10, 1863, meeting. He regarded Douglass "as one of the most meritorious men, if not the most meritorious man, in the United States." And Douglass called Lincoln "the king of American self-made men."[80]

Why the mutual affection and respect, despite their vast differences? Their meeting was the first time that an African American and U.S. president had met as near "equals" in the sense that they were cultural ambassadors of their respective races. They could help each other to vanquish slavery and create a new Union. They *wanted* to like and respect each other, and they were also alike in numerous ways. They shared strangely similar backgrounds.

ONE

Privileged Slave and Poor White Trash

The boy was sprung to manhood: in the wilds
Of fiery climes he made himself a home,
And his soul drank their sunbeams.

—LORD BYRON, "The Dream" (1816)

On New Year's Day 1834, a rebellious fifteen-year-old boy walked seven miles to a poor wheat farm in Talbot County on the Eastern Shore of Maryland. As he made his way across a rutted dirt road on a peninsula shaped like a three-taloned claw, he felt weary and despondent. The biting January wind echoed the bleak winter in his soul, and he likened himself to a fish in a net that had been "allowed to play for a time" but was now being "drawn rapidly to the shore, secured at all points."[1]

Frederick was about to begin life as a field-hand, the most common and brutal form of slavery in the United States. He was strong and fit and about six feet tall but knew nothing about fieldwork. He considered himself a city boy and still wore his soft cotton clothes from Baltimore, now thin and torn from overuse, rather than the coarse tow-linen shirt and pants of a fieldhand. As he approached the wheat farm he felt like a green country boy entering "the bewildering scenes" of a city for the first time.²

His initiation into fieldwork was a baptism of blood. On the third day of work his new master, Edward Covey, ordered him to hitch a wagon to a pair of oxen and retrieve a load of wood from the forest. It seemed like a simple enough task, but he had never been around oxen before. They were virtually untamed, and the instructions he was given for controlling them—"*woa*," "*back*," "*gee*," and "*hither*," Buck is the "in ox," Darby the "out ox"—all sounded like Greek to him.³ No sooner had he started when Buck and Darby ran off at full tilt for the woods, trampling over saplings, plunging into the underbrush, severing the wagon from its chassis, and finally coming to a halt against a stout tree. It took him hours to reconnect the wagon and untangle the oxen. Then he filled the wagon with a heavy load to prevent Buck and Darby from running off again and headed back to the farmhouse. But he had no idea how strong oxen were. As he neared the gate they started off again, charging like bulls, demolishing both wagon and gate and almost crushing him.

Frederick tried to explain what had happened, but Mr. Covey was not interested in explanations. He ordered him back into the woods, where Frederick watched as he cut three large shoots from a gum tree, a strong, tacky wood, and then expertly shaved off the bark and knotted the ends. Then he ordered the boy to take off his clothes. When Frederick refused he fell into a rage, rushing at him with the savagery of a wolf. He tore off Frederick's clothes and laid on the switches, one at a time, until he wore them out on the boy's back. "Under his heavy blows, blood flowed freely and wales were left on my back as large as my little finger," Frederick remembered.[4]

It was the cruelest beating of his life. He began to sympathize with the oxen, even though they had prompted the flogging. They were "the poor man's slave," according to a tradition that went back to Aristotle: "they were property, so was I; they were to be broken, so was I," Frederick concluded. "Break and be broken—such is life."[5] He too was a beast of burden and the sport of the slave gods. Little did he know that this baptism of blood would set him on the path to freedom. One day he would rip off his shirt and bare his scarred back to shocked white audiences, revealing the "indisputable proof" that he had experienced the "living hell" of slavery.[6] But today he was just one more slave getting whipped.

Until that moment Frederick had been a privileged slave. His first six years resembled those of a poor white boy; he lived in a log cabin with his grandmother at the edge of a small creek called Tuckahoe (pronounced "took-a-hoe") in Talbot County, where he ran wild, rarely saw whites, and was "freed from all restraint."[7] About the only thing that distinguished him from a poor white child was that he didn't know when his birthday was (February 1818, according to a slave inventory by Frederick's owner).[8]

His first owner, Aaron Anthony, was a Southern version of the self-made man. An orphaned son of an illiterate tenant farmer, Anthony became a ship captain and then chief overseer of the Edward Lloyd family, a Maryland dynasty. Edward Lloyd V, Anthony's employer, was one of the wealthiest men in the country, owning thirteen farms and five hundred slaves spread across ten thousand acres. Anthony had ascended to the master class by the time Frederick was born; he owned two hundred acres and some thirty slaves. On such an estate, planters could afford to let their slave children run wild under the care of an older slave woman until they were old enough to be put to work.[9]

Frederick's first job was as a "domestic,"

where he worked around the Big House and its gardens and stables. It was one of the most coveted positions in the plantation hierarchy. After a few years he received an even better position; he was sent to Baltimore to be the playmate of a white boy, a relative of Anthony's. In Baltimore, he dressed well, ate well, and even learned to read. Until arriving on the wheat farm, he had rarely been whipped, could boast of having had only three owners, all in the same family, and he had never seen a slave auction. This was rare indeed for a Chesapeake slave: it was far more common to be sold like so many bales of cotton into the high-growth markets of Alabama, Mississippi, and Louisiana, where the demand for slaves seemed insatiable.[10]

Even his name had the ring of privilege: Frederick Augustus Washington Bailey.[11] The surname, unusual among slaves, dated back to the eighteenth century, and his two middle names reflected the tradition of great republican leaders.[12] His mother, Harriet Bailey, a proud literate woman, had high hopes for her son, though Frederick barely knew her, for she worked as a fieldhand on a plantation twelve miles away and died when he was about seven.[13] There were numerous rumors that Harriet was part Indian, and Frederick hinted as much in his exotic description of her: "remarkably sedate and dignified," she looked "Hindoo" (an Indian from India), Hindus being thought of at the time as close racial kin of Native Americans.[14] As an adult he was sometimes asked "whether I was not part Indian as well as African and Caucasian?" And in one speech to Native Americans he announced, "I have been known as a Negro, but I wish to be known here and now as Indian."[15]

But aside from this rhetorical gesture, Frederick always publicly identified himself as black. Social customs at the time prevented people from declaring themselves black one day and Native American the next, or from self-identifying as both black and Indian. Race was defined by social custom and considered permanent. Moreover, Indians and blacks tended to distance themselves from each other: most Indians declared that they would die before submitting to bondage, and most blacks assumed that Indians were dying out, unable to live in "civilization." Without explicitly acknowledging any Indian ancestry, Frederick expressed pride in his mother and her genealogy, and he frequently said that most of what he inherited came from her.[16]

He never knew who his father was, but there had been whispers among the slaves that it was Aaron Anthony. Not only had Anthony never whipped him; he had acted "almost fatherly" toward the young boy, "gently leading me by the hand," "patting me on the head, speaking to me in soft caressing tones, and calling me his 'little Indian boy.' "[17] As Frederick knew, Anthony had made advances on slave women and had beaten them when they spurned him.

Such a paternity would help explain Frederick's privileged status. After Anthony died, Frederick became the property of his daughter Lucretia. She died in 1827, and since then he had been owned by Thomas Auld, Lucretia's husband. Significantly, Anthony and Lucretia, possibly his father and half sister, had both treated him with care and affection.[18]

The older, famous Frederick Douglass never admitted that he was a privileged slave. To him the phrase was a virtual contradiction in terms, for it implied that a master could be humane, whereas Douglass sought to convince his readers that slavery was everywhere evil and that even "good masters" were beasts who relied on torture to maintain the system. The closest he came to acknowledging his privileged status was to say that as a slave, "my troubles from the beginning had been less physical than mental."[19] To a strong and fit young man, the horrors of slavery were more in the mind than on the body.

Suddenly, however, Frederick's troubles were very physical indeed, for his privileged status had come to an abrupt halt. Nine months earlier, he had been ordered back to the town of St. Michaels on the clawlike peninsula of the Eastern Shore to live with Thomas Auld. Before that he had spent seven years in Baltimore working for Thomas's brother Hugh Auld and Hugh's wife, Sophia. But the brothers had quarreled and Thomas demanded his slave back. Frederick hated being back on the Eastern Shore. St. Michaels seemed filled with ignorant and vulgar whites who had no ambition, carried a jug or hipflask of rum everywhere they went, and lived in ugly unpainted homes. What a contrast from Baltimore, where he had interacted with people who sought to improve themselves through hard work, sharp dress, and reading! And he loathed living with Thomas Auld, a thin-lipped, white-haired forty-year-old whose "leading characteristics," according to Frederick, were "intense selfishness" and sanctimoniousness. Each morning Auld prayed that God would bless his home with bounty and basket; and then he starved Frederick while food rotted in the meat house.[20]

Thomas Auld thought that city life had ruined Frederick. The "happy slave" he sent to his brother had come back insolent and angry.

Frederick refused to address him as "Master," constantly forgot to follow orders, and dared to look him in the eye and challenge him. Auld had no idea how to discipline Frederick. He had spent most of his career working with whites and did not understand the protocol of slave management.[21] Reluctant to whip Frederick, he decided to rent him out for the year to someone well versed in the "art" of slave discipline.

Frederick's new master, Edward Covey, was legendary as a "nigger breaker."[22] His sadistic trick of ordering him to retrieve wood using untamed oxen was an example of his method. Unlike many of his peers, Covey was a man on the make, his goal being to get rich through his notorious practices. In his late twenties and recently married, he was too poor to own his own farm but he worked hard and made efficient use of rental slaves to cultivate neighbors' wheat crops. He owned one slave, a female, whom he bred: he locked her up each night with a rented slave and she soon gave birth to twins, thus tripling his investment.

Covey had "the cunning of the serpent" and the craftiness of the fox, according to Frederick. Among blacks he was known as "the snake," and he looked the part. A few inches shorter than Frederick, he was thin and wiry, with small green-gray eyes that were set deep into his forehead. Instead of hissing, he spoke from the side of his mouth in a low growl, Frederick said, like a dog "when an attempt is made to take a bone from him."[23] In essence Covey was a master at torturing and terrorizing slaves, and Auld considered him an ideal tenant for his "property": he would receive over $100 in annual rent (close to $7,500 in today's money); and Covey would break Frederick for him.[24]

Initially, Auld's hopes were fulfilled. Every week for six months Frederick was ritually flogged, either with a braided cowskin whip with flared knotted ends and a long handle for greater acceleration, or with a coarse wooden club about the length of a baseball bat but somewhat lighter. Often the beatings were more severe than the first encounter over the oxen. The old wounds did not even have time to heal before Frederick's flesh was ripped up all over again. He worked six days a week from dawn to darkness or longer, depending on the season, and Covey made him feel that he was spying on him, watching from the bushes or behind a tree to make sure that he was not slacking off. "A few months of this discipline tamed me," he said. "Mr. Covey succeeded in breaking me. I was broken in body, soul, and spirit." Sometimes he thought of killing Covey and himself but "was prevented by a combination of hope and fear." He hoped for something better in life and feared dying.[25]

Sunday was his only day of rest. He spent it "in a sort of beast-like stupor, between sleep and wake, under some large tree."[26] Often he was hungover. It was a tradition for masters to give their fieldhands whiskey on Saturday night and during the week off between Christmas and New Year's; and Frederick "loved drink." It was one of his few pleasures, and he consumed more than his share. After working for Covey all week, Saturday night was about the only thing he had to look forward to. The whiskey made him feel "like a president," confident and "independent." One night he drank so much that he passed out near a pigsty. At some point he woke up cold and shivering, "crawled into the sty," and went back to sleep. When the sow and her young returned, they tried to shove him out. He woke up and started yelling "order! order!" as if he were an overseer or president of an unruly meeting. Years later, after he had become a teetotaler, Frederick realized why masters gave their fieldhands liquor: it kept them "in a state of stupidity" during their days off, so that they would not think about freedom, or else would equate it with drunkenness and a hangover. Either way, liquor checked the impulse to run away.[27]

Aside from drinking, his only other solace
was to walk down to the banks of the Chesapeake near Covey's house on a summer's Sunday
and watch the ships sail down the bay toward
all corners of the globe. He was so struck with
the contrast between his scarred body and enslaved condition and these beautiful unmoored
vessels, moving freely across the water like
"swift-winged angels," that he often talked to
the ships, pouring out his "soul's complaint."
"You move merrily before the gentle gale and
I sadly before the bloody whip," he mumbled
to them. They seemed almost ethereal as he
watched them glide by, inspiring prayer: "O
God save me! God deliver me! Let me be free!"
His prayer to the ships was a Job-like lament
and a source of solace and hope. Talking to
them, he vowed to become like them and sail
away: "I *will* run away," he declared; "God helping me, I *will*. It cannot be that I shall live and
die a slave." His declaration briefly cleared his
mind and clarified his future. Yet like so many
prayers, this one seemed fleeting and invisible,
like a tear in the rain; he sometimes wondered
whether anyone heard it, and if so, whether it
would ever be answered.[28]

One day in August 1834 Frederick was threshing wheat with three other men.[29] It was an
assembly-line operation that required everyone

to work in unison: one man spread the wheat evenly over the ground in the treading yard; another man drove a horse over the wheat to crush it and separate it from the stalk; a third man fanned the wheat, sifting it through a large basket to separate the kernels from the chaff; and Frederick's job was to gather up the crushed wheat from the treading yard and bring it to the fan. Covey had promised the men that if they finished before sundown, they could go fishing, which spurred them on.[30]

In midafternoon, with only a few hours left to work, Frederick suddenly felt very sick. It was blisteringly hot, one of the hottest days of the year.[31] He was dizzy, his body trembled uncontrollably, and his head throbbed so badly that he could barely see. He tried to keep working but suddenly collapsed from heatstroke. Forcing himself up, he staggered on for a while but finally fell again and crawled toward some shade near a fence. His sickness brought the whole operation to a halt.

Covey, who had been watching from the comfort of his house, hurried over and asked what the matter was. As Frederick tried to explain, he kicked him savagely and ordered him back to work. Frederick tried to get up but couldn't, and Covey kicked him again, then picked up a heavy slab of hickory and clubbed him in the head. *"If you have got the headache, I'll cure you,"* he snarled.[32] As the blood flowed onto Frederick's face and clothes, Covey left him to his fate and took his place threshing wheat.

Soon Frederick began to feel better. The blows had strangely alleviated the pain in his head, and he resolved to walk the seven miles back to Thomas Auld's home, inform him of Covey's sadism, and request a new master. He hoped that Auld, seeing him so bloodied and battered, would worry about the loss of property value and agree to release him from Covey's charge.

It was dark when the boy arrived at Auld's place. Covey had tried to pursue him, but Frederick kept to the woods to avoid detection. He looked like he had just "escaped from a den of tigers."[33] His hair and shirt were caked with dried blood and new blood trickled down his legs from the briars and thorns. Auld was shocked at the sight of him, and Frederick saw a glimmer of humanity in his owner and hope for himself. As Auld paced the floor, he seemed to be grappling with a deep moral dilemma. Then suddenly he stopped, his mind made up.

"You deserved the flogging," Auld said. "Your sickness was pretense and your dizziness was laziness."[34]

"As sure as I go back to live with Mr. Covey

again, I [will] be killed by him," Frederick responded. Covey will "never forgive my coming to you with a complaint against him." He has "almost crushed my spirit," and if I go back to him, he will "ruin me for future service." My life is "not safe in his hands."[35]

"Nonsense," Auld said. There is "no danger of Mr. Covey killing [you]; he is a good man, industrious and religious." I "would not think of removing" you from Covey's home. "You belong to Mr. Covey for one year, and you *must go back* to him, come what will." Besides, "if you leave Covey now," with the year only "half expired, I should lose your wages for the entire year."[36]

Auld was willing to risk his property for the annual rent on his slave. And he did not want to cancel a contract with a "good man" who was industrious, religious, and a neighbor. He did concede, however, to let Frederick stay the night. He ordered him to "swallow a huge dose of epsom salts"—"about the only medicine ever administered to slaves"—and return to Covey's first thing in the morning.[37]

Despite his exhaustion, Frederick did not sleep that night. He was certain, as certain as night followed day, that Covey would beat him so severely that it would make all the other floggings seem trivial. He felt like a condemned

prisoner facing execution, and he pitied himself and hated the world for his futureless
state: "To be shut up entirely to the past and
present is abhorrent to the human mind," he
concluded; "it is to the soul—whose life and
happiness is unceasing progress—what the
prison is to the body; a blight and mildew, a
hell of horrors."[38] Even while facing the prospect of a life-threatening beating, he seemed
more concerned about his mental anguish
than his physical well-being. He would have
loved nothing more than a jug of whiskey that
night, to silence his soul and stifle his senses.
But there was no hope for the blissful oblivion
of drink: it was Friday night, not Saturday, and
there was no liquor around.

The next morning Covey was waiting for him
with a rope in one hand and a cowskin whip
in the other hand. When Frederick saw him, he
darted into the woods and hid all day in a corn-
field. He tried to pray but couldn't. He thought
of Covey and Auld, both religious men, praying
to the same God that he prayed to. It was hard
to ignore the notion that God was on *their* side.
Their "sham religion" made him doubt "all religion."[39] His body was still caked with blood;
he hadn't slept in almost forty-eight hours; and
aside from the Epsom salts, it had been even
longer since he had eaten anything. He knew

enough not to eat the corn, which was unripe and would cause diarrhea. If he stayed in the woods, he might starve; but if he returned to the farm, he would definitely have his flesh ripped up. He stayed put, wishing he could exchange his humanity "for the brutehood of an ox."[40] When night came he made a bed of leaves and tried to rest.

Then his luck began to change. Sandy Jenkins, a slave who worked on a nearby farm, was on his way to spend the Sabbath with his wife, a free black woman, when he spotted Frederick lying in the leaves. Sandy knew Frederick, liked him, and agreed to shelter him. It was a noble and risky gesture, for if caught Sandy would receive thirty-nine lashes and his wife a prison term.[41] While Frederick washed the blood off his body, Sandy's wife cooked a meal of ash cake made from cornmeal, water, and salt, on which she sprinkled a fine layer of ash. Frederick devoured it, and would always remember it as the best meal of his life.[42]

With food in his belly hope returned. He asked Sandy about his chances of running north to freedom. Sandy, who knew the area, said it was impossible; there was no escape from slave-catchers on this narrow claw of a peninsula. But he was not without a solution to Frederick's predicament: a believer in African magic, he gave Frederick the root of a common herb. Wear it on your right side, he said, and it will "be impossible for Covey to strike" you.[43] Frederick thought it absurd advice, but Sandy seemed so earnest in his belief and had been such a Good Samaritan that he put the root in his pocket to please him. And who knew? Perhaps Providence had led Sandy to him. Perhaps "the hand of the Lord" was in the root, Frederick thought.[44] God worked in strange ways, took many forms.

The root seemed to work. On Sunday morning Frederick walked boldly back to the farm and met Covey and his wife, who were on their way to church. Covey was smiling like an angel. How *are* you? he asked with genuine concern, and then politely told Frederick to drive the pigs into their sty. Covey's gracious manner astonished Frederick. His "extraordinary conduct" made him think that maybe there *was* something to Sandy's root.[45] Then he remembered that Covey considered himself a good Christian, which meant that he refused to whip a slave on the Sabbath.

Emboldened by his root and Covey's change of attitude, Frederick decided to put God to a test and make Him choose between the slaveholder and the slave: he would, if possible, "obey every order, however unreasonable"; but he vowed that if Covey still tried to beat him, he would "defend and protect myself to the best of my ability."[46] He would, in other words, renounce a central tenet of slaveholders' Christianity: never resist the master. And he would act on the supposition that in God's eyes all humans are equal.[47]

Early Monday morning the low growl had returned to Covey's voice. Frederick was in the stables, feeding the horses as ordered, when Covey snuck up on him and seized him by the leg. As he tried to get a slipknot on him, Frederick lashed back and knocked Covey down. "The fighting madness had come upon me," he noted, "and I found my strong fingers firmly attached to the throat of my cowardly tormentor, as heedless of consequences . . . as though we stood as equals before the law." As he well knew, the punishment for resisting a master was death. But "I had reached a point at which I was *not afraid to die.*" He felt "as supple as a cat and was ready for the snakish creature at every turn." He could have easily killed Covey, for he was bigger, stronger, and in better shape. But he went "strictly on the defensive, preventing him from injuring me, rather than trying to injure him." He flung Covey to the ground numerous times, like a wrestler humiliating his opponent, or a cat playing with a mouse. At one point he threw Covey into some cow dung, at another he "held him so firmly by the throat that his blood followed my nails." But he never seriously hurt him.[48]

The fight lasted two hours, a strange and epic pas de deux. "He held me and I held him."[49]

"Are you going to [continue to] resist?" Covey asked, trembling with fear and exhaustion.[50]

"Yes sir," Frederick politely responded.[51]

Midway through the battle, Covey called out for help, realizing that he could not vanquish Frederick alone. His cousin Bill Hughes, who lived and worked with him, came to his aid; but Frederick quickly turned aggressor and kicked Hughes in the crotch, which "sickened him." He staggered away, doubled over in pain, and didn't again interfere. Covey then yelled out for Bill Smith, another hired slave: "take hold of him—take hold of him!" he ordered. But Bill was not about to fight Frederick on Covey's behalf. "My master hired me to work, *not* to help you whip Frederick," he responded. When Covey saw his own slave Caroline, he ordered her to "take hold of him." She was a large, strong woman who "could have mastered me," Frederick noted, given how exhausted he was after fighting for over an hour. But she too refused to interfere. Such black solidarity made Frederick proud of his race and spurred him on.[52]

After two hours Covey was so exhausted he had to stop. Gasping for breath, he said, "Now, you scoundrel, go to your work; I would not have whipped you half so much as I have, had you not resisted." Frederick wanted to laugh at such pretense, for "the fact was, *he had not whipped me at all*."[53] It was Covey's way of trying to save face. He knew that he had been beaten and never again laid a hand on the young man.

Frederick frequently said that his fight with Covey was "the turning point in my 'life as a slave.'" As he explained, "I felt as I never felt before. It was a glorious resurrection, from the tomb of slavery to the heaven of comparative freedom. My long crushed spirit rose, cowardice departed, bold defiance took its place; and I now resolved that, however long I might remain a slave in *form*, the day had passed forever when I could be a slave in *fact*." A slave who refused to be flogged was already more than "half free."[54]

Of course Frederick's description of his fight as a "turning point" was essentially retrospective, written from the vantage point of having escaped slavery and looking back for clues to explain his rise. At the time, the fight gave him hope that this one victory might turn the tide after a string of beatings, much like an athlete feels after a big win. This hope (or belief) mattered greatly to Frederick, shaping his behavior and infusing him with confidence in the face of daunting odds.[55]

Covey never notified the authorities about the rebellious slave under his charge. He could have had Frederick publicly whipped or killed or both, but he sought to keep the fight a secret. Frederick suspected that he was ashamed to admit "that he had been mastered by a boy of sixteen."[56] After all, Covey wanted to protect his reputation as a "nigger breaker," which enabled him to rent slaves at below market rates. He also wanted to preserve his honor: a white man was not supposed to get beaten by a black boy in a fight. During the remainder of his stay with Covey, Frederick sometimes taunted him, trying to provoke him to attack. Next time, he said, he would seriously hurt him. But he was only posturing. Had there been another confrontation, he no doubt would have fought Covey in exactly the same way—on the defensive, deflecting blows and dealing few in return. He knew that if he seriously injured or killed Covey, there would be no way to cover up the fight, and public exposure would result in torture and death. As it was, Covey left him alone and pretended that nothing had changed, while Frederick's world suddenly looked much brighter indeed.

The fight taught Frederick a valuable lesson that would stay with him for the rest of his life: *always* resist a tyrant, and don't be afraid to die trying. But be pragmatic about it. The goal is to gain respect from your enemy and to instill pride in yourself, for if your enemy respects you, he will also fear you. Thus, do not turn the other cheek or befriend your enemy (unless he first converts to your cause), for this requires conciliation on your part and a loss of power over him. As Frederick put it, "A man without force is without the essential dignity of humanity."[57] Masters dishonored slaves by not allowing them to use force. Slaves should thus always resist by force.

Frederick tested his new philosophy on his next master. After his tenure ended with Covey, he was rented out to another wheat farmer named William Freeland. Freeland was Covey's opposite in almost every way. While Covey was poor, mean, and vicious, Freeland was "a well-bred southern gentleman," as Frederick put it; he had manners not money.[58] He was open and honest with his slaves, fed them well, and did not overwork them. And since he was not a churchgoer, he did not cloak crimes against humanity under a Southern Christian identity. Indeed, he was an ideal master, and he never beat or whipped Frederick.

But Freeland was still a master and thus a tyrant to be resisted. His mode of mastering, so different from Covey's, required a new form of resistance. Frederick summarized it this way: "Give [a slave] a *bad* master, and he aspires to a good master; give him a good master, and he wishes to become his *own* master. Such is human nature."[59] Shortly after Frederick began working for Freeland, he vowed to run away. It was a kind of belated New Year's resolution for 1836. Over the next four months he planned the escape and convinced five other slaves to go with him, including Sandy Jenkins, the "root man."[60]

The plan was relatively simple. On the night of Holy Saturday, with whites preparing for Easter, they would steal a canoe, paddle up the Chesapeake toward Baltimore, and then travel on foot until they reached the free soil of Pennsylvania. Since they didn't have a map they didn't know exactly where to go, but Frederick wrote out a pass for each of them, saying his master had given him "full liberty" to go to Baltimore for Easter.[61]

The scheme might have worked had someone not turned traitor. Frederick never knew who the turncoat was, but he suspected the root man. Sandy had withdrawn from the scheme one Friday night after having a bad dream, in which Frederick was being flown south "in the claws of a huge bird." It was an omen, he told Frederick: "Honey, watch de Friday night dream; dare is sumpon in it, shose you born; dare is indeed, honey."[62] Give up the plan, he was saying, otherwise you'll be caught and sent into the Deep South. Sandy had probably already divulged the plot to his master and now wanted to protect Frederick.[63] Such deceptions were not uncommon: in the American South the easiest way for a slave to become free was *not* to join a runaway scheme but to *expose* one to the master. Informers received either their freedom or special treatment in return for loyalty.[64]

It was clear to Frederick that someone had betrayed them, for on the day of the planned escape, he and his four comrades were suddenly rounded up and thrown in jail. They destroyed their passes and denied trying to run away, but almost all the whites assumed they were guilty and that Frederick was the ringleader. "You *long legged yellow devil*," you "put it into the heads" of other slaves "to run away," one woman yelled at him.[65] Some whites thought he "*ought to be hanged*," others said roasting him alive was the proper punishment, and almost everyone assumed that if he wasn't killed he would be sold into the cotton fields of Mississippi or Alabama, where escape was almost impossible.[66] Indeed, one neighbor warned Thomas Auld that unless he immediately removed Frederick from the Eastern Shore, he would personally "shoot [him] down." Frederick was too dangerous to be allowed to "tamper" with other slaves.[67]

When Thomas Auld retrieved Frederick from jail, he told him he had already made plans to send him to Alabama. But this was either a lie or else he changed his mind, for suddenly he ordered him back to Baltimore to live with Hugh and Sophia Auld, so that he could "learn a trade," as he said. Not only that, but if Frederick behaved himself, Thomas *"would emancipate me at age twenty-five."* Frederick could not believe his luck; "it seemed too good to be true."[68] Most other masters would have killed him, broken his will, or sold him down the river; and a prime fieldhand like Frederick was worth about $1,000 ($75,000 in today's money).[69] As Frederick sailed up the Chesapeake toward Baltimore, he began to feel that "there was something more intelligent than *chance*, and something more certain than *luck*" to explain his circumstance. One day he would quote Shakespeare and say there is a "divinity that shapes our ends."[70] But right now he was just happy to be leaving the Eastern Shore.

Baltimore felt like a new world of partial freedom. Hugh Auld, a shipbuilder by trade, was "a rough but manly-hearted fellow," as Frederick described him, and something of a father figure. Sophia (he called her "Miss Sopha") was a tender-hearted woman who often treated him like a son.[71] To be sure, Hugh and Sophia had their faults: Hugh drank too much, could be moody and impetuous, and tried to prevent Frederick from reading and writing. And when Sophia's temper flared up she became something of a termagant. But they neither beat Frederick nor justified their power over him with pious Christian bromides. Indeed, they revealed a sense of humility that most slaveholders lacked.[72]

Hugh got Frederick a job as an apprentice caulker in Baltimore's shipyards. The work was relatively easy, requiring more strength and endurance than skill; and Frederick now stood over six feet tall, with a muscular chest and legs from working the fields for three years. He quickly learned how to mix the oakum (tar and twisted hemp) and smooth it into the seams of ships to prevent leaking, and within the year he became an expert caulker, working in the shipyard where Hugh was foreman and bringing in as much as nine dollars a week, more than any other caulker and equivalent to lower-middle-class wages. But at the end of the week he had to hand over every penny to Hugh. When Hugh gave him a sixpence as a token of thanks, Frederick interpreted the gift "as an admission of my right to the whole sum." Despite Hugh's comparative humanity, Frederick viewed him as a thief and tyrant.[73]

Frederick hated living with Hugh and Sophia, and in May 1838 he took another step in his "career toward freedom," as he put it. It was not uncommon in Baltimore, a black metropolis with some ten thousand slaves, for bondsmen and -women to hire out their own time. They lived and worked where they wanted and enjoyed considerable freedom as long as they paid their masters a set amount each week. Any additional income was theirs to keep, and some slaves saved enough money to purchase their freedom. The system motivated slaves to work hard and provided masters with a guaranteed annuity, but it also depended on the master's trusting his slave. "I was not in very good odor," Frederick said of his reputation among masters. Surprisingly, Hugh agreed to let him hire out his time as long as Frederick paid him three dollars every Saturday evening and covered all his expenses.[74]

For four months the system worked beautifully and Frederick enjoyed greater independence than he had ever experienced.[75] Then he slipped up. In August he went away for a weekend with some free black friends to a camp meeting, a popular form of entertainment and religious expression that included singing, confessions, and converts who shook and quaked and fell prostrate after giving their bodies and souls to God. Although Frederick considered Christian slaveowners the most inhumane masters, he was himself a Christian and attended the A.M.E. church. Christ's message of freedom was the centerpiece of his faith and the camp meeting offered a way to enter into fellowship with other like-minded Christians. But in going to the meeting he was two days late in turning over his earnings to Hugh and thus broke his contract.[76]

Hugh was furious. He treated Frederick like a wayward son who had left home for the weekend and returned days later without any word or communication: the father, sleepless from worry, imagines the worst. Hugh thought Frederick had run away: "You rascal, I have a great mind to give you a severe whipping," he yelled. "You shall hire your time no longer. The next thing I shall hear of will be your running away."[77]

Hugh's fears were justified. With his partial freedom denied, Frederick attempted another escape. A year earlier, in 1837, the Baltimore and Ohio Railroad had completed a new line that ran north from Baltimore to Wilmington, Delaware (a slave state), with a connection to Philadelphia via steamboat. The B&O vigorously protected masters' property; as Frederick put it, "even *free* colored travelers were almost excluded." Any black passenger had to leave Baltimore by day and had to present "free papers," the equivalent of a passport that detailed the owner's appearance. Despite such obstacles Frederick calculated that the B&O offered the safest route to freedom. He borrowed a sailor's protection pass (certifying the owner's free status) from a friend who somewhat resembled him. Then he purchased a red shirt, black cravat, and tarpaulin hat to look like a sailor. And he bought a train ticket and arranged to have a hackman bring his baggage to the station on Monday morning, September 3.[78]

Although Frederick had never traveled by rail, he had heard enough about it to know what to expect. Passenger service was still in its infancy. There were no first-class cabins or sleepers and no one called the ride comfortable. Each car seated about thirty people on two rows of hard benches; it looked like a large dark rectangular wooden box with a few holes for windows. There was constant jolting and screeching, which made reading extremely difficult, and the noise was so bad that you had to yell. One contemporary said that the cars were more appropriate for cattle than people, and another passenger noted that the coal dust streaming through the windows was often so thick that it made breathing difficult. And in contrast to the Civil War years, the B&O in 1838 enforced segregation, with blacks relegated to the noisiest and dustiest car.[79]

Frederick used the jostle of the train and haste of the conductor to his advantage. He arrived at the station on September 3 a few minutes before his train departed in order to avoid the scrutiny of the station ticket agent. As the whistle blew his hackman tossed his small satchel into the car, and as the train left the station Frederick jumped aboard. He was halfway to Delaware before the conductor entered the colored car. Frederick knew how to impersonate a sailor from working in the shipyards, and though he was tense and agitated, he *performed* his freedom, acting confident and casual and waiting for the conductor to ask for his papers.[80]

"You have something to show that you are a free man, have you not?" the conductor asked.

"Yes sir," Frederick answered. "I have a paper with the American eagle on it that will carry me around the world."[81]

It was the perfect response, for Frederick exploited the respect for U.S. sailors then prevalent in Baltimore. The conductor merely glanced at his papers, took his fare, and went on his way.[82]

There were a few close calls. On the ferryboat ride across the Susquehanna River a black acquaintance noticed him and asked dangerous questions like, "When are you coming back?" which might have exposed Frederick. Then after boarding the train to Philadelphia he looked out the window and saw in the car next to him (on an adjacent track) a ship captain he had worked for just two days earlier. The man glanced toward Frederick but evidently did not see him. Even more harrowing, a German blacksmith he knew was on the train and "looked at me very intently" but said nothing, Frederick recalled. "I really believed he knew me but had no heart to betray me." To fugitives, even a large metropolis like Baltimore must have felt at times like a tiny village. The rest of the trip occurred without incident, however. From Wilmington Frederick took the steamboat to Philadelphia and then a night train to New York City.[83]

In less than twenty-four hours he had transformed himself from slave to free man, Southerner to Northerner. He would always remember the trip as the most glorious twenty-four hours in his life, as if he had been born again. "A new world had opened upon me," he recalled. Every other event, all other accomplishments, would pale in comparison to this. "I lived more in one day than in a year of my slave life. The dreams of my childhood and the purposes of my manhood were now fulfilled." For the rest of his life he would celebrate September 3 in place of his unknown birthday.[84]

For decades Frederick never expressed any gratitude to Thomas Auld for sending him north rather than selling him south, as most masters would have done. Nor did he publicly betray any appreciation to Hugh and Sophia Auld for their comparative kindness toward him, though privately he sought to reconcile with Hugh. He wrote him in 1857 saying, "I love you but hate slavery."[85] At the same time, however, he declared that if a slave "kills his master, he imitates only the heroes of the revolution."[86] Until the Civil

War he publicly vilified Thomas, Hugh, and Sophia. Although none of them owned slaves after 1848, they never became abolitionists, and so to Frederick they remained public enemies.[87] It wasn't until after the war that Frederick publicly reconciled with his former owner. He told Thomas Auld, "I did not run away from *you*, but from *slavery*."[88] In his public persona he remained true to the lesson he had learned from fighting Covey: always resist an enemy, even if he conciliates, unless he converts to your cause. With slavery gone, Frederick concluded, Auld was no longer his enemy.

As for Edward Covey, the snake, his reputation as a "nigger breaker" paid off. By the Civil War, he had become a wealthy gentleman planter, owning numerous slaves and property worth about $23,000 ($2 million in today's money).[89] While he got rich, Frederick made him famous, transforming him into one of the great villains of world literature, an equal of Simon Legree and Fagin. In each of his three autobiographies, Frederick cast Covey as the unforgettable demon of his story. Eastern Shore farmers sometimes protested; in 1847 one neighbor attacked Frederick's portrayal of Covey, calling "the snake" a good, honest, hardworking man and "a tried and faithful member of the Methodist Episcopal Church" who treated his workers well. "By his honest industry," Covey had "purchased a fine farm, and is now reaping the reward of his labor."[90] But Frederick's characterization stuck; for over a century Covey's old home has been known as "Mount Misery."*[91]

On a bitterly cold day in March 1830, a twenty-one-year-old man drove a two-yoke team of oxen across Indiana into Illinois. The roads froze at night and thawed into mud and slush during the day, making travel slow and difficult. He walked beside the oxen in his coonskin cap and buckskin breeches that came up to his knees, cracking his whip over their horns or into their hide, barking out commands—"gee," "haw," "g'lang," and "hi thar!"—to keep them moving.[92] While fording a stream he laid on the whip with more force. The oxen were not fully broken, and he used the lash liberally to prevent them from running off and injuring themselves or killing him. He was much less disciplined with his pet dog, who at one point jumped into a stream and started to sink. He waded into the icy water waist deep, "got hold of him," and

---

* "Mount Misery" is now owned by Donald Rumsfeld, the former secretary of defense.

"saved him," he recalled. "I could not bear to lose my dog."[93]

Abraham was moving to Macon County, Illinois, near a river the Indians had named Sangamon, for "the land of plenty to eat."[94] He was under no illusions that it would live up to its name. He was simply following his family farther west to another backwoods settlement. He felt like "a piece of floating driftwood," carried along by the currents of family and fate.[95] Little did he know that the move would set him free and give him a sense of purpose.

His father, Thomas Lincoln, had staked out a claim on the north bank of the Sangamon River, a few miles west of Decatur, and had asked Abraham to lead the wagon train.[96] (People called him Abe but he preferred Abraham, and his surname was pronounced "Linkhorn" or "Linkern" in the local dialect.)[97] The wagon train consisted of Abraham and his father, Thomas; Abraham's stepmother, Sarah Bush Johnston Lincoln; the families of Sarah's two daughters by a previous marriage; and two teams of oxen. The women sat in the crude covered wagons that Abraham had helped build, while the men walked beside the oxen.[98] They were leaving Pigeon Creek, a settlement in southern Indiana whose name reflected something of its backwoods rawness.

Pigeon Creek had not been kind to Abra-

ham. He had lived there fourteen years, having
moved from Hardin County, Kentucky, where
he had spent his first seven years.[99] Pigeon Creek
"was a wild region with many bears and other
wild animals still in the woods," he recalled. It
wasn't even a village; rather, a settlement with
about forty families living within a five-mile ra-
dius of Lincoln's home.[100] His life there seemed
like one tragedy after another: his mother died
from "milk sickness" (brucellosis) when he was
eight; his sister and only sibling died in child-
birth; he almost died after being kicked by a
horse and was for a while assumed dead; and
the skills he had learned consisted of farming,
fence-making, and a little carpentry, which he
hated.[101] His father decided to move to "the
land of plenty to eat" after the milk sickness returned. That was fine by Abraham, for he hated
the place. When he returned for a visit in 1846
he penned a poem that captured his sense of
sorrow at Pigeon Creek:[102]

I range the fields with pensive tread,
And pace the hollow rooms,
And feel (companion of the dead)
I'm living in the tombs.

About the only good thing that had happened
to him at Pigeon Creek was the arrival of his

stepmother, Sarah Bush Johnston, a widow with children from her previous marriage. Thomas married her soon after Abraham's mother died. Abraham was "wild, ragged, and dirty," but he immediately noticed changes.[103] She brought a featherbed and walnut bureau, as well as a table and chairs, spinning wheel, and silverware—all luxury items to Abraham. She cleaned him up and ordered Thomas to build a wall to close off the crude three-sided cabin. She also loved and nurtured Abraham and treated him no differently from her own children. She was "his best friend in this world," according to one relative; "no man could love a mother more than he loved her."[104]

Abraham's natural mother, Nancy Hanks Lincoln, had been a source of embarrassment. "My mother was a bastard—was the daughter of a [so-called] nobleman" from Virginia, he later told a friend. Even among poor white trash, the son of a bastard was a mark of shame. Understandably, Abraham wanted the knowledge kept a secret. There was one consolation about his mother's purported genealogy, however: "bastards are generally smarter—shrewder & more intellectual than" other poor whites, he said. He considered his mother much smarter than his father: she had inherited the nobleman's "qualities and I hers."[105] His belief in his noble blood fueled his ambition and mocked the idea that the poor were supposed to be content with their lot. In later years, he tried to forget about his early poverty: "it is a great piece of folly to attempt to make anything out of my early life," he told a biographer. "It can all be condensed into a single sentence" from Thomas Gray's *Elegy*: "The short and simple annals of the poor."[106] His poverty, like his mother, was a source of embarrassment.

Abraham did not get along with his father. He considered him ignorant and impoverished. So did some of his neighbors: one called Thomas Lincoln "an excellent specimen of poor white trash, lazy & worthless." Others remembered him as a hardworking, churchgoing Baptist but a bad businessman. He was "a tinkerer—a piddler—always doing but doing nothing great." A carpenter by trade, Thomas spent most of his time farming. In manners he was "backoodsish" (sic), or boorish. He could barely read or write, and he considered Abraham lazy because his son hated physical labor, loved to read, and was "always fooling hisself with eddication," thinking he could get ahead with it. He beat Abraham for acting smart or superior, one time knocking him off a fence for being too curious. Abraham never fought back. Thomas thought more of his stepson, who rather enjoyed manual labor, than he did of his own son.[107]

One of Abraham's greatest fears was that he would grow up to be like his father. He scorned Thomas's lack of education but at the same time was painfully aware that he himself had received less than a year of formal schooling. He hated that his father settled in places where "there was absolutely nothing to excite ambition for education," as he put it; and yet here he was, following him to another one of those places.[108]

If he wanted, he could strike out on his own right now. A month ago, on February 12, he had turned twenty-one, which meant that he had "reached his majority." He was a free citizen now: for the first time in his life he could not only vote but legally keep his earnings rather than give them to his father. And he could go where he pleased without needing his father's approval. Time and again, Thomas had rented out Abraham, much as Thomas Auld rented out Frederick. Abraham had to plow fields, split rails, and harvest wheat, and at the end of the week turn over every penny. Worse still, his father had yanked him out of school to rent him as a way to ease his own financial burdens. "I used to be a slave," Abraham recalled, "but now I am . . . free." Until he turned twenty-one, he felt little different from black boys: "we were all slaves one time or another," he noted.[109] But if Abraham were now free, why was he still following his father, working for him for nothing?

Perhaps he thought of this question as he walked the one hundred miles and more that March in 1830, goading the oxen across rivers and rain-rutted paths, hearing settlers tell how the Illinois soil was so hard that it could break a plow. He saw a few things on the trip that made him hopeful: a printing press (he had never seen one before); and a juggler performing sleight-of-hand tricks.[110] These were signs that life could be different from farmwork.

When he wasn't deep in his thoughts, he told jokes and stories. It was a family tradition and Abraham had a passion for dirty, juvenile jokes.[111] In one, a husband and wife conclude that Judgment Day is at hand and agree to divulge their sins:[112]

> "Well dear," said she, "our little Sammy is not your child."
> "Whose is he?" said the husband.
> "The one-eyed shoemaker. He came to see me once when you was away and in a vile hour I gave way."
> "Well," said the husband, "is the rest mine?"
> "No," said she, "they belong to the neighborhood."

When the wagon train finally reached Sangamon, it did not look to Abraham like a "land of plenty to eat." Their plot stood on a lonely bluff overlooking the river, filled with trees. The village of Decatur consisted of a handful of log cabins and did not appear much different from the other backwoods towns he had lived near. It seemed like one more place where "the best of society" consisted of men who "could boast of whipping somebody," as one former neighbor put it. This same neighbor summarized male social customs in the backwoods: "Knock down was the order of the day get up drink make Friends & all went on well."[113]

Abraham grew up in a world where fighting and heavy drinking were the main pastimes, the primary source of male status and sociability. In fights called "rough and tumbles," it was not uncommon to have a thumb, nose, ear, or lip bit off by an opponent; testicles ripped out; or an eyeball liberated from its socket and kept as a trophy by the victor. Not all fights were "no holts barred" rough and tumbles, however. Most were wrestling or boxing bouts, with rules and regulations. But even in a regulated match, "if you hooked up with the wrong antagonist, you could easily lose an eye or ear in what everyone considered a fair fight." Such bouts were not only a popular form of male entertainment; they were the way to gain status, preserve honor, and restore self-esteem.

While rich men fought duels, backwoods men brawled. In order to save face, you had to be willing to lose part of it.[114]

The Lincolns were a family of fighters. Abraham's mother, Nancy Hanks, could "throw most of the men who ever put her powers to the test." At five foot ten and 140 pounds, she towered over most men, who averaged five foot seven. And Abraham's father had been a legendary fighter. The same height as Nancy and a muscular 190 pounds, there was "not one bit of Cowardice about him." In one rough and tumble, he bit off the nose of his rival; in another, he whipped his opponent without himself receiving a scratch, and afterward they became "great good friends." At one point friends had proclaimed him a Kentucky champion. But there were also rumors that Thomas had been castrated, possibly from fighting, or made sterile. Whether or not these rumors are true is almost beside the point. What's important is that a culture of violence, in which a man might lose his testicles in a brawl, could fuel such apocryphal tales.[115]

When men weren't maiming each other they often killed themselves with drink. At Pigeon Creek and Sangamon, locally distilled whiskey flowed more readily than water. Indeed, during Abraham's formative years, America was an "alcoholic republic." The average man drank about eight shots a day of whiskey or rye (or their equivalent from a jug), usually in the space of a few hours; and over one-quarter of the adult male population sucked down twelve shots or more. Competition was part of the culture, the goal being to drink more and stay soberer than your opponent.[116]

Although fighting and guzzling whiskey might seem barbaric to us today, they were ways of flaunting your unconcern, or hiding your fears, about life's dangers in the backwoods. At any moment you could be struck down by wild animals, Indians, or sickness—and rarely were there doctors or ministers around to heal the pain. These pastimes were also manifestations of democracy, reflecting equal opportunity and the spirit of freedom. But mostly they were ways for base, ignorant men to become leaders in their communities.[117]

Abraham was of and from this culture; but as he came of age he gradually rejected it. At Pigeon Creek he had passed around the whiskey jug and had been in his share of fights, dislocating a man's shoulder in one bout. But by the time he arrived in Illinois, he had quit drinking and fought only regulated wrestling matches, which were less bloody but still violent.[118] To him, rough and tumbles and drinking were symptoms more of tyranny than of democracy. Though he rarely went to church, he had come to believe that an "over-ruling Providence" called for sobriety and peace. Besides, he had seen too many visible effects of these pastimes: faces scarred and disfigured, men wasted or dead at thirty-five. One winter night, he had come across a drunken man lying on the frost-covered ground. Realizing that the man was in danger of freezing to death, Abraham carried him home and built a fire so that he could sleep off the whiskey. Afterward, the man said Abraham had saved his life.[119]

Then too, Abraham didn't *need* to fight to prove his physical superiority. Most men challenged people their own size, and few could match Abraham. By his mid-teens he was already over six feet; and now, at six foot four and weighing over two hundred pounds, he towered over people. He was known for being able to lift a thousand pounds of rocks stacked in a box; and he could outrun, outthrow, and outjump all comers. Such shows of strength made men think twice before challenging him to a fight. When they did, Abraham often talked them out of it. One time, a scrawny little man challenged him to a fistfight; he agreed, provided the man would first "chalk out his size" on Abraham's body and count as a foul "every blow struck outside of that mark." The words hit their mark, for the man suddenly realized he had no chance against such a giant, and he wisely abstained. Just by looking at Abraham, you knew you would probably lose.[120]

The young giant spent the late spring and summer helping his father and cousin clear ten acres, plant corn, and build a log cabin and fence. His forearms and shoulders were so strong from railsplitting that he could extend a heavy axe horizontally in one hand, "holding it steady without even a quiver." Still, he hated the work and began looking for a chance to strike out on his own. He was open to anything as long as it wasn't farming or carpentry, his father's occupations.[121]

On the river Abraham found freedom. In the winter of 1830–31, a fast-talking businessman named Denton Offutt needed help taking a flatboat with provisions down the Mississippi River to New Orleans. Offutt, a hard-drinking "wild harum-scarum kind of man," offered ten dollars a month to build the boat and make the trip.[122] It sounded like good money, and Abraham signed on, as did his cousin and stepbrother.

River travel could be dangerous. Abraham had been down the Mississippi once before, when he was nineteen. His father had rented him out as a hand on a flatboat to New Orleans for eight dollars a month. One night, while they were lingering on the sugar coast near Baton Rouge, some slaves attacked the boat and tried to steal the cargo and kill the crew. Abraham picked up a club, started swinging, and drove them away, then quickly "cut cable, weighed anchor," and headed on. During the melee he was clubbed in the head, which left a deep gash above his right eye and a permanent scar.[123]

He liked being on the river, though. There was a lot of time to lie around reading, telling stories, or just gazing at the stars and listening to the bullfrogs a-cluttering on the shore. After returning from his first Mississippi trip, and handing over his earnings to his father, he had asked a friend to get him a job on a steamboat. "I want a start," he said. But the friend refused; Abe was not yet twenty-one, and working for himself without his father's permission would have been illegal.[124]

This second trip to New Orleans almost ended soon after it began. They were still on the Sangamon River when their flatboat, filled with barrels of corn and wheat, got stuck on a milldam at New Salem. The water level was low and the boat grounded on the lip of the dam like a log suspended over a waterfall, caught in a snag. The bow tilted up and water slowly poured into the stern. If they didn't dislodge the boat it would founder and destroy their cargo. Abraham convinced Offutt to transfer the cargo in the stern to another vessel to lighten the load and level their flatboat. Then he bored a hole in the bow to drain the water, and they finally eased the boat over the dam. The people of New Salem came out to watch the ordeal from the shore, and a few of them marveled at the cleverness of the strange giant in jeans rolled up to his knees, a striped cotton shirt (known as a hickory shirt), and a straw hat.[125]

No sooner had this disaster been averted when Offutt decided to purchase some thirty hogs to sell on the trip. The problem wasn't how to live on a flatboat with thirty live hogs; it was how to get the hogs onto the boat in the first place. Nothing seemed to work. Finally, Offutt came up with the crazy idea of sewing the hogs' eyes shut, hoping this would make them behave like horses with blinders on. While Abraham kept their heads steady, Offutt put needle and thread through their eyelids. Now chaos ensued; completely blinded, the hogs screamed in terror and refused to go anywhere. The men finally got them on board by tying their legs and hauling them on carts.[126]

Once on the Mississippi, they passed numerous flatboats, barges, keelboats, steamboats. The river was a main vein of American commerce, a vast, ever-shifting marketplace where everything from Bibles and bullets to whiskey and women were traded and transported. It "gave employment to hordes of rough and hardy men" who were big drinkers, frequent fighters, and "prodigious braggarts," Mark Twain remembered. Rivermen were legendary for their tall talk. Mike Fink, a contemporary of Abraham, was probably the most famous. A champion eye gouger and fearless hunter, he lived on or near the river and elevated tall talk to an art form: "I'm a regular screamer from the old Massassip!" he reportedly boasted. "I'm the very infant that refused his milk before its eyes were open and called out for a bottle of old Rye! . . . I can out-run, out-jump, out-shoot, out-brag, out-drink, an' out-fight, rough-an'-tumble, no holts barred, any man on both sides of the river." Abraham knew of Fink and had heard such language in Kentucky and Indiana, though perhaps nothing quite so eloquent. He also knew that rivermen were meaner and more murderous than landlubbers, and so he and the crew kept their distance from the other boats. Tall talk could easily slide into a bloody bout.[127]

New Orleans seemed like a foreign country. With a population of fifty thousand, including thirty thousand African Americans, it was a black metropolis to Abraham.[128] In all of Hardin County, Kentucky, there had only been about a thousand slaves (10 percent of the population); and Pigeon Creek, Indiana, was an all-white community.[129] Indeed, Indiana and Illinois both restricted black migration; the settlers were mostly poor Southern whites who hated blacks.[130]

In fact, New Orleans was the largest slave entrepôt in North America, with scores of auction markets where people were bought and sold like horses. It was almost impossible to be in the city and *not* experience the sights and sounds of slavery: the crack of a whip and a scream; the clanking of chains along the pavement; the leer of a white man at a dark-skinned woman. Abraham reportedly saw blacks chained and mistreated, and "his heart bled" for them. It wasn't so much the violence that upset him; after all, he had seen plenty of nasty fights. But in fights among whites, men *willingly* disfigured each other, partly to defend their honor. Slaves *had* no honor in the master's mind. They were unwilling participants in this culture of violence. Moreover, being newly free himself, Abraham was especially sensitive to the spectacle of slavery: "the horrid pictures are in my mind yet," he said some twenty years later. What shocked him, what he identified with, was the plight of others who were forever unfree.[131]

At the end of the trip, Denton Offutt was so impressed with Lincoln that he offered him the job of clerk at the general store he was opening in New Salem. Lincoln quickly accepted. The job would allow him to leave farming and railsplitting behind. And there would be more opportunities in New Salem, for it was larger than any community he had ever lived in. With about a hundred people and a dozen homes and stores, it was as large as Chicago in 1831 and served as a market center for farmers who came to sell grain and buy whiskey and other supplies. It had a church, a school, and two doctors, all within easy walking distance—a rare convenience for Abraham. And the people of New Salem seemed more refined than those at Pigeon Creek; there were more books around, and not quite as much drunkenness and fighting.[132] Still, it was a frontier town, and Abraham soon found himself in another scrap.

Word spread quickly about the new kid in town, partly because Denton Offutt bragged about the size and strength of his clerk. When Jack Armstrong got wind of it, he wanted to test Lincoln, perhaps to run him off and defend his honor in light of Offutt's boasting. Armstrong was the leader of the local gang from Clary's Grove, a nearby settlement. Stocky and "strong as an ox," he was "a regular bully" and was always looking for a fight.[133] He and his gang loved to lure strangers into card games and then beat them up and steal their money. He could be even meaner: he was known for having roasted a *live* pig, evidently enjoying the sounds of suffering before eating it.[134]

This kind of cruelty to animals was commonplace; cockfights, ganderpulling (ripping the head off a live gander), smashing a turtle against a tree or throwing it in the fire and watching it squirm—all were part of the territory. Lincoln had protested against such behavior at Pigeon Creek, saying that "an ant's life was to it, as sweet as ours to us." Unlike Armstrong, he was able to empathize with creatures who were very different from himself.[135]

Lincoln was reluctant to fight, but Offutt egged him on, for he wanted to win money on the bout. Lincoln agreed, but only on his terms: a regulated wrestling match, one in which you had to keep hold of your opponent in order to prevent the contest from descending into a fistfight or worse. Biting, eye-gouging, and testicle-ripping were not allowed. The goal was to "throw" your opponent, so that two shoulders and one hip touched the ground. Armstrong wanted to "tussle and scuffle," a more vicious genre, but Lincoln held firm.[136]

People came from all around to witness the

bout. Men bet knives and whiskey. Offutt wagered ten dollars on his clerk. It took place in front of Offutt's store (helping sales, no doubt); the crowd circled around the combatants, forming a ring. Exactly what happened remains unclear, owing to the haze of memories and the fact that with so many people watching, few had an unobstructed view.[137] But at some point, Armstrong "broke his holt" and Lincoln called foul. Armstrong may have thrown Lincoln; Lincoln may have grabbed Armstrong by the throat; and Armstrong's buddies may have tried to gang up on Lincoln, who stood his ground and challenged each one but refused to fight them all at once. By most accounts, Armstrong admitted to the foul and both men agreed to declare the match a draw. Neither man was seriously hurt, and no one lost money on the bout.[138]

The fight was "*the turning point*" in Lincoln's young life, according to his future law partner. Lincoln tacitly agreed. Years later, his campaign biographer called the fight "one of the most significant incidents of his early life." Lincoln read a copy, correcting errors of fact and interpretation in the margins, and he left untouched this conclusion about the significance of the fight. Of course, this was a backward glance while he was running for president. But even at the time, Lincoln hoped that the fight would improve his standing in the community. After all, when he first arrived he was a total outsider—"a strange, friendless, uneducated, penniless boy," as he put it.[139]

The fight immediately established Lincoln as a leader in New Salem. He earned the respect of Jack Armstrong and the Clary's Grove boys, who wielded considerable influence and admired his strength, courage, and boldness. Less than a year later, in the spring of 1832, the Clary's Grove boys helped elect Lincoln as captain of New Salem's volunteer company during the Black Hawk War.[140] Although Lincoln's company saw no action (the war lasted only three months), Lincoln fought other whites instead of Indians: he wrestled men from other companies, won all but one bout, and his men "idolized" him as a leader and fighter. Lincoln repeatedly said that being elected captain was "a success which *gave me more pleasure than any I have had since*," as he put it.[141] It is an extraordinary statement, for when he said it he was a nationally known figure, having already served a term in the United States Congress and debated Stephen Douglas. But he loved being respected by his peers. The fight and captaincy made him a leader, secured his honorable standing in the community, bolstered his confidence, and fueled his ambition. The new kid in town had proven his mettle.

Soon after the fight, and at the urging of his townsmen, Lincoln ran for the state legislature. He had no prior experience, but this was backwoods politics, where fights and drunkenness often added texture to the debates. He ran on a platform to improve navigation on the Sangamon River, which would stimulate growth and opportunity in New Salem, he argued. Lincoln said he was uniquely qualified to discuss the river, for he knew it well, had averted disaster on it in Offutt's flatboat, and could speak with authority about how to improve it.

Lincoln also emphasized education as the means to alleviate the vices of the backwoods, though he had no plan for making it more widely available: "I desire to see the time when education, and by its means, morality, sobriety, enterprise and industry, shall become much more general than at present," he said in a campaign handbill, which was printed and possibly ghostwritten for him. It is "the most important subject which we as a people can be engaged in." His own ambition was to be "truly esteemed by my fellow men." His fight with Armstrong had brought him some esteem; he now hoped to add to it a victory of another kind. But he lost this fight, even though he received a large majority of the votes in the New Salem precinct.[142]

Revealingly, Lincoln also became a fast friend of Jack Armstrong's. His skill and comportment in the fight, and Armstrong's willingness to admit his foul, induced mutual respect and honor. Had Lincoln responded to Armstrong's foul by pummeling or disfiguring him (which he probably could have done), he would have risked humiliating him and creating a lasting enemy. As it was, Armstrong "took him into his house" and "fed and clothed" him after the fight; and he served as Lincoln's first sergeant in their company during the Black Hawk War.[143]

Their friendship lasted decades, with Armstrong supporting Lincoln's political career and Lincoln providing crucial assistance to the Armstrong family. In 1857, when Armstrong's son Duff was charged with murder, Lincoln came to the rescue. Jack had died the year before, and Duff, a bruiser like his father, went out one night carousing with two friends. An argument ensued, and Duff and his partner crushed the skull of their former buddy, who died a few days later. A number of people witnessed the killing. Duff's accomplice (who went on trial first) was convicted of manslaughter and received an eight-year sentence. Lincoln, now a famous Illinois lawyer, agreed to defend Duff. He poked holes in the witnesses' testimony and emphasized the inherent goodness of the Armstrong family: they were "kind to him when he was young, lone, and without friends," he told the jury. Duff was found not guilty and walked away a free man, despite formidable evidence against him, including the murder weapon he had made—a lead ball sewn into a leather pouch, called a "slungshot." As the prosecuting attorney noted, "Armstrong was not cleared by any want of testimony against him. . . . Lincoln's speech and personal appeal to the jury saved" him. Lincoln did not charge the Armstrong family a legal fee.[144] Friendship and loyalty could exonerate a murderer.

Lincoln's fight and subsequent friendship with Jack Armstrong taught him something that would remain a central aspect of his career: "if you would win a man to your cause, *first* convince him that you are his sincere friend," as he said a few years after the fight.[145] Conciliate with your enemy, up to a point, and then put your foot down and fight. While Lincoln was willing to sacrifice principles for friendship, the young Frederick Bailey had learned a quite different lesson from his fight with Covey: never befriend an enemy unless he *first* converts to your side, for friendship depends upon common cause and shared principles. They would later apply these lessons in the testing years of the Civil War.

Lincoln never established a close relationship with his father. After moving to New
Salem, he rarely saw him, even though Thomas
lived nearby. He could neither befriend his father nor convert him to his cause of education
and refinement. In his mind, Thomas remained
an ex-master, someone who would try to keep
him from rising. And so he kept his distance,
though he did provide for him in old age. In
fact, he didn't even go to his father's funeral.
"If we could meet now," he wrote in 1851 as
Thomas lay dying, "it is doubtful whether it
would not be more painful than pleasant."[146] He
would always associate his father with manual
labor, ignorance, and bondage—memories that
were better left forgotten.

In the societies that spawned the young Frederick Bailey and Abraham Lincoln there was
verbal sparring as well, a world of words that
was no less real than the one of fighting and
drinking. In one literary bout, a master recap-
tures his slave, who has twice attempted to
run away. Before punishing him, he demands
to know why the slave tried to run away. He
has feelings for him, has treated him kindly and
humanely, and wants an apology. But his slave

says only, "I submit to my fate. I am a slave." This stoic response sparks a debate over the morality of slavery:[147]

> *Master:* It is in the order of Providence that one man should become subservient to another. It ever has been so, and ever will be.
>
> *Slave:* The robber who puts a pistol to your breast . . . makes just the same plea. Providence gives him a power over your life and property; it gave my enemies a power over my liberty. But it has also given me legs to escape with.
>
> *Master:* But it was my intention not only to make your life tolerably comfortable at present, but to provide for you in old age.
>
> *Slave:* Is a life like mine . . . worth thinking about for old age? No: the sooner it ends, the sooner I shall obtain that relief for which my soul pants.

At every turn the slave defends himself brilliantly, exposing the violence and inhumanity of slavery. In winning the debate, he wins his freedom.

The young Frederick Bailey and Abraham Lincoln both discovered this "dialogue" at the same time, between 1830 and 1831. It appeared in *The Columbian Orator*, a popular reader and elocution manual for young boys compiled by the Massachusetts educator Caleb Bingham. The *Orator* was one of the most popular books in the

new nation. From 1797 to 1860 it went through
some twenty-three editions and in many American homes it was one of a handful of essential
books, along with the Bible, a spelling book,
and a farmer's almanac. In subject matter it was
a radical book, for it used stories, speeches, and
poems to teach boys that all men are created
equal and entitled to the inalienable rights of
life, liberty, and happiness. It was considered
so radical, in fact, that in the 1850s, during the
height of the slavery crisis, the most prominent
Southern newspaper included it on a blacklist
of abolitionist books, effectively banning it from
Southern schools and homes.[148]

Frederick Bailey discovered *The Columbian
Orator* one day as a twelve-year-old boy in the
Baltimore shipyards. He heard about it from
some white boys he had met on the streets
while running errands for Hugh and Sophia
Auld. He already knew that words could be
weapons, for Sophia Auld had given him regular reading lessons until her husband found out
and put a stop to it: "knowledge unfits a child
to be a slave," Hugh had said. "Very well," Frederick thought, he would gain knowledge.[149] On
the streets of Baltimore he asked white boys for
spelling lessons, offering biscuits in exchange
for words. They practiced their spelling and
handwriting on cellar doors and flour barrels,

and he sometimes got the white boys to sympathize with his plight: "You will be free, you know, as soon as you are twenty-one, and can go where you like," he told them, "but I am a slave for life." They agreed that he had as much "right to be free as they had" and encouraged him to read. They introduced him to *The Columbian Orator*, which they were then studying. Frederick went into a bookstore on Thames Street owned by Mr. Knight (he would always remember the store) and purchased a copy with fifty cents he had surreptitiously earned polishing boots.[150]

The Columbian Orator "was indeed a rich treasure," he said, and he read it whenever he could and kept it hidden in the kitchen loft where he slept. He virtually memorized the "Dialogue Between a Master and Slave" but also had other favorites: a speech on Irish liberation by Daniel O'Connell, and the English statesman William Pitt championing American independence in the House of Lords. Frederick identified with the heroes: he imagined *himself* becoming the slave who argued his way out of bondage; now he was the black O'Connell or Pitt, standing up in the United States Congress to affirm universal freedom. The book not only improved his vocabulary, it enabled the young Frederick "to give tongue" to his thoughts that "had frequently flashed through my soul, and died away for want of utterance."[151] It enabled him to imagine a new world through words while fighting foes with fists and feet. It helped him speak to the conductor in a "calm and sedate voice," as Bingham instructed, as he fled north on the train to freedom.[152]

The young Abraham read *The Columbian Orator* during the winter of 1831, months after fighting Jack Armstrong.[153] Like Frederick, he was hungry for knowledge, and it was one of the few books he read during his formative years, along with a spelling book, the Bible, and one or two others. Like Frederick, he read deeply and for long hours, and reportedly remembered much of what he read. If so, then he could not help but see in the "Dialogue Between a Master and Slave" aspects of his own relationship with his father. And he learned from Bingham how to comport himself in a tense situation such as when he stood up to Jack Armstrong and called foul.[154]

The Columbian Orator was especially important to Frederick and Abraham because they were self-taught and the book was (and is) a brilliant self-help manual for speaking and debating. There were no schools for slaves, and Frederick was forbidden to read after Hugh Auld discovered his wife teaching him.[155] Lincoln had to learn on his own as well. He was denied a formal education because of the lack of accessible schools and competent teachers and because his father rented him out. When he arrived at New Salem he was still quite ignorant: "I did not know much," he said.[156] He had the equivalent (in today's system) of an eighth-grade education.

The Columbian Orator enabled both Lincoln and Douglass not only to imagine new worlds; it taught them the art of public speaking. This meant learning how to shed the sounds and gestures of an ignorant man. Democratic leaders were supposed to *sound* democratic, refined but not excessively so, like a gentleman but not an aristocrat.[157] Caleb Bingham told his readers how to accomplish this feat. Proper pronunciation was crucial, as was "a proper attention to accent, emphasis, and cadence."[158] Just here is where the book proved invaluable to Frederick and Abraham, for in 1830 they both sounded like ignorant hicks. In Abraham's world, fruit "spiled"; people "brung things back" from the woods; you got "eddicated" for "sartin"; and "skeeters" were thick as trees at the "crick." An early poem of Abraham's would have sounded this way:[159]

Ábrahem Linkern
his hend and pin
he weel be good but
god knows Whin

It is easier to reconstruct Frederick's dialect, for in a few private letters he evoked something of himself as a young boy on the Eastern Shore:

> I woulda kicked my grand 'dadda'! I was in a terrible mood—'dats a fact! Ole missus—is you got anyting for poor nigger to eat!!![160]

To the Dartmouth-educated Bingham, these were sounds of stupidity, not of great men in the making. But backwoods boys need not give up hope, for his book taught them how to speak like a democratic leader, so that their oratory would "assist and improve nature," as great language should.[161]

Books like *The Columbian Orator* would ultimately become much more important than fighting for Frederick Bailey and Abraham Lincoln. Still, their strength and skill as fighters should not be downplayed. Had they been scrawny weaklings, they never would have been able to rise in their vicious worlds. They would have lacked the self-confidence and esteem needed to remake themselves. Through fighting they defended themselves and their honor; now they would need to learn how to become democratic gentlemen.

TWO

Fugitive Orator and Frontier Politician

For Freedom's battle once begun,
Bequeath'd by bleeding Sire to Son,
Though baffled oft is ever won.

—Lord Byron, *The Giaour* (1813)

For a' that, an' a' that,
It's comin yet for a' that,
That man to man the world o'er,
Shall brothers be for a' that.

—Robert Burns, "Is There for Honest
Poverty" (c. 1795)

WHEN FREDERICK ARRIVED in New York City on September 4, 1838, the joys of freedom suddenly vanished. He felt like he had been watching a beautiful fire blaze out of control, consuming his surroundings and leaving everything charred and ruined in its wake. "A sense of loneliness and insecurity oppressed me sadly," he recalled. He was all alone in a strange place, with neither money nor food and no one to turn to for help. "In the midst of thousands of my fellowmen, and yet a perfect stranger!"[1]

New York seemed like a maze of streets and a cacophony of strange tongues. It was the largest city in the country, with a population of 350,000, and the sidewalks, filled with people, were a brightly colored montage of hats and coats. The streets whirled with hackney cabs, private carriages, and pigs, "the city scavengers,"

who trotted up behind the vehicles and pass-
ersby as if demanding recognition. Even the air
seemed different: it smelled of dung and per-
fume and body odor and fetid food.[2] And every
face was a foe. Frederick had long been accustomed to regarding unknown white men as the
enemy and strange black men as "more or less
under the control of" whites. But he was more
fearful of these New Yorkers rushing to and fro
than of a pack of "hungry wolves."[3]

A chance meeting with a black acquaintance
only fueled his fears. After wandering the streets
for a few hours, Frederick ran into Jake, a slave
from Baltimore and now a fugitive who worked
as a whitewasher. Jake was a man defeated by
his own suspicions. His former master had almost recaptured him, and the city, he warned,
was filled with wealthy Southerners on vacation and blacks who would betray you to slave-
catchers for a few dollars. "Trust no man," Jake
told Frederick, and do "not think of going either
on the wharves to work or to a boarding-house
to board," or you will be caught. Jake refused to
help Frederick, would not even tell him where
to go for help. Indeed, he suspected Frederick
of being the hired hand of a slave-catcher, and
soon disappeared into the crowd.[4]

Jake's fears, though exaggerated, were not
without foundation. New Yorkers got rich on

Southern slavery and cotton. The city "was virtually an annex of the South, the New York merchants having extensive and very profitable business relations with the merchants south of the Mason and Dixon line," wrote one South Carolinian who resettled in New York.[5] Some of the city's most respectable whites hoped for the expansion of slavery and the "extermination" of free blacks and abolitionists in order to improve commerce and their profits.[6] As a result, the growing numbers of fugitives in the city had to be on constant watch for their masters or slave-catchers.

Whites too lived in a constant state of fear. One of the worst depressions in American history had begun a year earlier, in May 1837. Prices plummeted after years of easy credit, and banks suspended payments in gold and silver to stay afloat.[7] Northeastern cities and towns were particularly hard hit, exacerbating the disparity of wealth that already existed in New York. Hard times dragged middle-class families into poverty and bankruptcy, fueling fears of ruin and riots. Frederick arrived in a city staggering under massive unemployment—about one-third of the city's workers had lost their jobs. And those lucky enough to work saw their wages suddenly cut by about 30 percent.[8] People likened the mood to "the shutting of a wild bird in a cage" or a natural disaster: "men awoke from gorgeous dreams in the midst of desolation. The harvest of years was swept away in a day."[9] It was not a good time to arrive in the city penniless and looking for employment.

At the end of his first day in New York Frederick slept among some barrels near the wharf. But with his hunger, fear, and sense of helplessness growing by the hour, he awoke frequently. He suddenly realized why more slaves did not run away: their known world of family, friends, and familiar paths, no matter how bad, was better than the prospect of permanent separation and a loneliness that gnawed at you like hunger. Frederick had never understood slaves who chose to return to bondage after successfully escaping to the North. Now he grasped that they preferred "the actual rule of their masters to the life of loneliness, apprehension, hunger, and anxiety which meets them on their first arrival in a free state."[10] If this was freedom, he thought, then perhaps slavery was not so bad by comparison: "I was indeed free—from slavery but free from food and shelter as well."[11]

Indeed Frederick might have been tempted to turn back were it not for one crucial fact: he was engaged to be married and his fiancée was ready to come to him as soon as he called.[12]

Her name was Anna Murray and she was a free woman, having been born free on the Eastern Shore of Maryland. She had almond-shaped eyes, a full round face, and dark skin, and she worked as a maid for the Wells family on South Caroline Street in Baltimore.[13] At twenty-five, she was five years older than Frederick and had moved to Baltimore at age seventeen. Quiet and hardworking, she was virtually illiterate but could read music, and when she played Haydn or Handel on her violin her hymns seemed to enchant the room. She taught Frederick the violin, he was a quick study, and soon they were playing duets. She also knew how to stretch a penny further than anyone Frederick had ever met. Although he never said as much, Anna Murray was partly responsible for his freedom and self-making.[14]

It was Anna's money that purchased Frederick's train ticket on the B&O, Anna's money that bought the red shirt and black cravat and waterproof hat that made him look like a sailor, and Anna's money that was given to the friend who resembled Frederick in exchange for the sailor's protection pass.[15] Soon after returning to Baltimore in late 1836, Frederick had boasted that "with money" he could "easily have managed the matter" of running away.[16] Anna's money, coupled with her independence as a free woman, made his escape possible.

Yet Frederick totally ignored Anna's role in helping him escape, both at the time and in his memories of the event. Recognizing it would have cut against his image of the self-made man and representative African American that even now, in his first days of freedom, he was already beginning to cultivate. In one of the first letters he wrote after reaching New York, he told a friend that he "felt as one might feel upon escape from a den of hungry lions."[17] It is a familiar image: the lone warrior, the American *isolatto*, fighting the savage enemy and emerging triumphant. He was participating in a tradition of self-made men that went from Ben Franklin and Natty Bumppo through Lincoln on up to Malcolm X—a tradition that dismissed the role of wives and women in shaping the man's success. What made Frederick's situation unique was that he established the tradition of the self-made African American.[18]

Frederick and Anna had met at a debating club called the Baltimore Mental Improvement Society, where ambitious free blacks from the shipyards met to hone their public speaking skills and hear lectures. Essentially a men's club, it also hosted respectable parties where black men and women could meet and court. Frederick had felt fortunate to be admitted to the society, for free blacks in Baltimore tended to keep to themselves, ostracizing slaves, much as white society was separated along class lines.[19] He had played a prominent role in the society's debates, offering tips on public speaking culled from his *Columbian Orator* while also learning how to parody slaveholders. While courting Anna and attending meetings his confidence soared; one night after a triumphant debate he went so far as to boast that he would never stop rising until he was a United States senator.[20] It was a revolutionary statement from a slave, reflecting the influence of Anna and the society on him.

Was Frederick in love with Anna? It depends on how you define love. Given his ambitions, he could not distinguish his feelings for Anna from her ability to help him realize his dreams: he could not separate her from what she represented. With her came access to money and other accoutrements of respectability—tableware and silverware, linens, good manners, and two featherbeds, one of which she sold to help defray the costs of Frederick's escape.[21] Moreover, as a free woman, any children Anna had would be free regardless of Frederick's status. And as an accomplished "household manager" she would enable him to devote all his energies to his career.[22] To a slave who had grown up sleeping on rough planks, dirt floors, and thin lumpy mattresses, often scavenging for food, Anna seemed almost regal, an "untouchable." Frederick must have been thrilled that she agreed to marry him, for in having his love requited he greatly expanded his opportunities. Love and opportunity were impossible to disentangle.

With Anna ready to come to New York when he called, Frederick had a special incentive to weather the loneliness and homelessness until he could find a safe haven from which to contact her. He wandered the streets for a few days, keeping a sharp lookout for a sympathetic face who would hear his plight and offer help. He found it in a sailor named Stuart who noticed Frederick's sailor outfit. Their meeting seemed almost like a pickup: Stuart saw Frederick "standing on the opposite sidewalk near the Tombs," the city's prison, and as Stuart walked over to him, Frederick "ventured a remark" and Stuart took an "interest in me." Frederick spent the night at Stuart's "humble home," presumably sharing his new friend's bed, as was the custom.[23] The pickup stemmed more from sympathy than any desire for sex, however, and the next day Stuart escorted Frederick to the home of David Ruggles, a free black journalist and activist who headed the New York Underground Railroad, which harbored hundreds of newly minted fugitives and helped them settle in Northern communities where they could find work.[24]

From Ruggles's home Frederick wrote Anna to say that he was safe in New York and to come at once. Anna made arrangements to ship her remaining featherbed and other furnishings. Then she packed a trunk containing her violin; some sheet music from Samuel Dyer and Ruel Shaw, compilers of hymnbooks; and a new plum-colored silk dress for the wedding. She arrived in New York within a few days. Frederick had brought a black suit for the wedding, now wrinkled from being stuffed in his sailor's satchel, and his *Columbian Orator*. They were married at Ruggles's home on September 15, 1838, eleven days after Frederick's escape. James Pennington, another runaway from the Eastern Shore and a newly ordained Presbyterian minister, presided over the ceremony. Frederick chose the surname Johnson and Pennington wrote out a marriage certificate declaring that he had "joined together in holy matrimony Frederick Johnson and Anna Murray as man and wife."[25]

On the advice of Ruggles they moved to New Bedford, Massachusetts, then the nation's whaling capital and an ideal place for Frederick to ply his trade as a caulker. They settled into a little two-room apartment on Elm Street a few blocks from the wharf, where the cobbled roads and row houses and Anna's furnishings faintly reminded them of Fells Point, the shipyard district of Baltimore where they had met. Anna was already pregnant with their first child, Rosetta, which would prompt rumors that she had conceived out of wedlock. But they were legally married—something forbidden of slaves—and they had new names and identities to consecrate their new life together: Mr. and Mrs. Frederick Douglass.[26]

Frederick discarded the surname Johnson after a New Bedford neighbor, Nathan Johnson, told him that there were already too many Johnsons in town and suggested "Douglas" instead. Nathan had been reading Sir Walter Scott's *Lady of the Lake* and was so impressed with the bravery of the protagonist, Douglas, that he recommended it to Frederick. Frederick agreed to the new name, even though he hadn't read Scott and didn't know how it was spelled. But he was familiar with Douglass Street in Baltimore, and so added an extra "s" to his (and Anna's) name.[27]

From the beginning of their marriage, which lasted forty-four years, Frederick and Anna lived in separate spheres, with Anna keeping house for Frederick and for other families when they needed extra income. About the only things that brought them together were their children and their love of the violin. Anna never learned to read and Frederick preferred reading to playing the violin and caring for children when he wasn't working. She essentially remained a domestic while he evolved from day laborer to orator, writer, newspaperman, and politician. He called Anna "my helpmeet" without ever referring to the particular ways she helped him, while Anna's identity "became merged into that of her husband." This was how they defined their love.[28]

Douglass was completely ignorant of Northern society. *The Columbian Orator*, "almost [his] only book," had done nothing to disabuse him of Southern views of free labor. He had been brought up to believe that slavery was the source of all wealth, that whites who did not own slaves were "*poor white trash,*" as he called them, and that Northern whites were thus impoverished, ignorant, and degraded. But New Bedford, which had largely escaped the ravages of the financial panic owing to its whaling trade, was thriving. Black men like

Nathan Johnson owned more books and worked harder "than nine-tenths of all the slaveholders of Talbot County, Maryland," Douglass noted.[29]

On his third day in New Bedford, Douglass went out on the wharves looking for work. His first job as a free laborer was to load barrels of whale oil onto a sloop. It was hard, dirty work, but he "went at it with a glad heart and willing hand," for no master was waiting to take his money at the end of the week. For the first time in his life he did not have to rely on a master, friend, or spouse in order to feel independent. "That day's work I considered the real starting point of something like a new existence," he recalled.[30]

But Douglass soon realized that escaping slavery did not mean fleeing racism. Despite its extraordinary tolerance and diversity, New Bedford was awash in prejudice, reflecting the plague that ravaged America. When Douglass sought a job as a caulker, a Quaker shipowner promptly employed him, but every white worker threatened to quit if he so much as lifted his caulking iron. They agreed to let him work as a day laborer for half their pay, but not as their equal.[31] A similar incident had occurred in Baltimore, in which white workers went on strike until management fired the free black workers. In Baltimore Douglass had heard whites

say that "*the niggers . . .* ought to be killed"
or else "they would take the country." And in
Baltimore whites had beaten him up so badly
that he almost lost an eye. At least in New Bedford his physical safety was not in jeopardy.[32]

For the next three years Douglass worked
as a day laborer sawing wood, digging cellars,
shoveling coal, sweeping chimneys, driving
coaches, waiting tables. He found two permanent positions, one in a candle factory and the
other in a brass foundry, which enabled him to
"nail a newspaper to the post near my bellows
and read" while he worked. "It was the pursuit
of knowledge under difficulties," he recalled.
He stood apart from most of his fellow workers,
white and black, who seemed little concerned
with the life of the mind.[33]

Mr. Cobb, the foreman of the brass foundry
where Douglass worked, would always remember the diligent (and dirty) worker. Twenty years
later Cobb attended a Douglass lecture, was invited onstage, and recalled how Douglass had
arrived at the foundry for the graveyard shift
covered in soot from sweeping chimneys by
day, then nailed up his newspaper and began
blowing bellows. Cobb had been awed by the
young man's work ethic and protected him
from one white worker who tried to assault
him with a shovel. He was thrilled to see the

former fugitive rise to "one of the intellectual men of the country."[34]

In New Bedford Douglass read whenever he could and became a preacher in the city's Zion Methodist church.[35] He was the happiest he had ever been, for he earned (and kept) a dollar a day, was a leader in New Bedford's black community, and had a devoted wife and two beautiful children (Lewis was born in 1840). But happiness was not his primary object.[36]

He was in quest of knowledge, and in this sense he resembled Herman Melville, who was also in New Bedford in 1840 waiting to sail on the whale ship *Acushnet*. A year younger than Douglass, Melville was as naïve, curious, and ambitious. He came to New Bedford not as a slave, even though he famously declared himself one: "Who ain't a slave? Tell me that." He came, like Douglass, to make his way in the world, his family's wealth having evaporated, and his experiences in New Bedford and on the whaling ship would form the basis of *Moby-Dick* (1851), a masterwork of world literature and an exploration of interracial friendship.[37]

New Bedford was a small town in 1840, with about three thousand residents, and with an easy walk from one end of town to the other, Melville and Douglass might have passed each other on the wharf. Both men described the same casks of whale oil piled upon the wharves, the whale ship at the dock, and the bellows at the forge where Douglass worked and read the newspaper. Melville might have inadvertently stumbled into the A.M.E. Zion church while Douglass was preaching or listening to a sermon.[38] Years later, the two men would read each other's works, respectfully borrowing phrases and ideas.[39] In 1864 President Lincoln would similarly borrow from Melville, using the metaphors of whaling to describe the problem of slavery: "We are like whalers who have been long on a chase—we have at last got the harpoon into the monster, but we must now look how we steer, or, with one 'flop' of his tail, he will yet send us all into eternity!"[40] While Douglass would eventually resemble Ahab in his radicalism, Lincoln became like Stubb, the good-humored conservative who "presided over his whale-boat as if the most deadly encounter were but a dinner."[41]

A more immediate influence on Douglass in New Bedford was the *Liberator*, the Boston organ of the American Anti-Slavery Society, edited by William Lloyd Garrison. Douglass subscribed a few months after moving to New Bedford even though he couldn't afford it, and paid the two-dollar annual fee in installments.[42] The *Liberator* was the most influential protest paper in American history. It relied on the

Declaration of Independence and the Bible as sacred texts and called for an immediate end to slavery and equal rights for all people. It envisioned a heaven on earth in which the government of God replaced human government. It advocated nonviolence, declaring that revolution would be achieved through moral suasion alone. And it refused to compromise: "I will not equivocate—I will not excuse—I will not retreat a single inch," Garrison had vowed in the first issue of the *Liberator* in January 1831.[43] He remained true to his word. To offset this message of breathtaking idealism, Garrison employed a style of "extraordinary physicality": in his pages oppressors trembled, nations quaked, statues leaped, and victims bled. While the romantic poets had "spiritualized the natural world," Garrison made palpable the moral repugnance against slavery.[44]

The publication of the *Liberator* outraged a nation whose citizens generally had no desire to end slavery. Human bondage had been a fact of life for millennia, and most Americans believed that ceasing slavery immediately was madness. At best, most white Americans saw slavery as a necessary evil, much like pollution today: you might be able to control it, but abolishing it required an act of God and lots of time—decades or even centuries, as Boston's mayor, Harrison

Gray Otis, and later Lincoln, declared.[45] Otis and most white Americans also believed that the Bible defended slavery in more places than it opposed it. Many Southerners, drawing on scripture and philosophers ranging from Aristotle and Saint Augustine to the Mississippi divine James Smylie, declared that slavery benefited society, masters, and slaves themselves.[46] Southerners suppressed antislavery literature and unsuccessfully tried to arrest Garrison. The Georgia legislature, for example, offered a $5,000 reward for his arrest and extradition to the state to be tried for libel. And South Carolina senator John C. Calhoun vainly tried to pass a national law banning the circulation of all abolitionist writings and images.[47]

The *Liberator*'s message was thus a radically new idea in Western culture.[48] Abolitionists were everywhere condemned as revolutionary fanatics who threatened to destroy American society. In 1835 Garrison was almost lynched in Boston, and throughout most of the decade mobs of "respectable" citizens, from bankers and lawyers to merchants, attacked abolitionist meetings. Understandably, the *Liberator*'s main support during its first few years of publication came from blacks, who made up about 75 percent of its readership.[49]

By the end of the decade abolitionists were

not quite as despised, even though they remained a fringe minority. This was because many white Northerners blamed the financial panic of 1837 on the "Slave Power"—the South's ruling elite. They believed that slavery depressed prices in free society and thus threatened their own livelihoods. Additionally, the famous congressional Gag Rules prohibited any discussion of slavery in Congress. As a result, abolitionism was increasingly identified with civil liberties, and subscriptions to the *Liberator* and membership in the American Anti-Slavery Society increased every year from 1834 to 1840.[50]

Douglass read the *Liberator* as devoutly as his Bible. To him both were sacred texts that echoed the Declaration in affirming universal freedom and equality. Every week he "mastered" the *Liberator*'s contents, as he put it, and was introduced to a community of like-minded men and women throughout the North.[51] He learned how to combat slavery with words and use punchy verbs. "The paper became my meat and drink. My soul was set all on fire," he wrote, quoting Garrison, his mentor, who had used the same line to explain why he refused to moderate his indignation: "I have need to be *all on fire*, for I have mountains of ice about me to melt."[52]

The *Liberator* inspired Douglass to attend

abolitionist meetings. Despite his working all day and often all night, the meetings enabled him to practice his oratory, debate new friends, and try out some of the phrases he read in the journal. At one meeting in 1839 he and a group of New Bedford black abolitionists lashed out at the American Colonization Society, which shipped free blacks to the African colony of Liberia as a conservative solution to the "problem" of blacks in America.[53] Most abolitionists hated colonizationists, and Douglass and his cohorts resolved never to be enticed by them: "we are *American citizens*, born with natural, inherent, just, and inalienable rights." They praised Garrison for advocating "immediate and unconditional emancipation."[54]

After reading the *Liberator* for three years, Douglass finally heard Garrison speak at a meeting in New Bedford on August 9, 1841. He had become something of a "hero-worshipper," after reading Thomas Carlyle's influential new book on heroes. He already loved Garrison "through his paper"; now he hoped to worship him. He was not disappointed: "no face and form ever impressed me with such sentiments."[55]

Garrison was another self-made man and in some respects a lot like Douglass. He had been abandoned by his alcoholic father while a boy and reduced to begging for food from neighbors. With virtually no formal education, his lucky break came when he got a job as an apprentice to a printer, which enabled him to learn a trade. He worked tirelessly, read voraciously, and was as proud, determined, and as much of a risk-taker as Douglass. For years Garrison had been threatened with murder and bankruptcy because of his paper and dream of freedom. Now, when he spoke, the words came out slowly, deliberately, as though priceless gifts from God; and his bespectacled bald head seemed aglow from the light of heaven (see figure 6).[56]

Douglass was not the only one to be impressed that day: to Garrison, this tall young black man, so beautifully dressed and poised and seemingly confident, stood out in a crowd and almost controlled the room by his looks. When Douglass began to speak, and he heard the rich baritone voice and saw the "large and attentive audiences" listening to him with such "deep interest," Garrison was deeply moved.[57]

The next day Douglass accompanied Garrison and forty black and white abolitionists to Nantucket for a large two-day convention. It was Douglass's first holiday since escaping slavery, and it began ominously. When the abolitionists boarded the ship for Nantucket, the captain refused to depart until the blacks dispersed to the "negro quarters." Holding their ground, the radicals protested against segregation and offered to debate every passenger on board, causing a long delay in the departure. The captain finally relented and allowed them all to sit on the upper deck.[58] The incident showed Douglass how moral suasion could lead to social change.

At the Nantucket convention, Douglass was urged to speak. With over five hundred people attending, the majority of them white, it was by an order of magnitude the largest audience that he had ever addressed. He was so nervous that he trembled with fear, and his fright recalled memories of slavery. "The truth was, I felt myself a slave." But after speaking for a few minutes he recovered his sense of freedom and the words flowed.[59]

Garrison took the stage next, riffing off Douglass's speech: "Have we been listening to a thing, a piece of property, or to a man?"

"A man! A man!" came the united response.

"And should such a man be held a slave in a republican and Christian land?" Garrison asked.

"Never! Never!" came the thunderous cry.

"Will you succor and protect him as a brother man—a resident of the old Bay State?"

"Yes!" shouted the audience with such force

that the walls and roof of the hall "seemed to shudder," according to one reporter.[60]

Douglass was stunned by the performance. Garrison captivated his listeners; they seemed to become "a single individuality," the image of Garrison's own soul. When Douglass spoke again at the evening session, he tried out some of Garrison's techniques. Now it was Garrison's turn to be amazed. Douglass's speech "would have done honor to Patrick Henry," Garrison declared. He was especially struck by Douglass's control of his rich baritone voice, like a singer achieving sublime power over his listeners.[61]

Before the convention adjourned, the general agent of the American Anti-Slavery Society invited Douglass to be a paid lecturer. Douglass was initially reluctant, for incredible as it may now seem, he was unsure of his talent. But he agreed to a three-month renewable contract at an annual salary of $450.[62] Little did he know that he had found his calling and was about to embark on a remarkable career. He would later note that public speaking was the most effective form of protest and his greatest accomplishment as an artist and activist: "I hardly need say to those who know me that writing for the public eye never came quite as easily as speaking to the public ear." Over the next few years he

Figure 6.
Liberator editor
William Lloyd
Garrison, around
1841. *(Library of Congress)*

would refine his talent and become one of the greatest orators in America.

The American Anti-Slavery Society needed Douglass more than Douglass needed it. In 1840 the society had split over differences in opinion about politics and women and was losing members and money. Garrison and his followers opposed voting and largely ignored political debates. They interpreted the Constitution as a proslavery document, considered American government incurably corrupt, and advocated disunion from the slave republic. As Douglass put it, they regarded slavery solely "as a creature of public opinion." They also demanded that women be allowed to have leadership roles in the American Anti-Slavery Society.[63]

One group of dissenters, believing in the efficacy of the ballot box, formed the Liberty Party in order to nominate antislavery candidates and seek change through political action. They "looked at slavery as a creature of law." A smaller group, opposing women's rights based on its reading of the Bible and social customs, organized the American and Foreign Anti-Slavery Society, which prohibited "promiscuous" meetings in which men and women both spoke.[64] There was so much infighting that abolitionists could not reconcile their differences. After the breakup, Garrison and his followers refused to accommodate dissenters, and each group went its separate way. The upshot of the schism was that the American Anti-Slavery Society saw its membership drop by half and its annual income plummet from $47,000 to $7,000. More than ever, the society needed a charismatic orator to champion its cause.[65]

It also needed someone who could speak about slavery firsthand. Southerners flooded the market with pamphlets, books, and images that depicted slaves as happy and content and masters as benevolent and fatherly. They accused abolitionists of never having seen slavery. Only Southerners could speak authoritatively about the institution, they argued, adding that Northern wage workers were far more oppressed than slaves. Indeed, white Southerners called themselves blacks' best friends; one pamphlet asserted that "of all the states," Maryland was "the first in friendliness toward the African."[66]

Partly in response to such criticism, Northern reformers wanted to hear from a *slave* what slavery was like. But most fugitives affiliated with the American Anti-Slavery Society were reluctant to become lecturers for fear of exposing themselves and being recaptured. And those willing to take such risks did not meet the society's strict standards for lecturing, which required "galvanism that can reanimate the dead as well as the steadfastness that can withstand" constant travel and frequent attacks.[67] Douglass was the first ex-slave to become a full-time lecturer for the society. The other black lecturers, from William Cooper Nell to Charles Remond, had been born free. Douglass's timing, in other words, was perfect.

Immediately he went on the road. His employer purchased a home for his family, conveniently located next to the railroad tracks in

Lynn, Massachusetts. But Frederick was rarely in Lynn, owing to his speaking schedule, and Anna and their two children remained in New Bedford until mid-1842. Anna obtained extra work as a domestic to supplement Frederick's income, and sometimes Frederick had to ask the society to send her an extra "$25 or $30" to "carry on household affairs." Their third child, Frederick Jr., was born in New Bedford in March 1842, but Frederick was not around to help care for the infant. For years the child barely recognized his father.[68]

Usually Douglass traveled with John Collins, a veteran white lecturer. They traversed New England in rude coaches or the railroad, sleeping in abolitionists' homes and speaking in churches, barns, schools, taverns, or on the town green when no building could be found. When Douglass covered a town by himself, racial prejudice was more pronounced and he often had trouble securing a venue and promoting his lecture. This happened in Grafton, Massachusetts. So he went into a hotel, borrowed a dinner bell, and walked through the main streets, ringing the bell and crying out, *"Notice!* Frederick Douglass, recently a slave, will lecture on American Slavery on Grafton Common this evening at 7:00." The strategy worked: a large audience came to hear him and the next day a church opened its doors to him.[69]

Douglass also fought prejudice on the railroads. In September 1841, while he was traveling with Collins on the Eastern Railroad, the conductor kicked him out of the cabin and into the freight car used for blacks.[70] Douglass told Collins to stay in the cabin, but Collins followed until the conductor pushed him back, ripping his clothes. Two weeks later Douglass and Collins boarded another Eastern Railroad car at Lynn and again sat together. The same conductor tried to separate them and Douglass stayed put and demanded to know why he should be forced out of the cabin after paying for it.

"Because you are black," the conductor said.

"That is no reason," Douglass retorted, and he and Collins clung to their bench. The conductor rounded up a half dozen toughs to "snake out the damn nigger." They finally ejected them, but in the process ripped out the floor bolts and destroyed the seat. Douglass and his comrades continued protesting such segregation, and eventually the Massachusetts railroad companies relented, abolishing segregated cars.[71]

From the beginning Douglass was a great success as a lecturer. He talked about his life as a slave, adding levity to the grim subject matter with humor, sarcasm, and mimicry. He dressed formally and paid close attention to how he was seen as well as heard, sometimes asking a sexton to turn up the gaslights so that people could see him better. He referred to his back being "covered with scars" and sometimes bared it, but to protect himself he withheld the names of his former masters and the locations where he had toiled. And since Garrisonians opposed violent resistance, he downplayed his fighting prowess. Audiences and reporters alike were spellbound by the form and content of his stories.[72] In December 1841, just three months after he started his new career, one journalist effusively described his performance: "This is an extraordinary man. He was cut out for a hero. . . . He has the 'heart to conceive, the head to contrive, and the hand to execute.' . . . As a speaker he has few equals." Douglass would use the same language a decade later to describe a fictional black hero whom he modeled on himself.[73]

Douglass's performances yielded results. He toured Rhode Island in late 1841, speaking out against a proposed state constitution that restricted suffrage to white men. His white comrades spoke first and offended the audience, and then Douglass came onstage and charmed them. The technique evidently worked, for voters passed a constitution that gave black men the vote. "Our labors in Rhode Island," Douglass said, "did more to abolitionize the state than any previous or subsequent work."[74]

The success in Rhode Island highlighted the fine line that existed between public opinion and law. Increasingly, Douglass wanted to couple moral suasion with political action to achieve the desired ends. He subtly endorsed political action when he paid tribute to the great antislavery statesman John Quincy Adams, who was struggling to overturn the congressional Gag Rules. As a slave he had come across an antislavery speech by Adams printed in the Baltimore newspaper. From it he had learned what "abolition" meant and discovered that a few Washington politicians were "pleading for us" and "moving for our freedom."[75] Antislavery politics could be as effective as moral suasion, he realized.

In 1843 Douglass and a group of lecturers embarked on an ambitious "100 convention tour" that began in New Hampshire and then moved west through Vermont, upstate New York, and down into Pennsylvania, Ohio, and Indiana. The performers traveled in pairs, and their goal was to abolitionize every community they visited, enlightening people to the horrors of slavery and "hastening its extinction." It was a grueling itinerary but the prospect of mass conversions filled Douglass with hope. He felt like one of Christ's disciples, compelling men to come into the fold. Rochester was one of his favorite stops. Even though it was a hotbed of political abolitionism and Douglass as a Garrisonian considered politics corrupt, he received a friendly reception and met numerous Liberty Party men.[76]

At times Douglass was left to abolitionize a town all by himself. In Buffalo, a city booming from the new steamboat trade, the prospects for conversion looked bleak, for the people seemed too bent on moneymaking to be concerned with reform. The hall where Douglass was scheduled to speak was a deserted old post office and his audience a handful of cab drivers, whips in hand and dirt covering their clothes. When Douglass's white colleague saw these "ragamuffins" he took the first steamer to Cleveland without even bothering to give a lecture, leaving Douglass to "do" Buffalo alone. Douglass spoke every day in the ramshackle old post office to audiences that "constantly increased in number and respectability." Within two weeks his listeners had grown from five to five thousand and no venue was large enough to hold them. His last Sunday there he spoke in the park to one-third of the city's population, the power of his word inspiring the multitude.[77]

The western leg of the "100 convention tour" did not go so well, however. Douglass quickly discovered that Indiana (Lincoln's old state) was almost as racist as Maryland. At Richmond, their first stop, they anticipated trouble, for a mob had almost killed a farmer for daring to ask Henry Clay, the presidential candidate from Kentucky (and Lincoln's hero), to free his forty slaves. Some of these same ruffians now mobbed Douglass and his colleagues, throwing rotten eggs and other missiles at them and ruining Douglass's suit.[78]

Then at Pendleton, Indiana, Douglass came as close as he ever would to being murdered. During the first day's meeting, a mob threatened to attack him and his partners and destroy a church. As a result, Pendletonians banished the abolitionists to the woods, where they built a platform from which to speak. On the second day some thirty backwoods boys, led by a young tough in a coonskin cap, attacked Douglass and his co-lecturers.[79] In temperament and behavior they resembled Lincoln's friend Jack Armstrong and his Clary's Grove gang.

The thugs tore down the speaking platform and hit one abolitionist in the mouth, knocking out several teeth. Another lecturer, William A. White, a recent Harvard graduate and a new

convert to abolitionism, suddenly disappeared.
Douglass, thinking White was in serious danger, picked up a club and went after the thugs.
He knew he was violating Garrison's principle
of nonviolence and the racial code that said a
black man should never attack a white man.
But he didn't care; such tenets were irrelevant
when a comrade's life was in danger. Now the
thugs were out for murder: "Kill the nigger,
kill the damn nigger," a few of them yelled.
Douglass fled for his life, but the gang leader
overtook him and clubbed him, breaking Douglass's hand and knocking him down. He raised
his club for another blow, this one aimed at
Douglass's head. But White, who had not been
hurt and saw Douglass fall, came to the rescue, body-blocking the tough and stopping
"his murderous pursuit." Other gang members
began pummeling White, until the townspeople, who had been watching up to this point,
broke up the riot.[80]

The incident haunted Douglass. Three years
later he dreamed about the brawl, and in the
morning wrote White to express his gratitude:
"I shall never forget how like two very brothers we were, ready to dare, do, and even die
for each other. You had left home and a life
of ease and even luxury that you might do
something toward breaking the fetters of the

slave and elevating the despised black man."
In protecting Douglass, White had shed "noble
blood—so warm, so generous" and "too holy
to be poured out by the rough hand of that
infernal mob."[81]

The attack haunted White as well. Indeed, he
quit lecturing after the "100 convention tour"
and returned to Boston to write poetry. In his
letter Douglass urged him to continue in the
cause: "Go forth, and scatter your eloquence
like sparks from the smitten steel. It will have
its influence." To further entice his friend, he
quoted from memory Lord Byron, whose work
he had recently begun reading:

> *Freedom's battle once begun . . .*
> *Though baffled oft is ever won.*

But not even Byron's words were persuasive,
for White never again put himself on the front
lines of battle.[82]

Despite such bonds of brotherly affection,
Douglass felt that most white abolitionists were
not immune to the prejudice that blanketed
the country. He received about half the pay of
white lecturers even though he was the most
effective speaker in the organization. After criticizing John Collins, he was reprimanded "for
insubordination to my superiors." His white

colleagues treated him as a spectacle or symbol rather than as a person: "I was generally introduced as a *'chattel'*—a *'thing'*—a piece of southern *'property'*—the chairman assuring the audience that *it* could speak." He hated the way some of his white colleagues patronized him: just "give us the facts," John Collins told him; "we will take care of the philosophy."[83]

But Douglass found it impossible to give the same lecture week after week. It felt "entirely too mechanical for my nature." He was now reading greedily, trying to make up for years of intellectual emptiness, and as his speeches grew in analytical and rhetorical power, he varied their content and form. "People won't believe you ever was a slave, Frederick, if you keep on this way," another white colleague warned. "Better have a little of the plantation manner of speech than not; 'tis not best that you seem too learned."[84]

Such advice felt like a slap in the face. Even though Douglass converted more people to the cause than anyone else in the organization, his white colleagues too often treated him like a child rather than an apprentice or master performer. "I was growing and needed room," he wrote, but some whites tried to contain him, wanting him to remain something of a slave.[85]

Some of this tension was a result of envy. After all, abolitionists devoted their lives to the cause and wanted to change the world. To be a great abolitionist was to be a great orator. They were nothing if not ambitious. And so when an upstart like Douglass suddenly began filling large auditoriums, receiving thunderous applause that shook the rafters while the efforts of white speakers fell on deaf ears, there was bound to be some resentment. The backlash occasionally took racist forms, from public reprimands to one private letter from a leading Boston abolitionist that referred to Douglass as "an unconscionable nigger."[86]

These ignoble examples should not diminish the heroic interracial efforts that led to the abolition of segregated cars in Massachusetts, or the state's repeal in 1843 of a ban on black-white marriages. Abolitionists accomplished what few people in American history have been able to do: integrate parts of society. One hundred years later, segregation and antimiscegenation laws would remain facts of life in American society.[87]

And in one sense, Douglass's colleagues were right to try to contain him. By 1844, after steeping himself in such authors as Byron, Burns, Shakespeare, Carlyle, Emerson, and Milton, he sounded nothing like a slave and audiences began accusing him of never having been one. Not giving details about where he came from further fueled doubts about his authenticity. Increasingly he heard people say that he neither looked, acted, nor spoke like a slave. One journalist, covering a large abolition meeting in Philadelphia in 1844, summarized Douglass's performance by saying, "Many persons in the audience . . . could not believe that he was actually a slave. How a man, only six years out of bondage, and who had never gone to school a day in his life, could speak with such eloquence—with such precision of language and power of thought—they were utterly at a loss to devise."[88]

Such doubts about Douglass's status as a fugitive threatened his career. And so he "threw caution to the wind" and wrote his life story, naming names, dates, places, creating a rogues' gallery of the Eastern Shore.[89] Having rehearsed his life story for years on the lecture circuit, he knew what to say and how to say it, and completed the manuscript during the winter months of 1844–45. After his friend Wendell Phillips, another brilliant orator, read it, he told Douglass that if he were him he "would throw it into the fire." If his owner hunted him down, Massachusetts could do nothing to protect him, Phillips said. He was right: a recent Supreme Court ruling (*Prigg v. Pennsylvania*) denied states any power to protect fugitives. The previous year, George Latimer, an ex-slave and father just like Douglass, had been captured in Boston and locked up in the Leverett Street jail, escaping reenslavement only because a wealthy abolitionist purchased his freedom.[90]

Douglass ignored these warnings. In May 1845, the American Anti-Slavery Society published *Narrative of the Life of Frederick Douglass, An American Slave, Written by Himself*, with introductions by Garrison and Phillips that vouched for its veracity.[91] Selling for fifty cents, it was a hard-hitting, lyrical, and ironic page-turner that soon became an international bestseller. Within three years it went through eleven thousand copies in the United States and nine editions in England, and by 1850 thirty thousand copies had been sold. Reviewers in England and Ireland lauded its "native eloquence," and one American reviewer called it "the most thrilling work which the American press ever issued—*and the most important*." Douglass became, like his new hero Lord Byron, famous almost overnight.[92]

But with fame his freedom was now in great jeopardy. Thomas and Hugh Auld, or any would-be kidnapper, could easily track his whereabouts in the antislavery newspapers. Indeed numerous slave-owners in Baltimore and on the Eastern Shore, including Thomas and Hugh, read the *Narrative*, despite laws prohibiting its circulation in Maryland and elsewhere in the South. The Aulds were outraged by Douglass's portraits of them. Thomas publicly called Douglass a liar, and Hugh sought revenge, vowing to "spare no pains or expense in order to regain possession of him" and "place him in the cotton fields of the South."[93]

But Douglass was already safe in the British Isles when Hugh issued his threat. He fled there three months after publishing his *Narrative*, seeking refuge "from republican slavery in monarchical England," as he put it. Anna and the children—they had four now, Charles having been born in October 1844—remained behind in Lynn and lived off the royalties from his book and Anna's part-time work as a domestic. Douglass spent almost two years in England, Ireland, and Scotland, speaking to ever larger audiences about the nature of American slavery and gaining thousands more converts to the cause.[94]

Antislavery sentiment was widespread in Britain. Britain had peacefully abolished slavery in England in 1772 and in its West Indian colonies on August 1, 1834; and Douglass considered West Indian emancipation, which freed 800,000 slaves at enormous financial expense to the British government, the "greatest and grandest" event of the century.[95] He viewed England as a beacon of humanity and hoped that British emancipation would inspire Americans to follow suit and inaugurate a new age of universal freedom. "There was something Godlike in this decree of the British nation. It was the spirit of the Son of God commanding the devil of slavery to go out of the British West Indies."[96]

Douglass fell in love with England and came close to staying there permanently. He loved English manners, the clean and comfortable trains, and the absence of hogs on the streets. He made a number of close friends, was feted by the British public, and for the first time in his life he experienced an utter absence of racism. From "the instant I stepped upon the shore and looked into the faces of the crowd around me, I saw in every man a recognition of my manhood, and an absence, a perfect absence, of everything like that disgusting hate with which we are pursued in" America, he said.[97] He could walk into a hotel, restaurant, or railcar without causing a fracas. And he could pass someone on the street without prompting a look of scorn. He went so far as to suggest that being black was a social advantage in Britain: "I find I am hardly black enough for British taste, but by keeping my hair as woolly as possible I make out to pass for at least half a Negro at any rate," he half-jokingly wrote one friend. He began to treat August 1, the anniversary of British West Indian emancipation, as more sacred than the Fourth of July.[98]

Douglass did not turn a blind eye to Britain's social problems, however, especially its rampant poverty. He realized that while social stratification in America stemmed primarily from racial distinctions, in Britain it came from class; and he forged alliances with Chartists, who advocated equal rights for the poor and laboring classes. He also acknowledged that the absence of racism stemmed in large part from the fact that so few blacks lived there. But at least in England, "there is Freedom, there is Liberty."[99]

The British Isles highlighted for Douglass the problems in America. He came to believe that the greatest obstacle to abolitionism was neither the wealth generated by slavery, nor the Constitution and laws defending it, but the horrible prejudice against blacks: whites "reconciled themselves" to black slavery and oppression "as things inevitable if not desirable."[100] Racism enabled slaveowners to feel good about themselves; it purged any guilt that came from treating humans as oxen and sex objects.

What finally convinced Douglass to return to the United States was his sense of duty to his fellow blacks and his desire to end the scourge of racism. "I have no love for America," he announced. "I have no patriotism. I have no country." But in loving England he did not hate America: "I love humanity all over the globe." What he hated were American laws, churches, newspapers, and legislatures that defended slavery. While he was abroad America had annexed Texas as a slave state and had made war with Mexico in order to acquire more slave territory. Douglass wanted to destroy these bulwarks of oppression, wanted to rip the Constitution into "a thousand fragments" and rebuild the government from the ground up in order to fulfill the principles of freedom and equality in the Declaration.[101] He wanted, in short, to import into America some of the humanity he had witnessed in England.

When Douglass left Bristol for the United States in early April 1847, he was a changed man. He had "spent some of the happiest moments of his life" in Britain and had "undergone a transformation. I live a new life," he declared.[102] Not only did he discover what it was like to live in a world without racism; he learned that brotherly love need not be dangerous. Unlike his bond with William White, the friendships he forged in Britain were not contingent upon the threat of death. In fact, Douglass made more friends during his two years abroad than he had in his entire life to date, including Julia Griffiths, Richard Webb, George Thompson, Thomas Clarkson, Elizabeth Pease, and Ellen and Anna Richardson. He was so popular (and famous) that he regularly filled auditoriums, some of which held over seven thousand people. At a public farewell party given for him in London, some fourteen hundred people attended, and during his travels countless others offered him "a friendly hand and a cordial welcome."[103]

Douglass's British friends also protected him in ways that his American friends had been blind to. After hearing of Hugh Auld's threat to reenslave him, they urged him to remain in England and raised $500 to bring Anna and the children. When Douglass decided to return to America, they contacted Hugh Auld, who now legally owned Frederick, and paid him £150 Sterling (just over $700) in exchange for Frederick's freedom. They raised an additional $2,000 so that Douglass (and Anna) would not have to worry about money for a while.[104]

Douglass didn't want the money. He thought it would alienate him from the mass of abolitionists who had to toil for their daily bread. Instead he suggested that they use it to buy him a printing press: he wanted to start his own newspaper. Previous attempts to run black newspapers having failed, he believed that a well-managed paper edited by a black man would be "powerful evidence that the Negro was too much of a man to be held a chattel."[105] He was confident he could succeed, for two of the most popular editors in America, Horace Greeley and Thurlow Weed, after reading his *Narrative* and published letters from abroad, called him "among the most gifted and eloquent men of the age."[106]

When Douglass arrived in Boston on April 20, he was legally a free man, famous throughout Britain and America, and ready to begin a new career as a journalist. He took the first train to Lynn and "within fifty yards of his house" was met by his two "bright-eyed" and curious sons, Lewis (age six) and Frederick Jr. (age five). His youngest child, Charles, had no idea who he was, and Anna seemed more like a maid than a wife. She complained of poor health and over-work, and said that she had worried so much about Frederick's safety that she "had not allowed herself to expect" him to come home, "for fear of being disappointed." But when Frederick walked through the door, his two boys clinging to him, she suddenly felt "exceedingly happy."[107]

The homecoming did not last long, for within days Douglass left for another lecture tour. Then he decided to uproot his family once more and move them to Rochester, a bustling young city and a railroad (and Underground Railroad) hub that burned with the fires of the Liberty Party yet lacked an abolitionist newspaper. Anna opposed the move, but he insisted, for it would enable him to start fresh. He would not have to compete for business with the *Liberator* and he need not be influenced by his former employer.[108]

The news of his intended move outraged Boston abolitionists. Garrison, who considered Douglass his protégé and found out about it secondhand, felt like a spurned lover and never forgave him.[109] The rift widened to include most other Boston abolitionists, who already considered Douglass an apostate. They had opposed the purchase of his freedom because it recognized the right "to traffic in human beings" and thus compromised abolitionist principles. They had wanted Douglass to publicly "disown" his manumission.[110] Now they considered it "absurd" for an ex-slave, "brought up in the very depths of ignorance," to pretend that he could be a successful editor. A fugitive orator who bared his back to shocked audiences was one thing; an editor who enlightened educated readers on the principles of liberty, justice, and humanity was something else entirely! The paper was not needed, they said, it could not succeed, and his usefulness was as a lecturer not a writer.[111]

Such criticism did not affect Douglass, though. He had already learned that as he continued to remake himself, he left friends and allies behind. Friends today too often became strangers tomorrow, especially abolitionists who were loath to compromise. While he constantly changed, they remained much the same or evolved in divergent paths. In a protean sea, love and friendship rarely survived.

When Lincoln returned to New Salem from the Black Hawk War in the fall of 1832, the general store where he worked had "petered out" and he needed a job. He wasn't worried, though, for he had his soldier's pay of $120 and numerous friends. He considered blacksmithing but remembered how much he hated manual labor. Law interested him but he felt he "could not succeed at that without a better education." He decided to speculate and bought a half interest in a general store with William Berry, his corporal from the Black Hawk War and a hard-drinking backwoodsman. He bought it on credit, signing a note "in payment for the whole."[112]

It was a bad investment, for there were three

stores in the village, two more than needed, and competition was fierce. Lincoln's buddies from Clary's Grove helped out by eliminating one competitor: they got drunk one night and wrecked a store owned by Reuben Radford, breaking the windows and destroying much of the merchandise and equipment. Lincoln neither encouraged his friends nor played a role in the destruction, but Radford, "fearing his bones might share the fate of his windows," decided to sell, and Lincoln and Berry bought the remaining merchandise on credit.[113]

Business continued to flounder. Lincoln and Berry sold dry goods and "groceries," meaning liquor, with most of the revenue coming from the liquor. Although Lincoln didn't drink and considered alcohol evil, he did not allow his moral scruples to interfere with business. In fact, in order to generate more income he and his partner purchased a license that allowed them to sell liquor by the glass, essentially turning their business into a combination tavern and store. Years later, when his political nemesis Stephen Douglas accused him of owning a "flourishing grocery" business in New Salem, Lincoln denied it: "I never kept a grocery anywhere in the world," he said. But numerous neighbors remembered him selling liquor and indeed referred to his store as a "grocery."[114]

Not even the liquor trade could save him, for within a year his store "winked out," and he was out of work again. Some friends got him the job as the New Salem postmaster, which paid about $55 a year, and he got a second job as a surveyor to make ends meet. But he was in debt for about $200, and when the note came due he couldn't pay, so his horse, saddle, bridle, and surveying instruments were sold at auction. Again he was saved by friends, who purchased his surveying instruments and gave them back to him.[115]

Lincoln's luck turned in 1834 when he was elected to the state assembly.[116] He ran partly for the salary but also because he loved politics and had the support of numerous New Salem friends. Politically he was a Whig, the party that had recently emerged under the leadership of Henry Clay to oppose President Andrew Jackson's Democratic Party. Clay created a Whig platform called the "American system," which supported a strong central government; a national bank; protective tariffs; and government-sponsored roads, canals, and other "internal improvements." Most Northern Whigs, including Clay, also championed conservative reforms such as temperance and colonization as ways to curb the excesses of American democracy (especially drunkenness and slavery). While Democrats were more likely to be proslavery and states' rights advocates, they also viewed themselves as the party of the common man and said that Whigs "favored the growth of aristocracy."[117]

In response, Clay argued that supporters of his system were more often "self-made men," a term he coined in 1832 that quickly caught on. For Clay, only white men could be self-made. Lincoln, who later referred to Clay as "my beau ideal of a statesman, the man for whom I fought all my humble life," endorsed every aspect of his American system and would remain a Whig in principle for the rest of his life.[118]

During his 1834 campaign Lincoln ignored his allegiance to Clay's American system. His district was divided between Whig supporters in New Salem and Democratic subsistence farmers in the countryside, and he would not have gotten elected running on a Whig platform. Instead of discussing politics he gladhanded voters. He frequently traveled around town as postmaster, stuffing letters in his hat and delivering them to recipients. These trips offered an opportunity to ask for votes. His work as a surveyor also helped. During one trip to survey some land about twelve miles west of New Salem, he saw thirty farmers harvesting a field, and after he introduced himself they told him that they could not vote for him unless he could offer a hand with the harvesting.[119]

"Well, boys," Lincoln responded, "if that is all, I am sure of your votes," and he took hold of the harvesting cradle and led the way around the field. "The boys was satisfied and I don't think he lost a vote," recalled one farmer.[120]

The campaign inspired Lincoln to study law. Until then, he had always felt inadequately prepared for such a profession, and some people in New Salem had laughed at the idea of his becoming a lawyer. Bowling Green, the corpulent justice of the peace, had once heard Lincoln offer amateur legal comments in court, and had laughed so hard that his fat sides began shaking spasmodically.[121] But during the campaign Lincoln received encouragement from the Whig politician and Springfield lawyer John Todd Stuart, the cousin of his future wife. After the election he borrowed Stuart's law books, "took them home with him, and went at it in good earnest."[122]

Lincoln began his law studies by reading Blackstone's *Commentaries*. This four-volume history of the laws of England, first published in 1765 and frequently republished, was required reading for aspiring lawyers; indeed it "ranked second only to the Bible as a literary and intellectual influence on the history of American institutions."[123] Blackstone explained the evolution of law as a rational, methodical, and scientific process, with "carefully delineated rules for everybody from kings to commoners." His focus was on theory and principle rather than procedure; and his vision of uninterrupted progress appealed to the status quo. His *Commentaries* were formidable even for educated readers, for his prose style, though elegant, was also dense, subtle, and richly ambiguous.[124]

Blackstone's *Commentaries* crucially influenced legal interpretations of slavery.[125] On the one hand, Blackstone argued that "the law of nature," being "dictated by God himself," was superior to all other laws. Natural law, or God's law, could override "positive," or man-made, law.* Blackstone's emphasis on natural law had contributed to the Somerset decision of 1772, which effectively abolished slavery in England (British lawyers had successfully argued that slavery was contrary to natural law). In the United States, Liberty Party abolitionists also relied heavily on Blackstone to declare that no governmental sanction of slavery could prevail over the natural law that forbade it. On the other hand, however, Blackstone suggested that natu-

---

* Positive law refers to those laws established or recognized by constitutions and government authorities.

ral law did not affect the contractual rights of a slaveowner.[126]

Most American lawyers and judges interpreted Blackstone conservatively. They prioritized positive law and common law (based on precedent) over natural law. As a result, American law in the decades before the Civil War attracted few radical reformers, since in order to change society you needed to dispense with legal precedent.[127] Typically, lawyers who became abolitionists either abandoned law as a profession (like Wendell Phillips) or became members of the Liberty Party.

Lincoln was deeply influenced by Blackstone. "I never read anything which so profoundly interested and thrilled me," he said. His opposition to the spread of slavery emerged partly out of his respect for natural law, which he considered antithetical to slavery. The positive law that sanctioned slavery was an exception to the natural law of freedom. But for Lincoln, natural law could not override positive law, which meant that slavery was protected in states whose constitutions sanctioned it. Nevertheless, the federal government should not support the spread of slavery into new territories that did not yet have constitutions.[128]

While most aspiring lawyers studied under a tutor in a law office, Lincoln "studied with nobody," as he said. He probably read Blackstone twice through and then supplemented it with procedural law books. As a postmaster and grocery store owner he often read on the job, from Robert Burns's poetry to Shakespeare and the newspapers. But this was "light" reading. His law studies required total immersion without interruption. On days that he didn't work, he sat against a wide oak tree and pored over Blackstone, "shifting his position as the sun rose and sank" in order to stay in the shade, "utterly unconscious of everything but the principles" of law. He became so absorbed in Blackstone that he skipped meals and lost about thirty pounds, his weight dropping to about 170.[129]

To most New Salem residents, Lincoln's studying for the law was a bit like a Yale graduate fighting in a rough and tumble. One day Russell Godbey, a New Salem farmer with a long goatee, saw Lincoln sitting against a woodpile reading. He thought it strange and asked, "What are you studying?"

"Studying law," Lincoln replied.

"Great God Almighty!" said Godbey. He was not the only one who worried that Lincoln's obsession with Blackstone had made him slightly "crazy."[130]

Lincoln remade himself visually before starting his new job at Vandalia, the state capital. He borrowed $200 ($15,000 in today's money) and with some of the money purchased the first suit he ever owned, including pants that actually fit, and other accoutrements of respectability: a white dress shirt and studs, silk vest, leather dress boots, and some underwear. "I want to make a decent appearance in the legislature," he told his creditor. But no matter how much he spent, he could not erase the signs of his backwoods upbringing: his clothes always seemed torn, frayed, or splotched; and the words most frequently used to describe him by educated and respectable people were "awkward," "shabby, "ugly," and "grotesque." Unlike Douglass, Lincoln never looked like a beautiful work of art.[131]

Besides, Lincoln was now overdressed for his job. Like countless other frontier buildings, the state capitol had not been built to last. Only ten years old, it already looked dilapidated. Chunks of plaster fell from the ceiling, endangering assemblymen, and the House chamber consisted of a large spare room with rough wooden tables, a pail and tin cups for water (or liquor), and a spittoon that looked like a litterbox for tobacco chewers, who made up a large portion of the lower house. So run-down was the building that in 1836 it collapsed, virtually imploding, and a new statehouse had to be built. The village of Vandalia, with its one thousand residents, was not much nicer: there were no proper hotels or boardinghouses, so assemblymen stayed at one of the numerous taverns, where drinking and fighting were part of the ambience.[132]

Lincoln spent three months of the year in Vandalia. In the first session he felt shy and insecure and rarely spoke, even though one-third of the House members were novices like him. But he soon learned how to introduce and pass bills in a frontier legislature; how to deal with stray and wild animals; how to raise money for new roads and canals; and how to promote the growth of businesses so that villages did not turn into ghost towns.

Lincoln's speaking style was strained. He spoke in a high-pitched voice that seemed almost absurd coming from such a large man, and his delivery, though much improved from reading *The Columbian Orator*, sounded terse, the words shooting out in staccato bursts. He often looked ill at ease as he spoke; he was known to speak with his hands in his pockets or gesticulate awkwardly. As a backwoodsman speaking to his own kind, he lacked the polish of Eastern orators.[133] But frontiersmen were suspicious of too much polish. Frederick Douglass and his comrades at Pendleton, Indiana, would have benefited from this knowledge; their refined civility was one reason why they got beat up by the backwoods boys.

In 1836, when Lincoln went up for reelection, New Salem voters demanded that candidates "show their hands" by stating their platform.[134] With Irish immigrants flocking to the state to help build canals, suffrage was a central issue. Canal workers typically owned no property and voted Democrat, so Lincoln didn't want them voting at all: "I go for admitting all whites to the right of suffrage who pay taxes or bear arms (by no means excluding females)."[135] Only white men who paid property taxes or served in the militia should be allowed to vote (there was no income tax). His parenthetical reference to women was meant as a joke, for as everyone knew, women had few rights and could neither pay taxes on property, serve in the militia, nor vote. While abolitionists such as Douglass and Garrison advocated equal rights for all, Lincoln followed a Whig platform and used women's second-class status as a source of humor. Blacks too were denied suffrage in Illinois, and Lincoln wanted to keep it that way. In fact, he later chastised Martin Van Buren for embracing black suffrage in New York State.[136]

On the suffrage issue Lincoln was being

pragmatic. To endorse blacks' or women's rights would have been political suicide.[137] But the other part of his platform was idealistic and visionary: he wanted his frontier state to have the kind of transportation network Massachusetts had spent a century implementing; and he wanted the federal government to pay for it from proceeds on the sale of public lands.[138]

It was an elitist platform. Immigrants would build federally funded roads and canals that benefited capitalists, but they would not be allowed to vote.[139] Ironically, Lincoln's platform ignored his own situation. He had more in common with subsistence farmers and canal workers, for he neither owned property nor had much to sell save his modest surveying skills. Only his militia service gave him the vote under his platform. He was aligning himself with other self-made frontiersmen and planning a fresh start. He got one soon after the August election, when he received his law license.

Lincoln's platform was also designed to save New Salem from extinction: the roads and waterways that ran through the village were horrible, and consequently business floundered and there was massive flight to larger towns. The exodus was so profound that property values dropped by as much as 90 percent in a year. Worries about the town's future helped

Lincoln win the election, though he lost the votes of subsistence farmers in rural areas like Clary's Grove. Even his friend Jack Armstrong, one of the poor farmers, decided not to vote for him.[140]

During the 1836–37 session, Lincoln established himself as a House leader.[141] He worked with a group of eight assemblymen to move the capital from Vandalia to Springfield and promote new roads and canals. Known as the "Long Nine" since they averaged six feet in height, they argued that Vandalia was too small and too far south in a state where the growth was in the north. They also raised $10 million in state bonds to build a series of railroads.[142]

The Panic of 1837 destroyed the Long Nine's grandiose roadbuilding plan and plunged the state into near bankruptcy. Bonds sold for fifteen cents on the dollar and the Illinois countryside was "littered with unfinished roads and partially dug canals" that were symbols of economic blight for years. People accused Lincoln of creating the mess, but he knew how to fight back and survived the attacks.[143]

The Long Nine accomplished its goal of moving the capital to Springfield, which was only twenty miles from New Salem. The move fueled Springfield's economy, benefiting Lincoln and other ambitious self-made men. In fact, Lincoln would follow the capital to Springfield, where he began practicing law with John Todd Stuart, a fellow Whig and legal mentor.

In one of the last acts of the 1836–37 legislative session, the General Assembly revealed just how conservative Illinois was with respect to slavery: almost unanimously, it passed a series of resolutions that censored abolition societies; defended the "sacred" and constitutional right to own slaves in the slave states; and argued that the federal government could not abolish slavery in the District of Columbia without the consent of its citizens.[144]

Lincoln and his fellow Whig politician Dan Stone were the sole dissenters. Yet while they issued a formal protest, their views of slavery did not differ much from those of the General Assembly. The main distinction was that Lincoln and Stone called slavery wrong: it had been "founded on both injustice and bad policy." But they clearly disliked abolition societies: "the promulgation of abolition doctrines tends rather to increase than abate [slavery's] evils." How abolitionists exacerbated the evils of slavery was never made clear, but in a state founded by Southerners, Lincoln and Stone could not afford to sympathize with the institution's opponents. Essentially they echoed the General Assembly's resolutions in arguing that any questions about slavery and emancipation should be left to slaveholders themselves. The Assembly's resolutions, and Lincoln and Stone's protest, were thus cautious and conservative responses to the problem of slavery. When Lincoln ran for president, he referred to this protest and said his position on slavery had not changed from 1837 to 1860. But this was a lie, a way of warding off accusations that he was a radical. Over the next twenty-three years he would become less conservative.[145]

Lincoln moved to Springfield on April 15, 1837. He left behind a dying village, soon to be a ghost town, and two failed marriage proposals. The first proposal had been to Ann Rutledge, the daughter of a tavern owner with whom he had boarded for a time.[146] Three years younger than he, Ann was short and plump and considered one of "the prettiest girls in the village."[147] She was also engaged to another man, John McNeil, which raised questions about how serious their engagement really was. Supposedly, McNeil left New Salem to visit his parents in New York. He was gone for months, questions were raised about his character, and in early spring 1835 Ann agreed to marry Lincoln if she could first obtain an "honorable release" from McNeil. Lincoln had just returned from his first General Assembly session at Vandalia. They were in no rush to marry: Ann needed time to get out of her engagement to McNeil, and Lincoln wanted first to complete his law studies and pass the bar. And so they set a rough date for late 1836 or 1837. But during the hot, rainy summer of 1835, Ann came down with "brain fever," probably typhoid, and she died on August 15. Her death plunged Lincoln into a severe depression (he was prone to them), and he dealt with it by immersing himself in his legal studies. Although Ann's death upset Lincoln, it may also have symbolized for him "the approaching death of New Salem."[148]

The other marriage proposal was to Mary Owens, a Kentucky woman whom Lincoln had first met in 1833 while she was visiting her sister in New Salem. Well educated, articulate and at times eloquent, and the same age as Lincoln (twenty-five), Mary came from a modestly wealthy family. She was "polished in her manners, pleasing in her address, and attractive in society," according to one neighbor.[149] With blonde hair and deep blue eyes, she was tall for a woman, about five foot five, and a muscular 150 pounds. Evidently Lincoln was smitten, for he boasted to a friend that if Mary came back he would marry her. Whether or not Mary's sister heard of Lincoln's boast, she played matchmaker, bringing Mary back to New Salem for a second visit in 1836, and the two began courting and were soon engaged.[150]

Mary liked Lincoln. She considered him "a man of fine intellect and (although crude) energetic and aspiring." She predicted that one day he would rise above his "humble and modest position in society."[151] But she had issues too: she thought Lincoln "ungainly and angular" in appearance (definitely not a looker) and "deficient in those little links which make up the great chain of woman's happiness."[152]

One day during their courtship, they went horseback riding with a few other couples and came across a fallen tree. While the other men courteously helped their partners across the branches, Lincoln insouciantly raced over them, "never looking back to see how I got along," Mary recalled. When she jokingly asked him about it, he replied that she "was plenty smart to take care of" herself.[153] She let the incident pass, however, for she concluded that Lincoln's boorishness stemmed from lack of training rather than meanness. In many things "he was sensitive almost to a fault," she said.[154] And sober, literate men were at a premium.

When Lincoln went to Vandalia for the

legislative session of 1836–37, he missed Mary. He anxiously awaited her letters and pined for her in his awkward way: "I really cannot endure the thought of staying here ten weeks," he wrote her. "Write back as soon as you get this, and if possible say something that will please me, for really I have not been pleased since I left you."[155]

But soon after moving to Springfield, Lincoln suddenly got cold feet. If he had attempted a love letter from Vandalia, now he penned a wily breakup note. "I am quite as lonesome here as I ever was anywhere in my life," he confessed. But he wasn't lonely for her: "I am afraid you would not be satisfied" in Springfield. "There is a great deal of flourishing about in carriages here, which it would be your doom to see without sharing in it. You would have to be poor without the means of hiding your poverty. Do you believe you could bear that patiently?"[156] Aware of Mary's comfortable upbringing and his own impoverished status, Lincoln worried about being able to support her in the lifestyle to which she was accustomed. In effect he was suffering from a crisis of manhood.

Lincoln was so insecure about marrying a woman of means that he wanted to call off the marriage. But he didn't want to lose face by breaking the engagement himself, and so his letter was designed to coerce Mary into doing it. He would "most positively abide by" his proposal to marry her, he wrote, "provided you wish it." Then he gave Mary some advice: "my opinion is that you had better not do it. You have not been accustomed to hardship, and it may be more severe than you now imagine."[157] Mary, by all accounts a classy lady, took the hint and broke off their engagement.[158]

Eight months later, his insecurities having abated and his manly honor still intact, Lincoln turned the ordeal into a joke. In an April Fool's letter of 1838 to Eliza Browning, a confidante and the wife of a Whig colleague, he recounted the affair without mentioning Mary's name. He said that he had agreed to marry her, for he had seen her "some three years before, thought her intelligent and agreeable, and saw no good objection to plodding through life hand in hand with her." But when he saw Mary again three years later he was horrified: "she did not look as my imagination had pictured her. I knew she was over-size, but she now appeared a fair match for Falstaff," Shakespeare's obese character. "I knew she was called an 'old maid,' . . . not from withered features, for her skin was too full of fat to permit its contracting into wrinkles; but from her want of teeth, weather-beaten appearance in general, and from a kind of notion that ran in my head, that *nothing* could have commenced at the size of infancy, and reached her present bulk in less than thirty-five or forty years."[159] Here Lincoln transposes his insecurities about marrying a classy, intelligent, and wealthy young woman into burlesque: he turns Mary into a toothless and obese old hag.

Lincoln went so far as to describe his near marriage to Mary as a form of bondage that was far worse than his former enslavement to his father. He vowed "never again to think of marrying."[160]

The bonds of matrimony threatened his manly honor, fueling insecurities about the duties and obligations of a husband. He had just moved to Springfield to begin a new career, and like frontier heroes in the American imagination, he needed elbow room, and did not want a woman tying him down.

Then too, Lincoln did not feel *comfortable* around eligible women. He was so tall and awkward—ugly, many said—that eligible women often made fun of him: "They'd laugh at him right before his face," recalled one girl. As a result, he preferred men, with whom he felt at ease joking, laughing, and fighting. As one New Salem neighbor observed, Lincoln "did not seem to know what to say in the company of [eligible] women. . . . While he was never at ease with women, with men he was a favorite companion." In fact he felt so awkward around women that as a general-store clerk he tried to avoid waiting on them, preferring instead to trade with the "men and boys."[161] If Lincoln was a leader among men, owing to his size, strength, and love of dirty jokes, with women these same traits made him seem like a freak.

Understandably, then, Lincoln's soul mate and the love of his life was a man named Joshua Speed. They met at a general store, and their relationship may have contributed to Lincoln's sudden aversion to Mary Owens.[162]

In April 1837 Lincoln rode into Springfield on a borrowed horse, with all his belongings (a few law books and some clothes) crammed into two saddlebags.[163] He stopped at Bell and Company's general store on the west side of town, set his saddlebags on the counter, and asked how much it would cost to buy a mattress, sheets, and pillow.[164] The slender young man behind the counter was Joshua Speed, the store's co-owner. He had a long tender face with high cheekbones, hair neatly combed and parted, full lips, and eyes that seemed both wise and playful (see figure 7). Five years younger than Lincoln, he looked cultured, even genteel. He was the son of a wealthy Kentucky planter who owned some sixty slaves, and he had come

Figure 7. Lincoln's Springfield friend and roommate Joshua Speed as a young man. *(Filson Historical Society)*

to Springfield to make his fortune. Though he had never met Lincoln, he knew of him, having heard him debate a Democratic opponent in Springfield in 1836. His first impression had been of "a long, gawky, ugly, shapeless man." But he shared Lincoln's Whig politics and had been dazzled by Lincoln's speech.[165] Now he took out his slate and pencil and tallied up the sum of $17.00.[166]

"It is probably cheap enough," Lincoln said. "But I want to say that cheap as it is I have not the money to pay. But if you will credit me until Christmas, and my experiment here as a lawyer is a success, I will pay you then. If I fail in that I will probably never be able to pay you at all."[167]

There was such pathos in Lincoln's voice that Speed "felt for him." And as he gazed at him now, he saw such melancholy in his face that he suggested an alternative: "I have a very large room, and a very large double-bed in it, which you are perfectly welcome to share with me if you choose."[168]

"Where is your room?" asked Lincoln.

"Upstairs," said Speed, pointing to the stairs leading to his room.

Without a word, Lincoln took his saddlebags, went up the stairs, and after a few minutes came back down, his face now beaming with joy. "Well Speed, I'm moved," he said.[169]

And so the two men became bedfellows. And for the next four years, long after Lincoln could afford his own room, they slept together in the same bed above the general store, sharing their most intimate thoughts. "No two men were ever more intimate," Speed himself said of their relationship; Lincoln "disclosed his whole heart to me." A mutual friend echoed this sentiment; Lincoln "loved this man more than anyone dead or living." Even Lincoln's son Robert Todd Lincoln later admitted that Speed was "the most intimate friend his father had ever had."[170]

Occasionally two of Speed's clerks, William Herndon and Charles Hurst, slept in the room as well. Other young men would sometimes stop by for an evening, "clustering around the big stove to listen" to tall tales, trade poems and stories, and stage informal debates. Speed called the group "a social club without organization."[171] But most of the time Lincoln and Speed had their room to themselves.

And in that room they shared their dreams and ambitions—Lincoln's for fame, Speed's for fortune. They gossiped about people in Springfield and the growth of the city. They discussed politics and championed Whigs. But mostly they talked about literature and themselves.[172] Speed introduced Lincoln to Lord Byron, the world-famous overnight sensation and Speed's hero—in fact Speed often wore a "Byronic collar" that funneled up his neck to his chin. Lincoln recited to Speed whole poems of Robert Burns and long passages of Shakespeare from memory. Through such sharing, they became passionate about each other's favorite writers. And they were both drawn to tortured romantic heroes such as Byron.[173] When one of them got depressed, the other acted as nurse and nurturer, helping to lift him out of his "hypos," as Lincoln called it. And they used humor as a way to manage their melancholy and cope with life's tragedies.[174]

In many respects Lincoln and Speed's romantic relationship followed the classical and Christian ideals of male friendship, which were widespread in the antebellum era. Intimate friends were soul mates, their two bodies uniting into one soul, according to Aristotle, who articulated an ideal of spiritual friendship that became incorporated into Christian and American traditions. To be sure, there were many different kinds of friendship, most of them utilitarian. But in spiritual or romantic friendship, the two men loved and respected each other, were fundamentally like each other, and expressed their affection in spiritual, emotional, intellectual, and often physical ways.[175]

The two most famous nineteenth-century male friendships embody this romantic ideal and shed light on the nature of Lincoln and Speed's relationship. Melville's Ishmael and Queequeg sleep together "in the most loving and affectionate manner." As "bosom friends," they are like "man and wife," opening "the very bottom of their souls to each other" and becoming, in their "hearts' honeymoon, . . . a cozy loving pair." There is also the suggestion of erotic affection, though muted: Ishmael and Queequeg's loving occurs in the same bed (at

the Spouter Inn) where the landlord and his
wife "were spliced," an erotic evocation of the
marriage bed.[176] Huck Finn and Jim, the other
famous friendship, call each other "honey" and
are "always naked, day and night," as they float
down the Mississippi River in the 1840s, not
too far from where Lincoln and Speed lived.[177]

As these examples suggest, sexual mores in
the years before the Civil War were in many respects less repressed than they are today. Gen-
der roles were extremely fluid, so much so that
the distinction between homosexuality and
heterosexuality did not even exist.[178] Moralists
characterized *all* explicitly sexual relationships
outside of marriage as sinful, and they treated
male-male sex no differently than male-female
sex. More general expressions of love (or intimacy) between two men (or two women)
were considered perfectly normal: "Women
hugged, kissed, slept with, and proclaimed love
for other women," and "men did the same with
other men" without anyone raising an eyebrow.
If passion was expressed in sexually explicit
terms, moralists called it wrong regardless of
whom it was with.[179]

Such openness about same-sex relationships
stemmed partly from people's interpretations
of the Bible, where male-male sex is neither unusual nor treated much differently than male-

female sex outside of marriage.[180] Then too, government had a hands-off attitude toward sex: laws regulating prostitution or "sodomy" were rarely enforced, and only four states had obscenity laws banning sexually explicit literature, whereas every Southern state tried to censor abolitionist literature.[181] As one historian has summarized, "In the free, easy social atmosphere of pre–Civil War America, overt displays of affection between people of the same sex were common."[182] The line between romantic and erotic friendship, between ardor and eros, love and lust, could be very blurry indeed.

In some cases, friends made their sexual passions explicit. A decade before Lincoln and Speed met, Thomas Jefferson Withers, a twenty-two-year-old South Carolina law student, told his friend James Henry Hammond how much he liked sleeping with him: "I feel some inclination to learn whether you yet sleep in your Shirt-tail, and whether you yet have the extravagant delight of poking and punching a writhing Bedfellow with your long fleshen pole—the exquisite touches of which I have often had the honor of feeling?" Withers playfully blurred the line between eros and ardor: "Sir, you roughen the downy Slumbers of your Bedfellow—by such hostile—furious lunges as you are in the habit of making at him—when he is least prepared for defence against the crushing force of a Battering Ram."[183] Significantly, their friendship threatened neither their sense of manly honor nor their social standing.[184] Indeed, Withers would later become a South Carolina appellate court judge and Hammond would achieve fame as a United States senator and governor of South Carolina. And both men would marry, raise families, and join the Confederacy.[185]

Male-male sex was also common in the military. Among sailors in the navy and marines, masturbating a mate was so widespread that men had a name for it: "shaking." Herman Melville named one of his characters "Shakings" in his narrative of life on board a navy ship, and he described sailors "polishing [their] *bright-work*" or "embracing the '*monkey-tails*' of the carronades, the screws, *prickers*, little irons, and other things."[186] These sailors ignored or laughed at the moralists who called masturbation a disease that could kill you. Another marine, Philip Van Buskirk, kept a diary that details his male-male sex encounters with such frequency that one wonders how his ship ever reached its destination.[187]

And Walt Whitman publicly and poetically "made love" to men and women as an aspect of his democratic vision: "all were lacking if sex were lacking, or if the moisture of the right man were lacking," he chanted. "I am for those who believe in loose delights, I share the midnight orgies of young men."[188] Such was the range of American romantic friendships.

There is no explicit evidence that Lincoln and Speed enjoyed carnal love, though Speed's letters to Lincoln during the era of their intimacy (the 1840s) have sadly been lost, and his purported diary has not yet surfaced.[189] But in one letter to Lincoln, Speed enclosed a violet, a flower symbolizing erotic intimacy. "The sweet violet you enclosed came safely to hand," Lincoln responded, "but it was so dry, and mashed so flat, that it crumbled to dust at the first attempt to handle it. The juice that mashed out of it, stained a place on the letter, which I mean to preserve and cherish."[190]

In general Lincoln's letters to Speed lack the effusive passion that is often characteristic of romantic friendship. But Lincoln *never* divulged this kind of romantic intimacy in his letters, not even to his wife or children. He preferred "short sentences & a compact style," as he told Speed one night, a form that discouraged intimate epistles.[191] In his letters he writes like a lawyer, not a lover.[192]

Still, the letters Lincoln wrote to Speed are the most intimate he ever composed.[193] He signed them "Yours forever" or "Your friend," and in other ways as well let Speed know how much he cared: "You well know that I do not feel my own sorrows much more keenly than I do yours, when I know of them," he began one letter. When Speed was away, Lincoln said he missed him and was anxious for him. "I want you to write me every mail," he said in one letter, and in another confessed, "I shall be very lonesome without you." In yet another letter he made clear his undying love: "You know my desire to befriend you is everlasting—that I will never cease while I know how to do anything."[194]

It was in his poetry and dirty jokes that Lincoln expressed a more explicit affinity for male-male love. In one poem, written as part of a prank when he was twenty, he describes how his neighbor Billy, having been spurned by women, finds happiness with a male lover, Natty:[195]

But Billy has married a boy.
The girls he had tried on every side,
But none could he get to agree.
All was in vain, he went home again,
And since that he is married to Natty.

So Billy and Natty agreed very well;
And mamma's well pleased at the match.

Years later, Lincoln would echo Whitman by playfully referring to his intimacy with Speed: "I slept with Joshua for four years, and I suppose I *ought* to know him."[196]

According to neighbors in New Salem and Springfield, Lincoln had a powerful, at times uncontrollable, libido. He once confessed to William Herndon, Speed's clerk and later his law partner and biographer, that in 1835 he had succumbed to his "devilish passion," hired a prostitute, and then worried that he had syphilis. Herndon went so far as to say that Lincoln "could scarcely keep his hands off" prostitutes, whom he treated differently than *eligible* women.[197] A New Salem neighbor remembered him patronizing a whorehouse with some buddies during the Black Hawk War.[198] Near the end of his life, Speed, himself a "lady's man," told Herndon that he had for a time kept a courtesan at Springfield. Lincoln, "desirous to have a *little*," asked, "Speed, do you know where I can get *some*?" Speed replied, "Yes I do, . . . I'll send you to the place with a note. You can't get *it* without a note or by my appearance."[199]

If these accounts of Lincoln's having sex with prostitutes are true, then there is no reason to suppose that he didn't also have carnal relations with Joshua Speed, the man he shared a bed with for four years. For if his sexual passions were at times uncontrollable, then he likely would have acted on them not only with strangers but with his most intimate friend in the world. After all, he did not consider the one form of sex to be substantively different than the other. The concept of sexual identities, defined by the binary opposition of "homo" and "hetero," was decades away.[200]

Regardless of how one interprets the nature of their intimacy, Speed "civilized" Lincoln in numerous ways, greatly contributing to his self-making. He was one of the most cultured men Lincoln had met, having grown up in luxury and comfort at Farmington, a beautiful plantation on the outskirts of Louisville. The Speed family home, a tall-ceilinged brick colonial, had been designed by Thomas Jefferson, a friend of the family. Joshua had been educated in "the best private schools in the West" and was as well-read as most graduates of Harvard or Yale. He showed Lincoln the meaning of respectability in manners, dress, and speech. Less than a year after Speed and Lincoln began living together, Lincoln's writing acquired a depth and sophistication that had previously been lacking. It began to resemble the clear and compact style of Speed.[201]

Lincoln's new public voice first emerged in his 1838 address to the Young Men's Lyceum of Springfield, a society devoted to education and uplift. It was the first speech he delivered as an intellectual rather than as a politician.[202] Entitled "The Perpetuation of Our Political Institutions," it warned that the major threat to America stemmed not from another nation but from the enemy within: mobs and the havoc they caused. Lincoln cited instances of vigilante violence that had resulted in the murders of an Illinois abolitionist (Elijah Lovejoy), a number of free blacks, and Mississippi gamblers who were "useless in any community." No matter how "obnoxious" the victims were, when mob violence replaced the rule of law, the government could not last. In evocative language he urged his listeners to "swear by the blood of the Revolution" and renounce the use of bloodshed. While the patriots of '76 affirmed the Declaration, citizens today needed to support the Constitution. And while "passion" helped the founding fathers, "reason, cold, calculating, unimpassioned reason must furnish" the materials for the future. "Let reverence for the laws . . . become the *political religion* of the nation."[203] Given Lincoln's new career as a lawyer, it was a rather self-serving speech. But it also reflected his stunning transformation of style, in which he employed passionate language to urge unimpassioned reason.

Lincoln repeated his appeal to reason over passion a few years later in a temperance speech. Likening drunkenness to slavery and tyranny, he called the recent temperance revolution (spearheaded by reformed drunkards) *more important* than the political revolution of 1776 in spreading liberty. For while alcohol incited people's fury, sobriety brought the "reign of reason." He looked forward to a new age, he said, when "there shall be neither a slave nor a drunkard on the earth."[204] Again Lincoln's speech used passionate rhetoric to invoke reason. And he asked Speed to read it.[205] He was proud of it and wanted to know what his mentor thought.

Lincoln's embrace of reason over passion had personal as well as national relevance. For if he could not always control his sexual passions, neither could he contain his zeal for Whig politics. In December 1840 he committed one of the more embarrassing faux pas of his political career. He had just returned to Springfield after a grueling three months of campaigning for the Whig presidential candidate William Henry Harrison. He had been constantly on the road, traveling on horseback, staying at rowdy taverns, sleeping two or three to a bed, and consuming "mean" coffee and "greasy food."[206]

He was worn out and now had to begin a legislative session in which the Democratic majority accused him and other Whigs of destroying the state's economy with their road-building schemes. Democrats wanted to kill the state bank, a Whig institution, and the only way for Whigs to oppose it was to pull a no-show and deny the Democrats a quorum. Lincoln and a few other Whigs attended the meeting to ensure a proper roll call, but when they arrived, they realized that their very presence constituted a quorum. Desperate, Lincoln and his comrades tried to escape, and after finding the door locked, they opened the window and jumped out. It was a stupid, panicky move, for Democrats destroyed the bank anyway and Lincoln was charged with "dereliction of duty." His "jumping scrape," as he called it, became so celebrated that he tried to absolve himself a few weeks later with a speech in the legislature, but the chair called him to order and cut him off.[207]

The incident humiliated Lincoln and possibly contributed to a severe bout of depression during the winter of 1840–41.[208] He was so incapacitated that he took to his bed. Speed said Lincoln "went crazy," and he was so worried about his friend that he removed "razors from his room" and took away "all knives and other such dangerous things." "It was terrible." According to Speed, about the only thing that prevented Lincoln from committing suicide was "that he had done nothing to make any human being remember that he had lived." Lincoln acknowledged his "deplorable state" of mind to his law partner John Stuart, adding, "I am now the most miserable man living. If what I feel were equally distributed to the whole human family, there would not be one cheerful face on the earth. . . . To remain as I am is impossible; I must die or be better, it appears to me." The nadir came on New Year's Day. Lincoln later referred to it as "that fatal first of Jany. '41." It was the worst day of his life, probably the closest he ever came to killing himself.[209]

There have been numerous theories seeking to explain the causes of "that fatal first of Jany. '41." But one fact is indisputable: it was on that day when Joshua Speed decided to move back to Kentucky and made plans to sell his interest in his general store.[210] His father had died in the spring of 1840, his mother wanted him home, and he had been contemplating the move for months. On New Year's Day 1841, Lincoln realized that his friend would be leaving him, and it crushed him.[211] As he later put it, "If we have no friends, we have no pleasure; and if we have them, we are sure to lose them, and be doubly pained by the loss."[212]

Speed was so worried about his friend that he waited until May 1841 to move back to Farmington. By then Lincoln had largely recovered and promised to visit Speed that summer. He came in August and stayed for almost a month.[213]

It was Lincoln's first vacation and his introduction to high Southern society. A family slave took care of his every need and he had a spacious room to himself. Lincoln so loved these indulgences that he considered his stay at Farmington "an idyllic time, . . . one of the happiest times in [my] life." The only uncomfortable incident occurred at dinner one night; a family member passed him the relish and he kept it, thinking it was for him alone rather than the entire table. But Joshua corrected Lincoln's mistake and taught him the nuances of formal dining: "Look at me Lincoln and do as I do," he said.[214]

While Frederick Douglass spent his first vacation at an abolitionist meeting at Nantucket, Lincoln spent his in the lap of Southern luxury, amid some sixty slaves, one of them his personal valet. He not only loved the experience; he never urged Speed to liberate the slaves he inherited from his father. And Speed felt no compunction about owning slaves; indeed, a few years later, when he began trading them, Lincoln said nothing and it did not appear to affect their friendship.[215] While Lincoln hated slavery, he was no revolutionary and was not about to destroy a friendship by chastising Speed. After all, his political hero, Henry Clay, was another wealthy Kentucky slaveowner.

After returning to Springfield, Lincoln betrayed his racial prejudice and absolved Joshua and his family for owning slaves. On his trip home he shared a boat with a slave trader and his coffle, and his description is quite revealing. "A fine example was presented on board the boat for contemplating the effect of *condition* upon human happiness," Lincoln wrote. Twelve slaves were chained together "like so many fish upon a trot-line. In this condition they were being separated forever from the scenes of their childhood, their friends, their fathers and mothers, and brothers and sisters, and many of them from their wives and children. . . . And yet amid all these distressing circumstances, as *we* would think them, *they* were the most cheerful and apparently happy creatures on board." Lincoln concluded that God "renders the worst of human conditions tolerable, while He permits the best, to be nothing better than tolerable."[216]

To Lincoln, God endowed blacks with the capacity to be happy and cheerful even in the worst of human conditions. His naïve description is both sympathetic to blacks and redemptive for whites, a delicate balance that he would try to maintain for the rest of his life.

Lincoln revealed a similar attitude toward blacks in Illinois. In 1840, 115 blacks lived in Springfield, about 4 percent of the city's population of 2,500. They were almost all laborers or domestics, and six of them were slaves, including a young female slave of Speed's business partner, also a friend of Lincoln's. Illinois was ostensibly a free state, owing to the prohibition against slavery's extension into Northern territories in the Northwest Ordinance of 1787.[217] But when the ordinance passed, a few slaves lived in Illinois Territory and masters illegally brought in a few more. The state's constitution of 1818 did not free any slaves. Instead, it only prohibited more slaves from entering.[218] As a result, some three hundred slaves lived in Illinois in 1840, and Lincoln did nothing to try to liberate them.[219] Nor did he seek to overturn the state's Black Codes, which dissuaded free blacks from entering the state.[220] Doing so would have been politically inexpedient, alienating him from the state's Southern sympathizers.

At the same time, however, Lincoln had a

close relationship with a number of Springfield blacks, especially William Florville, known as Billy the Barber.[221] He helped Billy acquire clients and later represented him in legal cases. And Billy's shop became Lincoln's "second home" in the late 1830s and early 1840s. A male hangout, it was a place to get a shave and a haircut, trade some jokes, gossip, and maybe read a little law when things were slow. In this sense it resembled the apartment he shared with Speed: a haven for cultured men amid the "dirt and discomfort" of Springfield.[222] Lincoln loved Billy's lightheartedness and sense of humor. But their relationship never threatened his political ambitions or his friendships with whites. After all, to someone like Joshua Speed, Billy was a Sambo (or ideal servant) and unthreatening to his understanding of white manhood. Had Frederick Douglass come to Springfield from Pendleton to give some abolitionist lectures, Lincoln almost certainly would have considered him insolent and obnoxious.

Slaveholding was so much a part of life in Illinois that if people came from money, the money often came from slavery. Indeed, two of the three women Lincoln was engaged to, including the one he married, were daughters of Kentucky slaveholders. Mary Owens returned to her slaveowning family in Kentucky after Lincoln spurned her, then married a wealthy slaveowner and moved to Missouri, where her two sons fought for the Confederacy.[223]

In some ways Mary Todd resembled Mary Owens and Ann Rutledge: she was the well-educated daughter of an aristocratic slave-owning Kentucky family; and like Ann, she was short (five foot two) and plump (see figure 8). (Lincoln loved plump women, perhaps because his own grotesque figure liberated him from classical notions of beauty.)

But in other ways Mary Todd was totally different—in fact, she acted like a man.[224] She was as ambitious for fame and as passionate about politics as Lincoln. Having been brought up in an ardently Whig family, she was a "violent little Whig," loved Henry Clay, who was a family friend and neighbor, and hated Democrats. At age fourteen she had reportedly ridden her horse to Ashland, Clay's estate, to tell him that she expected him to be the next president, adding that she too wanted to "live in the White House." That desire didn't die, for after moving to Springfield in 1839, she "declared her intention of marrying a future President of the United States." Vivacious and outgoing if a bit high-strung, she was very smart, loved poetry, and had a wit to match her future husband's.[225] She was, in other words, a perfect political and intellectual match for Lincoln.

They began courting during the 1840 presidential campaign and by the election were engaged. One Springfield neighbor remembered seeing them sitting in a room together while Mary led the conversation: "Lincoln would listen and gaze on her as if drawn by some superior power; irresistibly so: he listened—never scarcely said a word."[226] But after the election, and then Lincoln's humiliating window leap, his depression, and Speed's decision to move back to Kentucky, he called it off. He felt insecure about Mary Todd's wealth, uncomfortable about marriage in general, and unsure of his feelings toward Mary. This third failed engagement probably contributed to his depression.

Joshua Speed finally brought them together again. While Lincoln was vacationing at Farmington in August 1841, Speed proposed to Fanny Henning, a Kentucky woman. Then suddenly he too got cold feet, worrying that he didn't love Fanny enough. Lincoln helped Speed through the ordeal, telling him he thought Fanny "one of the sweetest girls in the world" and calling Speed's fears groundless. Days before the wedding Speed continued to have "forebodings" about his "dreams of Elysium far exceeding" earthly reality. Lincoln shared these apprehensions about marriage, and so when Speed went through with the ceremony (on February 15, 1842), and then told Lincoln a month later that he was *far happier than [I] ever expected to be*," he gave his friend the confidence to renew his courtship with Mary Todd.[227]

Their renewed courtship again focused on politics; but this time it led to a duel followed by marriage.

In August 1842, Lincoln attacked a political opponent in a way that crossed the boundaries of propriety. With Mary's help, he wrote a satirical essay that impugned the honor of James Shields, the Democratic state auditor.[228] Shields was an average-sized man with a big mustache who had been born and educated in Ireland, came to Illinois when his money ran out, and soon became a leading state Democrat who did not take insults kindly.[229] Lincoln published his satirical essay anonymously and titled it "The Rebecca Letter." It is narrated by Rebecca, a poor farmer's wife.[230] Technically a work of fiction, it anticipates *Huckleberry Finn* in its use of dialect and humor. It captures the sounds of Sangamon County (and of Lincoln): "a spell ago"; "mought be expected"; "desarnin set of men."[231] And it uses humor to attack Shields

Figure 8. Mary Todd Lincoln in an 1846 daguerreotype. (*Library of Congress*)

politically and insult him personally. Shields is a main character in the story. Lincoln calls him "a fool as well as a liar" and mocks his self-image as an irresistible ladies' man.[232] "Dear girls, *it is distressing*, but I cannot marry you all," he quotes Shields as saying. "Too well I know how much you suffer; but do, *do* remember, it is not my fault that I am *so* handsome and *so* interesting."[233]

Shields was outraged, and after finding out that Lincoln had written the essay, he ordered him to publicly retract "all offensive allusions" to his "private character and standing as a man."[234] When Lincoln refused, Shields challenged him to a duel. Lincoln accepted, for he "did not think it consistent with his honor to negotiate for peace with Mr. Shields," unless Shields withdrew his demands.[235]

While duels had largely died out in the more refined culture of the Northeast, they remained popular in the South and West, even though many states, including Illinois, outlawed them. Lincoln had violated the code of honor that protected a man's private character, and he knew that he would be dishonored if he declined Shields's challenge.[236] Eleven years earlier he had wrestled Jack Armstrong to defend his honor; now he was willing to die for it. On the frontier and in the South, as you became more refined the fighting became more brutal.[237]

Under the *code duello* the person challenged defined the terms of the fight. Lincoln chose as weapons "cavalry broad swords of the largest size." He designed a fighting field that resembled a miniature tennis court, with a plank twelve inches high for a "net"; a baseline on either side about sixteen feet from the plank; and sidelines that intersected the plank and baselines. Each fighter had to stay inside his box. If you stepped over the plank you forfeited your life, and if you stepped outside the baseline you fouled out and lost the fight.[238]

Lincoln's terms were designed to give enormous advantage to the man with the greatest reach and arm strength. As he knew, Shields was of average height, about five foot seven. And of course Lincoln was very tall, with unusually long and strong arms. Even with this advantage, he practiced his broadsword stroke before the duel. He planned to stand in his box and swing away until he hacked off a limb and "disarmed" Shields or induced a foul. "I did not want to kill" him, he supposedly said.[239] Still, this behavior is from a man who urged the rule of law and reason over "the basest principles of our nature," as he had emphasized in his lyceum speech.[240]

The miniature tennis court was built and the combatants were ready to begin when Springfield friends finally interceded. "You damned fools," a colleague of Lincoln's declared. He appealed to their "common sense" and "broke up the fight."[241]

Soon after the broadsword battle was called off, Lincoln and Mary Todd renewed their engagement. Lincoln had protected Mary, ensuring that her name would not be associated with "The Rebecca Letter." And Mary did not try to dissuade Lincoln from fighting. After all, she had been raised in Kentucky, where duels were a mainstay of society, and their mutual hero, Henry Clay, had been wounded in a duel. In Mary's mind duels signified manliness.[242] Perhaps the ordeal with Shields made them realize how much they had in common and the degree to which they were willing to sacrifice themselves for a Whig cause.

But as the date of their marriage approached, Lincoln again got cold feet. And so he wrote Joshua Speed: "Are you now, in *feeling* as well as *judgment*, glad you are married as you are?" he asked. Apparently Speed said yes, for Lincoln and Mary were married on November 4, 1842, in a small family ceremony.[243] Speed was not present, and one guest recalled that Lincoln "looked and acted as if he was going to the slaughter," though another woman said he was as "cheerful as he ever had been."[244]

While the nature of their marriage has been widely debated, one thing is certain: Lincoln's rise as a politician and lawyer accelerated after his marriage. In 1842 he declined reelection to the state legislature, having already been elected to four consecutive terms. He wanted to focus his energies on his law practice and national Whig politics. In 1844 he and Mary worked tirelessly (and vainly) to put Henry Clay in the White House; and two years later the voters of Sangamon and Morgan counties elected him to the U.S. Congress. He would be going to Washington.

If Lincoln's ambition was "a little engine that knew no rest," as William Herndon said, then Mary Todd fueled and lubricated it, though it cost him some happiness.[245] After the wedding he and Joshua began drifting apart. One would like to think that at the wedding Lincoln was thinking of him. After all, Joshua had taught him the meaning of love and had brought him and Mary together. As Joshua later acknowledged, "If I had not been married and happy, far more happy than I ever expected to be, he would not have married." Lincoln gave Mary a ring engraved with the words "Love is eternal."[246] Perhaps the engraving was as much an elegy for a friendship as hope for a marriage.

During his trip to the British Isles, Frederick Douglass made a special pilgrimage to Ayr, the birthplace of Robert Burns. He called it "one of the most gratifying visits" during his stay in Scotland, for he saw the humble cottage where Burns lived, walked the streets that had inspired Burns's poetry, and met the poet's sister. While conversing with her, he thought he saw "some lingering sparks . . . that called to mind the fire that ever warmed the bosom of Burns."[247]

Douglass recognized in Burns's life and poetry parallels with his own plight and that of other blacks. Both men had been born poor, were oppressed by elite whites and treated like brutes, and found in language a way to remake themselves and build a vision of humanity. Burns's verse taught Douglass to feel *proud* of his lowly origins. "The honest man, tho' e'er sae poor, / Is king o' men for a' that." Honest poverty was superior to the slavishness of the rich coward. And Douglass shared with Burns the dream of brotherly love: "that man to man the world o'er, / Shall brothers be for a' that."[248]

But if he identified with Burns, Lord Byron was his favorite writer. While the pleasures of Burns stemmed partly from his use of vernacular, Douglass had fled from provincial sounds. His two years in the British Isles helped him shed the lingering sounds of slavery. He wanted to sound cultured like an aristocrat or his wealthy British friends.

Lord Byron became for Douglass a model of the rebel aristocrat, in which aristocracy depended not on birth but on values. Byron was an emblem of radical cosmopolitanism. He had become a world-famous performer long before

Douglass, a "work of art" who helped Douglass remake himself in appearance, style, voice. Byron's mastery of irony and satirical irreverence shaped Douglass's own writings, and the poet's swift rise to ignominious fame echoed Douglass's ascent to insolent abolitionist. No wonder that Douglass so frequently quoted him.

Douglass saw in Byron a symbol of the great male freedom fighter. Here was an aristocrat turned rebel, a man who descended in social status in order to rise in spirit, and who sacrificed his life in the cause of freedom. There was something immensely appealing about Byron's tendency, in life and art, to set his face against society and seek to realize his ideals of freedom. Both Douglass and Byron believed that reality should continually aspire to the condition of the ideal. They lived for their dreams and were loath to compromise them.[249]

Lincoln, on the other hand, simply adored Burns. He found in Burns a literary soul mate and a vernacular style that spoke to his own efforts to elevate frontier talk to art. And Burns's life reflected back on Lincoln's own: a poor, provincial farmer who rarely traveled outside his known circle and sought to represent, poetically and politically, the voice of the people. Lincoln would have agreed with Walt Whitman, who said that Burns's poems and character "specially endeared him to America." Burns "would have been at home in the Western United States ['Western' referring to the Midwest] and probably become eminent there." Whitman could have been referring to Lincoln when he said of Burns, "He was an average sample of the good-natured, warm-blooded, proud-spirited, amative [amorous], alimentive [nourishing], convivial, young and early-middle-aged man."[250]

As for Byron, Lincoln did not read him as much as he did Burns, nor did he identify with Byron's genteel radicalism. In fact in his political views, friendships, and failed engagements, Lincoln recognized that the real *always* fell far short of the ideal. This was not a calamity. It was the way of the world. His insecurities about marriage had taught him that the "idealizing impulse" was itself the problem. As he told Speed, "The peculiar misfortune of both you and me" is "to dream dreams of Elysium far exceeding all that any thing earthly can realize."[251] Such pragmatism enabled him to tolerate slavery while hating it, or marry someone with whom he lacked the kind of intimacy already achieved. And it helped him reconcile his dreams of fame with his anonymous status. For while Douglass was internationally renowned, Lincoln was still a small-town lawyer and politician, utterly unknown outside of Illinois.

THREE

Radical Abolitionist and Republican

Hereditary bondsmen! know ye not
Who would be free themselves must
strike the blow?

—Lord Byron,
   Childe Harold's Pilgrimage (1812)

A kingdom divided against itself cannot stand.

—*Aesop's Fables* (c. 560 BCE)

FREDERICK DOUGLASS LOVED TO EXPOSE American lies. As soon as he moved to Rochester in late 1847, he began following politics closely, highlighting the hypocrisy of Americans yelping for freedom while seeking the expansion of slavery. He frequently contrasted the American condition with that in Europe. On August 1, 1848, while celebrating the anniversary of British West Indian emancipation, he praised France for having just abolished its monarchy and slavery. With remarkable suddenness, France lived up to its republican motto of "Liberty–Equality–Fraternity." By contrast, the United States defied the worldwide trend of emancipation and stood almost alone as an island of slavery in a New World of freedom.* In the punch line of his speech, Douglass

---

* In 1770 slavery was legal in every New World nation; eighty years later it had been abolished everywhere except the United States, Brazil, Cuba, and Dutch Guiana.

said that American statesmen wanted to rejoice with France "in her republicanism," but found it impossible to do so "without seeming to rejoice over abolitionism."[1]

Eminent statesmen like Henry Clay, Lincoln's hero, became a favorite target of Douglass's scorn. Soon after moving to Rochester, he undermined Clay's avowed hatred of slavery. Clay (like Lincoln) argued that slavery was the domain of each state and that only slaveholders could abolish it. Such a belief was like asking a pirate to voluntarily relinquish his booty. It allowed each state "to plunder, scourge and enslave any part of the human family within its borders," Douglass said. He belittled Clay's proposal to end slavery in his home state of Kentucky, since it would be 1885, almost forty years, before any slave was actually freed. Not only that, but Clay owned about fifty slaves, daily robbing them of their liberty. "Do you think that God will hold you guiltless if you die with the blood of these fifty slaves clinging to your garments?" Douglass asked the elder statesman.[2]

Douglass also exposed no-name congressmen like Lincoln. In January 1849 he published a tally of the votes in the House of Representatives on a resolution to prohibit the slave trade in the District of Columbia. Most Northern congressmen were shocked by the trade's visibility in the capital of a free country. One of the nation's largest slave markets stood just a few blocks from the Capitol, and congressmen passed the huge bleak warehouse on their way to work. They also had to confront the regular "train of slaves passing through" Pennsylvania Avenue from the Capitol to the White House.[3] Northern House members rallied around the resolution, voting for it and enabling it to pass.

Not Lincoln. He voted to *retain* the slave trade in the District.[4] Although he hated the trade and referred to Washington's slave market as "a sort of Negro livery-stable," he believed that the citizens of the District should themselves determine the fate of slavery and the slave trade there.[5]

Douglass was thrilled about the vote but thought "the news too good to be true."[6] He was right, for six days later the House reconsidered the resolution and voted it down. In both votes, Douglass duly noted, Lincoln supported the slave trade and cast his votes with such proslavery Southerners and future Confederate leaders as Howell Cobb, Alexander Stephens, Robert Toombs, and Albert Gallatin Brown.[7]

Such distortions of truth and perversions of freedom eventually led Douglass to endorse weapons over words. If the fate of slavery rested with the people in the slave states, as even antislavery men like Lincoln and Clay demanded, then so be it, Douglass said, as long as the "people" included slaves. He began instructing slaves what to do. A few months after Lincoln's vote he urged the slaves to "imitate the example of our fathers of '76." Slaveholders were *"sleeping on slumbering volcanoes,"* and the day may come when the lava would flow, he warned. He still hoped for a peaceful resolution to slavery and called himself a "peace man." And so he used the conditional tense ("may come"). His warning of an insurrection stemmed from scripture: "those who lead into captivity shall go into captivity" and "those that take the sword shall perish by the sword."[8] He defined slavery as a *"state of war,"* which implied that one should make war on slavery in order to bring peace.[9] Soon he would exchange the conditional for the declarative, abandon nonviolence altogether, and urge on the apocalypse. He would draw inspiration from Byron's Childe Harold, another self-made man, who declared, "Hereditary bondsmen! know ye not / Who would be free themselves must strike the blow?"[10] He would take up the sword to make war on those who distorted truth to protect slavery.

Douglass's newspaper became his bully pulpit. He named it the *North Star*, an astral guide for runaways and possibly also an echo of the *Northern Star*, the Chartist paper in England advocating workingmen's rights that Douglass had read during his stay there.[11] The *North Star* was a four-page weekly, modeled on Garrison's *Liberator*, and he borrowed from his former mentor by employing a punchy, fast-paced, and physical style. But where Garrison was unrelenting in his attacks, going for a knockout punch with every sentence, Douglass loved irony, humor, and ambiguity (he had to to admire Byron and Burns), and so his prose sounded more genteel. In content too he both borrowed from and moved beyond his mentor. Like the *Liberator*, the *North Star* sought universal emancipation and black uplift without ignoring other reform movements such as women's rights, temperance, and labor. But whereas Garrison downplayed politics, Douglass foregrounded it. The first issue, of December 3, 1847, featured Douglass's letter to Henry Clay, attacking him for compromising with slavery. In its variety of content and voices, the *North Star* imagined a new community that transcended the nation-state and envisioned "all rights for all," which later became the paper's motto.[12]

Launching a paper felt a bit like arriving in New York City fresh from slavery. You lived on hope and adrenaline, and if you could avoid the creditors (or kidnappers) for six months, then the chances of sustaining yourself as an editor (or freeman) rose dramatically. The venture was unpredictable, since no matter how carefully you planned the first issue (or escape) there were always unforeseen circumstances.

Douglass moved to Rochester in the fall of 1847 to launch his paper. He roomed with a friend and kept Anna and the children at Lynn so that he could devote all his energies to the task at hand. He rented an office at 25 Buffalo Street, in the heart of the city's thriving business district, and spent the entire $2,000 his British friends had given him in one fell swoop. Soon his new office was filled with the gleaming metal of a new press, types, cases, and stands.[13]

It was a bad, almost fatal mistake, for he had no idea how to run the equipment or oversee the apprentices he hired to set the type and lock the plates. He soon realized that it would be cheaper to contract with an experienced publisher. But he couldn't resell the equipment, and instead of having the equivalent in today's money of $150,000 on hand to build a subscription base, he went immediately into debt and the *North Star* survived its crucial first six months more due to Douglass's determination and steel will than anything else.[14]

Most editors had spent years apprenticing in a printing office. It was their school and trade. They learned how to set the laterally inverted type, watch their "p's and q's" to avoid spelling errors, and write clean, compact sentences. When they became editors they knew every aspect of the newspaper business and could identify good journalism when they saw it. Douglass had mastered the arts of speaking and writing, but he was lost when it came to editing and publishing.

In almost any other city, Douglass probably would have gone bankrupt. But Rochester, a manufacturing city of fifty thousand, was also a hub of radical reform. And with a direct route to Canada, it was one of the last stops on the Underground Railroad. It was, in other words, a city in need of a good abolitionist editor and conductor.

Indeed, Douglass's office became a central stop on the Underground Railroad. One friend remembered that Douglass had "a secret stairway built that led from a trap door in his office to a special hiding place" for fugitives.[15] The details of the story are probably apocryphal, for Douglass didn't have any money to build a hidden stairway, and stories of trapdoors and secret stairs were more often part of slavery's gothic memory than its history. Still, Douglass played a central role in Rochester's Underground Railroad: according to one estimate, he helped about four hundred fugitives gain their freedom.[16] He found them homes and showed them a safe route to Canada. In the first issue of the *North Star* he included the headline A SISTER RESCUED FROM SLAVERY, followed by a brief article describing an eighteen-year-old girl who had just left his office on her way to freedom.[17]

In early 1848 Anna and the children joined Frederick in Rochester. Anna was not pleased about having to move again, and initially she hated Rochester, for she had to live in a cheap rental tenement.[18] Her home was largely her world.

Domestic life improved in late spring of 1848. Frederick sold his home in Lynn, and with the proceeds and help from friendly abolitionists in Rochester he purchased a two-story, nine-room brick house at 4 Alexander Street, near his downtown office.[19] It was a terrific home for them, for it encompassed a large lawn for the children, a garden for Anna, and a study for Frederick, the first one he could call his own. His little "den-like upstairs study" contained a small table, books, and "a list of words he found hard to spell."[20]

Anna loved the new home and spent much of her time "keeping things straight." Friends called her "a model housekeeper," and according to one neighbor, her thrift helped Frederick sustain his paper as he struggled to gain subscribers. Soon after they moved, Anna got some relief, for her sister came to live with them and helped with the cleaning, cooking, and childcare.[21]

During their first summer on Alexander Street, Frederick asked an abolitionist friend to teach Anna and the children to read and write.[22] Anna was reluctant but tried it "for Frederick's sake." Soon, though, she felt overwhelmed, and when she began neglecting "housewifely duties for copybook and speller," her "experiment" in literacy ended forever.[23]

Frederick never expressed frustration over Anna's refusal to engage the power of the written word, but it must have upset him, for words were his first love and Anna knew it. About the only things they could enjoy together were their children and their love of music. Occasionally on a summer evening, the Douglasses gathered on their lawn, and Anna played her violin while Frederick led the children in singing "The Seraph" or another hymn from Anna's hymnbook. The neighborhood children, hearing Frederick's "rich baritone voice and good ear," gathered round as well, and after listening to a few more hymns, they would request a "popular" song. Frederick and Anna would then launch into a Stephen Foster tune such as "Nelly Was a Lady" or "Old Kentucky Home."[24] To Frederick, these popular Southern melodies seemed like elegies of a former self.

Douglass was so proud of his new home that on September 3, 1848, the tenth anniversary of his freedom, he wrote Thomas Auld, his old master, to say that he now had "as comfortable a dwelling as your own" and presided over a happy family consisting of "an industrious and neat companion" (Anna) and "four dear children" ranging in age from four to nine.[25] Despite his phenomenal rise, he thought constantly about his past. Indeed, his former life as a slave was now the source of his livelihood. While alone in his study, he would sometimes lay his pen in one of the gashes of his feet, which had been cracked open from frost while he was a slave.[26] His past was not only present; it was palpable.

Douglass fell in love with Rochester. It was one of the most abolitionist and feminist cities in the country, and it lacked the smugness of Boston's ruling elite. It was in the heart of the "Burned-Over District," a region in upstate New York along the Erie Canal that had been swept by the spiritual fires of revivalists, transforming it into a center of radical reform. Rochester was home to the Fox sisters, who in 1848 discovered the new religion of Spiritualism, which enabled people to communicate with the dead. And the city was only about sixty miles from Seneca Falls, the site of the world's first women's rights convention, also in 1848. Although there is no evidence that Douglass practiced Spiritualism, he attended, along with 30 other men and 110 women, the Seneca Falls convention. During a debate on a resolution for female suffrage, he gave an eloquent speech and saved the motion from defeat.[27]

Racial lines were comparatively fluid in Rochester. As a result there was an openness toward blacks that didn't exist in Boston. To be sure, Rochester wasn't England. But Douglass felt more at home there "than anywhere else in the country." As he later said, "I know of no place in the Union where I could have located at that time with less resistance or received a larger measure of sympathy and cooperation."[28]

Rochester's business and reform leaders had good reason to befriend and protect him: he was the city's most famous citizen and helped bring in money, business, and other luminaries. After the influential editor of a New York City daily told the people of Rochester to "throw the nigger printing press into Lake Ontario and banish Douglass to Canada," the city's reformers immediately came to his defense.[29]

Journalists also welcomed Douglass. In early 1848 Rochester's publishers invited him to their annual celebration of Benjamin Franklin's birthday at the Irving House hotel. When Douglass arrived, he was turned away at the door, the landlord calling him an intruder and saying it was "a violation of the rules of society for colored people to associate with whites." But one of the city's editors, seeing what was happening, called him inside and asked for a vote. With almost unanimous approval, Douglass was formally accepted into Rochester's publishing circle.[30]

The abolitionists Isaac and Amy Post became two of Douglass's closest friends. He had met them during a visit to Rochester in the early 1840s and they immediately bonded. Amy "loved me and treated me as a brother before the world knew me as it does now," Douglass noted. He reciprocated this affection, saying that he "loved and admired" Amy; and he called Isaac "as dear to me" as anyone. The Posts and

Douglasses came and went from each other's homes like family.[31]

Despite this community support, the *North Star* floundered and almost died in its first year. In May 1848, soon after purchasing his home, Douglass published an urgent appeal for financial help. He had obtained fewer than a thousand subscriptions and had to mortgage his home to stay afloat. In order to drum up subscribers and bring in money, he embarked on a series of lectures, which netted him from $25 to $50 per engagement ($1,875 to $3,750 in today's money).[32]

Aside from his lack of experience as an editor, Douglass faced a number of hurdles. One was that he miscalculated his subscriber base. His goal had been to reach the nation's half million free blacks: "Remember that we are one, our cause is one, and that we must help each other," he told them in his first issue.[33] He hired blacks to help him. Martin Delany, who had briefly studied at Harvard before being forced out, served as co-editor and was responsible for bringing in subscriptions. William Cooper Nell, a protégé of Garrison, came up from Boston to help. But Delany signed on few subscribers and Nell, who disagreed with Douglass about the uses of politics, eventually returned to

Boston.[34] Douglass failed to reach his imagined black community.

As a result he became frustrated and chastised blacks for not subscribing. "Every colored man should ask himself the question, 'What am I doing to elevate and improve my condition and that of my brethren at large?' " They weren't doing much, he concluded in July 1848. While the oppressed of Europe and the white workers of America were agitating, resisting, and uniting, "we, who are" the most oppressed, "are comparatively idle and indifferent about our welfare." Of the half million free blacks in the country, only two thousand were interested in self-help, fewer than fourteen hundred showed any interest in antislavery, and only about a hundred subscribed to his paper. "We say this in sorrow, not in anger."[35]

But Douglass was angry. He noted that while blacks spent lavishly on their fraternal organizations, they refused to subscribe to his paper. In July 1848, between four and five thousand blacks convened in New York City for the annual celebration of Odd Fellows, the nation's largest black fraternal order. With their formal dinner-dance, silken banners, and gilded regalia, they spent about $20,000, which averaged about four dollars per person. Yet they wouldn't spend two dollars for an annual subscription

to the *North Star*! Only later, when his paper
was on sound financial footing, did Douglass
realize that black fraternal organizations were
themselves a central source of race pride and
"mutual elevation."[36]

The lack of black support was a comparatively minor problem, however. Douglass's
greatest obstacle stemmed from factions within
the abolitionist movement coupled with resentment from former white allies. The *North Star*
sought to bridge the divide between Garrisonian nonresistance and the Liberty Party and attract readers from both groups. While it did not
condemn voting (as Garrison and his followers
did), neither was it a Liberty Party paper. It was
wholly independent in an age in which most
papers were aligned with a specific party or
association. As a result, neither group provided
the necessary base of support.

On top of this, Douglass's former Boston colleagues were still angry at him for leaving the
fold and starting his own paper. They called
the *North Star* "an unnecessary if not a useless instrumentality for promoting the cause
of the slave."[37] And they boycotted his paper.
Eight months after its first issue, the *North Star*
had fewer than thirty subscribers *in the entire
state of Massachusetts*, a state that was home
to Garrisonian abolitionism and ostensibly

the standard-bearer of freedom. A few Boston abolitionists went so far as to write letters to Douglass's British friends instructing them *not* to subscribe.[38]

Despite these trials, Douglass slowly established a base of influential readers. Harriet Beecher Stowe and Lucretia Mott were early subscribers, as was Lady Byron, the poet's widow. New friends from upstate New York signed on and read his paper religiously, as did old ones from Britain (despite the letters from Boston).

Two friends in particular set Douglass on the path to financial security. One was Julia Griffiths, whose parents had been intimately connected with the British abolition movement. Frederick and Julia had become close friends during his travels in England. She had helped him obtain his legal freedom and they corresponded after he returned to the United States. After learning that his paper was in jeopardy, she immediately wrapped up her affairs in England, came to Rochester with her sister Eliza, and moved into Douglass's home.[39]

Julia had a brilliant business sense. She separated Frederick's personal and business accounts and raised thousands of dollars by organizing antislavery fairs, making personal appeals for money and subscriptions, and creating a crucial base of support among women readers. She also taught Frederick the art of editing, beginning with the rules of grammar. Now he no longer had to rely solely on his sense of what sounded right. She was his tutor. She marked up his editorials "with careful blue-penciling," and he studied them as if they were math equations.[40]

Soon he learned how to write quickly and confidently without mistakes. "Think what editing a paper was to me before Miss Griffiths came," he remarked a few years later. "I had not learned how to spell; I wrote slowly and under embarrassment—lamentably ignorant of much that every schoolboy is supposed to know."[41] As an orator he hadn't needed to spell correctly, and while writing his 1845 *Narrative* he had been able to rely on others to clean up his prose.

The addition of an attractive young white woman in Douglass's home created a scandal. When he was in town Frederick spent most of his waking hours with Julia. They worked all day in his office and were often up late in the evenings. Most racist whites, who had been brought up to believe that all black men lusted after white women, assumed gross improprieties when they saw them together. The very sight of Frederick and Julia on Main Street in Rochester, arm in arm (as was the custom), created a stir, as if they had been naked, and "threats were openly made" if such "amalgamation" persisted.[42] But Frederick and Julia kept their heads high, ignoring the stares, and the threats eventually trailed off without incident. When a Rochester abolitionist mentioned the rumors, Douglass ignored them: "When the city, which you allege to be full of scandalous reports implicating Miss G. and me, shall put those '*reports*' in a definite shape, and present a responsible person to back them, it will be time for me to attempt to refute them."[43]

The worst rumors came from Boston abolitionists who considered Douglass a heretic. One former colleague called Julia "a Jezebel whose capacity for making mischief between friends would be difficult to match."[44] Garrison himself fueled the rumor mill by saying that since moving to Rochester, Douglass "has lost much of moral power. . . . He has had one of the worst advisors in his printing office, whose influence over him has not only caused much unhappiness in his own household, but perniciously biased his own judgment."[45] Douglass denied that Julia's presence had created unhappiness in his family. But according to another account, Amy Post said that Anna felt threatened by Julia and demanded that she live with another family: "I don't care anything about her being in the *office*—but I won't have her in my house," Anna reportedly told Frederick. Harriet Beecher Stowe, a friend of both Douglass and Garrison, tried to silence the rumors, "but her words were wasted on the leader of the American Anti-Slavery Society."[46]

There is no evidence of any sexual impropriety between Frederick and Julia. Douglass knew that if he were caught having an affair, it would ruin his career. And so whatever he did behind closed doors, he took every precaution to make sure that any unseemly behavior would not come back to haunt him. While Lincoln could hire a prostitute or sleep with his intimate friend for four years without anyone raising an eyebrow, the standards of decorum for black men, and the costs of violating them, were much higher.

If Julia Griffiths taught Douglass grammar and business skills, then Gerrit Smith transformed his political views and remade his paper. Gerrit (pronounced with a hard "G") had grown up in the village of Peterboro, about forty miles southeast of Syracuse, in one of the wealthiest families in the country. His father had been a business partner with John Jacob Astor and amassed over one million acres in New York State. As a young man Gerrit had idolized Lord Byron and dreamed of becoming

America's epic poet and aristocrat, living the ideals of unfettered freedom in his poetry. Indeed for most of his life Gerrit wore the "broad Byronic collar" (see figure 9). But a series of tragedies set him on the path to religious conversion and radical abolitionism. The Panic of 1837 almost bankrupted him, prompting him to empathize with the plight of the poor and devote his life to those in need. After recovering from near bankruptcy he became one of the nation's greatest philanthropists; he gave away about $8 million ($600 million in today's currency) worth of land and other assets, mostly to poor blacks. He forged close friendships with blacks, corresponding with them more frequently than any other white man. Essentially he sought to "make myself a colored man," as he put it.[47]

Smith's greatest act of philanthropy occurred a year before Douglass moved to Rochester. In 1846 he gave away 120,000 acres of land in the Adirondacks to some three thousand poor New York State blacks, amounting to forty acres per person. (There were no mules in the bargain, Smith being cash poor at the time but land rich.) Located in Franklin and Essex counties, the settlement became known as "Timbucto," after the fabled city in West Africa and a place beyond the pale of American prejudice. Smith

Figure 9. Douglass's friend and benefactor, fellow abolitionist Gerrit Smith, an engraving by A. H. Ritchie from a photograph. *(Author Collection)*

hoped his gift would enable recipients to become independent farmers and voters. (New York State required blacks to own $250 in property before they could vote.)[48]

Cynics and enemies accused Smith of being self-serving, for he was also a leading political abolitionist. He had helped found the Liberty Party in 1840 and its successor, the National Liberty Party, in 1848. The National Liberty Party was the only political party calling for universal emancipation and equal rights for all people, and in 1848 Smith was its presidential candidate. He attracted a following among black abolitionists, many of whom had become frustrated with Garrison's insistence on nonvoting and nonviolence. Since his gift increased the number of potential voters to his party, some people charged him with opportunism. But the National Liberty Party never attracted more than a few thousand voters. Its function was symbolic, serving as a beacon of democracy in a slave republic. Smith resembled most other white abolitionists in that he considered himself a prophet heeding God's will in battling the sin of slavery; he differed from them in the degree of his commitment.[49]

A few days after Douglass launched his newspaper, Smith welcomed Douglass to the state with a letter and a deed for forty acres at Timbucto. "In this, your new home, may . . . your labors of love for your oppressed race be greatly blessed of God."[50] They had never met, and Douglass could barely read the letter, as Smith's handwriting looked like chicken scratches from someone with a palsied hand. After deciphering the letter, Douglass published it in his newspaper (he probably sold the deed). So began their friendship. Smith seemed almost instinctively to know when Douglass needed help, for timely letters arrived with a check for $100 here or $200 there.[51]

Gerrit Smith was unlike any other white

man that Douglass had met. He gave away his wealth to blacks with few strings attached. He welcomed them to the state with forty-acre plots. He supported a black-owned newspaper with timely donations. He listened to blacks, trusted them, empathized with them, and respected what they had to say.[52] While Garrison had treated Douglass like a son, Smith became a friend and ideal colleague.[53] Douglass found that he could argue with and oppose Smith on important issues without recrimination.

The Constitution was one such issue. When they met, Douglass still clung to the Garrisonian belief that the Constitution was proslavery and corrupt. In fact, Garrison once publicly burned it, calling it "a covenant with death" and "an agreement with hell."[54] But Gerrit Smith endorsed it as a thoroughly antislavery document. The difference was important, for how you interpreted the Constitution shaped how you attacked slavery.

Smith and a few other theorists borrowed from William Blackstone to argue that natural law was incompatible with slavery and thus overrode any human law that defended it.[55] Instead of reading the Constitution from the perspective of the past, and thus having to deal with the long tradition of proslavery laws emerging out of it, they tried "to discern what the Constitution *might* be."[56]

This forward-looking perspective led Smith and other Liberty men to some beneficially creative interpretations. The very purpose of the Constitution, as stated in the Preamble, is to secure the blessings of liberty. The Constitution thus accords with the self-evident truths of equality and liberty in the Declaration. Moreover, it never even mentions "slave," "slavery," or "negro," and so it cannot sanction bondage or racial oppression. And it protects people's liberties in specific ways: the due process clause protects life, liberty, and property, prioritizing life and liberty over property; and the prohibition against bills of attainder ensures that every child will be born free, regardless of the status of the parent.[57] Those clauses often treated as pro-slavery have simply been misinterpreted. The "fugitive" clause refers to apprentices and children, not slaves. And the apportionment clause offers no protection to slaveowners.[58] And just in case there is any ambiguity or contradiction, natural law, or God's law, must prevail, rendering slavery null and void.[59]

Smith's interpretation of the Constitution was more than utopian; it was anarchic. It dispensed with seventy years of legal precedent.[60] And it encouraged people to fit the Constitution into their preconceived beliefs and define natural law according to their own laws.[61] In fact, most of the founding fathers and framers of the Constitution believed that slavery was a sin. But they compromised their ideals and established constitutional guarantees for slavery. In many respects they resembled Henry Clay: they opposed slavery in theory and sought its "ultimate extinction," as Clay (and Lincoln) said; but they were compromisers in practice, indeed were often themselves slaveholders.[62]

Initially Douglass called Smith's constitutional argument crazy. In 1849 he admitted that the Constitution, "strictly construed," was not proslavery.[63] But he emphasized that the framers' intentions made it a slaveholding weapon. He argued for a new Constitution and a new government. Smith's constitutional doctrine made government "nothing better than a lawless mob, acting without any other or higher authority than its own convictions." For if a government could ignore the original intentions of its Constitution "in one point, it may do so in all." There would be "no limit, or safety, or certainty" in how the Constitution was interpreted and applied.[64] Douglass was wedded to a model of law based on original intent.

But that changed over the next two years. Douglass frequently debated Smith on their different conceptions of law, and by early 1851 Douglass came around to Smith's view.[65] "I am sick and tired of arguing on the slaveholders' side" of the Constitution, he said. He still believed that the framers intended certain guarantees for slavery, even if most of them had hoped for slavery's ultimate extinction.[66] No matter. He was ready to "fling to the winds" the framers' intentions and legal precedent. He had recently read Blackstone's *Commentaries*, which told him that slavery was contrary to justice and could not be law. Now he only worried about the *morality* of creating your own legal rules "to defeat the wicked intentions of our Constitution makers."[67] Gerrit put these worries to rest, effectively telling him that the law was "always becoming," in a state of constant evolution.[68] Douglass supported this conception of law, for he too was always becoming, remaking himself.

A few months later, in June 1851, he turned his paper into an organ of Smith's National Liberty Party. The partnership made excellent sense, for Smith offered financial security through monthly subsidies in return for greater exposure of his party's platform. And Douglass retained considerable autonomy.[69]

With the merger he changed the name of his paper to *Frederick Douglass' Paper*. This too was a good decision, for his name had become a marketable commodity. He was thrilled that Gerrit wanted "a good-looking—as well as a good paper," and Douglass gave it a new look, purchasing "good clear white paper" and moving into a larger office in the Wilder Building on the corner of Exchange and East Main streets.[70] He projected himself into his paper to an even greater degree than he had done with the *North Star*. The paper's new name reflected that projection, as if to say, "this good-looking—as well as good paper is me." He also altered his identity as editor, dropping the "F.D." that came after his editorials.[71] Originally he had used the initials to allay accusations that he could not have written them. But now no one doubted his ability, so he conformed to custom and embraced "the right and dignity of *an Editor*—a Mr. Editor if you please!"[72] He was a gentleman with a respectable and successful profession. Douglass thanked Smith for transforming him and his paper: "You not only keep life in my paper but keep spirit in me," he said.[73]

Meanwhile, William Lloyd Garrison felt betrayed when he found out about Douglass's embrace of political abolitionism. "There is roguery somewhere," he announced, and he immediately struck *Frederick Douglass' Paper* from the list of approved papers he sent his readers.[74]

To Garrison and his Boston colleagues, Douglass had become an apostate, a wayward son in a strict evangelical family. They openly accused him of selling his soul and prostituting his mind to Smith's purse strings. Initially Douglass ignored this slander and tried to patch up their differences, but eventually he lashed back. For the next decade, the man he had once worshipped, and who had done so much for his early career, refused to speak to him.[75]

Now Douglass began using the declarative: the slumbering volcanoes *will* erupt; "the insurrection of the Southern slaves *shall* take place."[76] He urged slaves to endorse Virginia's state motto as their own: death to tyrants.[77] Political abolitionism justified the use of force, for it called on every loyal American to interfere with slavery wherever it existed. If Garrisonian nonresistance led to disunion from a slave republic, political abolitionism demanded war on tyrants.[78]

Significantly, Douglass's constitutional conversion coincided with the Compromise of 1850, a series of six laws passed by Congress that were intended to solve the sectional crisis over slavery.[79] The Compromise was the brain-

child of Henry Clay, who sought to allay Southern threats to secede from the Union. Most
Southerners demanded the extension of slavery into the territories newly acquired from
Mexico, and they threatened to secede if they
didn't get their way, while many Northerners
insisted on excluding slavery from these territories. Clay promised concessions to both sides,
but from Douglass's perspective he simply "secured everything to slavery."[80] Indeed, when
Clay died in 1852, Douglass wrote an anti-eu-
logy of sorts, saying he had done "more than
any other man in this country to make slavery
perpetual." He had dragged down "thousands
of the brightest luminaries," and countless
other no-name Whigs (like Lincoln), into the
slough of compromise and deception.[81]

The Fugitive Slave Act was the most outra-
geous part of the Compromise of 1850. Replac-
ing the previous law of 1793, it denied suspects
the right to a jury trial or even a hearing before a judge, and it excluded their testimony.
It appointed special commissioners, who were
authorized to send the suspect immediately
into slavery "without stay or appeal." And commissioners received a bonus for condemning
suspects to bondage ($10 instead of $5). Any
and all citizens in a community could be called
on to hunt down alleged fugitives, subject to a

$1,000 fine if they refused. Anyone caught aiding a fugitive faced a fine and prison term.[82]

The law transformed public opinion in the North. It made free soil "hunting ground for southern kidnappers" and convinced countless Northerners that they could no longer wash their hands of slavery.[83] It inspired Harriet Beecher Stowe to write *Uncle Tom's Cabin*, whose impact was so profound that it prompted President Lincoln to call Stowe "the little woman who wrote the book that started this great war" when he met her at the White House.[84] And the law sparked a mass exodus of Northern blacks to Canada.[85]

A number of influential Northern statesmen, including William Seward, Salmon P. Chase, and Charles Sumner, called the law unconstitutional and urged people to resist it.[86] Seward had already created a stir in the Senate when he said, "There is a higher law than the Constitution, which regulates our authority over the domain" of the territories.[87] Seward's higher law thesis resonated with Douglass's own belief that "the authority of God is greater than the authority of man."[88]

Douglass's response to the fugitive slave law relied on higher law as well and created even more of a stir. In 1852 he was invited to the national convention of the Free Soil Party, which sought to prevent the spread of slavery into the territories.[89] The convention was in Pittsburgh, and on the first day Douglass entered the majestic Masonic Hall, where a meeting of some two thousand delegates was in progress. A few members recognized him standing at the rear, wearing a blue blazer with brass buttons and white pants, and they urged him to speak. Douglass walked slowly to the platform "with the air and swagger of a man who said to himself—'I'll make you all hear, and feel me too,'" according to one journalist. He announced, to much applause and laughter, "The only way to make the Fugitive Slave Law a dead letter is to make half a dozen more dead kidnappers." When he added that "slaveholders not only forfeit their right to liberty, but to life itself," the applause became more solemn.[90]

If slavery was a kind of living death, as Douglass had sometimes suggested, he now demanded Old Testament retribution. The "lines of eternal justice" needed to be brightened with the blood of tyrants. This was God's law, he argued; and when human laws destroyed human rights, God's government needed to be erected in its place. He referred to Gerrit Smith's constitutional doctrine and said he was "proud to be one of [Smith's] disciples."[91]

Most of the major newspapers covered Douglass's speech, adding to his fame. During a layover on the way home, he stopped at a railside restaurant for dinner but the landlord refused to seat him. Douglass called for a vote among the diners, and as everyone recognized him, they unanimously voted in favor of having him eat with them, chastising the landlord for his "insulting conduct."[92] Being in the spotlight could erase racial barriers.

Douglass downplayed his militancy when speaking to women, however. A month before his Pittsburgh talk, Rochester's Female Anti-Slavery Society had invited him to deliver the 1852 Fourth of July address at the city's lavish Corinthian Hall. The celebration occurred on Monday, July 5, perhaps to highlight the nation's unfulfilled ideals.[93] His speech that day is probably his best known, and rhetorically it is masterful, employing a "double reversal." He opens by comforting his mostly white listeners, making them feel proud and hopeful about "your nation." The pronoun "your" foreshadows the sudden shift in tone that comes midway through: "pardon me, allow me to ask, why am I called upon to speak here today? What have I, or those I represent, to do with *your* national independence?" And then for the next hour he berates them, dramatizing the national sins of slavery and racism. The second reversal comes near the end: "I leave off where I began, with *hope*," he says, anticipating Barack Obama.[94] The speech is a jeremiad, a song of lament seeking to *restore* the ideals of the nation's founders. But unlike his other great speeches of the era, there is no talk of retribution or of killing kidnappers.*

In late June 1855 Douglass acted on his revolutionary rhetoric. At City Hall in Syracuse, a fortresslike stone structure, he helped found the Radical Abolition Party, the successor of the National Liberty Party. In many respects Radical Abolitionists grew out of the same tree that created Lincoln's Republican Party that same year: the conservative branch of the Liberty Party evolved into the Free Soil Party, which grew into the Republican Party; and the radical branch of the Liberty and National Liberty parties became the Radical Abolition Party.[95] Both parties hated slavery, but Republicans, believing that the Constitution protected slavery in the states, advocated its nonextension, while Radical Abolitionists urged an end to it everywhere.

---

* One reason "What to the Slave is the Fourth of July" is so well-known is that it lacks the militancy of his other great speeches of the era. White Americans like their black heroes virtuous and nonviolent.

The Radical Abolition Party was aptly named. At its inaugural convention, members embraced immediate and universal abolition; full suffrage for all Americans regardless of sex or skin color; the redistribution of land so that no one would be rich and no one poor; and violent intervention against the Slave Power. And they relied on "pentacostal visitations" (messages from God) to help them pave the way to their new free world.[96]

A few hundred people attended the convention, including three close friends of Douglass. Gerrit Smith, the party's chief organizer, was there. So was John Brown, a lean, gray-eyed, fifty-five-year-old militant whom Douglass had befriended soon after moving to Rochester (see figure 10). A bankrupt businessman, Brown had failed in every trade and business venture he had tried. Abolition was now his sole vocation, and he lived with the black settlers at Timbucto in upstate New York.[97] Douglass had been much impressed with Brown after their first meeting: "though a white gentleman," he wrote, Brown "is in sympathy a black man, and as deeply interested in our cause as though his own soul had been pierced with the iron of slavery."[98] Brown shared with Douglass and Gerrit Smith the conviction "that slaveholders had forfeited their right to live."[99]

Figure 10. John Brown in 1856, three years before his raid on Harpers Ferry. *(Boston Athenaeum)*

James McCune Smith was the third friend present. A frequent contributor to Douglass's newspaper, he was the nation's foremost black intellectual and its first black physician. From New York City, he owned a pharmacy and medical practice on fashionable Broadway. Like Douglass, McCune Smith had lived in Britain, having received his B.A., M.A., and M.D. degrees from the University of Glasgow after being rejected from American colleges owing to his race. He chaired the convention, itself a revolutionary act, for the next time a black man chaired a national political convention was in 1988.[100]

The party's true colors emerged during John

Brown's speech. Brown was on his way to Kansas to join three sons in the fight for freedom there. A year earlier the Kansas-Nebraska Act had become law, opening Northern territories to slavery. The new law applied the doctrine of "popular sovereignty" to the territories, which called on the settlers to vote slavery up or down. It effectively turned Kansas into a battleground between proslavery and antislavery emigrants. In his speech Brown quoted Hebrews 9:22, reminding his listeners that "without the shedding of blood there is no remission of sin."[101] He appealed for money and guns to bring with him to Kansas, and his speech electrified his listeners. A few people opposed his brazen request for weapons, but only one delegate formally dissented. Most members agreed that armed resistance was "the only course left to the friends of freedom in Kansas," prompting Douglass to ask for contributions, which yielded Brown about sixty dollars and a few guns.[102]

The fruits of this convention could be seen a year later, when Radical Abolitionists again met at City Hall in Syracuse to nominate candidates. Gerrit Smith became the party's presidential candidate and Douglass was nominated as vice president. A Smith-Douglass ticket didn't carry, though, partly because both men were New Yorkers, and the delegates, needing geographic diversity, elected Samuel McFarland of Pennsylvania as Smith's running mate.[103] Douglass and his comrades were under no illusions that Smith could get elected. In fact Douglass supported the Republican John C. Frémont, the dashing young Western explorer and California's first senator. Even Gerrit Smith supported Frémont, giving him $500. Their immediate goal was to agitate against slavery, help elect Frémont, and push Republicans toward a more radical anti-slavery stance.[104]

The convention was again quite spirited, for six days earlier (May 22) Charles Sumner, the abolitionist senator from Massachusetts, had been bludgeoned almost to death on the Senate floor by Preston Brooks, an arrogant young congressman from South Carolina. Sumner had been quietly working at his desk when Brooks, who had been drinking, entered the Senate chamber and without warning began pummeling him on the head with a cane made out of gutta-percha, which has the density of lead. Sumner was trapped at his desk, which was bolted to the floor, and in a heroic effort to rise and defend himself, he ripped the bolts from the floor and then collapsed.[105]

Although the session had just adjourned for the day, a number of senators remained in the chamber. But they were all anti-abolitionists, and not one came to Sumner's aid. As Sumner's blood began to pool on the carpeting, Robert Toombs of Georgia looked on approvingly, Stephen Douglas of Illinois casually sat down, ignoring the assault, and John Crittenden of Kentucky told Brooks, "Don't kill him."[106]

The provocation for the attack was Sumner's recent "Crime against Kansas" speech, which accused slaveholders of raping the virgin soil of Kansas. Sumner had singled out Senator Andrew Butler of South Carolina, Brooks's cousin and an architect of the Kansas-Nebraska Act: "The Senator from South Carolina has read many books of chivalry, and believes himself a chivalrous knight, with sentiments of honor and courage. Of course he has chosen a mistress to whom he has made his vows and who, although ugly to others, is always lovely to him; although polluted in the sight of the world, is chaste in his sight—I mean the harlot, Slavery."[107]

Preston Brooks was defending Southern and family honor. Immediately after attacking Sumner he became a Southern hero and every day received commemorative canes, silver pitchers, and gold plates from grateful fans for a deed well done. He endeared himself even more to Southerners when he said he was half inclined to "have the throats of every abolitionist cut."[108]

Congress did not even censure him, whereas Sumner's injuries were so serious as to require four years of painful treatment before he could return to the Senate.[109]

Things were even worse in Kansas. Missouri "Border Ruffians" and other Southerners were fighting a terrorist war against antislavery emigrants. President Franklin Pierce, a Democrat from New Hampshire and a close friend of Nathaniel Hawthorne, officially supported the corrupt proslavery legislature and proclaimed its opponents "treasonable."[110] Pierce thus sanctioned Border Ruffian outrages. One antislavery leader was hacked to death with hatchets and knives, and the Kansas proslavery paper announced, "In a fight, let our motto be, 'War to the knife, and knife to the hilt.' "[111] Then on May 21, the day before Sumner's beating, about 750 Border Ruffians, many of them drunk, attacked the town of Lawrence, an antislavery stronghold. They destroyed the newspapers, burned and looted homes, and blew up the Free State Hotel. The invaders wore red flannel shirts for uniforms and some of them carried flags or banners. A South Carolina battle flag, with a crimson star and the motto "Southern Rights," fluttered in the smoke-filled breeze, as did banners proclaiming THE SUPREMACY OF THE WHITE RACE and ALABAMA FOR KANSAS.[112]

Civil war had begun in Congress and Kansas.

Radical Abolitionists called for immediate retaliation. Frederick Douglass summarized the prevailing mood of his party: liberty "must either cut the throat of slavery or slavery would cut the throat of liberty," he announced to great applause.

These were precisely the sentiments on which John Brown had acted four days earlier, soon after learning about the assault on Sumner and the sack of Lawrence. On the night of May 24, he and seven men, including four sons and a son-in-law, entered the proslavery settlement along Pottawatomie Creek. The settlers there desired "the extermination of Abolitionists," but Brown and his men preempted these desires from becoming facts. They approached three cabins along the creek, woke up the settlers, dragged a total of five men out into the cold dark night, and hacked them to death with broadswords. They were the very same weapons Lincoln had selected for his duel against James Shields.* One victim was decapitated and another's windpipe "entirely

---

* Like Lincoln, Brown never used the broadsword. He issued the orders (and shot one victim in the head to make sure he was dead).

cut out."[113]

At the time Douglass did not know exactly what Brown had done. He knew that Brown had gone to Kansas to be a warrior and had encouraged him to go. When he eventually found out the details of the Pottawatomie massacre, he morally justified Brown's actions by saying it was "a terrible remedy for a terrible malady," not unlike "the execution of a murderer."[114] As Douglass knew, in a brutal environment one needed to be brutal or die.

As for the legal justification of their warfare, Radical Abolitionists relied heavily on the writings of former president John Quincy Adams. Douglass called Adams "the most renowned statesman America has produced."[115] Adams hated slavery, and as the son of John Adams, he was intimately familiar with the Declaration and the Constitution. As early as 1836, in response to belligerent Southerners, Adams had argued that Congress and the president, under the war powers clause of the Constitution, could end slavery in the states.[116]

Douglass and Radical Abolitionists latched on to this interpretation of war powers, but with a crucial revision: they defined slavery as a state of war. This meant that Congress and the president were obliged to free the slaves right now and end the civil war raging in the slave states. But since they did nothing, it was the "highest obligation" of the people of the free states to make war on slavery in order to preserve the peace and save the Union.[117]

Radical Abolitionists were only the first group to act on Adams's constitutional use of war powers. Immediately after Confederate troops fired on Fort Sumter in April 1861, Charles Sumner, who had been Adams's protégé, walked as fast as he could to the White House (he had only recently recovered from his beating) and told Lincoln that "under the war power the right had come to him to emancipate the slaves."[118] Union generals John C. Frémont, David Hunter, and Benjamin Butler also tried to use the war powers theory in their military campaigns. Congress drew on the same source to pass the Confiscation Acts of 1861 and 1862, which authorized the Union army to confiscate (and in the case of the 1862 act, to emancipate) slaves of disloyal masters. And of course Lincoln issued the Emancipation Proclamation by the power vested in him "as Commander-in-Chief of the Army and Navy of the United States *in time of actual armed rebellion* against authority and government of the United States, and *as a fit and necessary war measure* for suppressing said rebellion."[119] Frederick Douglass and his comrades had established an important precedent.

The war on freedom just kept getting worse. If the Mexican War sacrificed Northern boys to slaveowners' lust for land; if the fugitive slave law made Northerners hunt down blacks for the South's pleasure and pocketbook; and if the Kansas-Nebraska Act rubbed out the sacred line (36°30′ N) above which slavery could not extend and told settlers to decide for themselves whether or not to admit slaves; then the Supreme Court decision in *Dred Scott v. Sandford* (1857) capped a decade in which Southern leaders made slavery a national institution. Northern compromisers and Southern leaders had joined hands in a "conspiracy against freedom" that constituted an evil "Slave Power," according to Douglass, Lincoln, and countless other Northerners.[120]

The *Dred Scott* decision, with seven pro-Southern justices supporting it, declared that *any* attempt to prohibit the spread of slavery was unconstitutional.[121] It told slaveowners, "Go where you please; the land is all yours, the national flag shall protect you, and the national troops shoot down whoever resists you." It even implied that if slaveholders went into a free state, the Constitution would protect their property.[122] Not only that, but Chief

Justice Roger Taney (pronounced "tawny") said that blacks "were so far inferior, that they had no rights which the white man was bound to respect; and that [all blacks] might justly and lawfully be reduced to slavery."[123] This from the highest (human) judge in the land. According to Taney, Frederick Douglass (or any other black) could be stripped of his property and enslaved or killed like cattle with impunity.[124]

Ironically, Douglass was thrilled about the *Dred Scott* decision. Why? Because it would be the tidal wave that uprooted slavery and converted millions more Northerners to the antislavery cause. There were already more antislavery advocates than slaveholders in the nation, he argued. The *Dred Scott* decision would give Republicans enough votes to control Congress and the presidency. It would radicalize Republicans, making them realize that slavery was like a noxious weed that would spread everywhere if not stamped out immediately. And it would convince them to ignore the Supreme Court since the Court ignored natural law.[125] His hopes for a swift end to slavery "were never brighter than now."[126]

One year later Douglass commended Lincoln for a speech that made his hopes for ending slavery even brighter. Lincoln was contesting the Democratic incumbent Stephen Douglas for the Illinois Senate and just beginning to emerge as a nationally known figure.[127] In fact, Douglass misspelled his name, calling him "Abram."[128] But he liked what this Illinois Republican had to say.* Lincoln understood the implications of the *Dred Scott* decision, and Douglass quoted his "House Divided" speech at length: " 'A house divided against itself cannot stand.' I believe this government *cannot endure permanently half slave and half free.* . . . It will become all one thing, or all the other. Either the opponents of slavery *will arrest the further spread of it*, and place it in the belief *that it is in the course of ultimate extinction*; or its advocates *will push it forward till it shall become alike lawful in all the states*."[129]

"Well and wisely said," Douglass noted.[130]

He was engaged in his own response to the *Dred Scott* decision, helping John Brown plan a militant alternative to the Underground Railroad. Called the "Subterranean Pass Way," the plan was to terrorize the South by establishing a network of armed warriors in the Allegheny Mountains of Maryland and Virginia. These

---

* When Douglass recorded Lincoln's vote to retain the slave trade in Washington, D.C., ten years earlier, he listed only last names, and Lincoln appeared alongside all the other House members. It is thus likely, and understandable, that Douglass forgot that Lincoln had voted for the slave trade.

warriors would raid plantations and run fugitives north through the Alleghenies and Adirondacks to Canada.[131] The goal was to destroy the value of slave property: "if we could drive slavery out of *one county*, it would be a great gain—it would weaken the system throughout the state," forcing emancipation in the border states, Brown said.[132] Douglass agreed. The plan could be "very effective in rendering slave property in Maryland and Virginia valueless by rendering it insecure."[133]

In February 1858, a few months before Lincoln's "House Divided" speech, Brown spent three weeks at Douglass's home in Rochester responding to Chief Justice Taney by writing a "Provisional Constitution."[134] It was designed to govern the community of mountain warriors in Brown's Subterranean Pass Way. Douglass probably edited Brown's constitution, for it is more polished than almost anything else Brown wrote. In key ways it echoes Douglass's interpretation of the United States Constitution: it calls slavery a state of war; it seeks to fulfill "those eternal and self-evident truths set forth in our Declaration of Independence"; and it explicitly repudiates the *Dred Scott* decision, defining as citizens not only white men but blacks, women, and everyone else "degraded" by positive law.[135]

Occasionally Brown would talk about altering his plan for the Subterranean Pass Way. He would suddenly become grandiose and tell Douglass that he could, "with a few resolute men," capture the federal arsenal at Harpers Ferry, Virginia, "and supply himself" with the large cache of weapons housed there.

"I paid little attention to such remarks," Douglass said.[136]

Until September 1859, that is. That's when Brown wrote Douglass requesting an urgent meeting at an old stone quarry near Chambersburg, Pennsylvania. Brown told Douglass to bring money and a mutual friend, a fugitive named Shields Green, also known as "the Emperor."[137] Green was a man of few words but fearless and dignified. Brown knew "what stuff" Green "was made of" and wanted him at the meeting.[138]

Amid the quarry rocks, Douglass and Green listened as Brown and his secretary John Kagi, a zealous young journalist turned warrior, described the new plan. Brown did most of the talking. He and twenty men, including four blacks, were all set to invade the Harpers Ferry arsenal. They knew the terrain, had been in the area since July renting a farmhouse and passing as farmers (a fisherman in Brown's case). They would gain control of the arsenal at night, confiscate the weapons, and launch their attack on slaveholders. The capture of the arsenal would serve "as a trumpet" to rally slaves to their side.[139] Brown had already asked a number of blacks, including Harriet Tubman (Brown called her "General Tubman") and Martin Delany, to spread word of the invasion through the grapevine telegraph, so that the large slave and free black population in the area would be ready for them. At Tubman's suggestion Brown had planned the raid for July 4, but there had been unavoidable delays. He was ready now, though, had even brought a thousand pikes as weapons for those slaves who didn't know how to load a gun.

Brown urged Douglass and Green to go with him. "Come with me, Douglass," Brown said; "I will defend you with my life. I want you for a special purpose. When I strike, the bees will swarm and I shall want you to help hive them."[140] Douglass understood the metaphor; it came from the fable in Aesop where the bees turn on their master and attack him.

But he opposed the plan and tried to dissuade Brown from carrying it out. It would be fatal for everyone involved, he said, for Harpers Ferry was located in a steep gorge in the mountains. And since it was close to Washington, D.C., federal troops would immediately surround them. Besides, attacking the federal government "would array the whole country against us."[141]

That was fine with Brown: "something startling was just what the nation needed."[142]

They spent two days talking, debating. Finally Douglass told Brown that "he was going into a perfect steel trap and that once in he would never get out alive."[143] Unlike Brown, who was fifty-nine years old and ready to die for the cause of freedom, Douglass preferred to remain alive.

As he turned to leave, Douglass asked Shields Green what he was going to do. He was taken aback by the Emperor's response: "I b'leve I'll go wid de ole man."[144] And so they parted, the Emperor joining the two white men while Douglass returned home alone.

A few weeks later, on Sunday night, October 16, 1859, Brown and his twenty-one men entered Harpers Ferry and took the arsenal without resistance. But then Brown delayed unnecessarily. Possibly he was confused because the bees weren't swarming—the slaves did not rally to his side.[145] By Monday afternoon, surrounded by militiamen, Brown took refuge in the engine house of the armory. Two sons were with him and would soon die at his side. On Tuesday morning, as two thousand spectators looked on, a company of United States Marines led by Colonel Robert E. Lee and J. E. B. Stuart battered down the doors of the engine house. They captured seven survivors and severely wounded Brown in the process.[146] Lee and Stuart would soon become, like Brown, rebels and traitors. But on that day they were federal officers following orders.[147]

Brown and his survivors were tried for murder and treason and sentenced to hang. In prison, during the trial, and at the gallows, Brown performed brilliantly, becoming a heroic martyr to countless Northerners. In fact, the happiest moments of his life occurred while he was in prison waiting to die. His interviews, prison letters, and speech to the court circulated through Northern papers and were published as bestselling pamphlets. And he received a hero's eulogy from Ralph Waldo Emerson, the nation's leading intellectual and an acquaintance of Brown and Douglass. Emerson rarely weighed in on the social issues of the day, but when he did, his words had the power of an "avalanche." In November 1859, one month before Brown was scheduled to die (on December 2), Emerson borrowed the words of a friend and announced that Brown, "the new saint awaiting his martyrdom . . . will make the gallows glorious like the cross."[148]

The impact of Harpers Ferry transformed the nation. Indeed, it is not an exaggeration to say that John Brown helped elect Lincoln. In the wake of the raid, Southerners and Northern Democrats tried to link Brown to the Republican Party. As a result, many Republicans went out of their way to dissociate themselves from abolitionists and blacks. One of them was William Seward, the Republicans' front-runner for president. After Harpers Ferry he backed off his "higher law" doctrine, his assertion that there was "an irrepressible conflict" between freedom and slavery, and his demand that the Supreme Court rescind *Dred Scott.* In late February, three months after Brown was hanged and two months before the Republican nominating convention, Seward gave a speech in the Senate that "was so full of concession to the slave power" as to destroy his bid for the Republican nomination, according to Douglass: *"John Brown frightened Seward into making his last great speech.* In that speech he stooped quite too low . . . *and lost the prize that tempted the stoop."*[149] In Douglass's shrewd analysis, John Brown—or rather his soul, which was "marching on" in song—cost Seward the Republican nomination.[150]

This was fine by Douglass, for at the time he considered Lincoln "a man of unblemished

private character" and a "radical Republican"
who was "fully committed to the doctrine" of
an "irrepressible conflict" between freedom
and slavery that required immediate resolution.
Douglass had been immensely impressed with
Lincoln during his debates with Senator Stephen
Douglas: "he came fully up to the highest mark
of Republicanism, and he is a man of will and
nerve, and will not back down from his own
assertions."[151] Douglass was still a Radical Abolitionist and endorsed Gerrit Smith, again the
party's presidential candidate. Smith had been a
lead financier in Brown's raid on Harpers Ferry,
which endeared Douglass even more to him. In
fact Douglass told readers of his newspaper that
"ten thousand votes for Gerrit Smith . . . would
do more for the ultimate abolition of slavery
than two million for ABRAHAM LINCOLN or
any other" Republican.[152] But he also knew that
endorsing Smith would make Lincoln seem more
palatable. And he probably voted pragmatically
for Lincoln. After Lincoln secured the Republican nomination, Douglass joyously predicted
that he would be elected president, since the
Democratic Party had fractured along sectional
lines.

The split in the Democratic Party emerged
partly in reaction to Harpers Ferry. After Brown's
raid, Southern leaders argued that "had there

been no Republican Party, there would have been no invasion of Harpers Ferry."[153] Mississippi senator Jefferson Davis viewed John Brown as a touchstone of the Republican Party, which had been "organized on the basis of making war" on the South. Davis and other Southern Democrats demanded that the federal government live up to the *Dred Scott* decision and protect slaveholders' property everywhere. Northern Democrats refused, since such a policy undercut their own doctrine of popular sovereignty. And so the party split, with Northern Democrats nominating Illinois senator Stephen Douglas for president and Southern Democrats Vice President John C. Breckinridge of Kentucky. As Frederick Douglass predicted, the split assured Lincoln's election.[154] John Brown's soul was marching on.

But if Brown's soul helped elect Lincoln, it also helped kill him.

As John Brown swung from the gallows, a very handsome young man watched intently. He was close enough to see the slight grasping of Brown's hands and the twitching of his limbs as the rope jerked taut and the boards of the gallows creaked from the force of the 150-pound body coming to a sudden stop.[155] John Wilkes Booth was deeply moved.

Booth later said that he had helped capture

Brown, but he wasn't even in the military. At the time of Brown's arrest he was playing a stock character at the Marshall Theatre in Richmond, Virginia. He was fascinated by Brown, though, and "very anxious" to attend his hanging. On November 24, as a train of uniformed militia prepared to leave Richmond for Harpers Ferry, Booth asked if he could join them. After learning that only men in uniform were allowed on the train, he bought a uniform and boarded. At the hanging he became "extremely pale" and dizzy and asked a soldier if he had a flask. He needed a good stiff drink.[156]

Booth saw much of himself in Brown even though they had diametrically opposed visions of the good society. While Brown believed in a multiracial democracy, Booth thought of himself as a chivalrous and aristocratic Southerner. As an actor he was famous throughout the country but especially beloved by Southern belles, who wrote him fan notes, collected his *carte-de-visite* photograph, and waited for him after performances.[157] He considered slavery the bedrock of a virtuous society, and like Chief Justice Roger Taney, he believed that constitutional rights were for white men only. Still, Booth lauded Brown's pluck, his ability to turn words into deeds, and his composure and eloquence at Harpers Ferry.

According to Booth's sister, he "acknowledged Brown a hero when he saw him die."[158]

Indeed, Booth seemed envious of Brown's martyrdom. In December 1860, he said that Brown was justly executed for attempting "*in another way*" what Lincoln and the Republican Party were now doing (attacking slavery). Brown's method of "*open* force" was "holier *than . . . the hidden* craft" of the Republicans. It would not be long before Booth told his sister that Lincoln "was walking in the footsteps of old John Brown but no more fit to stand with that rugged old hero—Great God! No! John Brown was a man inspired, the grandest character of the century."[159] John Brown's soul was marching on, inspiring Booth to redeem *his* country and become a martyr to *his* cause.

When Frederick Douglass heard the news of Brown's raid, he was giving a speech in the grand National Hall in Philadelphia. The news hit him "like an earthquake. It was something to make the boldest hold his breath."[160] He would soon be breathless for another reason: authorities discovered in Brown's carpetbag a letter from Douglass to Brown. It was dated two years earlier (1857) and said nothing about Harpers

Ferry. But it was enough evidence for Governor Henry Wise of Virginia to charge Douglass with "murder, robbery, and inciting servile insurrection in the State of Virginia." Wise asked President James Buchanan and the postmaster general for help in arresting Douglass and sending him to Virginia for trial and execution. They complied.[161]

Suddenly, Douglass was the most wanted man in America. Had it not been for friends, he would almost certainly have been captured. The telegraph operator in Philadelphia, knowing that the feds were after him, urged him to flee. Douglass took the next train to New York City, spent the night with a female friend in Hoboken, New Jersey, and had a message wired home instructing his oldest son, Lewis, to hide or destroy incriminating documents such as his copy of Brown's Provisional Constitution. The Erie Railroad brought him safely to Rochester, but there he learned that New York's governor would surrender him to Virginia authorities on receiving a warrant for his arrest. So he crossed over to safety in Canada, following the path of the many fugitives he had helped. From there he went to England and Scotland for a prearranged lecture tour.[162]

For the second time in his life, Douglass fled the United States as a fugitive and returned from Britain as a free man. By June 1860, Governor Wise had dropped the charges against him. And the Senate committee investigating Harpers Ferry had decided to end the search for accomplices and put the affair to rest in the hopes of calming sectional tensions.

Douglass never criticized Brown for almost getting him killed. In fact he said he loved Brown and he frequently called him "THE man of this nineteenth century."[163] To be sure, he distanced himself from the Harpers Ferry raid and denied complicity in it. But this was partly because he had to: after all, in "a government recognizing the validity of the Dred Scott decision," Douglass had "no rights which the white man was bound to respect," as he noted.[164]

Although he considered Brown's military strategy misguided, he fully endorsed the *nature* of his warfare. "I am ever ready to write, speak, publish, organize, combine, *and even to conspire against slavery*, when there is a reasonable hope for success," he wrote from the safety of Canada.[165] And he was furious with those people, in both North and South, who said that Brown was insane. "Are heroism and insanity synonyms in our American dictionary?" he asked. Brown's conduct and actions were perfectly sensible: "He believes the Declaration of Independence to be true, and the Bible to be a guide to human conduct, and acting upon the doctrines of both, he threw himself against the serried ranks of American oppression."[166]

When Douglass said that John Brown began the war that ended American slavery, he should have included himself and a few other Radical Abolitionists, who supported Brown's actions with friendship, words, and money. In this sense, Douglass too assisted in electing Lincoln and in killing him.

It is a wonderful quirk of history that at the very moment Brown and his men were raiding Harpers Ferry, Douglass was speaking on the virtues of self-made men. As his friend was remaking himself into a martyr, Douglass was drawing lessons from his own radical re-fashioning over the past twelve years, from a bad speller and slow writer into a successful journalist, intellectual, and political revolutionary.[167] In his speech he outlined the templates of self-improvement: luck and pluck, environment, and self-reliance coupled with reliance on God. But the crux of self-making, Douglass said, was to remake your world as well. While it might be comforting to imagine a heaven free from all wars, wrongs, and vices, real self-made men waged war on those evils "so that the will of God may be done on earth as in heaven."[168]

The hallmark of self-made men were people like Douglass and Brown, who knew the will of God, acted on the injunction of the Lord's Prayer, and worked tirelessly to realize a heaven on earth.

Abraham Lincoln loved to expose American lies. In December 1847, in his first speech in the United States Congress, he attacked Democratic president James K. Polk for waging an unconstitutional war on Mexico.[169] President Polk had lied about "the particular spot of soil on which the blood of our citizens was [first] shed," Lincoln accused.[170] Polk argued that Mexicans had invaded *American* soil and fired on American troops, drawing first blood, so he declared war against Mexico.

Polk's evidence for claiming that first blood had been shed on American soil was "the sheerest deception from beginning to end," Lincoln argued.[171] The bloodstained soil was on disputed territory between the Nueces River and the Rio Grande. Everyone knew this, for when the United States annexed Mexican territory, Congress explicitly left "all questions of boundary to future adjustment."[172] Even Texans acknowledged the boundary dispute. Moreover,

Polk had declared war on Mexico without first obtaining congressional approval, as the Constitution stipulated.[173] The president was thus "in the wrong," Lincoln argued; "he feels the blood of this war like the blood of Abel . . . crying to Heaven against him."[174] A few days after his speech deriding Polk, Lincoln voted for a resolution declaring that the war had been *"unnecessarily and unconstitutionally begun by the President of the United States."*[175] He was gratified that the resolution passed.

Lincoln's attack on Polk stemmed as much from his efforts to discredit Democrats, elect a Whig president, and unify the Whig Party as from his antislavery sentiments. Since the Whig Party had many prominent proslavery Southerners, Lincoln hoped to conciliate with them and thus did not want to come across as being too antislavery. Whereas Frederick Douglass and other abolitionists condemned Polk for being a *slaveowning* president seeking to acquire more slave territory, Lincoln vilified him for being a *Democratic* president who acted unconstitutionally. He agreed with Southern Whigs in arguing that the war perverted the ideal of progress (by turning the United States into an "imperial power"), fueled sectional tensions, and threatened Whig unity. And he echoed Southern Whigs who said that the war gave President Polk and his party too much power.

Opposing the war was tricky business, however, since it was a military success. Most white American men supported President Polk's war. In fact, William Herndon, Lincoln's law partner and a fellow Whig, agreed with Democrats when he argued that President Polk, in ordering a preemptive strike against another country, did not violate the Constitution.[176] Lincoln dismissed such fallacies: "Allow the President to invade a neighboring nation, whenever *he* shall deem it necessary to repel [or preempt] an invasion, . . . and you allow him to make war at pleasure." Preemptive strikes turned presidents into "kings," Lincoln said, violating the Constitution and legal precedent.[177]

Eventually Lincoln would become much more vocal in his antislavery beliefs. Indeed he would dispense with legal precedent and the Supreme Court in opposing the spread of slavery. As a Whig, his antislavery principles often conflicted with party loyalty. But after the Whig Party dissolved and he became a Republican, his principles were in harmony with his party. Because of his political ambitions, Lincoln could never be as creative as Frederick Douglass in his constitutional arguments. But he would follow other antislavery Northerners and give preference to natural rights over positive (or man-made) law, transforming the Constitution into an antislavery document that was subordinate to the ideals of the Declaration.

Most congressmen went to Washington alone and left their families behind. But Mary, thrilled by her husband's election, wanted to "share his success" by going with him.[178] They brought their two children, four-year-old Robert Todd (Bob), and one-year-old Edward (Eddie), who was already showing signs of the consumption that would kill him three years later. It was a long trip, some sixteen hundred miles. It involved a stagecoach, a steamboat down the Mississippi and then up the Ohio River at Cairo* that followed Huck Finn's intended route, another steamer down the Kentucky River, and a train into Lexington, where they stopped at Mary's childhood home to rest for three weeks before finishing the journey.[179] The Todd family slaves helped them relax, working as mammies for the two boys and washing their soiled clothes.[180]

In 1847 cross-country travel was not meant for

---

* Pronounced "Kay-row."

families with small children. Riding in a stage-coach felt like being imprisoned in a cramped and creaking wooden barrel. Steamboats, while more spacious and luxurious, carried a motley crew of men who, especially in the mid-Atlantic and Southern states, indulged in the pleasures of tobacco. Invariably you would find a few young men who, after planting themselves in the middle of the deck, would take out their tobacco boxes for a chew and while casually squirting their plugs would create "a copious shower of yellow rain" that formed a "magic circle, within whose limits no intruders dared to come," according to one passenger.[181]

The Lincolns felt more comfortable on the trains that brought them into Lexington and then Washington, for they sat in the "ladies' car," which prohibited tobacco.[182] There were still inconveniences: frequent jolting; the screeching of metal on metal; and red-hot embers fluttering up from the stove in the middle of the carriage. But at least they didn't have to dodge tobacco juice.

When the Lincolns arrived in Washington in December 1847, the nation's capital seemed huge and incomplete. With some forty thousand people, including two thousand slaves and eight thousand free blacks, it was the largest city either of them had ever seen.[183] Many Americans referred to Washington as "the City of Magnificent Distances," but Charles Dickens, who had visited a few years earlier, termed it "the City of Magnificent Intentions" because it was only half developed. There were no streetlamps anywhere. Empty roads went nowhere waiting for buildings to give them life. And everywhere were public buildings that needed "a public to be complete."[184] Pennsylvania Avenue, the main thoroughfare, had been partly paved with cobblestones. The rest of it was a mudhole after a heavy rain.[185] Pigs roamed the streets and "garbage, dead animals, and human waste littered every neighborhood." The sewage from the Capitol spilled onto the Mall from gullies and became a "fetid marsh."[186]

Not even the classically elegant Capitol was finished. Its dome, yet to be gilded, looked like a large phrenological chart of the head, with steel wires crisscrossing around it as if to draw attention to the mental and moral faculties of the nation's character. (The most prominent parts of the dome seemed to correspond with those areas in phrenology responsible for acquisitiveness and combativeness.) The Capitol faced east, but as the city had grown west, it had "the appearance of turning its back on" the people and the city.[187]

Dickens called Washington "the headquarters of tobacco-tinctured saliva," and he did not exaggerate. Chewing was allowed in all public places, and the marble columns of the Capitol and the carpeting in the House and Senate were stained with it. Spittoons were everywhere, but chewers often ignored them or missed their mark. "Even steady old chewers of great experience are not always good marksmen," Dickens noted after meeting some of them. Many esteemed members of the House and Senate, their cheeks swelled with plug, would shoot an airball, missing the spittoon entirely. One New York representative hated serving in Congress because of so many colleagues who "squirted their tobacco juice upon the carpet" and drank on the job. In fact he likened Congress to a "dramshop" or pub, especially during night sessions.[188] Neither Abraham nor Mary drank or chewed (many women did both); but they were used to these habits from Springfield.

The Lincolns lived at Mrs. Spriggs's boardinghouse, which was filled with Whig congressmen and looked out onto the lawn of the Capitol. There were about twenty other boarders, all of them men unused to rooming with women and children. One boarder complained that young Bob was a brat and got "his own way" around the house. Lincoln agreed that his son "has a great deal of that sort of mischief that is the offspring of much animal spirits."[189]

Soon after arriving in Washington Mary hired one of Mrs. Spriggs's slaves to care for the children while she and her husband attended a performance of the Ethiopian Serenaders, a blackface minstrel show.[190] The Serenaders painted their faces "jet black," created clown-like "ruddy lips and large mouths," and sang and danced to such negro melodies as "Old Dan Tucker," "Lucy Neale," and "Railroad Overture."[191] The Lincolns enjoyed the show enough to return for a second performance.[192]

Frederick Douglass hated the racist imitations of blackface minstrelsy. These white performers grossly exaggerated the singing, dancing, and acting of blacks, he said, and he urged actors to "represent the colored man rather as *he is*, than as Ethiopian Minstrels usually represent him *to be*." Minstrelsy may have humored whites, but it disgusted blacks and widened the racial divide.[193]

Joshua Giddings, one of Lincoln's fellow Whig colleagues and a boarder at Mrs. Spriggs's, frowned upon the Lincolns patronizing a blackface minstrel show. A large, white-haired congressman from Ohio, Giddings looked and sounded like a preacher. He was a fervent abolitionist and had already made a name for himself in Congress for his passionate orations against slavery and his friendship and collaboration with John Quincy Adams, also a member of the House. After intense struggles with Southern congressmen, Adams and Giddings heroically repealed the Gag Rules that had silenced public discussion of slavery for almost a decade. Giddings frequently got into arguments over slavery at Mrs. Spriggs's mess table, usually with Southern Whigs but sometimes with Lincoln. When an argument began, Lincoln often changed the subject by telling a joke or story to deflect tension. It was his way of conciliating at the dinner table. Giddings thought Lincoln "had rather timid ideas about how to deal with the South." Lincoln believed Giddings's antagonism toward slaveowners exacerbated rather than abated slavery's evils.[194]

Lincoln also viewed John Quincy Adams as too extreme in his antislavery views. The former president looked harmless, for his body was bowed by time and his bald head speckled with age spots (see figure 11). But his age and feeble physical condition did not stop Southerners from issuing an occasional death threat against him for his fierce opposition to slavery. He not only argued that "in case of war" the government could legally abolish slavery in the states; he maintained that "the people had a right to reform abuses of the government." The people could take government into their own hands and reorganize it in order to align it with the ideals of the Declaration. For this Adams was formally censured and accused of treason.[195] He responded by pointing to the Constitution's definition of treason and the "puny minds" of the Southern men who had accused him.[196]

Adams became a radical late in life. For almost twenty years in Congress, he had withstood "insult, bullying, and threats" from slaveholders.[197] In the early 1840s, when he was in his mid-seventies, he finally began calling himself an abolitionist. His conversion stemmed from John C. Calhoun's "open and brazen avowals" to acquire Texas and perpetuate slavery. "When I see the Constitution of my country struck down by the South for such purposes as are openly avowed, no alternative is left me" than to become an abolitionist, Adams said. "I must oppose them [Southerners] with all the means within my reach. I must fight the Devil with his own fire."[198] Adams sounded more like Frederick Douglass than Lincoln. No wonder Douglass respected him so much.

Lincoln kept his distance from Adams and never got to know him. When he started his congressional term, Adams still lived up to his nickname, "Old Man Eloquent." Despite his advanced age, he could deliver brilliant speeches. On February 21, 1848, a few months after the term began, he stood up in the House to oppose a resolution of gratitude to Congress and Mexican War generals for their "gallant" efforts in Mexico. His ringing "No" was the last word he spoke in Congress and his last protest against slavery. He immediately collapsed at his desk and died two days later.[199] Adams was a tangible link, through his father, to the founders and his death marked the end of an era. Yet Lincoln pretended that he didn't exist, for he mentioned neither him nor the lavish obsequies honoring him.

Lincoln was much more respectful of Southern slaveholding Whigs. This should not be surprising, for his closest friends were also slaveholding Whigs (or their children), and he felt more comfortable around them than Northern abolitionists. After hearing Alexander Stephens, his Whig colleague from Georgia, denounce the Mexican War, Lincoln was so moved that he wrote William Herndon a quick note to say that Stephens, "a little slim, paleface, consumptive man . . . has just concluded the very best speech, of an hour's length, I ever heard. My old, withered, dry eyes are full of tears yet."[200] Perhaps what so moved him was Stephens's succinctness, which was also what he loved about John C. Calhoun's "short sentences and compact style."[201] Still, when Giddings or Adams spoke out against slavery with greater eloquence, Lincoln treated it as a nonevent.

Lincoln dissociated himself from Adams until the Civil War. When he edited his presidential campaign biography, he crossed out the line that said he had been a staunch "Adams man" and instead called himself a staunch "anti-Jackson, or Clay" man.[202] His self-conscious effort to distance himself from Adams is ironic, for both men sought the ultimate extinction of slavery and opposed its expansion into the territories. And of course Lincoln would eventually act on Adams's understanding of the war powers to abolish slavery. But as a congressman and presidential candidate, he considered Adams a liability rather than an ally, owing to his extreme antislavery views.

Lincoln wanted to distinguish himself in Congress.[203] He did not feel intimidated serving in the same chamber with such luminaries as John Quincy Adams, Joshua Giddings, and Alexander Stephens. He was undaunted by the Corinthian columns surrounding the House chamber and the elevated and canopied Speaker's chair that resembled a pulpit.[204] He attended almost every session and was no more scared speaking in Congress than in an Illinois courthouse.

He was confident of the skills he had honed as a lawyer. He had been living in "the courts of justice" for years and had learned how to distinguish truth from lies. "I have sometimes seen a good lawyer struggling for his client's neck in a desperate case, employing every artifice to work round, befog, and cover up, with many words, some point arising in the case, which he *dared* not admit and yet *could* not deny," he noted in one speech. Indeed at times Lincoln had been that "good lawyer," employing artifice on a client's behalf.[205] He hoped that these skills would enable him to rise to eminence by exposing the deceptions of President Polk and his Democratic Party.

But Congress and the president essentially ignored him. Part of the problem was timing. The Mexican War was almost over when he launched his attack against Polk, and he essentially echoed what eminent Whigs had been saying for two years. People were tired of hearing about the war's being unconstitutional. And if they had to listen to such arguments, they preferred them coming from John Quincy Adams, Joshua Giddings, or Alexander Stephens.

Figure 11. John
Quincy Adams,
by Southworth
and Hawes.
*(Metropolitan
Museum of Art)*

Lincoln was also called inconsistent in his antislavery views, especially in relation to Giddings and Adams. Unlike them, he had not opposed the annexation of Texas, which provoked the war in the first place owing to its boundary dispute with Mexico. "I never was interested in the Texas question," Lincoln said. And "I never could very clearly see how the annexation would augment the evil of slavery."[206] No matter that annexation increased the size of the slaveholding states by about one-quarter. For Lincoln the point was that Texas would have the same number of slaves whether it was an independent republic or part of the United States.

But there were other, more serious contradictions in Lincoln's war record that threatened his legitimacy. When the war broke out in 1846, he had *supported* it to placate Illinois voters. As Illinois men rushed to enlist, he encouraged them with a "warm, thrilling, and effective" war speech.[207] Then when he arrived in Congress, he called the war unconstitutional, accused Polk of lying, and demanded to know the exact spot on which first blood was shed. Then a week later he supported the war by voting to supply the army and honor its officers.[208] As a result, Lincoln acquired the epithet "spotty Lincoln," which evoked not only a "pettifogging lawyer," as one newspaper complained, but a flip-flopping politician.[209]

In his efforts to unite Northern and Southern Whigs, Lincoln virtually abandoned antislavery politics. He refused to participate in the heated debates over the Wilmot Proviso, which prohibited slavery from expanding in the newly acquired territories from Mexico. He voted for the proviso (which was defeated), but he didn't want to upset Southern Whigs and so kept silent during the debates. And of course he voted with Southerners to retain the slave trade in Washington, D.C. It was an embarrassing vote for someone who considered himself a foe of slavery, and Frederick Douglass exposed him in his newspaper.

As part of his compromise efforts, Lincoln created his own proposal for ending slavery in Washington. His bill fully compensated masters for their property. It imposed an "apprentice-ship" period on slaves that effectively delayed freedom until 1870–75. It encouraged freed blacks to emigrate to Liberia. And it required a special election in which white citizens in the District could vote on the proposal.[210]

The bill's most sinister feature demanded greater enforcement in capturing fugitive slaves who escaped to the District. This provision was particularly callous because on January 17, 1848, as Lincoln drafted his bill, three armed men forced their way into Mrs. Spriggs's boardinghouse, violently seized a black waiter working there, "and in the presence of his wife, gagged him, placed him in irons, and with loaded pistols, forced him into one of the slave prisons of this city," from which he was reportedly sent to the slave market in New Orleans to be sold to the highest bidder. The waiter had worked at Mrs. Spriggs's for several years and was well liked by congressmen boarding there (presumably including Lincoln). A few years earlier, he had contracted to purchase his freedom from his master for $300. He had paid all but $60 when his master suddenly ripped him away from his family, his job, and his future. Joshua Giddings was so upset that he immediately introduced a resolution in the House proposing either to ban the slave trade in the District or to move "the seat of government to some free state." Such outrages were too common an occurrence to ignore.[211] But Lincoln never mentioned the incident, nor did he alter his fugitive slave clause.[212]

His abolition bill was so conciliatory that no one endorsed it. It resembled (and was possibly modeled on) Henry Clay's plan to abolish slavery in Kentucky. Much like Clay, Lincoln hoped to emancipate slaves without disrupting the pocketbooks of masters. Nevertheless, Southerners viewed it "as a first step toward abolishing slavery throughout the country." And antislavery Northerners found it equally intolerable. Giddings was furious over the bill's fugitive slave provision. The Boston abolitionist Wendell Phillips started calling Lincoln "that slave-hound from Illinois," a term that stuck among some abolitionists.[213]

What most infuriated Giddings and other abolitionists, however, was Lincoln's support of General Zachary Taylor for president. Lincoln had befriended Alexander Stephens, the future Confederate vice president, and together they helped organize a "Taylor for President Club" that stirred up national interest. Taylor knew nothing about politics, had never even voted, and owned about 130 slaves. And unlike Henry Clay, he did not even consider slavery morally wrong. But Lincoln and Stephens thought that nominating Taylor would regenerate the Whig Party and soothe sectional tensions.

Antislavery "conscience" Whigs felt abandoned by Taylor's candidacy and defected to help form the Free Soil Party. How could they remain members of a party that opposed the Mexican War and then nominated the general who helped win it? How could they endorse for president a man who owned hundreds of slaves and didn't even consider slavery a sin? And how could they support a presidential candidate who saw no ethical problem allowing slavery to spread? At the Whig nominating convention in Philadelphia, Joshua Giddings, Charles Sumner, Henry Wilson, and Charles Francis Adams (John Quincy Adams's son) led the flight out the door and into the new Free Soil Party. Had Quincy Adams been alive, he almost certainly would have joined them.[214]

Lincoln supported Taylor for president for reasons of expediency. While some Whigs wanted to nominate Henry Clay, Lincoln believed that Clay could never get elected. "Our only chance is with Taylor," he said. "I go for him not because I think he would make a better president than Clay, but because I think he would make a better one" than a Democrat.[215]

Lincoln clearly valued party loyalty over antislavery principles. He hated the new Free Soil Party, despite its antislavery focus, much as he despised the Liberty Party. The only good thing anti-slavery parties did was to help elect proslavery Democrats, he argued. The Liberty Party had cost Henry Clay the presidency in 1844, and now the Free Soilers might elect the proslavery Democrat Lewis Cass. Lincoln also argued that Whigs were as anti-slavery as Free Soilers, ignoring the fact that such leading Whigs as Henry Clay, Alexander Stephens, Robert Toombs, and Zachary Taylor were all slaveowning Southerners. In contrast, not a single leading Free Soiler was a slaveowner.

Lincoln's support of Taylor was a shrewd political move, however. After all, he helped elect the second (and last) Whig president. And President Taylor was willing to stand up to greedy Southerners who wanted more land for slavery.[216]

At the end of Lincoln's congressional term he got a taste of the sectional powder keg that would soon destroy his beloved party. One day in March 1849, Joshua Giddings was casually conversing with a fellow Free Soiler when

Representative Richard Meade of Virginia went up to him, shook his fist in Giddings's face, and said, "God damn you, we ought to and will compel you by violence to do *right* [support the South], if there is no other way."[217]

Such threats were nothing to Giddings. Southern congressmen had already menaced him with clubs, bowie knives, and revolvers. And so he simply laughed and said, "You will not hurt us."[218]

Meade turned white with rage. He grabbed Giddings by the collar, again waved his fist at him, and "uttered a volley of oaths."[219] Giddings laughed in his face. Before Meade had a chance to hit him, Thomas Henley of Indiana intervened and sent Meade sprawling.

No sooner had this fight been averted when Robert Johnson, a drunken Democrat from Arkansas, suddenly attacked Lincoln's colleague Orlando Ficklin of Illinois. Their confrontation quickly devolved into a fistfight on the floor of the House. Then Samuel Inge of Alabama entered the fray and began bludgeoning Ficklin on the head with his cane, "causing the blood to flow profusely." Eventually the brawl was broken up and Ficklin was carried out, "his face covered with blood."[220] Lincoln witnessed the ordeal but made no effort to interfere. Perhaps he wanted to ignore the fact that a little civil war had erupted in the House.

Mary Todd, who liked to sit in the gallery and listen to the debates, missed the excitement. Tired of boardinghouse life and her husband's long hours, she had taken the two boys to the family home in Lexington, where slaves helped with the childcare. After Lincoln's term ended, she met him back at Springfield.

Lincoln's term in Congress was a failure. He did not run for reelection owing to a prearranged agreement to open his seat to another Whig candidate; but he could not have been reelected, for he lost the support of his constituents.[221] In fact, his replacement lost the election, and colleagues blamed Lincoln for giving up a "safe" Whig seat.[222] He seemed unprepared for the national spotlight, and opponents drew attention to his speaking style: "His awkward gesticulations, the ludicrous management of his voice and the comical expression of the countenance, all conspired to make his hearers laugh at the mere anticipation of the joke before it appeared," wrote one Democratic journalist.[223] The forty-year-old Lincoln left Washington with his hopes for national eminence dashed. Had he died the following year he would not even have made the history books.

When he returned to Springfield in the spring

of 1849 he was distraught. Mary soothed his damaged ego by showering him with praise and predicting great things for him. She wrote letters to help him obtain a patronage position in return for his support of President Taylor. The Whig Party offered him the governorship of the Oregon Territory for $3,000 a year, a respectable salary. He was tempted but Mary opposed it, so he turned it down.[224] He effectively retired from politics, neither running for nor holding office from mid-1849 through most of 1854.[225]

During these six years Lincoln "practiced law more assiduously than ever before," as he said.[226] As his law practice with William Herndon grew, he became a case lawyer and quit traveling as much on the Illinois circuit court. He accepted all kinds of clients: he defended railroad companies in some instances and opposed them in others; he represented a black girl who sought her freedom one day, a slaveowner who demanded his "property" back on another. As Herndon noted, he was "purely and entirely a case lawyer."[227] But he made good money during these years, and by 1854 he had ascended to Springfield's upper class.

-*->==) (==*-

Despite the Lincolns' new financial security, there were bumps in their marriage that sometimes felt like an avalanche. Their home, a quaint one-story Greek revival on the corner of Eighth and Jackson streets in downtown Springfield, often masked turmoil within.* Mary had "an ungovernable temper" that could quickly turn violent. She hated her husband's "boon companions," down-home jokes, and "uncouth manners and appearance."[228] To someone who still thought of herself as a Southern aristocrat, her husband's behavior was a source of embarrassment.

What most infuriated Mary was when Abraham ignored her and the children. One Sunday he was driving his son home on a wagon and became so preoccupied with his thoughts that he failed to notice when his son tumbled out. He probably would have continued on home oblivious to what had happened had Mary not been standing in the street and seen the accident. She became furious and publicly upbraided him.[229]

On another occasion Abraham was in their sitting room reading and either didn't hear or ignored Mary's repeated requests to put more wood on the fire. Exasperated, she picked up a log and addressed him formally, which was her custom: "Mr. Lincoln, I have told you now three

---

* In 1856 they added a second story to accommodate their growing family. William (Willie) was born in 1850 and Thomas (Tad) in 1853.

times to mend the fire and you have pretended that you did not hear me. I'll make you hear me this time." He kept reading as she approached, slowly raising the log. Then suddenly he felt like his nose was exploding. She had clubbed him so hard that his nose bled for days and he had to go to work with a bandage on his face.[230]

Another source of tension was their very different views about domestic help. Having grown up with slaves, Mary considered it almost beneath her to have to pay wages to servant girls. As a result she was stingy with them, and she was not used to the insolence of the "wild Irish" girls who thought nothing of talking back to her.[231] Her family's slaves had worn the mask of obedience out of fear of being whipped. She probably thought that sparing the lash spoiled the help. After a disagreement with one servant girl, she reportedly told a friend, "If Mr. Lincoln should happen to die, his spirit will never find me living outside the boundaries of a slave state."[232]

Lincoln, however, sympathized with Mary's servants. Having grown up a poor white boy who had to give all his wages to his father, he could understood what working for a tyrant felt like. He offered to increase the servants' pay to make their work a bit more bearable. One girl, who received $1.25 a week (about $5,000 per

year in today's wages), threatened to leave unless she received an extra 25 cents weekly. Mary
thought her impudent but Abraham pulled her
aside and quietly said, "Don't leave. Tell Mrs.
Lincoln you have concluded to stay at $1.25
and I'll pay the odd 25¢ to you." But Mary overheard the conversation and became incensed.
She told the girl to leave immediately and then
turned to her husband and said, "As for you, Mr.
Lincoln, I'd be ashamed of myself."[233] Lincoln
hired a replacement and promised to give the
girl a 75–cent-per-week bonus on top of whatever Mary paid. And he warned her "not to fuss
with Mrs. Lincoln."[234]

Lincoln thus learned how to use subterfuge
to keep the peace at home. When a neighborhood boy asked him to give money to the fire
department fund drive, he responded, "I'll go
home to supper and ask Mrs. Lincoln what she
has to say. After supper she will be in good
humor, and I will ask her if we shall give fifty
dollars. She will say, 'Abe, when will you learn
some sense? Twenty dollars is enough.' Come
around in the morning and get your money."[235]
The boy got his twenty dollars. With Mary, he
knew how to negotiate and still get what he
wanted.

Despite these bumps, Abraham and Mary's
mutual love of politics kept them relatively

content as a couple. Her outbursts partly reflected her desire to be heard in a society that all too often silenced women and treated them little better than servants. Given her ambition for her husband, she insisted on participating in his world. When he ignored or patronized her, or refused to treat her as he did other men, she let him know it.

Then too, fate had a way of relieving some of the tension. When four-year-old Eddie died in 1850, Abraham and Mary were both devastated. They came together in their grief, and within a few weeks of Eddie's death Mary was pregnant with William.

In late June 1852 they similarly grieved over the death of their hero Henry Clay. Clay was "the man for whom I fought all my humble life," for he believed in "ultimate emancipation" and had brokered compromises without losing sight of that goal, Lincoln said. Mary too considered Clay her "beau ideal" of a statesman, though she expected her husband to surpass him and reach the White House.[236]

On July 6, 1852, the day after Frederick Douglass delivered his "Fourth of July" oration at Rochester, Lincoln gave a eulogy on Clay at the capitol in Springfield. While Douglass described a country in decline, Lincoln offered a paean to the man and a nation in ascendance. He linked

Clay's birth to national birth: "The infant nation and the infant child began the race of life together; . . . and now the nation mourns for the man."[237] He called Clay the nation's greatest self-made man and highlighted his brilliance as a compromiser: "no one was so habitually careful to avoid all sectional ground."[238] In negotiating the Compromise of 1850, Clay "exorcised the demon which possessed the body politic, and gave peace to a distracted land."[239] Whereas for Frederick Douglass, the "demon" was slavery and racism, for Lincoln it was sectional strife. Clay's life symbolized for Lincoln national health and progress. But in a few years he would follow Douglass and resort to the jeremiad.

Indeed, what Lincoln did not yet understand was that Clay's death signified the end of an era of compromise. At the very time Lincoln and Douglass gave their speeches, the Fugitive Slave Act and Harriet Beecher Stowe's *Uncle Tom's Cabin* were mobilizing the North against slavery and dividing the country. And Lincoln's beloved Whig Party, which had masterfully united proslavery and antislavery men, was irrevocably fragmenting along sectional lines. Southern Whigs were outraged by the party's refusal to nominate Millard Fillmore.[240] Many Northern Whigs, including Lincoln, saw

Fillmore as a Northern "puppet of the Slave Power" and nominated the military hero Winfield Scott as the Whig candidate for president in 1852.[241] At the very moment that Lincoln delivered his eulogy of the Whig founder and leader, the party was unraveling. The November election four months later was the last time that a Whig appeared on a presidential ticket.

Long after the Whig Party was dead, however, Lincoln followed its tradition of conciliation with the Slave Power. Even after he became a Republican, he often referred to himself as an "Old Line Whig."[242] And unlike many of his antislavery colleagues, he never questioned the validity of the Fugitive Slave Act of 1850, either politically or constitutionally. It was a necessary concession to the South, he said, much as Southern congressmen believed that ending the slave trade in Washington, D.C., was a concession to Northerners, who did not like seeing slave auctions on their way to work. Lincoln believed that the Constitution called for "an efficient fugitive slave law."[243] He offered to give to the South *any* legislation to reclaim fugitives as long as free blacks were in no more danger of being enslaved than innocent whites were of being executed.[244] He even argued that the Fugitive Slave Act *was as fair to blacks as criminal laws were for whites*, ignoring the fact that suspected fugitives were denied the constitutional rights of a jury trial and due process of law.[245]

Lincoln also continued compromising with the nation's founding principles. While he endorsed the abstract ideal of equality, he abandoned it as a practical solution to slavery. "If all earthly power were given me, I should not know what to do" about slavery, he confessed in 1854. "My first impulse would be to free all the slaves and send them to Liberia—to their own native land."[246] But this was unfeasible. He also opposed freeing blacks and making them "politically and socially our equals." Why? "My own feelings will not admit of this; and if mine would, we well know that those of the great mass of white people will not." Such feelings might be unjust, but a "universal feeling, whether well or ill-founded, can not be safely disregarded. We can not, then, make them [blacks] equals."[247]

In certain respects, Lincoln remained a Whig for the rest of his life, but in other ways, the collapse of the Whigs liberated him from the impulse to compromise simply for the sake of party. It led to his emergence as a brilliant politician whose founding principle was, like Douglass's, the natural law of universal freedom.

Lincoln remade himself once he began to identify Stephen Douglas as his chief adversary and
enemy. The Democratic senator from Illinois authored the Kansas-Nebraska Act of 1854, which
"aroused" Lincoln "as he had never been before."[248] Four years younger than Lincoln, Douglas was the most famous man in Illinois and
among the most successful young politicians in
the nation (see figure 12). Born in Brandon, Vermont, he had received a good education, learning Latin and Greek, even though his physician
father had died when he was an infant. He studied law for six months before moving at age
twenty to Illinois, where admission to the bar
was less stringent than in the East. At twenty-
seven he became the state's youngest supreme
court judge and thereafter was known as Judge
Douglas. He was thirty years old when he was
elected to the House and thirty-four when he
moved to the Senate. By the early 1850s he was
one of the Senate leaders, and when people discussed future presidents his name was usually
near the top of the list.[249]

In many respects Douglas was Lincoln's opposite. At five foot four he was a foot shorter
than Lincoln, walked with a strut as opposed
to Lincoln's long loping strides, and had a pug-

nacious temperament. His combativeness coupled with his deep baritone voice (some said "roar") prompted friends to call him "the little Giant."[250] While Lincoln lived frugally and abstained from alcohol and tobacco, Douglas was extravagant. He loved expensive wines and fine cigars, drank too much, and liked to speculate in real estate.[251]

Their debating styles were as different as their looks and personalities. Lincoln almost always appeared composed (or stiff) and relied on carefully chosen words for his weapons. Douglas acted like a wily fighter in a barroom brawl, often putting his whole body into the bout. "He has excellent prize-fighting qualities," wrote one journalist.[252] Sometimes he seemed out of control. In the midst of one congressional speech he got so worked up that he ripped off his cravat, unbuttoned his waistcoat, "and had the air and aspect of a half-naked pugilist," as John Quincy Adams noted with horror. "His face was convulsed, his gesticulation frantic, and he lashed himself into such a heat that if his body had been made of combustible matter it would have burnt out."[253]

While Lincoln was comparatively sympathetic toward blacks, Douglas was a virulent and representative racist. The word "nigger" rolled off his tongue like water (there is no

record of Lincoln ever uttering it), and he loved
to pander to American prejudice. One of his favorite insults was to call his opponent a friend
of "Fred Douglass." His obsession with Frederick Douglass seemed personal even though the
two men had not met. They shared the same
name until 1846, when Stephen Douglas deleted the second "s," possibly in reaction to
Frederick Douglass's sudden fame following
the success of his *Narrative of the Life of Frederick Douglass*.[254] The white Douglas wanted
to make sure that no one mistook him for the
black Douglass. In fact, he hated the very sight
of blacks. Lincoln by contrast felt comfortable
around them (despite his political callousness
toward them). He even characterized himself
as "a long black fellow" to a former acquaintance.[255]

Even at the level of personal relationships
the two men were opponents. One of Douglas's
closest friends, and the best man at his wedding,
was James Shields, Lincoln's old broadsword adversary.[256] Like Shields, Douglas fancied himself
a ladies' man, and he had even courted Mary
Todd before she met Lincoln. Springfield residents had often seen Stephen Douglas and Mary
Todd walking around town or talking at a party.
Similar in temperament and size, they evidently
liked each other, but Douglas's advances never

reached a marriage proposal, for Mary was too passionate about the Whig Party to allow herself to become enamored of a Democrat, no matter how successful.[257]

For years, then, Stephen Douglas had been Lincoln's *unacknowledged* rival. They had met in 1834, when both men were in their twenties. In the 1840 presidential campaign, Lincoln heard and "tried to answer many of [Douglas's] speeches," combating his "shirks and quirks" with facts and logic.[258] Yet Lincoln did not explicitly identify Douglas as his chief enemy, or define himself against him—until 1854, when the Kansas-Nebraska bill became law.

Then Lincoln experienced an awakening. It was as though his outrage over the expansion of slavery and his own failings as a politician were embodied in Stephen Douglas. His self-image became clarified through his rival. Suddenly, slavery became the great issue of his life, and his political goals became sharply focused: challenge and defeat Douglas in order to put slavery on the path of ultimate extinction. To accomplish this would mean a great leap forward in his political career without sacrificing his principles.

Douglas became for Lincoln what Andrew Jackson had been to Henry Clay, what John C. Calhoun had been to John Quincy Adams, what

Figure 12. Illinois senator Stephen Douglas. *(Library of Congress)*

slaveholders were to Frederick Douglass: a cosmic rival such that each man holds the other in his orbit while both revolve around a common center of antagonism, giving both strength and spirit.[259]

Lincoln began defining himself against Stephen Douglas soon after the passage of the Kansas-Nebraska Act: "we were both ambitious" as young men, he wrote, "I perhaps quite as much so as he. With *me*, the race of ambition has been a failure—a flat failure; with *him* it has been one of splendid success. His name fills the nation; and is not unknown even in foreign lands. I affect no contempt for the high eminence he has reached. So reached, that [if] the oppressed of my species might have shared with me in the elevation, I would rather stand on that eminence, than wear the richest crown that ever pressed a monarch's brow."[260] Political success for Lincoln hinged upon his halting the spread of slavery so that someday it might die a natural death, whereas for Douglas success served only himself, so his ambition was regal and unprincipled rather than democratic.[261] Lincoln realized that he had to defeat Douglas to elevate the oppressed and realize his ambitions. Defining himself against his rival in this way soon catapulted him to the White House.

With his Kansas-Nebraska Act Stephen Douglas altered the progress and destiny of the nation. Or so Lincoln believed, and this was why his enemy needed to be vanquished. The year 1854 became a historical fulcrum for Lincoln. Before that date, he (and in his mind most other Northerners) believed "that slavery was in the course of ultimate extinction." From the nation's founding until the Kansas-Nebraska Act, "the public mind" considered the nation to be morally progressing.[262] Its graph was slowly rising. As a result, Lincoln had been relatively quiet about slavery, because he believed that if it were contained it would die a natural death. The masses would increasingly recognize the virtues of free labor and the evils of slave labor. And the number of slaveowners would slowly diminish over time, he assumed. Limiting the supply of land would deplete Southern soil and prevent slaveowners from being able to capitalize on their property. Eventually, there would be little economic incentive to own slaves, leading slaveholders to acknowledge their evil and end it.

How long would it take for slavery to end in this organic way? "I do not suppose that in the most peaceful way ultimate extinction would occur in less than a hundred years at the least" (the 1950s), Lincoln said in 1858.[263] And he believed that a peaceful end to slavery, "in God's own time," was the best solution "for both races."[264] Frederick Douglass and other abolitionists felt quite sure that God wanted slavery to end immediately, but Lincoln's God had more patience and was more inscrutable.

Stephen Douglas derailed this vision of progress. He signed a devil's pact with Southerners and in his Kansas-Nebraska Act repealed the Missouri Compromise, which had prohibited slavery from spreading north of the 36°30' parallel in the Louisiana Territory.[265] Suddenly the nation's destiny was no longer on a trajectory of upward moral progress. It had peaked and was now regressing. The United States was in decline. Abruptly Lincoln felt that the only way he could tell the national story was as a rise and fall, which hopefully would mobilize the masses and restore the nation to its former glory.[266]

A lot of Northerners agreed with Lincoln in believing that Stephen Douglas's Kansas-Nebraska Act marked a new era of descent. The Republican Party emerged in its immediate wake, uniting diverse groups of Northerners under the explicit goal of prohibiting the spread of slavery. They concurred when Lincoln said there was "a vast difference" between *tolerating* slavery and *extending* it over a territory "already free and uncontaminated with the institution."[267] They yelled "that's right" when Lincoln said, "Let no one be deceived. The spirit of seventy-six and the spirit of" Judge Douglas's Kansas-Nebraska Act "are utter antagonisms; and the former is rapidly displaced by the latter."[268] They cheered when he talked about how much he hated slavery and how evil it was.

It was not that Northerners necessarily sympathized with blacks, particularly in Illinois.

Rather, their hatred of slavery reflected fears about their own well-being. Powerful Southerners threatened to turn Northern territories into slave states, thus depressing land values, creating unfair competition with slaveowners, and destroying their opportunities. Most Northerners believed (like Southerners) that access to new land was a prerequisite to self-making and economic growth. But they demanded land uncontaminated by slavery, which prevented free laborers from becoming "fatally fixed for life," as Lincoln noted.[269] You might be a hired hand today, but with access to "free soil" you would soon be able to enjoy the fruits of your own labor.[270]

In the immediate wake of the Kansas-Nebraska Act (which became law in May 1854) Lincoln's speeches attracted "more marked attention than they had ever before done," as he noted.[271] Buoyed by his newfound popularity, he went on the offensive, attacking Judge Douglas like a boxer who jabbed away at his opponent, slowly wearing him down. In the autumn of 1854 he ran for the state legislature and was easily elected. Immediately he set his sights much higher: the United States Senate. The incumbent was none other than his old broadsword nemesis James Shields, Douglas's right-hand man who had helped him push through the

Kansas-Nebraska Act. Defeating Shields would put Lincoln in the same ring with Judge Douglas, where he could battle him for the nation's destiny. As an assemblyman he was prohibited from running for the Senate, so he resigned his newly won seat to take on James Shields and Judge Douglas.[272]

Lincoln's timing was perfect, for Northerners were furious with Douglas for opening their territories to slavery. When the judge returned to Illinois in the fall of 1854 to campaign for Shields and other Democrats, he quickly realized how bitter the resentment was: "I could travel from Boston to Chicago by the light of my own effigy," he said.[273] In his first campaign speech in Chicago, he was shouted down with boos, hisses, and screams as soon as he walked onstage. A few people threw rocks and rotten eggs, and each time he opened his mouth to speak "the tumult was renewed."[274] He lost his temper and began shaking his fist at the crowd, "which only intensified the din."[275] Then he tried staring the crowd into silence like a parent fed up with his three-year-old child, but the crowd kept yelling. For two hours he endured the insults, waiting for the people to lose their voices or get tired so that he could educate them about the virtues of the Kansas-Nebraska Act. But the crowd wouldn't relent and so he finally stomped offstage and retired to the luxurious Tremont House hotel, where one imagines him comforting himself with a bottle or two of claret.

During the campaign Lincoln tracked Douglas like a hound pursuing wounded prey. He followed him from town to town as the judge stumped for his Democratic faithful, and he challenged him on every point: "popular sovereignty" was a euphemism that masked Douglas's coalition with Southerners to gain power; Henry Clay's Compromise of 1850 did *not* annul the Missouri Compromise; the Kansas-Nebraska Act *did*, overturning eighty years of laws governing slavery in the territories; and Douglas's epithet for the new Republican Party, "*Black Republicans*," pandered to popular prejudice.[276]

About the only points on which they agreed related to the role of blacks in American society. Lincoln quoted Judge Douglas as saying, " 'This government was made for the white people and not for the negroes.' Why, in point of mere fact, I think so too," he noted. And he agreed with Douglas in opposing black suffrage in Illinois and racial commingling, especially interracial marriage. But they differed on racial issues nonetheless. As Lincoln emphasized, Douglas refused to acknowledge that blacks were humans and thus had no moral qualms about "whether a new country shall be slave or free." Lincoln spoke for "the great mass of mankind," who "take a totally different view." They considered slavery "a great moral wrong" and their opposition to it "is not evanescent but eternal. It lies at the very foundation to their sense of justice."[277] Lincoln wanted to elevate the oppressed without collapsing racial hierarchies.

Frederick Douglass joined Lincoln and other antislavery men in Illinois that fall in 1854. He knew that in the northern part of the state, Democrats were especially vulnerable to upsets by Republicans, so he arrived with Joshua Giddings, Salmon P. Chase, and other political abolitionists to stump for Lincoln and other antislavery candidates. There is no record of Lincoln and Douglass meeting, but Lincoln probably did not want to be seen with him, for to be associated with a black abolitionist would have destroyed his chances. With great eloquence and satire Frederick Douglass hammered away at Judge Douglas, and the "white Douglas" was so outraged by the presence of the "black Douglass," as journalists called them, that the judge canceled a scheduled appearance at Aurora because the great orator planned to be there and respond directly to his speech.[278]

Frederick took a "peculiar interest" in Stephen. This interest was "quite natural," he said, for "no man likes to read in a newspaper of the hanging of a man bearing his own name" (in reference to the lynched effigies of the senator).[279] Since Stephen now regarded himself as the "most abused man in the United States," Frederick hoped that he would learn to empathize with the three million slaves who suffered far greater abuse by the very men Judge Douglas was in league with.[280] And he emphasized that the Kansas-Nebraska Act created a situation in which one of two things must happen: "The South must either give up slavery, or the North must give up liberty."[281]

Lincoln had not quite reached the same conclusion. But a few months after Douglass's speech he raised the same question: "Our problem now is 'Can we, as a nation, continue together permanently—forever—half slave, and half free?' The problem is too mighty for me. May God in his mercy superintend the solution."[282] Soon he would agree with Douglass.

Lincoln almost defeated James Shields. He was the front-runner on the first ballot in the state assembly (which elected senators), receiving forty-four votes to Shields's forty-one. But the winner needed a majority vote (as opposed to a simple plurality), and Lincoln realized that to prevent a proslavery victory he must surrender his votes to another antislavery Democrat who had polled only five votes in the first ballot. "It was rather hard for the 44 to have to surrender to the 5—and a less good humored man than I, perhaps would not have consented to it. . . . I could not, however, let the whole political result go to ruin, on a point merely personal to myself."[283]

Even though Lincoln lost the election, he had accomplished a number of things. He and Frederick Douglass helped rout proslavery Democrats in Illinois. Lincoln's speeches were now more incisive than ever before, and a few opposition journalists began to acknowledge him as "a fine speaker" and one of the "ablest black Republicans."[284] And he received some national exposure for his attacks on Judge Douglas. The official Lincoln-Douglas debates would not begin until 1858. But in essence Lincoln began debating him in the fall of 1854, a few months after the Kansas-Nebraska Act.

Judge Douglas was a serious contender in the 1856 presidential campaign. In the Democratic nominating convention he and James Buchanan became deadlocked after the sixteenth ballot without either man securing the necessary majority. Buchanan, who was even more willing to do the South's bidding than Douglas, had received more votes. In a move that resembled Lincoln's a year earlier, Douglas instructed his delegates to vote for Buchanan: "Mr. Buchanan . . . is, in my opinion, entitled to the nomination."[285]

Lincoln canvassed the state for the Republican candidate, John C. Frémont.[286] Illinois was a swing state, and most pundits believed that if it and Pennsylvania went Republican, Frémont would win. Lincoln gave more than fifty speeches, addressing crowds as large as thirty-five thousand at Alton and ten thousand at Princeton.[287] (He and Frederick Douglass both had strong vocal cords.) He emphasized that the difference between Frémont and Buchanan was that Buchanan wanted to extend slavery into those territories *"now legally free"* and Frémont did not. "That is the *naked* issue and the whole of it."[288] By framing the campaign in this way he denied that Republicans were a sectional party that antagonized the South.

Indeed, Lincoln tried to avoid exacerbating sectional tensions. He said nothing about the civil war then raging in Kansas or Preston Brooks's caning of Charles Sumner. He defended Frémont against accusations that he was a bastard, a secret Catholic, and a radical who wanted to repeal the Fugitive Slave Act and abolish slavery in the states. Judge Douglas and his cohorts tried to intimidate voters by saying that if Frémont won, the Union would be dissolved.[289] Preston Brooks, whose confidence rose with every new trophy cane he received, threatened to invade Washington if Frémont were elected and "lay the strong arm of southern freemen upon the treasury and archives of the government."[290] Numerous reports warned that slaves throughout the South were planning a massive revolt timed to the election. People assumed that if Frémont won, slaves would instantly stage "a bloody revolt," as one Northern paper phrased it.[291] Northerners were terrified by these stories but they still cast more votes for Frémont than for any other candidate. Buchanan prevailed, however, sweeping the South and winning the swing states of Illinois and Pennsylvania.[292]

While stumping for Frémont at Galena Lincoln vowed to uphold the Constitution and respect the authority of the Supreme Court. Responding to charges that restricting slavery was unconstitutional, he said, "*I grant you that an unconstitutional act is not a law.*" But he refused to accept the Democrats' interpretation of the Constitution. "The Supreme Court of the United States is the tribunal to decide such questions, *and we will submit to its decisions.*"[293]

Of course he would uphold the supreme law of the land. There was no reason to suppose he wouldn't. He had devoted his career to defending man-made laws and was opposed to the anarchic "higher law" of abolitionists. He would not have joined the Republican Party had it endorsed a "higher law" or repudiated the Fugitive Slave Act.[294] He had been brought up to believe that without the Supreme Court, "the Constitution would be a dead letter."[295] The Court "settled" the great legal questions of the day.[296] Chief Justice Taney's predecessor John Marshall had declared in *Marbury v. Madison* (1801) that the Court's rulings were "supreme law" and "must prevail over" Congress and the president.[297] Lawmakers had accepted this decision. To most white Americans, Supreme Court justices did not so much *interpret* the Constitution as *clarify* it; instead of *making* law they *found* it.[298] But they were also dependent upon public opinion, as the Frenchman Alexis de Tocqueville shrewdly noted. If they acted imprudently they could "plunge the Union into anarchy or civil war."[299]

This is essentially what happened.

Eight months after vowing to uphold the Supreme Court, Lincoln contradicted himself. In March 1857 the Court announced its decision in *Dred Scott*, which effectively declared the

Republican Party platform unconstitutional. It was as though Lincoln and the Republicans thumbed their noses at the Court, for they clamored even more to exclude slavery from the territories.

Now Lincoln demanded that an unconstitutional act become law. To him, the Court did not properly understand that slavery was an evil that needed to be contained. It did not properly understand the *natural law* that said *"all men are created equal."*[300] The founders meant what they said.[301] Lincoln firmly believed that God considered slavery wrong: "our good Father in Heaven" made the evil of slavery "so plain" that "all *feel* and *understand* it, even down to brutes and creeping insects."[302] But the Court echoed Judge Douglas in ignoring the immorality of slavery and calling the ideals of the Declaration "self-evident lies."[303] And so Lincoln rejected the Court as the nation's supreme authority.

Suddenly he began to rely on natural (or "higher") law and follow the path that Frederick Douglass had long ago taken. It was a stunning reversal from his plea twenty years earlier, in the Young Men's Lyceum address, when he had urged people to uphold the Constitution and revere the laws. He had always thought like a lawyer, had always shown enormous respect for the law and

legal precedent, and had been horrified at
the thought of ignoring the law and resisting
the highest tribunal in the land. But now he
repudiated the Constitution and legal precedent and defined the Declaration to be the
centerpiece of government. He appropriately
borrowed from scripture to clarify his newfound faith in natural law: the Declaration
was "the apple of gold" within the Constitution's "picture of silver," he wrote. "The picture was made *for* the apple—not the apple
for the picture."[304]

Understandably, Judge Douglas attacked Lincoln and his party for so baldly resisting the Supreme Court.[305] Lincoln denied that he and his
party resisted the Court. "We believe as much
as Judge Douglas (perhaps more) in obedience
to and respect for the judicial department of
government," he said in a speech at Springfield
that was printed and widely circulated.[306] Yet
he also called the *Dred Scott* decision "errone-
ous" and vowed to do what he could to have
the Court overrule its own decision.[307] His Republican audiences cheered him for defying
the Court.[308]

Sensing blood, Judge Douglas attacked. He
asked his Democratic audiences, "The Supreme
Court is the ultimate tribunal, the highest judicial tribunal on earth, and Mr. Lincoln is going

to appeal from that?"[309] They had a nice laugh as Lincoln squirmed.

Lincoln probably wanted to say, "Yes, I appeal to God over the Supreme Court." But that would have been politically inexpedient. He knew that to endorse a "higher law" thesis would lead to charges of anarchy. For how could one know what God wanted? Southern planters believed that God defended slavery, and their ministers cogently argued that the Bible sanctioned it. As Lincoln himself acknowledged, slavery had been considered a "meritorious" institution for thousands of years.[310]

Instead of appealing publicly to God's law, Lincoln relied on history for his defense. He argued that President Andrew Jackson, Douglas's hero and the patron saint of every Democrat, had disregarded the Supreme Court. After the Court declared a national bank constitutional, Jackson vetoed a bill to recharter it, partly on constitutional grounds: "each public functionary must support the Constitution *as he understands it*," Lincoln quoted him as saying.[311] It didn't matter that Lincoln hated Jackson; to him and most other old-line Whigs, Jackson had been a tyrant who preferred gunfighting and dueling over debating. It was irrelevant that Jackson had not actually violated the Constitution when he vetoed the bank.[312] What mattered was that Lincoln could declare that his understanding of the Supreme Court was identical to that of Douglas's hero.

When Judge Douglas ran for reelection Lincoln formally challenged him. Here was the opportunity to be in the same ring as his foe and fight him head-to-head. The Illinois Republican Party took the unusual step of formally nominating Lincoln for the Senate.[313] (It was unusual because senators were elected by the state legislature.) Lincoln's "House Divided" speech was his formal challenge to Judge Douglas.

The speech was nothing less than revolutionary. It declared that the former and current presidents of the United States (Franklin Pierce and James Buchanan); the chief justice of the Supreme Court (Roger Taney); and the architect of the Kansas-Nebraska Act (Stephen Douglas) were *conspiring against the United States* in their quest to nationalize slavery and extend it into every state and territory. These powerful statesmen were at the head of a secret "political dynasty" known as the Slave Power.[314] They were evil men, disloyal to the nation's ideals and traitors to their country. "Stephen, Franklin, Roger, and James" were conspiring to overthrow freedom everywhere, even in the free states.[315]

Indeed, Lincoln warned of another Supreme

Court decision—a "second Dred Scott"—that would open every state to slavery.[316] Soon Boston and New York and Philadelphia and Chicago would be filled with slaveowners *and their slaves*. Free laborers would have to compete with slaves for jobs. And jobs were already scarce because of another depression that had swept the North a year earlier. (Many Northerners blamed the depression on the South, which had barely suffered.)[317] A "second Dred Scott" decision was suggested in the first one and not far away.[318] "We shall *lie down* pleasantly dreaming that the people of *Missouri* are on the verge of making their state *free*; and we shall *awake* to the *reality*, instead, that the *Supreme* Court has made *Illinois* a *slave* state," Lincoln said.[319]

No wonder Frederick Douglass loved the speech. It was subversive, powerful, breathtaking.[320]

Lincoln had the benefit of being correct. His "House Divided" speech was accurate. He wasn't simply stirring up people's fears about the Slave Power. Advocates of slavery were attempting to make it lawful "in *all* the states, *old* as well as *new—North* as well as *South*," as he warned.[321] Proslavery newspapers argued that the *Dred Scott* decision protected slaveholders' property if they moved to free states.[322] And a "second Dred Scott" case was slowly working its way through the courts.[323]

The case, *Lemmon v. People*, involved a Virginia master, Jonathan Lemmon, who in 1852 had brought eight slaves to New York City, a major port, in order to ship them to Texas. Authorities set them free since state law prohibited masters from bringing their slaves into the state. Lemmon appealed on the grounds that he was merely in transit and that the state must respect Virginia property.[324] The *New York Tribune* predicted that once slaveowners won the right of transit, "we shall see men buying slaves for the New York market and there will be no legal power to prevent it."[325] Samuel Foot, a judge on New York State's highest court, similarly warned that if the Lemmon case reached the Supreme Court, it would be the end of free soil in the North.[326] And the New York lawyer George Templeton Strong said that "a decision of the United States Supreme Court in the Lemmon case . . . will entitle every Southerner to bring his slaves into New York and Massachusetts and keep them there."[327] These were rational observers, not crazy conspiracy theorists. Had the Lemmon case reached the Supreme Court, it probably would have legalized slavery in every state, but the Civil War intervened.[328]

With his "House Divided" speech Lincoln ascended onto the stage of national politics.[329] He was forty-nine years old, twice the age Frederick Douglass had been when he had soared into the national spotlight. Now Lincoln issued a formal challenge by inviting Stephen Douglas to canvass the state and "address the same audiences." It was "the usual, almost universal western style of conducting a political campaign."[330]

Douglas demurred, for Lincoln lacked prestige. The *Chicago Tribune* said that if he declined he was a coward, and that got his blood up.[331] He realized that he had a lot to gain in debating Lincoln. His reelection was anything but secure, and he hoped to use the campaign to reunite his party. Southern Democrats saw him as too soft on slavery's opponents, but his Northern base had shrunk as well, since voters increasingly considered him a pawn of the South.[332] By routing Lincoln in a debating contest, he could appeal to both sides, add luster to his state, and revive his own reputation. "The battle of the Union is to be fought in Illinois," one Illinois paper declared.[333]

They agreed to seven debates from August to October 1858. Each would last three hours, and the two men would alternate who opened.[334] "I shall have my hands full" with him, Douglas told a friend. "He is the strong man of his party."[335]

A week before the debates began Douglas challenged Lincoln to a fistfight.[336] He was livid with Lincoln for accusing him of conspiring with the Slave Power, and so "he said something about *fighting*, as though referring to a pugilistic encounter." Lincoln exploited it for laughs: "A warlike proceeding" would only prove who was "the more muscular," Lincoln joked, but it would do nothing to settle their argument over slavery.[337] Behind his joke there was dead seriousness. Lincoln still believed that the problem of slavery could be settled peacefully, despite all the evidence to the contrary.

The debates were a study in contrasts. Douglas traveled by special train in a private car stocked with wine and cigars. He looked presidential in his new blue suit with silver buttons and cleanly pressed linen shirt. His beautiful (and very young) wife, Adèle Cutts, accompanied him. She was half his age, and men called her the "handsomest woman" they had ever seen.[338] Lincoln traveled by passenger car and got to know some of his audiences and their concerns. He wore his "everyday clothes," a tattered black frock-coat with sleeves that were much too short, and black pants that showed off his ankles and large feet. No one called Mary handsome. She stayed home anyway on Lincoln's orders. He did not think her aristocratic airs would fit well with his down-home persona.[339]

The contrast was even greater when they began speaking. The stage resembled a boxing ring. It was an elevated platform surrounded by linen, with flags draping from the sides. Instead of chairs being placed in each corner, they were set side by side with a small table between them (see figure 13). Douglas exploded off his chair as if anxious to score another point. Pugnacious and audacious, he exuded confidence and at times sounded like a demagogue. "His voice rolled forth in a fierce if monotonous bulldog bark," but it did not carry. Lincoln's voice had phenomenal range, but it sounded shrill and rose to "a high treble" when he got excited. And he didn't know what to do with his arms. Sometimes he would wring his hands together as he spoke, "first in front and then behind." At other times he would gesture, but his arms moved awkwardly, as if he were stiff in the joints. Occasionally he would accent a syllable by bending his knees, which made him look almost clownish. He relied on common sense rather than style, poetics instead of pugnacity. And he was always in control.[340]

Most of the debates attracted huge crowds— ten thousand at Ottawa, fifteen thousand at Freeport, about eleven thousand at Charleston,

Figure 13. Lincoln-Douglas debate. *(Library of Congress)*

twenty thousand at Galesburg, and twelve thousand at Quincy.[341] At Freeport the crowd was so dense that officials had to use a battering ram to open a path to the platform. Railroad companies offered special excursion trains with banners and bands. People traveled by carriage and steamboat as well, sometimes as an entire family.[342] For many families, attending a debate was summer vacation, a brief respite at the end of harvest before planting the winter wheat. The debates combined the gravity of a courtroom with the excitement of a rock concert. No wonder voting rates were over 80 percent. People were passionate about politics and public speaking, and the two went hand in glove.

For those who had been following Lincoln's and Douglas's speeches, the campaign was mostly performance, for the issues had not dramatically changed. Lincoln jabbed away at Douglas's doctrine of popular sovereignty, calling it the root cause of national decline and part of a grand conspiracy to nationalize slavery. And Douglas labeled Lincoln a renegade who rejected the supreme tribunal and an abolitionist who would destroy the Union.

In essence their differences could be reduced to this: Judge Douglas championed the rights of the majority (of white men), including the right of one man to enslave another, while Lincoln defended "minority rights" without altering existing hierarchies. To him, elevating the oppressed also raised up the majority. They were two fundamentally different views of the white American experience.[343]

Throughout the debates Judge Douglas taunted Lincoln for being a friend and ally of Frederick Douglass. Lincoln was "worthy of a medal from Fred Douglass" for his abolitionism. And he exploited Douglass's praise of the "House Divided" speech: Lincoln was the "perfect embodiment" of Douglass's principles. The Democratic papers also picked up on Douglass's support of Lincoln. "An Ally of Lincoln—The Nigger Chief Out for Him," one Illinois editor declared.[344]

Time and again Lincoln denied any adherence to racial equality and intermarriage, and he denounced the idea that blacks were whites' equals. He offered an analogy from scripture to clarify his views. Christ instructed the multitude to be perfect, even though He knew that all humans sinned. Similarly, the principle that "all men are created equal" was an *ideal* to strive for, even though it could never be realized. "If we cannot give freedom to every creature, let us do nothing that will impose slavery upon any other creature."[345]

Lincoln lost the election, but his performance in the debates established his national reputation.[346] In 1859 a few supporters began suggesting him as a contender for high office. "I do not think myself fit for the Presidency," he told friends in mid-1859.[347] Thirty years earlier he had said much the same thing about his prospects as a lawyer. But he was right to consider himself unfit, for compared to every other president, he was totally unprepared. With virtually no formal schooling, he had served only one unsuccessful term in Congress and had twice lost a bid for the Senate. He had no friends in the East, his allies were all in the West, and the Republican front-runners, Salmon Chase of Ohio and William Seward of New York, were political giants by comparison, with powerful backers throughout the North.

But after John Brown's raid on Harpers Ferry, Seward and Chase suddenly started to seem like damaged goods. They already had reputations as radicals. For years both men had brazenly resisted the Fugitive Slave Act, declaring it unconstitutional. But now they were linked with high treason and murder. Democrats and Southerners called John Brown "Seward's pawn," prompting Seward to backpedal from his "higher law" thesis and raising questions about the content of his character. Chase had known Brown and supported his militancy. In 1856 he had given Brown twenty-five dollars and recommended him "to the confidence and regard of all who desire to see Kansas a free state." The following year Brown asked Chase for money for *"secret service and no questions asked."* These details became front-page news after Brown's raid, and conservative Republicans threatened to "bolt the party."[348]

Lincoln suddenly became more appealing to Northern voters, for he was much more conservative than Seward and Chase. He used Brown's raid as an opportunity to affirm his faith in law and order. The way to express "our belief in regard to slavery . . . is through the ballot box—the peaceful method provided

by the Constitution," he told a Kansas audience on December 1, 1859.[349] Two days later
he warned Southerners not to break the law.
"Old John Brown has just been executed for
treason against a state. We cannot object, even
though he agreed with us in thinking slavery
wrong. . . . If constitutionally we elect a President, and therefore you undertake to destroy
the Union, it will be our duty to deal with
you as old John Brown has been dealt with."[350]
Brown's execution indicated what the appropriate response to treason should be.[351]

A few months later, in February 1860, Lincoln
became almost prophetic in describing the effect
of Brown's raid. During a speech in New York
City he compared Brown to the many fanatics
throughout history who attempted to assassinate a nation's leader in the name of a greater
good. "An enthusiast broods over the oppression
of a people till he fancies himself commissioned
by Heaven to liberate them. He ventures the attempt, which ends in little else than his own execution." The speech was published and widely
circulated, and it is nice to imagine John Wilkes
Booth, then performing in Richmond, reading it
and then tossing it away in disgust.[352]

Lincoln's prophecy was part of an important
address at the Cooper Union in Manhattan. It
was his first trip to the Northeast, and some of

the most influential men of the Republican Party were in attendance, including the editors Horace Greeley, Henry Raymond, William Cullen Bryant, and Noah Brooks. He wore a new black suit for the occasion, properly tailored, which had cost $100.[353] Before the speech he stopped at the studio of Mathew Brady, the nation's foremost photographer, and sat for his "shadow," as he called it. The photograph made him seem presidential. Standing in front of a column with his hand on a book, he looks beyond the camera lens in a visionary gaze (see figure 14).[354] The portrait is the perfect complement to the "Wide Awakes," a club of young Republicans so named for its constant vigilance against the Slave Power. The "Wide Awake" emblem, a large single eye, seems almost an enlargement of Lincoln's eye in the Brady photograph (see figure 15).

The speech was also presidential. It reads as a well-argued lawyerly brief against the *Dred Scott* decision. Appealing to the court of public opinion, Lincoln undermines the arguments of Judge Douglas and Chief Justice Taney, who claimed that the framers of the Constitution had sanctioned the spread of slavery into the territories. He presents evidence showing that no fewer than twenty-one of the thirty-nine framers, "a clear majority," voted to *exclude* slavery from the territories.[355] And none of

Figure 14.
Lincoln before
his Cooper
Union speech.
*(Library of
Congress
/ Author
Collection)*

them said that doing so would be unconstitutional. Douglas and Taney and their clique had
turned the Constitution into a document that
would have horrified the framers.

Lincoln ends his speech with an appeal to
Republicans to be firm but tolerant toward
the South, like a father toward a prodigal son.
Southerners were again threatening to secede
unless they got their way, adding that the
breakup would be the North's fault. "That is
cool," Lincoln said, by which he meant auda-

Figure 15. A New York rally of the Wide Awakes, a Republican campaign club. *(Library of Congress)*

cious. "A highwayman holds a pistol to my ear and mutters through his teeth, 'Stand and deliver, or I shall kill you and then you will be a murderer.'" He hoped his brief would quell the recklessness: "LET US HAVE FAITH THAT RIGHT MAKES MIGHT."[356]

The speech was a smashing success. Handkerchiefs waved, hats flew into the air, and the cheering lasted ten minutes. The *New York Tribune* editor Noah Brooks was so excited that he called Lincoln "the greatest man since St. Paul," and a Harvard Law School student said it "was the best speech I ever heard." Another reporter was no less restrained: "No man ever before made such an impression on his first appeal to a New York audience." Brady's photograph and copies of the speech (with footnotes) sold by the thousands, and Lincoln later said that "Brady and the Cooper Institute made me President."[357]

Three months later he acquired a slogan that broadened his appeal even more. In early May the state nominating convention was held at Decatur. Delegates convened in a large wigwam, a barnlike structure with a canvas roof. The state campaign manager, Richard Oglesby, felt that Lincoln needed a slogan. He found it after consulting with Lincoln's cousin John Hanks, who had helped Lincoln build a fence after moving to Illinois thirty years earlier. On the first day of the convention, Oglesby and Hanks marched down the aisle of the wigwam carrying two rails from the fence. They were decorated with streamers and a banner hung from them that read:

ABRAHAM LINCOLN
The Rail Candidate
FOR PRESIDENT IN 1860
Two rails from a lot of 3,000 made in 1830 by
Thos. Hanks and Abe Lincoln—whose father
was the first pioneer in Macon County.

The crowd erupted, cheering wildly and throwing things into the air with such frenzy that the canvas roof became detached from the rafters. "The roof was literally cheered off the building," said one observer. Lincoln was called to the front and admitted that he had indeed "*split rails* and cultivated a small farm" on the Sangamon River near Decatur. He didn't know whether these were his rails, but "he had mauled many and many better ones since."[358]

As an epithet, "the Railsplitter" rivaled "Old Hickory" and "Tippecanoe"* in popular appeal. It captured Lincoln's folksy image, his rise from poor white trash to presidential candidate, and his embrace of the free-labor ideal that entitled every man to "better his condition," as he said.[359] It was also the perfect image to combat an enemy dependent upon slave labor for its sustenance.

Increasingly, Northerners of all classes felt threatened by the Slave Power. Stocks were in a bear market but the slave market was booming. Slave prices had doubled in less than a decade, whereas an acre of free soil or a Wall Street stock had remained steady or fallen, prompting many Northerners to blame hard times on slavery.[360] Demand for slaves was so intense that many Southerners, including Lincoln's old friend Alexander Stephens, sought to reopen the African trade, which had been banned since 1808.[361] Slaveholders on the Eastern Shore of Maryland had recently proposed legislation to enslave or

---

* For presidents Andrew Jackson and William Henry Harrison respectively.

exile all free blacks in the state.[362] Many Southerners wanted to annex Cuba as a slave state,
and some were even greedier, wanting all of
Central America. Under the leadership of Jefferson Davis, the Senate was in the process of
passing legislation that banned Congress from
excluding slavery in any territory.[363] The prominent planter George Fitzhugh wanted to extend
the "benefits" of slavery, as he put it, to white
Northerners. And in the wake of Harpers Ferry,
most Southern congressmen brought concealed
weapons with them to work (usually "a revolver
and a knife"), just in case an argument got
out of hand.[364] The image of the Railsplitter—
patient and hardworking, firm and fatherly yet
broad-minded—seemed to many people an
appropriate choice for presiding over the prodigal South.

On May 18, the day Republicans nominated
their candidate for president, Lincoln got up
early and walked the few blocks to his clut-
tered law office. The convention was in Chicago, in a huge newly built wigwam, but by
tradition candidates stayed home. He was too
nervous to work, however, and so he headed
to the office of the *Illinois State Journal*, a
hub of news gossip. Some friends were playing "fives," a form of handball, in a vacant lot
next to the *Journal* office, and Lincoln joined

them for a game. When the votes started coming in he walked over to the telegraph office. On the first ballot he received 102 votes and was in second place behind Seward. On the second ballot he almost doubled his votes, and on the third ballot he topped the 233 votes needed for a majority. He knew he would win when he saw the second ballot. Men started congratulating him. He shook a few hands but then turned for home: "Gentlemen there is a little woman at our house who is probably more interested in this dispatch than I am."[365]

The next day he and Mary got in an argument over liquor. Mary insisted on serving it to visitors; it would be gauche not to. But Lincoln ignored her demands. "Having kept house sixteen years, and having never held the 'cup' to the lips of my friends then, my judgment was that I should not in my new position change my habit in this respect."[366] It turned out to be a needless fight because their house was too small to accommodate all the visitors, and so Lincoln set up an office in the state capitol.

His old friend Joshua Speed wrote to congratulate him. They had grown apart over the years, owing to Speed's move to Kentucky, his dislike of the Republican Party, and the fact that Mary did not like him. Indeed, it sometimes seemed as though she felt threatened by him. Lincoln and Speed rarely saw each other and infrequently corresponded, and Speed's note was a touching reminder that friendship and intimacy could still transcend political differences. "Allow a warm personal friend, though as you are perhaps aware a political opponent, to congratulate you. Should you be elected, and I think you have a fair chance for it, I am satisfied that you will honestly administer the government and make a lasting reputation for yourself."[367]

Most Southerners felt differently. Had Lincoln campaigned in the cotton states, they probably would have arrested or lynched him. Southern newspapers hinted as much. They also spread rumors that his running mate, Hannibal Hamlin of Maine, was a mulatto owing to his dark complexion. And they vowed to secede "immediately" if he were elected.[368]

Lincoln was unfazed by these threats. In fact, he felt confident he would win the election, for it was a four-way race, with Southern Democrats choosing John C. Breckinridge, Northern Democrats selecting Judge Douglas, and the Constitutional Union Party nominating John Bell of Tennessee, who was strong in the border states. "The prospect of Republican success now appears very flattering, so far as I can perceive," Lincoln wrote Hamlin in July.[369]

On election day he went to his office in the statehouse to follow the returns. In the morning he chatted "with three or four friends as calmly and as amiably as if he had started on a picnic," according to one observer. To some supporters he seemed more interested in local elections than the presidency, but asking about some small-town district attorneyship was his way of easing stress. A large crowd followed him into the courthouse to vote, cheering wildly. They followed him back to the statehouse when the returns began coming in. He moved his office to the legislative chamber where he had worked twenty years earlier. A few minutes after midnight a telegram arrived saying that victory was assured. Church bells tolled and people caroled in the streets, singing "Old Abe, old Abe." Lincoln admitted that he was "a very happy man." Folding up the telegram, he hurried home. "Mary, Mary," he shouted as he approached his house, "we are elected."[370]

The election results revealed the degree to which "we live in revolutionary times," as one Illinois Republican put it. Lincoln carried every free state save one (New Jersey), but he received less than 40 percent of the popular vote and only 500,000 more votes than Judge

Douglas, the runner-up.* And in ten Southern states *Lincoln did not receive a single vote.*[371] For more than two generations slaveowners had controlled national politics. Now their winning streak was over, the "charm of invincibility" gone. Lincoln would become the first antislavery president since John Quincy Adams.[372] "The great revolution has actually taken place," Adams's son Charles wrote in his diary after learning of Lincoln's victory. "The country has once and for all thrown off the dominion of slaveholders."[373] Or to borrow Frederick Douglass's metaphor, the slumbering volcano was beginning to erupt.

Aesop was an indispensable guide for such times. Having been sold into slavery in Greek antiquity as a prisoner of war, he understood the nature of both slavery and civil war and captured the psychology of a slave society. His fables reveal a society of savagery and spite, where rulers are tyrants and survival depends upon cunning and self-reliance. His stories about animals resonated in a world where men

---

* Had blacks and women been able to vote, Lincoln would have won in a landslide.

were reduced to brutes and the "law of the jungle" was the way of life. No wonder Douglass and Lincoln (and countless other Americans) loved him.[374]

Douglass and Lincoln read Aesop when young and committed many of his fables to memory. In the revolutionary 1850s especially, Aesop helped them articulate central aspects of American society. Both Douglass and Lincoln drew from the fable of the lion and the bulls, where the lion separates the bulls through deceit in order to eat them. The moral was clear: "a kingdom divided against itself cannot stand." Douglass borrowed from another fable to define Democrats (and some Republicans) as wolves in sheep's clothing. Perhaps his favorite was the story about the bees rebelling against their master.[375]

In paraphrasing Aesop, Douglass and Lincoln also drew attention to their personas as self-made men.[376] Since Aesop's fables were children's stories, quoting them was analogous to a statesman today referring to a Bugs Bunny episode: it suggested bad (or an absence of) formal education. You had to be a very good orator to get away with it.

Douglass and Lincoln used Aesop as satirical set pieces. By the 1850s Douglass had mostly abandoned his brilliant use of mimicry, which drew howls of laughter, because he increasingly felt it inappropriate to his subject. "One of the hardest things I had to learn," he noted, "was to stop telling so many funny stories. I could keep my audience in a roar of laughter—and they liked to laugh. . . . But I was convinced that I was in danger of becoming something of a clown and that I must guard against it."[377] Now he wrote out his speeches and presented himself as an intellectual, with hardly a trace of his former dialect. A fable from Aesop or parable from the Bible could still draw laughter (though more refined); instead of mimicking one slaveholder, it satirized the Slave Power.

Lincoln usually reserved his satirical and comical stories, whether from Aesop or his own imagination, for smaller audiences. His "House Divided" speech satirizes Stephen Douglas, Franklin Pierce, Roger Taney, and James Buchanan, who form the frame of the Slave Power. His famous opening, "A house divided against itself cannot stand," is indebted to Aesop and Mark 3:25. But these one-liners are not meant to provoke laughter or even smiles. His stories to friends and supporters best capture the cadence and form of his humor.

Lincoln never lost his accent. In 1862 the New York attorney George Templeton Strong captured the sound of Lincoln speaking by recording it in dialect in his diary after meeting with him. Lincoln was responding to pressure from abolitionists, who called for legislation to emancipate the slaves. "Wa-al [well]," Lincoln responded, "that reminds me of a party of Methodist parsons that was traveling in Illinois when I was a boy thar, and had a branch to cross that was pretty bad—ugly to cross, ye know, because the waters was up. And they got considerin' and discussin' how they should git across it, and they talked about it for two hours, and one on 'em thought they had ought to cross one way when they got there, and another another way, and they got quarrellin' about it, till at last an old brother put in, and he says, says he, 'Brethren, this here talk ain't no use. I never cross a river until I come to it.' " Strong greatly respected Lincoln; he called him "a barbarian, Scythian, yahoo, or gorilla in respect of *outside* polish, but a most sensible, straightforward, honest old codger. . . . His evident integrity and simplicity of purpose would compensate for worse grammar than his."[378] The story resembles Aesop in contrasting talk and action, or "being put to the test."[379]

Lincoln's folksy style was part of what endeared Douglass to him when they met. He was used to that kind of grammar and humor. The sound of Lincoln's voice, especially when telling a story, suggested to him that for all their differences, their backgrounds had more than a little in common.

FOUR

Abolitionist Warrior and War President

On the day of atonement you shall
send abroad the trumpet throughout
all your land.

—LEVITICUS 25:9

IN LATE MARCH 1861, with seven states in the lower South having already seceded and traitors celebrating the new Confederate States of America with lavish parties, bad brandy, and victory shots fired at the heavens, Frederick Douglass finally abandoned hope that his nation would ever fulfill its glorious ideals.[1] He was planning a trip to the black Republic of Haiti, he told readers of his newspaper, with an eye toward emigrating there and encouraging other American blacks to do the same. He would leave New Haven, Connecticut, on April 25 and arrive at Port-au-Prince, Haiti's capital, by May 1. If Haiti met his expectations of being the new "city set on a hill," if it reflected "a light of glorious promise," and if its government was "free and independent" in word and deed, then he would move there and proudly call it home.[2] At the very least, he would visit the site of the world's largest and most successful slave rebellion, where in 1791 half a million slaves had risen up against their masters, fought off Napoleon's army, and in 1804 declared themselves a republic and forever free from slavery. At the very least Haiti's tropical beauty would be a welcome respite from the bitter winds of Rochester.[3]

He was relieved to be going. It was as though the weight of a nation had suddenly been lifted from his shoulders. For twenty years in speeches and essays he had fought slavery and racism with all his might. He had encouraged blacks to follow his example and rise up through resistance, self-reliance, and ceaseless work. He had presented himself to the world as an emblem of hope and a model to follow. Now, suddenly, all of his efforts seemed in vain. "Slavery has touched our government and the virtue has gone out of its arm," he mourned.[4] The friends of freedom had lost the means of defending themselves. "History shows that the North has never been able to stand against the power and purposes of the South."[5] The slaveowning South was like the devil: its riches were too tempting, its threats too frightening, its influence too corrupting. Satan had conquered goodness and God was telling Douglass to leave this land and start anew.

It was a startling transformation. For years Douglass had mocked slaveowners as they turned Northern soil into hunting grounds for the South's pleasure. He became even more hopeful when they opened Northern territories to slavery. And he cheered after the nation's highest human tribunal desecrated the sacred Constitution. He ended his second autobiography, published in the wake of the Kansas-Nebraska Act, with a testament of his faith: "Old as the everlasting hills; immovable as the throne of God; . . . it is the faith of my soul that this anti-slavery cause will triumph."[6] The book was a runaway best-seller, more popular even than his first autobiography, of 1845. Its success, he assumed, was a sign not only of his ever-growing stature and the public's interest in his ability to continually remake himself, but of his nation's mounting intolerance to slavery.

While tens of thousands of his fellow black men and women left America's shores in search of better homes, he had resisted this impulse. In fact just one month earlier, in response to a letter from a subscriber, who had asked him if he ever expected to emigrate to Haiti, Douglass responded with a firm "No; I do not expect to emigrate to Haiti under any circumstances now existing or apprehended."[7]

What caused him to change his mind? What

induced him to suddenly abandon his faith in America?

The answer was the new president, Abraham Lincoln.

Douglass was never so demoralized as when he read Lincoln's Inaugural Address. It "is little better than our worst fears," he complained. Instead of firmly rebuking the South, Lincoln "courted their favor."[8] He vowed to uphold the Fugitive Slave Act, suppress slave insurrections, and *never* interfere with slavery in the slave states. Lincoln essentially told slaveholders that he was "an excellent slave hound."[9]

Worse still, the Inaugural was a "double-tongued" address. Lincoln had been elected on a platform to confine slavery "where it is, 'where the public mind shall rest in the belief of its *ultimate extinction*,' " as Douglass quoted him.[10] Lincoln affirmed his promise to contain slavery but in the next breath gave away the greater goal of ultimate extinction.

Congress had just passed a proposed Thirteenth Amendment in the hope of wooing the traitors back into the Union.[11] Although it was never ratified, this "first" Thirteenth Amendment was the exact opposite of the "actual" one that abolished slavery (in 1865). It was an *unamendable* amendment guaranteeing slavery in the slave states *forever.** Lincoln refers to it in his Inaugural: "I understand a proposed amendment to the Constitution . . . has passed Congress, to the effect that the Federal Government shall never interfere with" slavery in the slave states. *"I have no objection to its being made express and irrevocable."*[12]

Lincoln's having "no objection" to the amendment was intellectually and morally dishonest, for it negated his belief in the "ultimate extinction" of slavery.[13] In that one sentence he agreed to desecrate the Constitution.[14] In that one sentence Douglass lost faith in Lincoln and his nation.

Part of Lincoln's problem, Douglass concluded, was that he did not properly understand the meaning of law. He believed in the "original intent" of the lawmaker, much as Douglass had before being converted to the antislavery interpretation of the Constitution. "The intention of the law-giver is the law," Lincoln declared in his Inaugural, which led him to defend the Fugitive Slave Act and support the amendment guaranteeing slavery in the states forever.[15]

---

* "No amendment shall be made to the Constitution which will authorize or give to Congress the power to abolish or interfere, within any State, with the domestic institutions thereof, including that of persons held to labor or service by the laws of said State."

Not necessarily true, Douglass responded. It "depends upon whether the intention itself is lawful." After all, a law authorizing murder was no law at all. "The very idea of law carries with it ideas of right, justice, and humanity."[16] Reread your Blackstone! Douglass told Lincoln. Blackstone reminds us that law "forbids that which is wrong."[17] Lincoln knew this too, for he happily renounced an unjust Supreme Court ruling in *Dred Scott*, and he declared secession treasonous, "the essence of anarchy," even though the Supreme Court deemed it constitutional and right.[18]

Why did Lincoln defend unjust laws protecting slavery? Because he wanted to conciliate with slaveholders in order to save the Union. "We are not enemies, but friends," Lincoln told the South in his Inaugural.[19] But in calling treasonous slaveholders his friends, Lincoln sacrificed the rights of blacks.[20] Northern friends of the South were no more moral than a Stephen Douglas or a James Buchanan. Just three years earlier, Lincoln had accused them of conspiring to overthrow the government. Then suddenly he got elected president, became the first "modern antislavery president," as Douglass put it, and he conciliated with slaveholders almost as much as these conspirators had.[21]

Indeed, the poetic ending of Lincoln's Inaugural probably made Douglass feel sick to his stomach: "We must not be enemies. Though passion may have strained, it must not break our bonds of affection. The mystic chords of memory, stretching from every battlefield, and patriot grave, to every living heart and hearthstone, all over this broad land, will yet swell the chorus of the Union, when again touched, as surely as they will be, by the better angels of our nature."[22] To Douglass, those mystic chords of memory ignored the cries of blacks in chains. Unless the traitors were tried and prosecuted, any reunion between North and South would leave blacks forever unfree. In seeking to save the Union, Lincoln almost destroyed its ideals.

Douglass had expected so much more from Lincoln.[23] He understood how difficult it was for the president-elect. Days after the election and four months before Lincoln took office, South Carolina announced plans to secede. By February 1, seven states had left the Union, and twenty-one days later, on George Washington's birthday, Jefferson Davis was inaugurated president of the Confederate States of America.

During this crisis President Buchanan was unable to respond effectually. His only goal was to avoid war. While he viewed secession as unconstitutional, he did nothing to prevent it. Indeed, he virtually encouraged it by assuring the South that the federal government had no right to use force. He blamed secession on the antislavery movement and urged a constitutional convention to create amendments that would protect slavery in the territories and states and prevent Northern states from interfering with the Fugitive Slave Act.

Douglass thought that Buchanan should be tried for treason, and he knew that Lincoln could do nothing until he took office.[24] He lauded Lincoln's "stately silence" as he waited to take office on March 4. He admired Lincoln's "stern refusal" to endorse any compromise scheme that would violate the Republican pledge to prohibit the extension of slavery. And he considered Lincoln's nickname, "Honest Old Abe," to be a sincere and accurate reflection of the president-elect's words and actions.[25]

Douglass joined thousands of fellow citizens early in the morning on February 18 to welcome Lincoln's private train as it stopped briefly at Rochester's New York Central station during its meandering journey from Springfield to Washington. A band was playing and the president-elect appeared on the balcony at the rear of the train and bowed to the throng. It was a stiff, awkward bow; his chin rose while his body seemed to break in two at the hips. He looked like a wooden nutcracker.[26]

Douglass already knew what Lincoln was going to say, for his railroad speeches were essentially the same at every stop.[27] "I am not vain enough to believe that you are here from any wish to see me as an individual, but because I am, for the time being, the representative of the American people," Lincoln said. "I appear merely to see you, and to let you see me, and to bid you farewell."[28]

Douglass, remembering how nobly Lincoln had challenged Stephen Douglas a few years earlier, expected him to stand up to the South in much the same way. He must order the "haughty slave masters" to lay down their arms and return to the Union or face charges as traitors (a capital crime). He must respond to this crisis as sternly and inflexibly as President Andrew Jackson had in a similar emergency in 1832, when South Carolina nullified federal law and refused to pay a tariff. Jackson had immediately taken action, declaring disunion to be treason, threatening to invade the state and hang the traitors, and causing the nullifiers to back down. Lincoln must do these things "or be the despised representative of a defied and humbled government." Do the right thing! Douglass repeatedly urged Lincoln. "Let the conflict come and God speed the right."[29]

Douglass even entertained hopes that the secession crisis would radicalize Lincoln. After all, the president-elect had entered the nation's capital under threats of assassination. Allan Pinkerton, a brash, bearded abolitionist and the head of the Pinkerton National Detective Agency, persuaded Lincoln to leave Baltimore for Washington in disguise at night after uncovering reliable evidence of a plot. Lincoln suddenly became a "poor, hunted fugitive slave," Douglass noted, "seeking concealment, evading pursuers, . . . crawling and dodging under the sable wing of night." Indeed, the president-elect left Baltimore on a train very much like the young Frederick Bailey had some twenty-three years earlier, as a fugitive and in disguise. Unlike many Northerners, who lampooned Lincoln for his cowardice, Douglass sympathized with him. "He only did what braver men have done." It was no doubt "galling to his very soul to be compelled to avail himself of the methods of a fugitive slave."[30] Perhaps the ordeal would prompt Lincoln to empathize with blacks and identify with the plight of the slave far more than he previously had.

And so Douglass had gotten his hopes up only to have them crushed. During his first month in office Lincoln acted little better than President Buchanan had. Much like Buchanan, he promised not to attack: "The government will not assail *you*," he told the South. He comforted the Southern people, assuring them that they "shall have that sense of perfect security which is most favorable to calm thought and reflection."³¹ He endorsed the constitutional amendment forever protecting slavery in the states. And he echoed Buchanan in pledging only to "hold, occupy, and possess" federal forts and arsenals in the South.³²

Fort Sumter was one such fort. It was an unfinished brick structure standing on a slab of granite a few miles from downtown Charleston, South Carolina. One of the first dispatches Lincoln read after assuming his new duties was from Major Robert Anderson, the Union commander of Fort Sumter, who said that his supplies were running out and that in a few weeks his men would be out of food. Over the next month Northerners became obsessed with Sumter, wondering what Lincoln would do. Upholding his pledge, Lincoln informed South Carolina governor Francis Pickens that he would supply the fort with food but not men or ammunition. He was baiting Southerners, inviting them to commit another act of aggression against the Union, which they did. On April 12, shortly before supply boats arrived,

Confederates opened fire on Fort Sumter and bombed it for thirty-three hours until Major Anderson surrendered his garrison.[33]

"God be praised!" Douglass said. The war "has come at last."[34] Here was the chance to destroy slavery. "Let the long crushed bondman arise! and in this auspicious moment snatch back [his] liberty."[35] In their belligerence slaveholders had finally overreached, forcing the American government to "put down this slaveholding rebellion."[36]

The bombing of Fort Sumter revolutionized the nation. Before the smoke had settled, Lincoln issued a proclamation asking for seventy-five thousand troops for ninety days to put down the insurrection.[37] The response was so overwhelming that he could have raised five times that number. Douglass was thrilled: "the dead North is alive, and its divided people united," he proclaimed.[38] In fighting the Confederacy, Northerners also fought slavery, he believed. He canceled his trip to Haiti.

And then Lincoln disappointed him once again. After closely reading Lincoln's call for troops, Douglass realized that the president was going out of his way to protect slaveholders' property: "the utmost care will be observed, . . . to avoid any devastation, any destruction of, or interference with, property."[39]

"We all know that means that no attempt will be made to destroy slavery," Douglass sneered.[40]

Not only that, but as soon as the call for troops went out, the Lincoln administration turned away thousands of blacks who were eager to shoot down slaveholders. Douglass alone could raise ten thousand black troops within thirty days, he said with bravado, and he emphasized that one black regiment marching on Southern soil would be "the full equal of two white ones."[41] Blacks with guns would terrify Southerners. The election of Lincoln had already caused "many a matron throughout the South" to go to sleep at night dreading what her slaves, newly empowered with ideals of freedom, might do to her and her children.[42] And it had caused many a master to stay up all night, shotgun in hand, ready for an uprising that in most cases did not come.

The problem was that the mass of racist Northern whites were almost as terrified of a slave insurrection as were slaveholding rebels. Even the huge, ferocious-looking Union general Benjamin Butler seemed scared after hearing of a plot among Maryland's slaves to rebel. A proslavery Democrat from Massachusetts, Butler liked to wear his hair long in the few places it remained on his head, perhaps to add to his look of toughness. Stationed at Annapolis and in command of a regiment of Massachusetts troops, he wrote Maryland governor Thomas Hicks on April 23, two weeks after Fort Sumter, to assure him that his forces would not "in any way" interfere with slaveholders' property. "I am therefore ready to cooperate with your excellency in suppressing most promptly and effectively any insurrection against the laws of Maryland."[43]

Butler's statement outraged Douglass. But what most galled him was hearing that Union officers happily returned runaways to their masters. Even before Fort Sumter, slaves began fleeing to Union troops, offering their services in exchange for protection and freedom. In March eight slaves ran away from a plantation near Milton, Florida, having heard that the government sought to protect its forts in the South. They traveled through bogs, bayous, and swamps for thirty miles without resting and finally arrived in stolen canoes at Fort Pickens, at the mouth of Pensacola Bay. Hungry but relieved, the men calculated that their services would be gladly accepted in return for being sent north as free men. They were right to assume that Fort Pickens badly needed reinforcements. But the commander of the fort, Lieutenant A. J. Slemmer, put the men in irons and "delivered them to the city marshal to be returned to their owner."[44] According to one eyewitness, their owner made an example of them, whipping them unmercifully for hours to dissuade hundreds of other slaves from following suit. Some were literally whipped to death, and the survivors were so badly injured that two weeks later they still could not stand up.[45]

This torture occurred because the federal government enforced a fugitive slave law for the benefit of people who had just committed treason against them. It was tantamount to Southerners' returning to John Brown deserters from his army. It was absurd, in other words, and never would have happened to white men. When Lydia Maria Child, a petite and elderly abolitionist, read about the incident at Fort Pickens in Douglass's newspaper, she felt like trampling on the national flag: "God knows I *want* to love and honor the flag of my country; but how *can* I, when it is used for *such* purposes?" Douglass felt the same way. Until the Union decided to "strike down slavery," it didn't "deserve the support of a single sable arm."[46]

But slaveholders were also growing more belligerent against whites, murdering some and raising the ire of the North. Within a month of Lincoln's call for troops, Virginia, North Carolina, Tennessee, and Arkansas also joined the

Confederacy. On May 24, the day after Virginia formally seceded, Union colonel Elmer Ellsworth led a regiment into Alexandria. Ellsworth was not only stunningly handsome (he resembled John Wilkes Booth) but a close friend of Lincoln's. Indeed, Lincoln treated him "like a son"; he mentored him in law and invited him to travel in the president's private car to Washington. At Alexandria Ellsworth captured the telegraph office and then noticed a Confederate flag flying atop the nearby Marshall House Hotel, a boxy three-story brick building. Outraged, he burst into the hotel, ran up the steps to the roof, and tore it down. On his way out, the hotel's Confederate owner was waiting for him with a shotgun and blew him away at point-blank range.[47]

There were also reports of Confederates poisoning federal troops, of pirates sending Northern arms to the South, and of Unionists in the South being mobbed and lynched. Maybe after a few more Elmer Ellsworths were killed the government would begin to treat rebels like enemies rather than friends, Douglass said. Maybe then the Lincoln administration would begin treating blacks as humans.[48]

Things began to change after Ellsworth was killed. On May 24, Benjamin Butler experienced a change of heart toward blacks, perhaps because he had been reprimanded by

John Andrew, the abolitionist governor of Massachusetts, for his willingness to suppress slave insurrections. Butler was now stationed at Fort Monroe, Virginia, and admitted into his camp three slaves who were about to be sent into the rebel army to build fortifications. Butler needed men and put them to work. Soon the slaves' owner sent an agent, who referred to the Fugitive Slave Act and Butler's constitutional obligation to deliver up fugitives.

"Virginia passed an ordinance of secession and claims to be a foreign country," Butler replied, "and I am under no constitutional obligations to a foreign country."

"But you say we can't secede and so you cannot consistently detain the Negroes," the agent countered.

"You say you have seceded, and so you cannot consistently claim them," said Butler, pleased to win any kind of argument. "I shall detain them as *contraband of war.*"[49]

The term became lodged in the North's memory, and word of the contrabands immediately circulated through the slave community's grapevine telegraph. Within three days Butler had $60,000 (in today's dollars) worth of contraband on his hands, and by August over a thousand men, women, and children.

By then the Republican-controlled Congress

had acted. On August 6 it signed into law the First Confiscation Act, authorizing the Union army to confiscate slaves aiding the Confederate war effort.[50] Reports that thousands of slaves had been pressed into service for the Confederacy, contributing to its victory at the first battle of Bull Run in July, helped convince the administration of the military need to confiscate slaves. According to Douglass, slaves not only did the rebels' dirty work, building fortifications and working as teamsters; they also fought as rebel soldiers in militia units, having been forced by their masters to bear arms against the North. It was an embarrassment, Douglass complained. While the rebel army used blacks "as real soldiers, having muskets on their shoulders, and bullets in their pockets, ready to shoot down loyal troops," the Lincoln administration looked the other way, pretending that the nation's four million slaves and half a million free blacks did not exist.[51]

Then at the end of August Douglass experienced another spark of hope. John C. Frémont, now a Union general in command of the Western Department, was stationed in Missouri, a border state experiencing some of the worst guerrilla fighting of the war. There were some sixty-five thousand secessionists, many of whom roamed the state in small bands murdering farmers, stealing horses, cutting telegraph lines, and destroying railroad tracks and bridges.[52] With Missouri in a state of anarchy, Frémont took "decisive action."[53] On August 30 he issued the nation's first emancipation proclamation. Declaring martial law in the state, he ordered all armed secessionists to be court-martialed and shot if found guilty. And all slaves of disloyal citizens "are hereby declared free men."[54]

Frémont understood that the only way to win the war was to forever deprive rebels of their property. His abolitionist advisers Owen Lovejoy and John Gurley, and his wife, Jessie, agreed with him. As Lovejoy put it, "why take a costly and weary way" to put down the rebellion "when a cheap short one is at hand? . . . Let the President, in his capacity as commander of the army, proclaim such liberation and the war would end in thirty days."[55] From the outset of the war, then, Frémont wanted to transform the conflict into a social revolution rather than preserve the status quo.[56] To him it was a moral and military fight for universal freedom, not a war to save the Union by ignoring the plight of blacks.

Frémont's proclamation thrilled Republicans throughout the country. Northern cities held rallies and torchlight parades to honor him, and one Republican editor called it the most exciting event of the war to date. Harriet Beecher

Stowe spoke for many when she said that "the hour has come, and the man." And Secretary of War Simon Cameron was so moved that he telegraphed Frémont congratulating him for his courage.[57]

Twelve days later Lincoln rescinded Frémont's emancipation proclamation. He was worried about losing the border states, he told Frémont in a private letter, and so he asked him to modify his proclamation to conform to the Confiscation Act, which did not free a single slave. Frémont courageously refused. If he retracted his proclamation, he told Lincoln, "it would imply that I myself thought it wrong and that I had acted without the reflection which the gravity of the point demanded. But I did not. I acted with full deliberation and upon the certain conviction that it was a measure right and necessary and I think so still."[58] Lincoln was thus forced to publicly retract Frémont's emancipation proclamation, which caused him more than a little embarrassment. As if to retaliate, he soon relieved Frémont of his command.[59]

Douglass called Lincoln a genuine proslavery president. He did not mean any ill will, he emphasized. But revoking Frémont's emancipation proclamation was the largest blunder of the war to date, worse even than Lincoln's insidious Inaugural. "The action of Frémont was the hinge, the pivot upon which the character of the war was to turn," he declared in his newspaper. Lincoln had the opportunity to shape public opinion, not to respond slavishly to it. He should have thanked Frémont for the chance to announce to the world his earnestness and refusal to compromise with traitors. For a brief moment Douglass thought the war would be waged by a "determined warrior" rather than "a crafty lawyer."[60]

To Douglass, Frémont was sacrificed to "appease the proslavery sentiment of the border states."[61] It was one more disappointment in a war that had been nothing but disappointments. Nevertheless, Douglass felt sure that Frémont's brave words would soon rise Christlike from the altar to destroy the monster slavery.[62] Frémont's sacrifice underscored for Douglass the inevitable outcome in an epic struggle that had long ago been foretold in Revelation, where Michael and his angels battled against "the infernal host of bad passions."[63] Despite the many disappointments Lincoln had caused him, he never regretted not going to Haiti. He believed that the forces of righteousness would eventually prevail.

Frémont inspired Douglass to speak out more forcefully against Lincoln. His was only "one humble voice," but Douglass knew that speaking truth to power could change the world.[64] In essay after essay he railed against Lincoln, urging him to free the slaves and recruit black troops. "The Negro is the stomach of the rebellion," he wrote, and every slave who escaped from the rebel states "is a loss to the Rebellion and a gain to the Loyal cause." Refusing to arm blacks was like fighting "with only one hand."[65] He also understood that the quickest way for blacks to gain equal rights was for them to become Union soldiers.

The nation's four million slaves, plus another half million free blacks, were equivalent to a quarter of the North's population and represented a potent source of power. Indeed, there were half as many blacks in the country as rebel whites![66] Utilizing them would thus satisfy the demand for troops, prevent the need for conscription, and more than offset the attrition of white soldiers who refused to fight for black freedom. As a military strategist Douglass favored demography over geography.

Douglass also challenged Lincoln's assumption that the border (slave) states of Maryland, Kentucky, Missouri, and Delaware would secede if the slaves were freed. The border-state dilemma hinged around a simple question: did slaveholding Unionists value their country over slavery? Douglass thought they did, which meant that the border states would not secede. And if he was wrong, if border-state men loved slavery more than their country, then let them go! Good riddance! They were wolves in sheep's clothing.[67]

To be sure, there would be a lot more guerrilla warfare in the border states if Unionists chose slavery over their country. But Missouri, Kentucky, and Maryland were already engaged in guerrilla warfare, and Douglass felt Lincoln could handle it.[68] When Maryland's secessionists caused riots and threatened to secede in mid-1861, he declared martial law, suspended the writ of habeas corpus, and arrested secessionist politicians before they could vote on an ordinance of secession. The result was "a smashing victory for the Union party."[69] In Missouri Lincoln *approved* Frémont's declaration of martial law; he just told him not to kill any prisoner without his consent.[70]

The important point about the border states was not the official status of the state but Unionists' ability to control transportation routes, manufacturing facilities, and armories amid the guerrilla warfare. If the Union army could not control these resources, they would have trouble defending Washington, D.C., and they would lose crucial manufacturing plants and the strategic Ohio River to the rebels. But as long as Lincoln ordered his generals to imprison anyone advocating secession, then border-state guerrilla warfare was a manageable problem.[71]

Such actions were constitutional, Douglass argued. Beginning in September 1861 he reprinted on the front page of his paper, just under the masthead, John Quincy Adams's war powers argument. During civil war, *"the military authority takes, for the time, the place of municipal institutions, slavery among the rest."* According to one of the nation's wisest legal authorities, declaring martial law, suspending the writ of habeas corpus, and emancipating all the slaves were constitutional during civil war. *"Not only the President of the United States, but the Commander of the army has the power to order the universal emancipation of the slaves."*[72] John Quincy Adams would have endorsed Frémont's proclamation, Douglass was telling Lincoln. Why can't you?

Not only was Lincoln's policy of condoning slavery to protect the border states morally wrong and constitutionally misguided; from a military perspective it was disastrous. Douglass sketched out four basic problems with Lincoln's policy. First, it encouraged England and France to intervene on behalf of the Confederacy. The Union blockade that prevented rebels from sending cotton to Europe had caused widespread unemployment in England and France. These countries would not "long endure a war whose only effect is to starve thousands of their people, slaughter thousands of our own, and sink millions of money." Make it an abolition war, "and you at once unite the world against the rebels, and in favor of the Government."[73]

Second, slaves would soon conclude that if they had to remain slaves, as Union policy dictated, they would rather fight *against* the Union than for it. They would only be protecting themselves, choosing a *known* master over an unknown tyrant. "They hesitate now, but if our policy is pursued," they will deem it better "to endure those ills they have, than fly to others they know not of."[74]

The third problem with Lincoln's border-state policy was that it *inspired* the rebels. It gave them the moral high ground, enabling them to say that this war was about the right to govern oneself, not slavery. And of course the idea of self-government was a potent principle with roots in the Revolution. It was a cause that the masses were willing to fight and die for. Make it an abolition war, however, and suddenly the Union was fighting for *freedom* rather than the right to control the South, and the rebels were fighting for slavery, not independence.[75]

Finally, the current policy invited more compromises with slavery. Republicans like William Seward had already promised numerous
concessions to the South and would no doubt
offer more to end the war. Yet as Lincoln himself had so eloquently noted, "a nation divided
against itself cannot stand." Continue compromising with the slaveholders and it would become all one thing, till slavery was lawful in all
the states.[76]

Douglass was almost lynched for his harsh
critique of Lincoln. In November 1861 he went
to Syracuse to give a lecture on "The Rebellion,
Its Cause and Remedy." When he arrived at Syracuse's New York Central station he saw "at
every corner" advertisements for his talk alongside handbills seeking to silence him: NIGGER
FRED COMING, they announced. "Shall his vile
sentiments again be tolerated in this community by a constitutional liberty-loving people?
or shall we give him a WARM reception at this
time for his insolence, as he deserves?"

The lynch mob chose the wrong city in
which to attack Douglass, however, for Syracuse was among the most abolitionist places in
the country. The mayor, police force, and many
citizens all gave Douglass ample protection as
soon as he arrived. Dr. Wieting, the slim and
rather frail owner of the beautiful new the-

ater where Douglass spoke, personally ushered him inside despite the mob's threat to sack the place. When the mob taunted Wieting as a "nigger-lover," he responded that his "principles of freedom applied to humanity not to color." Douglass spoke to a full house and received a standing ovation.[77]

The war unified abolitionists and accorded them far more respect than ever before. Douglass had long been filling auditoriums to capacity, but now his audiences included many conservatives and Democrats who enjoyed not only the magic of his performance but the content of his message.[78] And for the first time in fifteen years, William Lloyd Garrison and his clique no longer saw Douglass as the enemy for his political abolitionism. Indeed, when the war broke out they abruptly abandoned their advocacy of disunion and hatred of the Constitution and began to agree with Douglass that "freedom should be fought *within* the Union, and not out of it." Douglass was thrilled about his former comrades' change of heart and quickly joined a national Emancipation League that united abolitionists of all stripes. He knew that a unified voice was the most effective weapon against Lincoln's obstinance.[79]

In early 1862 Douglass filled the Cooper Union in New York City, much as Lincoln had two years earlier. Like Lincoln's earlier address, his discussed America's destiny. There the similarities ended. Combating Lincoln's policy of black colonization, Douglass declared that the destiny of the African American "is the destiny of America." He likened the nation to an open book, its black ink giving meaning to the white pages and offering lessons about "wisdom, power, and goodness" and the sacredness of "human brotherhood."[80]

The changing zeitgeist even penetrated the nation's Capitol. Now congressmen were regularly voicing sentiments at least as revolutionary as those of Douglass. The stern, clubfooted House leader Thaddeus Stevens outdid even Charles Sumner in the Senate: "Free every slave—slay every traitor—burn every rebel mansion, if these things be necessary to preserve this temple of freedom," Stevens intoned. We must treat "this war as a radical revolution and remodel our institutions."[81]

European radicals also took a keen interest in America's new spirit of emancipation. Karl Marx wrote extensively on the war from Vienna, possibly read Douglass in translation, and certainly echoed him: the border states "have constituted the chief weakness of the North," Marx declared. "Tender regard for the interests of these ambiguous allies has smitten the

Union government with incurable weakness" and "spared the foe's most vulnerable spot, the root of evil—*slavery itself.*"[82]

It was as though universal emancipation was an idea whose time had finally come, as Victor Hugo, another fan of Douglass, noted.[83] For decades, Douglass and his comrades had been spit upon or beaten up and accused of threatening the Union. But after rebels fired on Fort Sumter the masses suddenly began to see them as Cassandras who had long been trying to expose the evils of slavery and save their country.[84] Slowly, very slowly, Lincoln began to listen.

In 1861 Douglass devoted himself largely to journalism. He wrote more essays and gave fewer speeches than during any other period since 1843. It was as though he wanted his critiques of Lincoln to be permanent; if he couldn't speak to the president in person, he could at least send issues of his paper to the White House. The new motto under the masthead from Proverbs 31 suggested that his paper rather than his voice had become his main mouthpiece: "open thy mouth, judge righteously, and plead the cause of the poor and needy." And the new name, *Douglass' Monthly*, reflected the new format.

Since 1860 the paper had become a sixteen-page monthly rather than a four-page weekly, allowing him to save money and still publish as many pages each month. Douglass sequenced the essays as he wrote them, so that readers could trace his thoughts over the course of the month. The effect was a kind of serial book-of-the-month, with each issue critiquing the state of the nation.

Douglass' Monthly was an appropriate form for a nation experiencing radical social upheaval. Time passed differently during civil war. A week or a month rushed by like the blur of Niagara to the untrained eye or the rat-tat-tat of the telegraph to a new operator. But then a single moment would linger like an afterimage or photograph, in which time stood still. People remembered exactly where they were when they read Lincoln's Inaugural. And when they scanned a list of casualties in their daily paper after a battle, the death list seemed to flow like a river "down the pale sheet" until suddenly their eyes and their world stopped on the name of a loved one.[85] *Douglass' Monthly* gave focus and fixity to the blur of events. It functioned like a photographic album, freezing some moments while evoking through the arrangement of stories the onward rush of the war. Many Northerners wanted time to speed up in order to restore order and soothe the grief over lost sons. "Ah God! may Time with happy haste / Bring wail and triumph to a waste, / And war be done," Herman Melville wrote in one evocative poem.[86] But Douglass wanted social revolution; his world was not changing quickly enough.

He spent most of his time at home in Rochester writing or at his office, which still carried the name "The North Star." A few years earlier he had moved his family to a larger house at 1023 South Avenue in Pinnacle Hills, a half-hour carriage ride from downtown.[87] Their new home looked like a European villa, surrounded as it was by an extensive garden and overlooking rolling hills with landscaped fruit trees. One friend described it as having "a singularly poetic appearance and, in a way, [resembling] an island, a small separate world, where those who have the courage to defy disgraceful prejudice find a rich intellectual life and are received with great kindness, generosity, and a rather un-American heartfelt warmth."[88]

At one level his new home suggested a black bourgeois household. Douglass was more financially secure than ever before, for over the past decade he had commanded almost as much money from lecturing as the most sought-after white orators, at a time when public lecturers made a good living.[89] But then, as if to offset this façade of security, he isolated himself from white bourgeois society and acquired the look of a radical intellectual, letting his hair grow out and experimenting with a new goatee. For many white intellectuals, hair was a sign of self-expression, an outward manifestation of one's inner spirit. Muttonchops, footlong beards, goatees, mustaches that drooped below the chin, and hair that stood on end, suggesting a mind so electric that its current coursed through the skin and split the hair ends, were all common styles of the day. Even with his new goatee and long hair Douglass looked rather staid compared to many of his friends. He did not want to go too far with his new look, did not need to draw any more attention to himself and risk being alienated from white bourgeois parlors.[90]

Anna was not doing well. In 1860 their youngest child, Annie, had died at age ten, and it was as though the "baby's" death had crushed her physically and emotionally. She suffered from "neuraligia" (shingles), which kept her at home and in a sour mood. "I am sad to say that she is by no means well," Frederick wrote to one friend, "and if I should write down all her complaints there could be no room to put my name at the bottom, although the world will have it that I am actually at the bottom of it all." To Frederick she was a nag who used her "powers of speech with great ease and fluency" to highlight the flaws "in my temper and disposition as a husband and father, the head of a family."[91]

Anna had good reason to be upset with him. Although Julia Griffiths was no longer a threat, having married a British clergyman and returned to England a few years earlier, another foreign white woman was vying aggressively for Douglass's affections. Ottilie Assing had come to America from Germany in 1852 to begin life anew. A year younger than Douglass, she resembled him as a social outsider who fled her homeland for New York City, and she became a romantic intellectual. But she lacked his pragmatic sensibility.[92]

Ottilie was raised in Hamburg, the daughter of a Jewish father and Gentile mother, both of whom were bourgeois intellectuals. She was also a devoted child of German romanticism, and her circle of friends and acquaintances in Germany were writers, visual artists, or actors. Ottilie tried her hand at all three and described herself as "almost an actor." Art was her life, including the art of abolition. In fact she so internalized the German romantic tradition that even as an adult she saw herself in fictional characters and treated her favorite novels as guidebooks to what her life would be like.[93]

The first major climax in her life occurred one night in 1843 when she was twenty-four. Her parents had died and she and her sister had moved to Berlin to live with an uncle. The uncle and sister got along well, but Ottilie hated both of them, and during an argument her uncle slapped her. Ottilie stormed out of the house and decided that the only courageous response to such humiliation was to follow the example of Goethe's Werther. She ran to Berlin's Tiergarten, the city's large public park, hid in the shrubs, and stabbed herself three times with a knife. She survived but clung even more tenaciously to her faith that life should imitate art.[94]

The second climax in her life occurred in 1856, when she made a pilgrimage to Rochester to meet Frederick Douglass. She was living in Hoboken and working as an American correspondent for the progressive German paper the *Morning Journal for Educated Readers*.[95] Having already established herself in abolitionist circles, she had seen Douglass's engravings and read his books and knew how attractive and eloquent he was. Her purpose in going to Rochester was to ask permission to translate into German his best-selling second autobiography, *My Bondage and My Freedom*. When she met him at his home at 1023 South Avenue she was even more impressed with his looks and voice. And when she first saw Anna she mistook her for a maid.[96]

From the beginning of their relationship Assing idealized and exoticized Douglass.[97] In her introduction to the German translation of *My Bondage and My Freedom*, she casts him as the living embodiment of "an imagined hero" and the "perfect master" of the art of oratory, with as "mellifluous, sonorous, flexible a voice speaking to the heart as I have ever heard." When Douglass spoke, his listeners were swept away, Assing says, "as if a new apostle had revealed to them for the first time a truth that had lain unspoken in everyone's heart." Like Saint Paul, Douglass converted the masses. According to Assing, the growth of antislavery thought was largely due to his accomplishments and personality. In describing him physically she became almost rapturous: a "light mulatto of unusually tall, slender, and powerful stature," he has a "prominently domed forehead" betokening genius, "an aquiline nose," and "narrow, beautifully carved lips."[98]

Assing was completely in love with Douglass. Once again she saw life echoing art, but this time it was a different story. Now Assing saw herself as the beautiful and brilliant heroine from another one of her favorite novels, *Aphra Behn*

(1849), by the German writer Clara Mundt.[99] In the climactic scene of Mundt's novel, the heroine Aphra becomes the lover of a sublime black revolutionary.[100] In the drama that Assing was creating for herself, as in Mundt's novel, the black hero is already married. No matter. For in great literature, as in a life fully lived, the heroine must consummate her love and sacrifice herself for her hero. It is the only true plot. No wonder, then, that Assing publicly dismisses Anna in her introduction to *My Bondage*: "Douglass' wife is completely black," she writes, in striking contrast to her description of her hero's exotic light-skinned features.[101] Privately she referred to Anna as "Border State," a millstone around her (and in her mind Douglass's) neck.[102]

Assing *did* sacrifice herself for her hero. It was her apartment in Hoboken where Douglass sought refuge in the immediate wake of John Brown's raid, a wanted man with federal authorities from the president down searching everywhere for him. And it was Assing who hurried to the telegraph office to send Douglass's coded message to his son telling him to destroy or hide sensitive documents relating to Brown. Without her help Douglass may well have been captured and sent to Virginia for trial and almost certain execution.[103]

Assing consummated her love with her hero, at least in her imagination. "When you are so intimately connected with one man as I am with Douglass, you will get to know men . . . from a perspective that would never be revealed to you otherwise," she told her sister in one letter. In another she boasted that she and Douglass were "united in a deeper love than many who are married."[104] She spent most summers in Rochester living with the Douglasses, and when she returned to Hoboken in the fall she looked forward to her "weekly allowance," her term for Douglass's letters to her.[105] When Douglass planned his trip to Haiti, Assing said she made arrangements to go with him. It would be just the two of them, since Anna and the children would remain home in Rochester. Assing had looked forward to spending time with Douglass in an exotic land without "Border State" Anna interfering with their love.[106]

Undoubtedly Douglass and Assing were intimate friends, but how deep and sexual was their love is unknown, for the only surviving sources suggesting sexual intimacy stem from a collection of letters Ottilie wrote her sister Ludmilla after the war.[107] In Assing's mind she consummated her love. But she hated her sister; in fact Anna was "amiable compared to Ludmilla."[108] Her sister was her rival, and it is significant that Assing told Ludmilla about her intimacy with Douglass after learning that she had married a German aristocrat. Her descriptions of a love deeper than marriage could thus reflect wishful boasting. With rivals and strangers Assing cloaked her insecurity and jealousy with intellectual arrogance.[109]

In Douglass's writings Assing appears as a shadowy friend. He was much more overt about his feelings toward other close friends, from Julia Griffiths and Amy Post to Gerrit Smith. In fact he rarely mentioned Assing in his public and private writings except in letters to Gerrit Smith, who was also a friend of Assing's. This silence may have stemmed from Douglass's need to hide something. He could have had a sexual affair with Assing without much risk of getting her pregnant and destroying his career, for in 1861 she was forty-two years old.

There were factors other than Anna that prevented Douglass and Assing from achieving a lasting and intimate union, however. One was Assing's elitism. She was wholly unsympathetic to America's poor and ignorant classes, especially immigrants. She called New York City "the home of the scum of all nations thanks to the masses of rude and ignorant Irishmen." And in one letter to Douglass she casually suggested that it would be easier to teach a cat grammar than "Border State."[110] Despite the strain on their marriage, Douglass still had affections for his wife.

Their respective faiths also kept them apart. Douglass believed in a living God who could alter the affairs of the world. "All things are possible with God," he declared. "I believe in the millennium."[111] Assing was horrified by such sentiments, for she was an avowed atheist and had little sympathy for anyone else's religious belief. She effectively replaced religion with the truth of art and aesthetic experience, and she acknowledged the spiritual chasm separating them. "Personal sympathy and concordance in many central issues brought us together; but there was one obstacle to a loving and lasting friendship—namely, the personal Christian God."[112]

Perhaps it is not coincidental that at the very time Assing entered Douglass's life and began her private war on Anna, the nation was splitting apart. Many Americans thought of their nation as a family. "We are separated because of incompatibility of temper," the Southern aristocrat Mary Chesnut wrote in her diary after secession. "We are divorced, North from South, because we have hated each other so."[113] Douglass saw a close correlation between family and nation and opposed disunion and divorce.[114]

If destroying slavery was the quickest way to end the war, then halting the rebellion at home was much harder to manage, for in this sphere Douglass's ability to distinguish between good and evil was not so clear-cut. While he was uncompromising in his opposition to slavery and insistence that Americans must cast their loyalties with the nation or with slavery, in individual relationships he sought reconciliation and compromise. He reunited with William Lloyd Garrison during the war, putting aside their decade-long bitter feud. He wrote affectionate letters to his former master Thomas Auld, telling him he loved him. He divided his loyalties and affections between his wife and Ottilie Assing for over twenty years. And he would befriend Lincoln even as he criticized his policies.

The tide was slowly turning. At the end of February 1862, Douglass compiled a list of Union and Confederate victories and concluded that from a military perspective the Union had crushed the rebels, winning three battles for every one for the enemy. Unionists were "everywhere jubilant," while rebels were despondent. The victory trend would continue, since Union forces had roughly three times more eligible men than the Confederacy.[115] The rebel boast that one Southern man was equal to five Northern men had largely disappeared from Southern newspapers, replaced by "the cry of disaffection." From a military perspective, the rebellion had plainly failed, Douglass concluded.[116]

The "popular heart" of the North was also in the right place. In February 1862 Douglass went on the road for a whirlwind two-week trip covering a thousand miles. He spoke on behalf of the Emancipation League and met tens of thousands of people, treating it like a political campaign. As a conversation-starter, the war and slavery were more popular than the weather; and so it was easy to engage people, despite his being black. He spoke to passengers at train stations and river landings and in cars and steamers. While eating at restaurants he went round the tables to find out how people felt about the war and slavery. In the evening he went into people's homes and sat round the fire to chat about the nation's destiny. And in churches and meeting halls he mingled with people after his lectures to gain a sense of public opinion. Despite the grueling nature of the trip—the bad food and smoke-filled train air and an occasional drunken Democrat who dismissed him with a turn of the head and the mutter of "nigger"—the trip filled him with encouragement. "The people are all ready to sweep slavery from the country would the government lead off or stand out of the way," he concluded. Public opinion was on his side. The Union victories and the Emancipation League were converting the North against slavery.[117]

Then in April 1862 Congress passed a bill to abolish slavery in Washington, D.C. It was the first time since 1846, when New Jersey abolished slavery, that an emancipation law had been passed in the nation.[118] Since then the number of slaves had increased by 1.5 million.

Douglass wrote Charles Sumner to thank him for his efforts in spearheading the bill. They had recently become friends. Sumner's caning had humbled him, eliminating much of the Boston Brahmin elitism that had gotten in the way of his personal relationships with blacks. They corresponded regularly and sent each other collections of their writings. Sumner was the "best embodiment of the Anti-Slavery idea now in the counsels of the Nation," Douglass said in his congratulatory note. "May God sustain you."[119]

Despite these recent successes, Douglass regarded Lincoln as an impediment. Whatever his intentions, Lincoln's actions had been "calculated in a *marked* and *decided* way to shield and protect slavery," Douglass told a crowd of over two thousand at an outdoor Fourth of July celebration at Himrod in New York's Finger Lakes region.[120]

He stood like a prophet amid the pine trees in his speech, the people gathered around him in a circle. He wore a light blue suit to match the sky, which periodically seemed to send off sparks from the sun. In the distance a band was playing softly, as if to accompany his rich and discordant litany of the president's misguided policies.[121]

From the beginning of the war, Lincoln had been guided by the border states rather than the free states. He wanted only "to reconstruct the Union on the old and corrupting basis of compromise," in which slaveholders would retain all the power they had ever had.[122]

Consequently, he refused to arm blacks or free the slaves. He revoked the emancipation proclamations of General Frémont and more recently of General David Hunter, who in May 1862 had announced martial law in South Carolina, Georgia, and Florida and declared slaves in those states forever free. While he forbade antislavery generals to interfere with slavery, he allowed proslavery generals like Henry Halleck and George McClellan to "violate the spirit" of Congress's Confiscation Act that forbade the Union army to return fugitives to disloyal masters. Then, as if to add insult to injury, on the same day that Lincoln revoked General Hunter's emancipation proclamation, he publicly told Maryland's slaveholders that he would rigorously defend the Fugitive Slave Act.[123]

Lincoln's policies were all the more tragic because the nation was now more capable than ever before of realizing its ideals. "There are principles in the Declaration of Independence which would release every slave in the world and prepare the earth for a millennium of righteousness and peace," Douglass noted. But for Lincoln! "But alas!"[124]

The Union could not be saved. It could not be reconstructed as it was. You must recognize this fact, Douglass told his listeners. He offered two very simple strategies for destroying the twin monsters of rebellion and slavery. First, Congress should pass a "stringent Confiscation Bill" that would declare all slaves of rebel masters "forever free."[125] And second, the president, as head of the nation, should issue his own emancipation proclamation to give teeth to the Confiscation Act.

Many of those listening to Douglass in the pine grove on July 4 would later declare him a prophet. For just thirteen days later, on July 17, Congress passed the Second Confiscation Act, which declared all slaves within Union lines "forever free" and urged the president to emancipate all other slaves of rebel masters.[126] The act instructed the president to give all rebels sixty days to return to the Union or else face prosecution and seizure of property. And it authorized the president to employ and arm blacks in the military and provide voluntary colonization in "some foreign country" for those slaves freed during the war.[127]

The Second Confiscation Act was potentially revolutionary despite its provision for colonization. Its influence depended on Lincoln. As Douglass noted, "the sole power of putting life into this law is vested in the President." If Lincoln ordered his generals to confiscate all rebel property, if he issued an emancipation proclamation, and if he ordered the army and navy to employ blacks, then the act, coupled with Lincoln's supporting actions, would transform the nation. If Lincoln did nothing, the act would be little better than a dead letter.[128]

Douglass waited anxiously to see what Lincoln would do. On July 25 the president issued a proclamation warning Southerners to cease their rebellion and pledge allegiance to the United States or else have their property subject to confiscation.[129] To Douglass the proclamation did not go far enough, for it said nothing about the status of slaves and was silent about employing and arming blacks. Lincoln was still too tentative, too slow to act.

One source of encouragement came from Charles Sumner, who said he knew the president intimately and urged abolitionists to have faith in him. "I wish that you really knew the President, and had heard the artless expression of his convictions on" slavery, Sumner said. You might wish he "were less cautious, but you would be grateful that he is" at heart a firm opponent of slavery. Stand by Lincoln, Sumner said, even if you have to nudge him along. Douglass published Sumner's letter in his newspaper.[130]

Then a few weeks later Douglass lost faith in Lincoln all over again. In August the president met with a delegation of free blacks from Washington and strongly encouraged them to emigrate. Douglass may have felt snubbed that *he* hadn't been invited to the meeting. He was incensed with Lincoln's message that blacks had caused the war, that they could never be equals of whites, and that they should emigrate to some tropical country. "I don't like you, you must clear out of the country," was Lincoln's response to blacks, Douglass concluded.[131] The president had no interest in listening to what blacks had to say. Every step of his presidential career relating to slavery proved him *active* for its support and *passive* "to the cause of liberty to which he owes his election."[132]

And then suddenly on September 22, like a burst from the heavens, Lincoln announced his preliminary Emancipation Proclamation. He declared that on January 1, 1863, all slaves of rebel owners would be "forever free" and he ordered military personnel to recognize their freedom.* He even went a step further than the Second Confiscation Act, urging Congress to emancipate slaves in the border states by compensating masters. And two days later he suspended the writ of habeas corpus for all rebels and their abettors, effectively treating them as prisoners of war.[133]

News of the preliminary Emancipation Proclamation was the happiest moment of Douglass's life. He was working at home in Rochester when he heard the announcement, and he wrote a response that appeared on the first page of his newspaper. Lincoln had almost broken his heart from "slothful deliberation," plunging him into the depths of despair.[134] But like Job being restored, his hopes for the nation were suddenly renewed. "We shout for joy that we live to record this righteous decree," he an-

---

* The final Emancipation Proclamation authorized the military to employ blacks.

nounced.[135] He had devoted almost every waking hour of his adult life to ending slavery. As a small child on the Eastern Shore of Maryland he had wondered why blacks were slaves, and from that moment on, "the cry that has reached the most silent chambers of my soul, by day and by night, has been 'How long! How long oh! Eternal Power of the Universe, how long shall these things be?' "[136] Now he knew. The deliverance of millions was at hand.

Douglass had no doubt that Lincoln's Emancipation Proclamation, coupled with the Second Confiscation Act, would lead swiftly to the end of slavery *everywhere* in America. "Slavery once abolished in the rebel states will give the death wound to slavery in the border states. When Arkansas is a free state Missouri cannot be a slave state."[137]

What Douglass doubted was whether or not Lincoln would actually *follow through* with his Emancipation Proclamation. For in the days and weeks after September 22 the president rarely mentioned it. Moreover, his motives seemed to stem purely from military necessity. And in all his prior actions he had shown an apparent lack of "any vital hostility toward slavery."[138]

But Douglass also recognized that neither Lincoln nor any other individual had control over emancipation. Events far greater than the president "had wrung this proclamation from him," Douglass said, and these same events would carry him forward to sign the final emancipation decree.[139] Every day slaves fled their masters for Union lines, abolitionists spoke out in one united voice, Republicans in Congress worked to dethrone slavery, and Union soldiers killed traitors to the country. They were all part of a providential wave of progress sweeping the globe. It was thus absurd to assume that one man could emancipate four million. Abraham Lincoln would take no step backward. Even if he tried, he would be silenced, swept under the wave of progress.

As the day of deliverance approached, Douglass seemed at a loss for words. On December 28, 1862, the Sunday before emancipation was scheduled to go into effect, he spoke at his A.M.E. Zion church in Rochester. It was one of his favorite venues, for he knew the congregants and loved the stately gothic stone building with its intricate stained-glass windows, which now seemed especially vibrant. The sky was cloudless with "brilliant sunshine" and the air was balmy, "making December as pleasant as May." The day "was in harmony with the glorious morning of liberty about to dawn upon us," Douglass said. The congregants expected a normal two-hour performance but instead received a ten-minute homily. It was one of the shortest speeches of Douglass's life. "This is scarcely a day for prose," he began. "It is a day for poetry and song, a new song."[140]

Here was one of the greatest orators in the world, beginning a speech by saying it was no time for speeches! A speech could not convey the message and emotions he wanted to convey. It could not adequately capture the new age at hand. His newfound hope for the country had overwhelmed his faith in the power of stories.[141]

On New Year's Day 1863, Douglass gave an even shorter speech. The hundreds of celebrations throughout the North captured the sense of a new age, and Douglass was not alone in preferring music, poetry, and shouts of joy to lectures. In Boston three thousand people, including most of New England's literati, attended a jubilee concert at the Music Hall. Douglass preferred a less refined celebration at the nearby Tremont Temple, a Baptist church that stood a block from the Common. The Temple was one of the few integrated churches in Boston and it had a storied reputation among radicals. Almost every major abolitionist had spoken there, from William Lloyd Garrison and Wendell Phillips to John Brown and Gerrit Smith. Even Lincoln had lectured at the Temple, his western twang resounding off its walls in 1848 as he stumped for Zachary Taylor. Douglass had spoken at the Temple on numerous occasions, most recently two years ago, on the anniversary of John Brown's martyrdom. A mob had tried to prevent him from speaking but he had fought his way to the rostrum "like a trained pugilist" and delivered his eulogy.[142] If hatred had been unable to silence him then, now joy left him almost speechless.

Over three thousand black and white abolitionists met at the Temple in the morning. The black historian William Cooper Nell gave a lecture on the meaning of New Year's Day for slaves. Traditionally it marked the end of a week-long drinking binge and respite from work. It was also known as "Heartbreak Day" because of so many families being sold and separated. But henceforth New Year's Day would be invested with "imperishable glory in the calendar of time," Nell said.[143] Throughout the day there were numerous short speeches and music but no announcement of the final emancipation decree. Douglass wrapped up the afternoon session by saying that this moment represented a sharp break from the sins of the past. "We have had a period of darkness, but are now having the dawn of light, and are met today to celebrate it."[144]

In the evening there were more talks and
music and presentations as everyone waited
anxiously for word from Washington. At 11:00
p.m. Douglass said, "we won't go home till morning." He was feeling glum and starting to lose hope
all over again. Why was Lincoln *always* so tardy?
Then suddenly a messenger burst into the hall
and announced, "It is coming! It is on the wires."
The Temple erupted in cries of joy. "I never saw
enthusiasm before," Douglass said. "I never saw
joy before. We gave three cheers for Abraham
Lincoln and three cheers for almost everybody
else." And then Douglass spontaneously began
singing the somber, slow, and melodic "Blow Ye
the Trumpet, Blow," a millennialist hymn that
had been John Brown's favorite:[145]

> *Blow ye the trumpet, blow!*
> *The gladly solemn sound*
> *Let all the nations know,*
> *To earth's remotest bound:*
>
> *The year of jubilee is come!*
> *The year of jubilee is come!*
> *Return, ye ransomed sinners, home.*

With emancipation Douglass's attitude toward Lincoln suddenly and dramatically
changed. Never again would he so harshly crit-

icize the president, even though he continued to disagree with him on many things. He knew that the Proclamation was a revolutionary document that turned the war into a "contest of civilization against barbarism" rather than a struggle for territory. It acquired for him "a life and power far beyond its letter" and became another sacred text, which restored the Declaration to its rightful place at the center of the nation's laws. Henceforth, he said, January 1 and July 4 would rank as the twin birthdays of liberty.[146]

Time was what Lincoln needed. Everything was moving too quickly, jumbling and spinning out of control. His entire world seemed to be a swirl of constant motion, and he wanted everyone in the country, especially Southerners, to gain control of themselves and just *slow down*.

He set an example of a statesman who was in control of time and his emotions. During the four months between his election and his arrival in Washington he acted as though he had all the time in the world. In fact, he and Mary treated this period like a presidential honeymoon. Mary went to New York City and then St. Louis to purchase a new wardrobe. Since her husband would soon be making $25,000 per year, five times more than his previous average annual salary, she no longer worried about prices. She loved shopping and the attention she received from the merchants, who were all too eager to extend her credit and convince her to buy another dress.[147]

Lincoln remained in Springfield and entertained the swarm of visitors with tall tales, bad jokes, and quotes from Aesop. Countless office-seekers heard his Irish bull story about Patrick and his new boots: "I shall never git em on," said Patrick, "till I wear em a day or two, and stretch em a little." And then Lincoln would slap his thigh or "draw his knees up almost to his face" and laugh uproariously, his high-pitched chortle echoing through the Springfield state-house.[148]

He even took time out from work to visit his stepmother, Sarah Bush Johnston Lincoln, whom he hadn't seen in years. She lived in Coles County in the southeastern part of the state, and to get there he had to travel on a cold and filthy freight train and then a one-horse buggy. Sarah cried when she saw him. She hadn't wanted him to run for president and now worried that "something would happen to him" at Washington. "No No Mama," he assured her. "Trust in the Lord and all will be well. We will see each other again soon."[149]

He started growing a beard in response to Republican advisers and well-wishers, though initially it looked like deformed muttonchops since he had so few whiskers on his cheeks. What partly convinced him to try the new hirsute look was a letter he received a few weeks before the election from eleven-year-old Grace Bedell of Westfield, New York, near Lake Erie. Grace promised to get her brothers to vote for Lincoln if he grew a beard. "You would look a great deal better for your face is so thin," Grace wrote. "All the ladies like whiskers and they would tease their husbands to vote for you and then you would be President." Lincoln was touched by Grace's suggestion and responded with a personal note. He told her that unfortunately he had no daughters but that he had three sons, one seventeen, one nine, and the youngest seven. "As to the whiskers, having never worn any, do you not think people would call it a piece of silly affectation if I were to begin it now?"[150] He heeded her advice anyway. Perhaps he thought that whiskers gave him a more venerable look. Or maybe he agreed with Grace that his face was too thin.

Numerous people commented on Lincoln's levity during the months between election and

taking office. Many visitors could not understand it or concluded that he was unfit to govern the country. But humor was Lincoln's way
of dealing with a grave crisis.

During dinner one night at a restaurant, a
young admirer came up to Lincoln and told
him that he was willing to lay down his life to
protect him. Lincoln smiled and then launched
into a story about a soldier whose sisters em-
broider a belt for him, with the motto "Victory
or death" on it.

"No, no," the soldier says. "Don't put it quite
that strong. Put it 'Victory or get hurt pretty
bad.' "[151]

Lincoln also used humor on politicians who
called on him. The former governor of Kentucky
traveled to Springfield to urge him to concede
to secessionists' demands. Again Lincoln smiled
and then told him the fable from Aesop about
the lion who falls in love with the plowman's
daughter. Totally smitten, the lion asks for her
hand in marriage. The plowman consents if the
lion will rip out his teeth and remove his claws
to lessen his daughter's fright. The lion agrees,
but as soon as he removes his teeth and claws,
the plowman attacks him with a club and drives
him away. The Kentuckian liked the satire but
not the parallel between a club-wielding farmer
and slaveholders.[152]

Part of Lincoln's levity stemmed from his assumption that secessionists were bluffing and would soon return to the Union. Ever since the Missouri Compromise of 1820, slaveholders and their allies had strutted and bluffed their way around Washington until slavery had become a national institution and freedom a sectional luxury. In the face of numerous compromise plans swirling through Congress, and death threats that Lincoln ignored, he maintained a "stately silence," as Douglass phrased it, except for reassuring the South that he would not interfere with slavery in the slave states.[153]

In his "private and confidential" letters Lincoln abandoned the tone of levity. To Republican colleagues throughout the country he repeatedly said, "let there be no compromise on the question of *extending* slavery. If there be, all our labor is lost, and ere long, must be done again. . . . The tug has to come and better now than later."[154] The object of all the compromise plans was "to put us again on the high road to a slave empire."[155] Unless slavery were vigilantly contained, Southerners would once again try to conquer or annex vast new territories to satisfy their lust for the evil.

Lincoln had no problem offering other concessions to the South. He agreed to repeal personal liberty laws in Northern states that obstructed enforcement of the Fugitive Slave Act.[156] It was a large concession, for while he refused to interfere with slavery in Southern states, he was willing to curtail black freedom in Northern states. "As to fugitive slaves," he said, "I care but little." He even agreed to admit New Mexico as a slave state "if further extension were hedged against."[157]

These schemes and negotiations all took place in private and confidential letters. Publicly he presented himself as a model of the assured statesman waiting patiently for Southern tempers to subside.[158]

The closest Lincoln came to losing control during the secession crisis occurred as he prepared to leave Springfield for the White House. He secured the family trunks himself and labeled them A. LINCOLN, THE WHITE HOUSE, WASHINGTON, D.C., apparently oblivious to the fact that everyone knew exactly where he was going.[159] He had spent half his life in Springfield and here had risen from a poor, ignorant, and lonely young man into the first self-made president. Packing his belongings prompted a rush of emotions that made past and present suddenly seem like a chaotic swirl, like photos taken from a family album and tossed in the air.

Before leaving on February 11, two days after his fifty-second birthday, he said good-bye to his law partner William Herndon. Pointing up at the law shingle hanging outside their office, he said, "Let it hang there undisturbed." Then he lowered his voice and added, "Give our clients to understand that the election of a President makes no change in the firm of Lincoln and Herndon. If I live I'm coming back some time, and then we'll go right on practising law as if nothing had ever happened."[160]

He gave a farewell speech to his neighbors and became so choked up that he had to pause to collect himself. "To this place, and the kindness of these people, I owe every thing," he said. "Here I have lived a quarter of a century, and have passed from a young to an old man. Here my children have been born, and one is buried. I now leave, not knowing when, or whether ever, I may return, with a task before me greater than that which rested upon Washington. Without the assistance of that Divine Being, who ever attended him, I cannot succeed. With that assistance I cannot fail. . . . To His care commending you, as I hope in your prayers you will commend me, I bid you an affectionate farewell." He boarded the presidential train and never saw Springfield again.[161]

Lincoln's farewell speech reflected his growing faith in God as the fundamental source of value. His unqualified reverence for the law and

the Constitution as the *"political religion* of the
nation," as he had long ago phrased it, had been
shattered by Stephen Douglas and Roger Taney
and other leaders of the Slave Power. The laws
of nature and of nature's God now replaced
these more secular sources. But unlike Frederick Douglass, he generally did not define himself as a prophet heeding God's will, or even
claim to know precisely what He wanted. God
was inscrutable rather than indwelling. The
most one could hope for on earth was to discover signs of God's presence and to establish
a covenant (or sacred agreement) with Him.
By "trusting in Him who has never forsaken
this favored land," God would reciprocate this
trust by guiding the faithful toward righteousness.[162]

Lincoln hoped for a similar covenant between
his constituents and him. During the twelve-
day trip to Washington, the presidential train
stopped at every town and village, and Lincoln
would go out to the balcony of his car to give
a brief speech. He asked the people to stand by
him so long as he stood by his country and its
laws as he understood them.[163]

The Lincoln car was the most luxurious form
of transportation he (or almost anyone else)
had ever seen. An 8–by–40–foot luxury coach,
it became a model for first-class business travel

after the Civil War. It looked like a long, narrow apartment, with an entrance and hallway at one end, an enclosed master bedroom, bunk beds for young Willie and Tad, a sofa bed for Robert, who was a student at Harvard, and a large sitting room at the other end, with a door that led out to the balcony where Lincoln greeted his constituents.[164]

Lincoln spent more time with his family on the train than he had since his marriage. Robert, who had often felt abandoned by his father, loved the attention. He lost his shyness, flirted with the girls, drank too much wine (without his father knowing it), "and even took a turn at driving the locomotive."[165] Perhaps because he drank too much, he shirked the one duty his father had asked of him, which caused Abraham to lose his temper and yell at him.

Lincoln had put Robert in charge of guarding the bag containing the draft of his Inaugural Address. He had labored more tediously over it than anything else he had ever written, and had printed copies to circulate among Republicans for suggestions. During an overnight layover, Robert stupidly gave the bag to a hotel porter, who tossed it on a pile of unclaimed luggage. Lincoln frantically waded through the bags and fortunately found the satchel with all the copies intact.[166]

On February 16 the presidential train stopped at Westfield, New York. Lincoln remembered that young Grace Bedell was from Westfield, and when he appeared on the balcony he told the crowd that he had received a letter from her three months earlier. "It was a very pretty letter, and she advised me to let my whiskers grow, as it would improve my personal appearance," Lincoln said. "Acting partly on her suggestion, I have done so." He paused so that the crowd could admire his new beard. "And now," he continued, "if she is here, I would like to see her." A small boy who sat atop a fencepost "with his mouth and eyes both wide open" scanned the crowd and suddenly cried out, "there she is, Mr. Lincoln." He pointed to "a beautiful girl with black eyes who was blushing all over her fair face."[167]

Lincoln stepped down from the car, made his way over to where Grace was standing and blushing, and "gave her several hearty kisses." Then, amid the "yells of delight from the excited crowd, he bade her good-bye," and on he went to the next stop.[168]

The honeymoon ended in Baltimore, when Lincoln was informed of a plot to assassinate him. A Baltimore barber and a few rebel comrades planned to ambush him during the changeover to the Baltimore and Ohio line that went to Washington. On the advice of Allan Pinkerton and numerous other advisers, the president-elect snuck into the capital like a fugitive to thwart the would-be assassins.[169] When news got out that he had entered Washington at night and in disguise, many Northerners (with the notable exception of blacks) accused him of cowardice.

Meanwhile, Jefferson Davis had been inaugurated as president of the Confederacy a week earlier to great fanfare. And over the past three months, one congressman after another had stood up in the Capitol, resigned his seat, and announced his intention to secede—without anyone even arresting or detaining him.

Lincoln now had ten days to finish preparing his Inaugural Address, finalize a cabinet, meet hundreds of people, and figure out how to coax the rebels back into the Union without forsaking his pledge to prohibit the spread of slavery and seek its ultimate extinction. They were among the busiest ten days of his life to date.[170] He slept only a few hours each night, a practice that would become routine over the next four years, greatly exacerbating the aging process.

On his first day in Washington he met Stephen Douglas and a delegation of other Illinois politicians at Willard's Hotel, a large six-story building near the White House where the Lincolns stayed until inauguration. The meeting with his old rival was "peculiarly pleasant."[171] Lincoln had asked to see Douglas. He was hoping for his support. It was the first time in his political career that he and Douglas actually shared the same political strategy, in this case saving the Union. Suddenly Douglas was no longer a rival, and Lincoln felt somewhat unmoored, as though his political orbit of the past seven years had abruptly fragmented.

Lincoln circulated his Inaugural Address for suggestions. His aim was to placate the upper South,* those states that had so far remained in the Union. He also hoped to "cool passions and buy time."[172] In his draft he vowed to protect federal property, and he told rebels that the choice between peace and war lay in their hands. Overall, this first draft was far less conciliatory than the one he delivered.[173] He opposed congressional efforts to amend the Constitution, saying he was "not much impressed" with them. "I am, rather, for the old ship, and the chart of the old pilots," meaning a Constitution untampered by hysterical conciliators.[174] He vowed to *reclaim* federal forts that had been captured by rebels,

---

* Virginia, Maryland, Delaware, North Carolina, Tennessee, Kentucky, Arkansas, and Missouri.

rather than simply *protect* those forts still under Union control, as the final draft states. And he ended by contrasting his *sacred* duties with the *secular* ones of the rebels: "*You* have no oath registered in Heaven to destroy the government, while I shall have the most solemn one to 'preserve, protect, and defend' it. . . . With *you* and not with *me*, is the solemn question of 'Shall it be peace, or a sword?'"[175] He was treating the rebels with a firm but understanding hand.

Had Lincoln delivered this draft, Frederick Douglass would have been far more sympathetic to him and his dilemma.

A few colleagues offered suggestions, including the Missouri Republican Francis Blair Sr., his Springfield friend Orville Browning, and William Seward, who had agreed to serve as secretary of state. Blair loved the document. It reminded him of the firm hand of Andrew Jackson when he had stood up to South Carolina nullifiers years before. Browning found it "able, well considered, and appropriate" and recommended only one change. He urged Lincoln to delete his vow to reclaim the federal forts taken by rebels. "On principle the passage is right as it now stands," Browning wrote in the margin. "The fallen places ought to be reclaimed. But cannot that be accomplished" without broadcasting it in the Inaugural?[176]

It was Seward who had serious problems with the document. Although he considered its basic argument "strong and conclusive," he thought its tone far too strident and warned Lincoln that if he delivered it, Virginia and Maryland would immediately secede, leaving Washington surrounded.[177] Seward was not shy about his willingness to compromise. Since John Brown's raid on Harpers Ferry he had essentially abandoned the Republican platform of containing slavery. Now he simply wanted to pacify rebels and achieve a peaceful reunion. He was ready to sacrifice every piece of federal property to them, and even suggested threatening a war with Spain and France in order to defuse sectional tensions.[178]

On almost every line of Lincoln's draft Seward recommended changes. He was as aggressive with his quill as Preston Brooks had been with his cane. All told he proposed forty-nine changes, ranging from deleting or inserting one word to adding an entire paragraph. He told Lincoln to "strike out the whole sentence" that opposed a constitutional amendment protecting slavery, which Lincoln did.[179] And he wanted to soften the ending and suggested a final paragraph: "The mystic chords which, proceeding from so many battlefields and so many patriot graves, . . . will yet again harmonize in their ancient music when breathed upon by the guardian angel of the nation."[180]

Lincoln had a much better ear than Seward. He agreed to the new ending and borrowed many of Seward's words, but created a far more elegant plea for reunion that ignored the plight of blacks. Lincoln's "chorus of the Union" was still lily-white.[181] As Douglass noted, the beauty of the language masked the ugliness of its message.

Lincoln delivered his revised Inaugural beneath the portico of the Capitol, its still unfinished dome looming up behind him. A new bronze statue of liberty stood on the lawn facing the Capitol. She held a sword in one hand and a wreath of flowers in the other. The thousands of spectators gathered around the portico to hear Lincoln's address seemed to ignore her. She stood all alone, staring at their backs, like an orphan. She was waiting for the dome of the Capitol to be completed, where she would then find a home.[182]

Scores of rumors circulated that Lincoln would be killed before taking office or shot during the ceremony. Some men wagered bets about whether he would live to be inaugurated. One journalist traveling south from New York overheard some Southern ladies talking of assassination:

"I am glad Lincoln has not been killed," said one.

"Why so?" asked her friend.

"Because if he had been, Hannibal Hamlin [who had dark skin] would become President, and it would be a shame to have a mulatto at the head of the government."[183]

On March 2, two days earlier, Congress had passed the Thirteenth Amendment, guaranteeing slavery in the states forever. Lincoln felt he could support it because he had never sought to interfere with slavery in the slave states.[184]

Despite his efforts to placate the South in his Inaugural, rebels interpreted it as a declaration of war. One South Carolina editor used a racist epithet to characterize Lincoln. "The Ourang-Outang at the White House" had sounded "the tocsin of battle," which was also "the signal of our freedom," he declared. Another editor from Richmond said Lincoln's message "inaugurates civil war." Yet another told his fellow Virginians that they now must choose between "invasion by Lincoln's army or Jefferson Davis's."[185]

Seward's hope that a more conciliatory Inaugural Address would prevent Virginia and Maryland from seceding came to naught. Virginia seceded a week after Fort Sumter's bombing, and Maryland probably would have followed suit had not Lincoln boldly imposed martial law in the state to silence secessionists.* Here he took a cue from Southerners: during civil war, whether between North and South or between master and slave, the only way to maintain stability was to suspend basic freedoms.[186]

Stephen Douglas became an avid supporter of Lincoln. He stood near him during the Inaugural Address, and as Lincoln "fumbled awkwardly with his hat," he kindly held it for him. During the address Douglas frequently muttered his assent: "Good . . . That's so . . . No coercion . . . Good again." After Lincoln finished, he immediately congratulated him and then rigorously defended the speech. "He does not mean coercion," Douglas told one reporter. "He's all right." To another journalist who accused Lincoln of rescinding his platform by supporting the constitutional amendment, Douglas said, "Well, what of it? It shows that Mr. Lincoln has the nerve to say what is right, platform or no platform." He had urged Lincoln to support the amendment as soon as it passed Congress![187]

---

* Roger Taney declared Lincoln's suspension of the writ of habeas corpus unconstitutional, but Lincoln ignored the chief justice.

Douglas escorted Mrs. Lincoln to the Inaugural Ball, which was held in a new building on Judiciary Square. The ballroom had been decorated with flags from every state and brilliantly lit from five large gas chandeliers. At 11:00 p.m. the Marine Band began playing "Hail to the Chief" and Douglas marched with Mary "arm in arm." At midnight they danced the quadrille. Mary wore a new blue gown with a matching blue feather in her hair. Douglas and his wife, Adele, introduced her to some of the women in Washington society.[188]

On April 14, as telegraph dispatches flooded Washington with the news that Union troops had surrendered Fort Sumter, Stephen Douglas met with Lincoln at the White House for two hours. Their interview was marked by "a cordial feeling of a united, friendly, and patriotic purpose." Again the senator vowed to "stand by" the president. Lincoln showed him a draft of his proclamation to raise 75,000 volunteers. "I would make it 200,000," Douglas said. He was among the few who believed that it would be a long war. He never knew how long it would last, though, for a month later he died, partly of complications from heavy cigar-smoking and drinking. He was forty-eight years old.[189]

Douglas's friendship with Lincoln during his last months reflected the enormous bipartisan support among Northern whites who were eager to fight the rebels and save the Union. Lincoln could have raised 200,000 troops. But the reconciliation of these former rivals also reflected their shared terms for saving the Union. Slavery would not be affected and blacks would play no part in the Union army. Douglas was still the mouthpiece for bitterly racist whites who considered blacks subhuman and saw nothing wrong with slavery. And Lincoln, as an antislavery conservative, was horrified of social revolution and hoped to preserve the old hierarchies. As he put it in his annual message to Congress in December 1861, "In considering the policy to be adopted for suppressing the insurrection, I have been anxious and careful that the inevitable conflict for this purpose *shall not degenerate into a violent and remorseless revolutionary struggle.*"[190] The war focused solely on white men and their nation. Stephen Douglas could not have agreed more. And so in coming together, the two rivals ignored the very questions (slavery and race) over which they had fought for years.

No wonder, then, that Lincoln revoked John C. Frémont's emancipation proclamation in September 1861.[191] It threatened his vision of trying to save the Union. Most Republicans approved of Frémont's proclamation, including Orville

Browning, Lincoln's conservative friend from Illinois. It "was necessary and will do good," Browning told him. "It has the full approval of all loyal citizens of the West and North West."[192] And legally it was justified by international law and "the laws of war as acknowledged by all civilized nations."[193] Most Republicans had already come to believe, like Frederick Douglass, that saving the Union necessitated an emancipation policy.

Lincoln was hurt by Browning's response. Frémont's proclamation was clearly unconstitutional, he said. The recently passed Confiscation Act enabled generals to *confiscate* slaves, not free them. If Frémont needed slaves he could seize them "and use them; but when the need is past, it is not for him to fix their permanent future condition." Emancipation needed to be decided by lawmakers, not generals. More importantly, Frémont's proclamation would not *save* the government. "On the contrary it is itself the surrender of the government."[194]

Lincoln believed that any emancipation policy threatened border-state loyalty, especially Kentucky's. Frémont's proclamation may have been popular in *some* quarters, but Kentuckians were ready to secede over it. In fact Lincoln had heard that an entire company of Kentucky volunteers "threw down their arms and disbanded" after learning of Frémont's proclamation. Had he not revoked the proclamation, Kentucky rifles would be aimed at Washington, not the South. "I think to lose Kentucky is nearly the same as to lose the whole game," he told Browning. "Kentucky gone, we can not hold Missouri, nor, as I think, Maryland. These all against us, and the job on our hands is too large for us. We would as well consent to separation at once, including the surrender of this capitol."[195]

Lincoln was terrified of losing Kentucky. His fear sounded conspiratorial, a domino theory of the border states. If Kentucky went, then Missouri and Maryland, and the war would be lost. But he never explained exactly how secession in Kentucky would cause the same in Missouri and then Maryland. Nor did he mention how secession might affect Kentucky on the ground, especially given the intense guerrilla warfare raging there. His fear about Kentucky is striking when compared with the majority of Republican statesmen, from conservatives to radicals, who believed with Orville Browning that Frémont's proclamation "was necessary and will do good."

Lincoln's sensitivity to Kentuckians stemmed in part from close friends living there and regularly advising him. Of these, none was closer or more influential than Joshua Speed.

Speed was now a wealthy slaveowner and sometime slave trader. He had voted against Lincoln but their bonds of affection had not been severed and each had enormous respect for the other. Lincoln offered Speed a cabinet post, but Speed turned it down, partly because he wanted to stay in Kentucky. He served as Lincoln's ad hoc Kentucky adviser, writing frequently of the situation there and on occasion coming to Washington to consult with the president.

Speed was outraged with Frémont's proclamation and immediately urged Lincoln to revoke it. Not only was it unconstitutional, but it would incite a slave insurrection. "All of us who live in slave states, whether Union or loyal, have great fear of insurrection," he told Lincoln. Frémont's proclamation would incline all the slaves "to assert their freedom," causing "the women, whether loyal or not, and the whole community [to] suffer."[196] He was hinting of rape and plunder.

Speed was so distressed that he went days without eating and sleeping. It was as though he had just been told that a gang of rapists and murderers had been let loose in his community. If Frémont's proclamation were allowed to stand, it would "crush out every vestige of a Union party in the state," he warned. He and a handful of friends would be the only Union men left in the entire state. "Cruelty and crime would run riot in the land."[197] By invoking the specter of a slave insurrection, and the rape and plunder that went with it in the white imagination, Speed made clear to Lincoln that no virtuous citizen of Kentucky *or any other slave state* would tolerate an emancipation policy.[198]

Frémont's wife, Jessie, did her best to convince Lincoln to let her husband's proclamation stand. She was the daughter of Missouri senator Thomas Hart Benton and the most politically connected woman in the country. She had met nine previous presidents at the White House, including Andrew Jackson, who had tousled her hair as a girl, and she had been "a spy and a translator for two of Jackson's successors." She made a special trip to Washington from St. Louis and was hopeful that she could persuade Lincoln. After sending up her card asking when she could see the president, he replied, "Now, at once." It was 9:00 p.m. and she was exhausted but complied. When Lincoln saw her he silently nodded and failed to offer her a seat, "an insult they both understood." She handed him a letter from her husband explaining why his emancipation proclamation was a military and diplomatic necessity. Echoing Frederick Douglass, she said that a war for emancipation would deter Britain, France, and Spain from recognizing the Confederacy.[199]

Lincoln cut her off: "You are quite a female politician." Then he said that he had already made up his mind: General Frémont "should never have dragged the Negro into the war. It is a war for a great national object and the Negro has nothing to do with it."[200]

But every day "the Negro" forced himself into the war, demanding to be part of the "national object." Every day contrabands came into Union lines. Every day Union officers recognized the military necessity of freeing slaves and employing blacks. Every day Republicans, from the conservative to the radical, echoed Orville Browning in urging Lincoln and the administration to save the Union by emancipating slaves. And every day Frederick Douglass and black leaders spoke out in unison with white abolitionists, bearing witness to the fact that "the Negro" was inextricable from saving the Union. As Douglass phrased it, the destiny of the African American "*is* the destiny of America."[201] The wave of public sentiment for emancipation was slowly growing.

On top of this, the Confiscation Act passed on August 6, 1861, was ambiguous and needed clarification. The status of contrabands was vague. They were no longer slaves. "But were they free? The law did not say."[202]

In early 1862 Lincoln finally began to change his views about emancipation. Indeed, he experienced the equivalent of a conversion. Perhaps it started with his son Willie's death in February. In the midst of a gala to show off Mary's expensive White House renovations, Willie suddenly became feverish. It was probably typhoid caused by the city's sewage system. Their youngest son, Tad, also came down with a fever but quickly recovered as Willie's condition steadily worsened. For two weeks Lincoln stayed with his son, putting cold compresses on his forehead and transacting virtually no business. On February 20 Willie died. "Well, Nicolay, my boy is gone—he is actually gone," Lincoln told his secretary. Then he broke down and cried. "He was too good for this earth . . . but then we loved him so," he mourned. Mary was so devastated that Lincoln worried about her health as well. She took to her bed for three weeks, and for months "the mere mention of Willie's name sent her into paroxysms of weeping." She cloaked herself in black mourning dresses and began inviting Spiritualists to the White House so that she could communicate with her dead son.[203]

Perhaps Willie's death fueled Lincoln's

sympathies for parents throughout the North who had lost a son. Every week the war got bloodier and the death lists in the daily papers grew longer. Almost everyone knew of someone who had been killed or wounded in the conflict, and yet Lincoln had been waging a war that sought "minimal disruption of civilian life." It was a self-defeating policy, for by its very nature civil war disrupted civilian life. The need to emancipate the slaves *in order* to save the Union weighed upon Lincoln, a heavy burden.[204]

He turned to God for help, relying "upon the Divine arm, and seeking light from above." He hoped that he "might be an instrument in God's hands of accomplishing a great work," as he told a delegation of Quakers who urged him to issue an emancipation decree.[205] And he continued to quote *Hamlet*: "There's a divinity that shapes our ends, / Rough-hew them how we will." Lincoln never described his transformation as a conversion experience. Rather, he said that he underwent a "process of crystallization" in his religious beliefs.[206]

In March 1862 Lincoln drafted a proposal for "the gradual abolishment of slavery." His plan followed the tradition of abolition that Northern states had adopted since the Revolutionary War. Emancipation would require the approval of voters; it would free the slaves over the course of a generation or so; and it would compensate slaveowners for the loss of their property. "In my judgment, gradual and not sudden emancipation is better for all," Lincoln said.[207] His proposal also constituted sound military policy, for if the border states accepted it, they would no longer be tempted to join the Confederacy. He hoped to buy border-state loyalty, and the costs of doing so would be less than "three months of war expenditures."[208]

He called Charles Sumner to the White House and showed him his proposal. "I want you to read my message," he told him in an eager voice. "I want to know how you like it. I am going to send it" to Congress today. Sumner was so excited that he read the document over and over until Lincoln said, "There, now, you've read it enough, run away. I must send it in today."[209] Congress immediately adopted it.

To Frederick Douglass, Lincoln's proposal was so conservative and had such little chance of being adopted that he dismissed it. Slaveholders were totally opposed to freeing their slaves, even with the inducement of money. This was because slaves generated far higher rates of return than stocks, bonds, or real estate. And it was hard to satisfy one's sexual lust on a stock

certificate. As Douglass predicted, none of the
border states acted on Lincoln's proposal.

In April the Republican Congress, apparently
inspired by Lincoln's gradual abolition plan,
went a step further and passed an emancipation act for the District of Columbia. Lincoln
was not entirely satisfied with the bill, for it *instantly* (rather than gradually) liberated three
thousand slaves, and it was forced upon the
District, without the consent of its voters. But
it adhered to Lincoln's cherished "principles of
compensation and colonization," as he said. It
paid slaveholders $300 per slave and allocated
$100,000 to ship them to Central America, and
so he signed the bill.[210]

In May Lincoln revoked General David Hunter's emancipation proclamation partly because
it violated *all* of Lincoln's principles of emancipation: it instantly freed slaves; it neither compensated owners nor allowed them a say in the
matter; and it did not come with a commitment
to colonization.[211] In revoking Hunter's decree
Lincoln pleaded with citizens of the border
states to adopt his proposal of compensated
emancipation. Doing so would *preserve* stability, he said, for it would bring a swift end
to the war and introduce freedom slowly and
gently. Masters would receive just recompense,
and blacks could be sent to South America. The

change contemplated by his plan "would come gently as the dews of heaven, not rending or wrecking anything," Lincoln emphasized. "Will you not embrace it?"[212] If not, he would not be able to help in the future, he implied. Social revolution and immediate abolition were upon the nation, and he was out of step with his party in seeking gradual change.[213]

Then on July 22 Congress formally requested Lincoln's support in seizing rebel property and freeing the slaves. The Second Confiscation Act called on the president to issue a public warning to rebels, which would offer them a sixty-day grace period to return to the Union. If they refused, all their property would be subject to seizure, and indeed the president would be *obligated* to seize it.[214] In a separate section the act said that confiscated slaves would be "forever free," but it was unclear whether a presidential proclamation to *seize* rebel property also implied *emancipation*.[215]

Lincoln almost vetoed the Second Confiscation Act on the grounds that it was unconstitutional. What most troubled him was the emancipation clause, but his objection to it stemmed primarily from its confusing language. In fact the entire bill had been horribly written. After working with a senator to revise some of the bad language, Lincoln signed it into law. But he took the unusual step of sending Congress a long critique, a kind of presidential amicus brief.[216]

Five days later, on July 22, he drafted an emancipation proclamation. Following the terms of the Second Confiscation Act, he gave rebels sixty days to return to the Union. If they complied, he would encourage them to free their slaves by offering compensated and gradual abolition, similar to his offer to the border states. But if rebels persisted in their "insurrection" and "treason," all their property would be subject to seizure, and on January 1, 1863, their slaves would become "forever free." He effectively held up an olive branch with gradual abolition in one hand, war and immediate abolition in the other, and he told the rebels to choose, much as he had done in the first draft of his Inaugural Address.[217]

Lincoln then asked his cabinet what they thought of his emancipation proclamation. Members were divided, some urging him to issue it right away and others worried that it would cost Republicans votes in the fall elections. Once again Lincoln followed the advice of William Seward, who told him to wait for a decisive military victory before issuing it. Emancipation should reflect Union strength, not weakness, Seward said.[218] And so Lincoln tucked the document away in his desk drawer.

Instead, on July 25 he issued a "Proclamation to Suppress Insurrection." It adhered to the Second Confiscation Act in that it gave rebels sixty days to return to the Union "on pain of the forfeitures and seizures" of their property.[219] But the document said nothing about emancipation. To Frederick Douglass and other abolitionists, it left the status of slaves in a limbo of half-freedom. And it said nothing about employing blacks in the army.

Elsewhere Lincoln agreed with Congress that blacks should be employed as laborers in the army, but he vehemently opposed arming blacks as soldiers. His views on this issue had not changed since the beginning of the war, and he again warned of border-state rebellion if blacks were allowed to shoot whites. "The nation cannot afford to lose Kentucky at this crisis," he said in August 1862. "To arm the negroes would turn 50,000 bayonets from the loyal border states against us that were for us."[220] What he did not say was that arming blacks would turn 150,000 more bayonets against the rebels.[221]

Lincoln spent the summer of 1862 waiting and praying for a Union victory, which would enable him to make public his intention to emancipate the slaves. He repeatedly urged the arrogant George McClellan to attack Lee's army and force a showdown. But McClellan, a meticulous organizer, was a terrible strategist. He grossly exaggerated the strength of his enemy and showed more respect to rebels than to Republicans. For example, he refused to confiscate Mrs. Robert E. Lee's house for a field hospital, prompting the army's physician to ask Lincoln, "Are our brave soldiers to die off like rotten sheep because General McClellan chooses to protect the grounds of a rebel?"[222] McClellan even ignored some of Lincoln's orders. His troops loved him, but this was partly because he protected them from fighting while also telling them how brave they were.

On August 14, Lincoln invited a delegation of Washington, D.C., blacks to the White House to promote his plan for colonization. It was the first time a group of blacks met with a president on "a matter of public interest." The Reverend James Mitchell arranged the meeting. Mitchell was from Indiana, he and Lincoln had been active in Midwestern colonization societies, and Lincoln had recently appointed him commissioner of emigration. Now that emancipation was becoming a reality, Lincoln hoped to convince Washington blacks to accept the government's offer to send them to Central America.[223]

The delegation did not include a single black leader, though press reports ignored this point. In fact, four of the five men were recently freed slaves and probably illiterate. The selection was in keeping with Lincoln's purpose. He did not want a discussion. He wanted an opportunity to speak to blacks like a teacher lecturing obedient students in order to enlighten them on the virtues of colonization.[224] Frederick Douglass was the last person he wanted at such a meeting, for he would have challenged Lincoln on every point.

Many blacks endorsed the idea of emigration and agreed with Lincoln that in America blacks and whites could not live together harmoniously. The black leader Henry Highland Garnet supported Lincoln's vision of colonization as "the most humane, and merciful movement which this or any other administration has proposed for the benefit of the enslaved."[225] But unlike Lincoln, black emigrationists had essentially abandoned their faith in America as a democratic nation.

The meeting was a success in the sense that Lincoln's lecture was widely circulated and discussed in the black community. Reactions to it were divided, but opponents "were far more numerous and certainly more vocal," prompting numerous protest meetings in Washington and other Northern cities.[226]

Perhaps Lincoln also hoped that the meeting would make emancipation more palatable to the border states.[227] If so, he knew he was fighting an uphill battle. Every time he had proposed gradual and compensated emancipation with colonization, slaveholders and border-state representatives had rejected his plan outright.

On August 22 Lincoln issued his most important statement to date about emancipation. It was in response to an editorial by the Republican Horace Greeley entitled "The Prayer of Twenty Millions." Greeley spoke on behalf of Northerners and took Lincoln to task for ignoring "the emancipating provisions" of the Second Confiscation Act and heeding border-state politicians.[228]

Lincoln responded with a forthright enunciation of his policy. "My paramount object in this struggle *is* to save the Union, and is *not* either to save or to destroy slavery," he wrote. "What I do about slavery, and the colored race, I do because I believe it helps to save the Union."[229] It was a sincere letter, as Lincoln later said, and consistent with everything he had said and done.[230]

Frederick Douglass published Lincoln's reply

to Greeley after the Emancipation Proclamation came out, and he urged his readers to read it again. "In it are stated in the most clear and concise words the reasons for issuing the late Proclamation," Douglass said. Lincoln had finally recognized that saving the Union required emancipation.[231]

In mid-September Lincoln got the battle he had been waiting for. Lee's invasion of Maryland would finally force a major showdown with McClellan. Lincoln was still unsure about issuing his proclamation. He wished he knew what God wanted: "In great contests each party claims to act in accordance with the will of God. Both *may* be, and one *must* be wrong. God can not be *for*, and *against* the same thing at the same time. In the present civil war it is quite possible that God's purpose is something different from the purpose of either party."[232]

He especially wanted to know the will of God in the matter of emancipation. *"If I can learn what it is I will do it!"* he declared. But God remained inscrutable, since these were not "the days of miracles."[233] And so he searched for a *sign* of God's will. With the news of Lee's invasion, one suddenly appeared. As he told his cabinet, he "made a vow, a covenant, that if God gave us the victory in the approaching battle, he would consider it an indication of Divine will, and that it was his duty to move forward in the cause of emancipation."[234]

On September 17 McClellan declared a tenuous victory over Lee at Antietam, which blunted the Confederacy's invasion threat. Five days later, on September 22, Lincoln called his cabinet together and announced his intention to issue his Emancipation Proclamation.

Before showing his cabinet the document, he read them a story from a new collection by the humorist Artemus Ward. Evidently he wanted to add levity to this momentous event.[235] The sketch he recited, "High-Handed Outrage at Utica," is written in first-person dialect. A showman goes to Utica, New York, to display his wax figures of the Last Supper. One young man after seeing the arrangement begins pummeling Judas Iscariot.

"Sez I, 'You egrejus ass, that air's a wax figger—a representashun of the false 'Postle.'

"Sez he, 'That's all very well for you to say, but I tell you, old man, that Judas Iscarrot can't show hisself in Utiky with impunerty by a darn site!' with which observashun he kaved in Judassis hed."[236]

The story richly draws attention to someone who speaks with a provincial accent and confuses a sacred sign for the real thing. Lincoln was humorously warning his cabinet, and himself, about the dangers of presuming to know God's will.

Having told his cabinet the parable, Lincoln showed them his preliminary Emancipation Proclamation. Dated September 22, it encouraged colonization of freed blacks and compensated emancipation in the border states, reflecting his conservative approach to emancipation. But it also declared that on January 1, 1863, the slaves of all rebels "shall be then, thenceforward, and forever free."[237] The Second Confiscation Act's sixty-day grace period for rebels to return to the Union was now over.

It is richly symbolic that the three most important documents on emancipation written by Lincoln in 1862 were all dated on the twenty-second day of a month: the first draft of his Emancipation Proclamation on July 22; his reply to Horace Greeley on August 22; and his preliminary Emancipation Proclamation on September 22. As everyone knew, the man who had presided over the nation's *first* revolution and had publicly freed his slaves in his will as a symbolic gesture of voluntary and gradual abolition, George Washington, was also born on the twenty-second (of February, 1732). Perhaps Lincoln was paying tribute to Washington in these three documents by finally turning the war into a *second* revolution that would pursue the ideals set forth in the first one.[238]

Frederick Douglass was not the only one who worried that Lincoln would not issue the final Proclamation. Harriet Beecher Stowe did not attend any New Year's celebrations owing to her suspicions that Lincoln would "put off or evade the proclamation." Lydia Maria Child thought the president was under the spell of William Seward, whom she called "a snake" and a "crooked and selfish hypocrite" who could not be trusted. And Samuel Gridley Howe, whose wife, Julia Ward, had turned the John Brown song into "The Battle Hymn of the Republic," also worried. "The President has set his face steadily Zionward, though he is as yet rather ashamed of his Lord," she said.[239]

But Lincoln never looked back. "I may advance slowly," he said. "But I don't walk backward." In November he told some Kentuckians that he would "rather die than take back a word of the Proclamation."[240]

The final Proclamation reflected Lincoln's continued evolution on emancipation. It no longer mentioned colonization and explicitly called on blacks to serve in the armed forces, though not as soldiers. Lincoln had not abandoned colonization, nor his faith in gradual, compensated, and voluntary emancipation. But there was nothing gradual or gentle about this document. Its aim was to crush the rebellion and its unintended consequence was social revolution. It declared all slaves in rebel territories immediately and forever free. It defended the emancipating provisions of the Second Confiscation Act. And it explicitly relied on the war powers clause of the Constitution. Emancipation was a "fit and necessary war measure for suppressing said rebellion."[241] His use of the war powers clause was consistent with his understanding of rebellion. He had never dignified rebels by calling them Confederates or a government. The closest he came was to use the term "so-called Confederacy," since he considered them anarchists and traitors. The Emancipation Proclamation enabled Lincoln and his generals to fight the rebels with both hands, as Frederick Douglass phrased it, and prosecute them as traitors.

On New Year's Day almost every government officer, including the diplomatic corps in their gold-braided uniforms, came to the White House for a reception. Lincoln shook hands almost continuously for three hours and his arm was so stiff that his hand began to shake when he held up the pen to sign the Proclamation. "I never in my life felt more certain that I was doing right, than I do in signing this paper," he said. Then he joked that people would see a trembling hand in his signature and assume that he "has some compunctions." After signing it he gave his pen, slightly dented with teeth marks, to the Massachusetts Historical Society for preservation.[242]

Outside, blacks and whites gathered together in crowds along Pennsylvania Avenue and listened as preachers read them the Proclamation. "Men squealed, women fainted, dogs barked, white and colored people shook hands, songs were sung," the black minister Henry Turner said. "It was indeed a time of times and a half time. Nothing like it will ever be seen again in this life." For countless people that day, national ideals and scriptural prophecies were being fulfilled. The line between present and future, heaven and earth, seemed suddenly to vanish.[243]

In summarizing the evolution of his thinking about emancipation, Lincoln said that he had always been firmly antislavery: "If slavery is not wrong, nothing is wrong." But unlike John Quincy Adams, Frederick Douglass, Charles Sumner, and many others, he did not believe that the presidency gave him the "unrestricted right" to act on that judgment, even during civil war. Proclaiming freedom became lawful only by "becoming indispensable to the preservation of the Constitution." For over a year he hadrevoked emancipation proclamations because he did not think they were "indispensable necessities" to saving the Union. He emphasized that he had no control over the events that led to emancipation. "I claim not to have controlled events, but confess plainly that events have controlled me."[244] He might also have quoted Edmund Burke, the shrewd critic of revolutions, who had said that the leader of a nation "must oftentimes be content to follow."[245]

It is a rich and wonderful irony that a *conservative* Republican would preside over the most radical transformation of the nation's history. Frederick Douglass was not the only one who understood this. No less an authority on radicalism than Karl Marx emphasized the revolutionary nature of Lincoln's Emancipation Proclamation. Writing from Vienna, he called it "the most important document of American history since the founding of the Union, a document that breaks away from the old American Constitution. . . . Never yet has the New World scored a greater victory than in this instance, [when] *ordinary* people of goodwill can carry out tasks which the Old

World would have to have a *hero* to accomplish."[246] It is a strange convergence of Marx and Lincoln. But an even stranger one, in the form of an interracial friendship, was soon to come.

FIVE

Friends

Forgive, I pray you, the transgression
of your brothers and their sin, because
they did evil to you.

—GENESIS 50:17

IN EARLY AUGUST 1864 Lincoln looked like a man defeated. There was a "tired spot" in his eyes and his tall gaunt frame seemed ready to collapse from the burden of war.[1] The news had been bleak all summer. Grant's star had fallen since his stunning victory at Vicksburg and now many called him a "bloody-handed butcher." Mired in the Wilderness campaign, he had vowed to "fight it out on this line, if it takes all summer." But he had recently lost forty-four thousand men in less than a month, a staggering figure that forced newspapers to print "extras" of the casualty lists.[2]

At a June fund-raiser for soldiers, Lincoln tried to rally the nation. "War, at the best, is terrible, and this war of ours, in its magnitude and in its duration, is one of the most terrible. . . . It has carried mourning to almost every home, until it can almost be said that the 'heavens are hung in black.' " He promised to vanquish the rebels "if it takes three years more"; this did not inspire confidence.[3]

A daring attack on Washington further shook Union confidence. In July 1864 Confederate general Jubal Early's troops had come within five miles of the White House and burned down the Silver Spring home of Postmaster General Montgomery Blair. During the raid on Washington, Lincoln visited Camp Stevens just outside the city to see what combat looked like. Wearing his signature stovepipe hat, he looked over the parapet as bullets whistled by. He seemed to be courting death. The veteran soldier and future Supreme Court justice Oliver Wendell Holmes Jr. took him for a naïve civilian and yelled, "Get down, you damn fool, before you get shot!"[4]

Washington's hospitals choked with disease and death, and the stream of ambulances coming into the city caused traffic jams. That August Walt Whitman tried to capture the "terrible realities" of hospital life by focusing on the fate of a young Wisconsin man, small and bearded, "a splendid soldier" and "almost an ideal American." The man was a veteran of three years with only a few days to go before being discharged. While bringing in a wounded sergeant during a skirmish, he was shot in the knee. His leg was amputated and an infection set in. "Today the doctor says I must die," he wrote in his diary; "all is over with me—ah, so young to die."[5]

Even Lincoln's sense of humor turned morbid that August. According to one anecdote, he went for a walk in Lafayette Park and stopped at the bronze statue of Andrew Jackson astride his upreared horse. A thin, hungry-looking man approached and, not recognizing the president, begged for money. Lincoln asked him why he didn't join the army. "They won't let me in," the man said. "I'd be glad enough to die for my country, sir, if they would give me a chance."

Lincoln said he could help. He took out a piece of paper and wrote, "The bearer is anxious to go to the front and die for his country. Can't you give him a chance?" Then he sealed it in an envelope and told the man to take it to the local recruiting office. The man disappeared and Lincoln never heard from him again.[6]

The story, though apocryphal, captures the state of the Union in early August 1864. Volunteers had dried up despite Lincoln's call for another 500,000 men. The martial spirit had vanished from popular songs and was replaced by the elegiac: "We are tired of war on the old camp ground, / Many are dead and gone." The Treasury Department had spent all its gold, causing greenbacks to fall to forty cents on the dollar. And everywhere people were clamoring for peace.[7]

Even loyal Lincoln men found it hard to keep the faith. They thought he would lose his bid for reelection in November owing to military losses coupled with his insistence on making emancipation "a fundamental article in any negotiation for peace." If he had been too slow to embrace abolition in the first seventeen months of war, he was now too firmly attached to it, most Northerners said. "A stiff upper lip can be maintained these days only by the liveliest faith, such as removes mountains," wrote one supporter.[8]

Lincoln felt sure he would lose reelection. "I am going to be beaten, and unless some great change takes place *badly* beaten," he said.[9] He was being attacked from both sides. The ranks of antiwar Democrats, known as "Copperheads," burgeoned.[10] They demanded peace immediately at any price, which would almost certainly leave slavery intact and grant amnesty to all rebels. Copperhead newspapers, some subsidized by rebel spies, pandered to American prejudice in their effort to end the war and preserve slavery. "Tens of thousands of white men must yet bite the dust to allay the negro mania of the President," said one editorial. And more than a few soldiers felt they were fighting and dying "for a nigger."[11]

Race had become a central issue in the campaign. Democratic editors coined the term "miscegenation" (race-mixing) and accused Republicans of championing interracial marriages and cohabitation and thus polluting the white race. In one widely reprinted political cartoon, Lincoln appears with blacks and other radicals in a park and bows politely to the black lover (or fiancée) of Charles Sumner. "I shall be proud to number among my intimate friends any member of [your] family," he tells her (see figure 16).[12]

Lincoln and Frederick Douglass were also intimate friends, Copperheads accused. Democrats exploited Lincoln's White House meeting with Douglass from a year earlier. They quoted Douglass as saying "the President of the United States [had] received a black man at the White House just as one gentleman received another."[13] Had Democrats known about his relationship with Ottilie Assing, they no doubt would have created a cartoon depicting them at a White House soiree. Stephen Douglas's race-baiting had been mild by comparison. With slavery in its death throes, racism reached new levels of intensity to maintain white supremacy.

While Democrats assaulted Lincoln from the

right, members of his own party were abandoning him from the left. At the end of May 1864 radical Republicans formed a new Radical Democratic Party and nominated John C. Frémont for president and Thomas Cochrane, the nephew of Gerrit Smith, as his running mate.[14]

What prompted the defection was Lincoln's Reconstruction plan, which radicals considered too lenient. It promised amnesty to all rebels except for a few high-ranking officers and allowed states to reenter the Union if only 10 percent of the voters swore an oath of allegiance to the government. These terms were consistent with Lincoln's desire to avoid uprooting society. If there must be a revolution, it should not be too radical and needed to be controlled; otherwise a counterrevolution would ensue. Union-occupied Louisiana offered a test case for Lincoln's lenient Reconstruction policy. To him and his commander Nathaniel Banks, the transition from slave to wage labor had been comparatively smooth and successful.[15]

Radicals disagreed. They called Banks "a born slave-driver" and argued that Lincoln's model of Reconstruction in Louisiana put "all power in the hands of an unchanged white race."[16] While black laborers were nominally free, their status most closely resembled that of serfs. They were tied to the land and could not leave the plantation without a pass. They had to work as wage laborers for whites, with wages capped at $10 per month. While they could choose their employer, they were bound to one-year contracts that required "faithful service" and "perfect subordination" to their employer.[17] The laws thus prevented them from carving out forty acres for themselves with a mule and living independently as subsistence farmers, which some radicals encouraged.

In July radical Republicans in Congress passed an alternative plan for Reconstruction. Called the Wade-Davis bill, it required over 50 percent of voters to swear loyalty before a state could reenter the Union. It restricted suffrage only to those men who could take an "ironclad oath" saying they had never aided the rebellion. And it denied blacks the vote to satisfy congressional moderates and conservatives. Lincoln vetoed it.[18]

Debates over Reconstruction divided the Republican Party and would remain a major source of contention for the next twelve years. Republicans could agree on only two aspects of Reconstruction: a constitutional amendment abolishing slavery; and unconditional surrender of the Confederacy. Conservatives wanted the president to control a smooth and quick reunion but a slow transition to black freedom, with generous terms for the traitors. Radicals wanted Congress presiding over the South's future, granting blacks immediate freedom and stripping rebels of power.

The Frémont platform went even further than the Wade-Davis bill in securing black rights. It sought to "secure to all men absolute equality before the law."[19] It called for redistributing land to freedmen formerly owned by rebels. And it criticized Lincoln's willingness to suspend habeas corpus and throw in jail editors sympathetic to the rebels. This last plank was a cheap shot, however, for Frémont and other radicals felt no compunction declaring martial law in order to silence rebels and their sympathizers.

Frémont's platform looked a lot like the Radical Abolition Party platform of 1855 in its egalitarianism. Understandably, Frederick Douglass endorsed Frémont, although he did not attend the nominating convention. He was sharply critical of Lincoln's Reconstruction plan. Since it required only one-tenth of the whites in a rebel state to declare their loyalty to the Union in order to reorganize their government, it contradicted the very idea of democracy.[20] Moreover, Lincoln's silence on black suffrage suggested to Douglass that the president opposed it. This was shameful, he said; blacks were men enough to fight and die for their country but not to vote in it! He was impressed with Frémont's platform of "perfect equality" before the law, including suffrage for black men and retaliation against rebels for enslaving and murdering black prisoners of war.[21]

These divisions in the North profoundly threatened the war effort. After three years of bloodshed and roughly 200,000 Northern deaths, military victory now hinged on an election. The Republican Party had effectively split, and Democrats would have their nominating convention at the end of August. If their candidate won, as Lincoln and most Republicans now believed, the rebels would effectively win the war.

Amid these divisions, Lincoln understood as never before that the fate of the Union hinged around the role of blacks. He had publicly acknowledged that "the emancipation policy and the use of colored troops constitute the heaviest blow yet dealt to the rebellion." Crucial military victories could not have been achieved "but for the aid of black soldiers."[22] Perhaps blacks could help him out of his current predicament. And if they could not save the Union, perhaps they could help him secure emancipation. He was also open to alternative Reconstruction plans (though nothing so radical as Frémont's), which could defuse infighting among Republicans.[23]

On August 10, with these issues on his

mind, Lincoln met with John Eaton, an earnest
young Dartmouth-trained minister. Eaton had
achieved great success supervising freedmen
at Davis Bend, Mississippi, a 400–square-mile
peninsula south of Vicksburg that Grant had
confiscated from Jefferson Davis's family. Grant
had great faith in Eaton and had hoped Davis
Bend would "become a Negro paradise." In this
he was not far wrong, for blacks thrived there,
growing corn, vegetables, and cotton for the
Union army. The community offered a wonderful alternative to Louisiana as a model for Reconstruction.[24]

Eaton's job was essentially that of engineer.
He secured the land at the Bend for the freedmen, created a "self-directed labor and enterprise" system, as he called it, and then made
adjustments as necessary.[25] The freedmen controlled their own community based on Eaton's
design. They worked as independent farmers,
with the more experienced supervising the novices. They presided over their own court and
justice system. And Eaton had started schools.

Davis Bend was more productive than any
other plantation in the Mississippi Valley, Eaton
told Lincoln. William Wells Brown, a black abolitionist and friend of Douglass's, had visited
the community in July and called it "a sort of
earthly paradise for colored refugees."[26] And

Figure 16. "Miscegenation," an anti-Lincoln Democratic political cartoon. *(Library of Congress)*

freedmen elsewhere in the Mississippi Valley were so impressed that they hoped to start a new colony using Davis Bend as the blueprint.

Lincoln was thrilled with Eaton's report, and over the next week the two men met frequently to discuss the nature and destiny of the freedmen.[27] Eaton agreed with Lincoln's belief that "negroes, like other people, act upon motives."[28] They would aid whites if whites helped them. And the sooner blacks in the South could secure their freedom, the faster they could aid the Union, Lincoln told him.

Then Lincoln asked Eaton if there were a way to tap into blacks' "grapevine telegraph" in order to urge them to leave the plantations and "seek the protection of our armies."[29] Such a move would greatly strengthen Union forces and destroy the source of rebel labor. It might even prevent a negotiated settlement that would leave countless blacks still in bondage.

Eaton had no idea how to access this strangely effective source of black communication. But he was struck with how accurately Lincoln understood "the situation in the South."[30]

Then Lincoln "alluded to John Brown's raid" on Harpers Ferry.[31] He said that he had opposed Brown's method and his timing, since people had associated Brown with Republicans in order to discredit them. (Lincoln obviously had no idea that Brown's method and timing had together helped him get elected.) But now that the war was upon them, Lincoln added, perhaps they could find a way to borrow from Brown in order to free more slaves and aid the Union. But he didn't elaborate.

Frederick Douglass also came up in their conversation. Lincoln mentioned his critics "with the utmost frankness." This prompted Eaton to describe a recent talk he had heard by Douglass, an unsparing detractor.[32]

Eaton had met with Douglass a few weeks earlier in Toledo, Ohio, where he had stopped to visit his brother on his way to Washington.

Hearing that Douglass was scheduled to speak in Toledo, Eaton attended and afterward the two men "found much to talk about."[33]

In his Toledo speech Douglass attacked Lincoln's Reconstruction plan for being too lenient and ignoring the issue of black suffrage.[34] And he was furious with the president for not extracting eye-for-eye retribution against rebels whose policy was to murder or enslave captured black soldiers. A year earlier when Douglass had met Lincoln at the White House for the first time, Lincoln had promised retribution. But he had been reluctant to kill whites in retaliation for murdered blacks. Eaton agreed with Douglass's critique, for as a Union officer in charge of freedmen, he knew that he would face the same fate as blacks if he were captured by rebels.[35]

Douglass and Eaton had good reason to be upset. A few months before the Toledo speech, a heinous example of rebel barbarism had occurred at Fort Pillow, on the Mississippi River about forty miles north of Memphis. The rebel commander Nathan Bedford Forrest had a long history of torturing blacks, and after the war he would help found the Ku Klux Klan.

Forrest was a self-made man and Southern counterpoint to Lincoln. Born dirt poor in a Tennessee log cabin, he received virtually no education and earned money as a railsplitter.

In his early twenties he worked on a plantation with an uncle, saved enough money to buy a slave, and within a few years set up a "nigger yard in Memphis," as he called it, and made a fortune trading slaves and real estate.[36] At the beginning of the war he earned about $30,000 per year, roughly equivalent to $2.25 million in today's currency.

At the Fort Pillow massacre, Forrest's six thousand troops surrounded some six hundred Union soldiers, who took refuge in the fort and promptly surrendered. Blacks constituted about half of the captured soldiers, but Forrest viewed black troops and their allies as slave insurrectionaries. He thus ordered no quarter and his men massacred about three hundred, mostly blacks, including some civilians who were in the fort. According to testimony from survivors, the Southerners' yell to "Kill all the niggers!" resounded through the fort. Forrest boasted to his adjutant general that the river near the fort "was dyed with the blood of the slaughtered for 200 yards. . . . It is hoped that these facts will demonstrate to the Northern people that negro soldiers cannot cope with Southerners."[37]

Six days later on April 18, Lincoln referred to the massacre during a talk in Baltimore. "Having determined to use the negro as a soldier, there is no way but to give him all the protection given to any other soldier," he said. He promised retribution if the accounts of the murders could be substantiated, which they were. But he refused to issue a retaliatory order.[38]

Now Lincoln listened attentively as Eaton detailed Douglass's criticisms.[39] One imagines the "tired spot" in his eyes growing more pronounced.

In response to criticism of his Reconstruction plan, Lincoln asked Eaton if Douglass knew anything about his recent letter to Louisiana governor Michael Hahn. Probably not, Eaton said, because he himself didn't even know about it.[40]

Lincoln went to his desk and pulled out a copy of his March 13, 1864, letter to Hahn. Perhaps he did not need his steel-rimmed oval eyeglasses that looked too small on his large head, for it was a short letter. He read it to Eaton. "I barely suggest for your private consideration, whether some of the colored people may not be let in [allowed to vote]—as, for instance, the very intelligent, and especially those who have fought gallantly in our ranks. They would probably help, in some trying time to come, to keep the jewel of liberty within the family of freedom."[41]

Eaton was stunned. Not even radicals in

Congress had been able to pass a Reconstruction bill granting blacks suffrage. Lincoln said that if he offered universal *amnesty*, he also needed to provide universal *suffrage*, "or at least suffrage on the basis of intelligence and military service."[42]

He put the letter down and then asked Eaton, "with that curious modesty characteristic of him," whether or not Frederick Douglass "could be induced to come see him."[43]

Eaton replied that "he rather thought he could."[44]

Lincoln then told Eaton about his meeting with Douglass a year earlier and said he considered him "one of the most meritorious men in America."[45]

When Douglass disembarked at the Baltimore and Ohio station on New Jersey Avenue and C Street, a White House messenger was there to meet him.[46] Lincoln had asked Indian Commissioner William P. Dole to make sure Douglass arrived safely. On August 18 Dole informed the president that Douglass had been expected the day before on the 11:00 p.m. train but had not arrived. He "is yet expected today. I will send him to you when he comes."[47]

Douglass was thrilled that Lincoln wanted to see him. His first meeting with the president had been one of the great honors of his life. Being in the White House had been almost magical. He personally liked Lincoln, considered him sincere, and felt "quite at ease" in his presence.[48] Lincoln had treated him like a man rather than a black man. In fact, the president had shown him the respect of one self-made man to another.

But that hadn't stopped Douglass from lashing out at Lincoln for his misguided policies. As Douglass well knew, some conservatives endorsed racist policies but treated blacks with respect when interacting with them. And some abolitionists were haughty and patronizing toward blacks. Political beliefs did not necessarily correlate with personal behavior.

Douglass's attack of Lincoln's Reconstruction plan and apathy after Fort Pillow had been comparatively mild. In his signature speech over the last six months, "The Mission of the War," delivered to tens of thousands of people, he called Lincoln's absence of "all moral feeling" the chief danger to the Union.[49] After all, Lincoln had famously told Horace Greeley that he was *indifferent* to slavery, and he had said much the same thing in his recent annual message to Congress.[50] When his archrival Stephen

Douglas had expressed a similar indifference to slavery in 1858, "Lincoln denounced that sentiment as unworthy of the lips of any American statesman." Stephen Douglas wanted popular sovereignty; "Mr. Lincoln wants the Union." There was little difference between them.[51]

Nothing personal, Mr. Lincoln, Douglass might have added. It was how politics was played.

At the White House the messenger ushered Douglass into the reception room. Lincoln was in another meeting and Douglass took a seat in the corner and began reading. Soon he felt the familiar stare of a white man who was outraged at having to share the same space with a black man. Douglass "raised his flashing eyes and caught [him] in the act." The culprit, Judge Joseph T. Mills from Wisconsin, tried to overcome his embarrassment by mocking Douglass. "Are you the President?" he asked.

"No . . . I am Frederick Douglass," he responded with calm dignity.[52]

When Mills met with Lincoln he told him what had happened and then race-baited him by asking, "Now Mr. President, are you in favor of miscegenation? That's a democratic mode of producing good Union men & I don't propose to infringe on the patent."[53] Lincoln apparently ignored the joke.[54]

Douglass found Lincoln "in an alarmed condition." Since their meeting a year earlier the president had aged a decade, his face more lined and his cheeks hollowed out.[55] He was distressed at his gloomy prospects for reelection, as he told Douglass, adding that most people felt his antislavery policy prevented a peaceful settlement with the rebels. He referred to a recent letter he had written to Horace Greeley, who was hoping to negotiate a settlement. In it Lincoln made clear that any proposition for peace was contingent upon "the abandonment of slavery."[56] It raised an outcry. People now accused him of refusing to negotiate. Moreover, Lincoln feared that his former general George McClellan would become the presidential candidate at the coming Democratic convention at Chicago, and if so, he felt certain that McClellan would win.

Lincoln wanted Douglass's advice. He showed him a letter he had drafted (but not sent), in which he defended himself against "the peace clamor raised against him."[57] Since no Confederate had ever submitted a peace proposition, it was wrong to say that Lincoln was unwilling to negotiate. The letter also made clear that he would not revoke his Emancipation Proclamation and reenslave those who were faithfully serving the Union cause. "As a matter of morals, could such treachery . . . escape the curses of Heaven, or of any good man? As a matter of policy, to *announce* such a purpose would ruin the Union cause itself."[58]

But what if Lincoln had no authority to continue an abolition war? This is essentially what he said, and it disturbed Douglass. In the letter Lincoln abdicates control, and thus responsibility, over the abolition of slavery. Ultimately the people would decide. They had agreed to fight slavery *only* as a means to save the Union. But what if the people demanded peace without abolition and the rebels agreed? Then there was nothing Lincoln could do about it, for they would vote him out of office and Congress would not support him. He could not make abolition a condition of peace even if he wanted to. His letter was an ingenious way of appeasing peace advocates without repudiating his policies.[59]

"Shall I send forth this letter?" Lincoln asked.

"Certainly not," Douglass replied. "It would be given a broader meaning than you intend to convey; it would be taken as a complete surrender of your antislavery policy." And if you talk about your "want of power" it will be misconstrued.[60]

Lincoln never sent the letter.

On another matter Lincoln needed Douglass's help. He had a plan to bring more slaves into Union lines, but he wanted Douglass to carry it out. His plan resembled John Brown's efforts to invade the South and free the slaves. He wanted Douglass to organize a band of black scouts "to go into the rebel states, beyond the lines of our armies, carry the news of emancipation, and urge the slaves to come within our boundaries," as Douglass summarized. If the plan worked, it could help preserve the Union and end slavery.[61]

Douglass was amazed by the plan, for he knew that Lincoln had considered Brown a criminal and madman. Yet now Lincoln was borrowing from his old friend, conceiving a similar plan to raid the South and liberate the slaves. It resembled Brown's original Subterranean Pass Way plan, the one that Douglass had thought would work.[62]

Lincoln's John Brown plan both alarmed and thrilled Douglass. It alarmed him because it suggested that the Emancipation Proclamation would have no force after the war. It thrilled him because it revealed that Lincoln genuinely hated slavery and had issued his Emancipation Proclamation not merely as a military necessity. No wonder Lincoln demanded a constitutional amendment to abolish slavery.[63]

Suddenly Douglass saw Lincoln in a new

light. The president was willing to go to far greater lengths in the cause of freedom than Douglass had thought possible. His John Brown plan "showed a deeper moral conviction against slavery than I had ever seen before in anything spoken or written by him."[64] Lincoln had long lagged his party; now he was ahead of it.

The two men talked for hours, and by the end of their meeting they considered each other friends. Twice during their conversation Lincoln's secretary announced that Governor William Buckingham of Connecticut was waiting to see him. "Tell Governor Buckingham to wait, for I want to have a long talk with my friend Frederick Douglass." Both times Douglass offered to step outside but Lincoln objected.[65]

Douglass assumed that this meeting was the first time "in the history of the Republic" a president had shown such impartiality toward a black man.[66] He was right, and it was not just him that the president was impartial to.

Lincoln met with more blacks at the White House (not counting slaves and servants) than any other previous president. Bishop Daniel Payne was introduced to him in 1862 and contrasted Lincoln's graciousness with the haughtiness of President John Tyler, whom he had met years earlier when giving a eulogy for one of Tyler's servants. The Reverend Henry Highland

Garnet also got to know Lincoln, who asked him to give a sermon in Congress to commemorate emancipation. Douglass's former co-editor Martin Delany became the first black major in the Union army and met with Lincoln in early 1865 to propose a scheme similar to the John Brown plan Douglass and Lincoln had discussed.[67]

Black women similarly emphasized Lincoln's compassion. Mary Todd Lincoln's dressmaker Elizabeth Keckly frequented the White House for measurements and consultations. She became Mary's confidante and gave her the name of a Spiritualist after Willie died. Keckly called Lincoln "far from handsome"; but she said he was as kind and considerate of her "as he was of any of the white people about the White House."[68] And Sojourner Truth was so excited to meet the president that she brought her autograph book and asked him to sign it. Truth said she was "never treated with more kindness and cordiality than I was by that great and good man."[69]

Once blacks and whites began working together to achieve their separate goals of ending slavery and saving the Union, interracial friendships and alliances flourished. Fighting the rebels with both hands effectively meant that one hand was white and the other black.

The flow of blacks to and from the White

House became so regular as to prompt the *Washington Chronicle* to comment on it in early 1864. "Years ago had a colored man presented himself at the White House at the President's levee, seeking an introduction to the Chief Magistrate of the nation, he would have been, in all probability, roughly handled for his impertinence."[70]

The closest antecedent to this kind of White House interracialism had happened fifty-two years earlier, when the wealthy black shipowner Paul Cuffe had met with President James Madison. Cuffe was a Massachusetts Quaker who championed colonization as an antidote to American slavery and racism. In 1812 customs officials illegally impounded his brig and threatened to ruin him. Cuffe responded by taking his case to the president.[71] Madison was a slaveowner who, with most other founders, called slavery a sin and sought gradual abolition. Like Cuffe, Madison was an advocate of colonization. At their meeting Cuffe supposedly addressed Madison in the simple, unadorned language of his Quaker faith: "James, I have been put to much trouble, and have been abused. . . . I have come here for thy protection." Madison complied with Cuffe's request for help in recovering his ship, in part owing to their similar visions of removal for African Americans.[72]

It was the first time an African American had met with a U.S. president on terms other than those of servant or slave. Yet how different was Cuffe's interaction than Douglass's! While Madison and Cuffe shared a vision of black uplift that depended on colonization, Douglass and Lincoln came together in the cause of interracial Union.[73]

Meanwhile John Eaton, having been informed of Douglass's meeting with Lincoln, visited him afterward. Douglass was pacing the floor in the parlor of a friend's house where he was staying, lost in thought and evidently agitated. Papers and an open ink bottle were on a nearby desk. He had already begun outlining the John Brown plan and seemed surprised when he saw Eaton. "I have just come from President Lincoln," he told him excitedly. "He treated me as a man; he did not let me feel for a moment that there was any difference in the color of our skins! The President is a most remarkable man."[74]

A few days later a White House messenger arrived to invite Douglass to tea with the president. A carriage was waiting outside to take him to the Soldiers' Home. Douglass had to decline, for he had already agreed to give a lecture later that day.[75] He hoped there would be many more opportunities for tea with the president.

Back in Rochester he worked on the John Brown plan. He consulted a number of other black leaders, all of whom eagerly supported it. On August 29 he sent Lincoln his report. Conceptually it resembled Brown's Subterranean Pass Way and anticipated the army's Special Forces. A general agent (no doubt Douglass) would assign agents to various locations throughout the South, each one familiar with his region, to conduct squads of slaves into Union lines. The agents would report directly to department generals who would enable them "to pursue their vocation unmolested." Slaves would be fully provided for until fit for service, and the agents would be paid liberally. Douglass reminded Lincoln that "every slave who escapes from the rebel states is a loss to the rebellion and a gain to the loyal cause."[76]

On August 29, the same day he sent his proposal to Lincoln, the Democratic convention met in Chicago and nominated McClellan for president. The platform was one "Jefferson Davis might have drawn," wrote a Lincoln supporter.[77] Now there was even more urgency in the John Brown plan.

Douglass shifted his support to Lincoln, and Frémont abandoned his candidacy in order to unite Republicans. Douglass wanted to canvass for Lincoln but Republican committees were sensitive to the charge of "being the 'Nigger' Party," as Douglass noted, so he continued working behind the scenes.[78]

The John Brown plan was never implemented, for on September 2 General William T. Sherman took Atlanta in the most important victory since Vicksburg. His famous words, "Atlanta is ours and fairly won," echoed throughout the North.[79] Lincoln ordered hundred-gun salutes throughout Washington and proclaimed a day of Thanksgiving and Prayer.[80] By the time Sherman began his march to the sea, the air had gone out of Copperhead peace efforts. It soon became apparent that Lincoln would win reelection, rendering the John Brown plan unnecessary, since almost every Northerner believed that the war would soon be over.

John Eaton considered Lincoln's friendship with Douglass a testament to the president's bipartisan diplomacy. One of the president's great skills, he said, was "in handling the men who were inclined to find fault with his policy." Eaton had no way of knowing that Lincoln had developed this skill on the Illinois frontier with adversaries ranging from Jack Armstrong to Stephen Douglas. "If you would win a man to your cause, first convince him that you are his sincere friend," he had declared twenty-two years earlier.[81] The doctrine had served him well, for he had done exactly that with countless blacks.

Douglass could befriend Lincoln because the president had finally converted to his abolition cause. He too had remained faithful to his principle of friendship, which depended upon a shared cause. The two men needed each other. Lincoln needed Douglass to help him save the Union, and he served Douglass's own goal of freeing the slaves. At their August 1864 meeting both men recognized that these twin goals were mutually reinforcing.

But their friendship also hinged on their capacity to *forgive*.[82] As self-made men who continually transformed themselves, Douglass and Lincoln understood that former enemies may become future friends and vice versa. They refused to see themselves as fixed or static. In order to achieve transformation, they needed to forgive their former enemies of wrongdoing and credit them with the potential for change. Their faith in the power of forgiveness led to the possibility of rapprochement and gave them the strength to continue evolving.

❖⟫◯⟪❖

When Douglass and Lincoln met for the third time on March 4, 1865, the mood was celebratory. Douglass came to Washington to attend Lincoln's second inauguration. The war was almost over; 170,000 blacks were in uniform, marching triumphantly across the South; and Congress had recently passed the Thirteenth Amendment, abolishing slavery throughout the United States.[83]

The day was bleak and rainy. Mud covered the unpaved streets and people "streamed around the Capitol in most wretched plight." Many of them had been up all night, having taken special inaugural trains that arrived in Washington that morning. Between the cinder dust from trains and the mud and rain, the thirty thousand people attending the ceremony looked gray and worn out. "Crinoline was smashed, skirts bedaubed, and moiré antique, velvet, laces and such dry goods were streaked with mud from end to end."[84]

Douglass had arrived a few days early and on March 3 took tea with Salmon P. Chase, Lincoln's former secretary of the Treasury and now the chief justice of the Supreme Court. Douglass had met Chase on the abolition lecture circuit before the war and liked him. He was thrilled that Chase had replaced Roger Taney, whose *Dred Scott* decision had been partly responsible for the war. A new robe had been made for the chief justice to administer the oath of office, and Douglass helped him try it on.[85]

The new iron dome now sat proudly atop the Capitol. Renovations had stopped briefly in 1861 but Lincoln ordered work on the dome to proceed. Completing it symbolized hope for reunion, he believed.[86] But to many Democrats, including Herman Melville, the new iron dome was a far more ominous symbol.

> *Power unanointed may come—*
> *Dominion (unsought by the free)*
> *And the Iron Dome,*
> *Stronger for stress and strain,*
> *Fling her huge shadow athwart the main;*
> *But the Founders' dream shall flee.*

Melville worried that the iron dome would "fling her huge shadow athwart" the Main Streets of America and impose unprecedented dominion on communities and towns, thus destroying the founders' dream of a loose confederation of states and a decentralized government.[87]

The bronze statue of liberty stood proudly atop the dome. She looked a little strange wearing a helmet rather than a cap, as the Greek goddess typically did. But Jefferson Davis, who as secretary of war had overseen the design of the statue, knew that in ancient Greece a cap on a woman was "a badge of the freed slave," and so he had suggested a helmet instead.[88]

While Douglass stood in the crowd waiting for the ceremonies to begin, a friend pointed out Andrew Johnson, Lincoln's new vice president. Johnson noticed Douglass, and his expression immediately turned to "one of bitter contempt and aversion." When he saw Douglass watching him he assumed "a more friendly appearance." For Douglass it was one of those moments when "the doors of a man's soul open" and his "true character" emerges. He turned to his friend and said, "Whatever Andrew Johnson may be, he certainly is no friend of our race."[89] Although Lincoln's and Johnson's policies on Reconstruction were quite similar, their personal behaviors toward blacks were worlds apart.

With so many people gathered around the Capitol, Douglass worried about an assassination attempt. In this he was not alone. Since the fall of 1864 reports of conspiracies had circulated through the North, and Lincoln had recently hired a personal bodyguard. During the inauguration plainclothes policemen stood at his side armed with .38 Colt revolvers. John Wilkes Booth was also there, watching Lincoln from the right balcony. Douglass stood directly in front of Lincoln and had an excellent view (see figure 17). Perhaps he should have worried

Figure 17. Lincoln's Second Inaugural, 1865.
(Library of Congress)

about himself, for one year later in Baltimore someone did try to assassinate him.[90]

As it turned out, the ceremony was "wonderfully quiet, earnest, and solemn," Douglass noted. There was a "leaden stillness about the crowd" as Lincoln delivered his address, and Douglass thought it sounded more like a sermon than a state paper.

In his speech Lincoln emphasizes God's inscrutability. "Both sides read the same Bible, and pray to the same God; and each invokes His aid against the other." He imagines a wrathful

God wreaking vengeance against slaveholders but carefully avoids presuming to know God's will. Such presumption would be hubris, he implies. "The Almighty has His own purposes." The proper attitude toward people and nations should be one of humility, tolerance, and forgiveness. "With malice toward none; with charity for all."

After the ceremony Douglass went to the reception at the White House. As he was about to enter, two policemen rudely yanked him away and told him that no persons of color were allowed to enter. Douglass said there must be some mistake, for no such order could have come from the president. The police refused to yield, until Douglass sent word to Lincoln that he was being detained at the door.

Douglass found the president in the elegant East Room, standing "like a mountain pine in his grand simplicity and homely beauty."[91]

"Here comes my friend," Lincoln said, and took Douglass by the hand. "I am glad to see you. I saw you in the crowd today, listening to my inaugural address." He asked Douglass how he liked it, adding, "there is no man in the country whose opinion I value more than yours."[92]

"Mr. Lincoln, that was a sacred effort," Douglass said.[93]

The Second Inaugural became for Douglass

one of the great works of American literature. He frequently quoted from it and never criticized it. And yet it ends on a note of reconciliation similar to that of the First Inaugural.

Douglass now realized that reconciling with the rebels was not *in itself* a misguided policy. Perhaps this understanding was partly due to his relationship with Lincoln. Like the president, he placed great faith in the power of forgiveness that could lead to reconciliation. But forgiveness had moral force only if rebels acknowledged wrongdoing. Otherwise it empowered them, allowing them to continue sinning and committing outrages. Forgiveness would then lead to reconciliation with whites but no change in behavior toward blacks. In the end, of course, this is what happened.

One month later, on April 9, Lee surrendered to Grant at Appomattox. Lincoln heard the news that night and the next morning he ordered a five-hundred-gun salute to announce the victory. Thousands of people gathered around the White House to celebrate. Bands were playing, flags were flying, people sang, laughed, shouted. "All, all jubilant," wrote one reveler. The crowd began chanting for Lincoln, and eventually he appeared at a second-story window. He asked the band to play "Dixie," a minstrel tune that had become associated with the rebel cause. It is "one of the best tunes I have ever heard," Lincoln told the crowd. "Our adversaries over the way attempted to appropriate it, but I insisted yesterday that we fairly captured it." And so the band played "Dixie," then it launched into "Yankee Doodle."[94]

Five days later on April 14, John Wilkes Booth sent a letter to the Washington newspaper the *National Intelligencer*. Over the past few months Booth had recruited a small band of Confederate soldiers to kidnap Lincoln and demand in exchange for him thousands of rebel prisoners of war.[95] The original plan was to ambush Lincoln during his carriage ride to the Soldiers' Home and hustle him into Confederate Virginia. Booth had met with Confederate spies in Montreal, Canada, and had probably received from them "both money and intelligence."[96] One of his men had also met with Confederate secretary of state Judah P. Benjamin, who oversaw Confederate secret service operations.[97] After Lee surrendered to Grant, Booth had to change his plan, for he could no longer barter for prisoners. But he refused to believe that the South was defeated and slavery abolished. "Our cause being almost lost, something decisive & great must be done," he wrote in his diary.[98]

Booth's letter to the *National Intelligencer* was a call to arms for the rebels. "The country was formed for the white, not for the black man," he said. Slavery fueled economic growth, elevated blacks, and represented the greatest blessing God had ever bestowed "upon a favored country."[99] Lincoln threatened to exterminate everything virtuous in the South. Booth likened Lincoln to Julius Caesar, a character both of them knew well from their mutual love of Shakespeare. Indeed, in March 1864 Lincoln had seen a production of *Julius Caesar* starring John's brother Edwin Booth.[100] And in November 1864 John had played Mark Antony in a benefit performance of the play to raise money for a statue of Shakespeare in Central Park.[101]

But Booth preferred the role of Brutus. He ended his letter to the *National Intelligencer* by saying, "When Caesar had conquered the enemies of Rome, and the power that was his menaced the liberties of the people, Brutus arose and slew him. The stroke of his dagger was guided by his love of Rome. It was the spirit and ambition of Caesar that Brutus struck at." Caesar must bleed for his actions, Booth said.[102]

The night of April 14, Abraham and Mary arrived late at Ford's Theater in Washington for *Our American Cousin*, a third-rate comedy. They had invited General Grant and his wife, Julia, but the Grants had left for New Jersey to see their children. Earlier in the day Mary had had a headache and said she wanted to stay home, but her husband "was fixed upon having some relaxation and bent on the theater." The Lincolns went with a young couple whose company they enjoyed, Major Henry Rathbone and his fiancée, Clara Harris, the daughter of a New York senator. As they entered the presidential box near the stage, the orchestra began playing "Hail to the Chief," stopping the show. Lincoln went to the railing of the box, bowed, and smiled as the audience cheered wildly.[103]

Suddenly, Ford's Theater seemed like a cozy family, a metonym of the nation. At least that's how it felt to Julia Shephard, who sat center-stage watching the show and provided her father with a vivid description: "The President is in yonder upper right hand private box, so handsomely decked with silken flags festooned over a picture of George Washington. The young and lovely daughter of Senator Harris is the only one of his party we see, as the flags hide the rest. But we know Father Abraham is there, like a Father watching what interests his children, for *their* pleasure rather than his own. . . . How sociable it seems, like one family sitting around the parlor fire. Everyone has been so jubilant for days that they laugh and shout at every clownish witticism, such is the excited state of the public mind."[104]

One member of this family had shirked his duty, however. John Parker, the police officer who had been assigned to keep constant guard at the entrance to the presidential box, had deserted his post. He wanted to see the play, and after watching it for an hour, he went outside for a drink. Parker had a history of bad behavior; on numerous occasions he had been charged with drunkenness, and at other times he had missed work for up to a week in order to enjoy houses of prostitution.[105]

A little after 10:00 p.m., John Wilkes Booth showed his card to a footman at the bottom of the stairs leading up to the presidential box. The footman evidently recognized him and let him through, for Booth had performed at Ford's on numerous occasions. Earlier that day, Booth had bored a peephole through the door to the box. Now, as he looked through his peephole, he saw Lincoln from behind, sitting in a rocking chair. Quietly entering the box, he pointed his derringer at the president's head from two feet away and pulled the trigger. It was about 10:30 p.m.[106]

Major Rathbone tried to seize Booth, but the assailant slashed him with his dagger and then jumped to the stage. Booth's spur caught on the flag bunting decorating the box, and he landed on one leg, breaking his ankle. Waving his bloody dagger, he shouted *"Sic simper tyrannis!"* ("Thus ever to tyrants!" the Virginia state motto), and escaped through the rear of the theater. Then, above the din, everyone heard Mary's wail: "They have shot the President! They have shot the President! Oh, my God, and have I given my husband to die?"[107]

It was Good Friday.

Once doctors realized that Lincoln would not die immediately, they took him across the street to a private house owned by William Peterson, a merchant-tailor. At the rear of the first floor was a narrow room with a small bed. Since the bed was too small for Lincoln's tall frame, the doctors placed him diagonally across it. Although they knew that Booth's shot was fatal, they did not want the president dying in a theater, an unseemly if not blasphemous site in the minds of many Americans.[108]

Over the next nine hours, Mary waited for her husband to die. For a few hours she sat at his side, and through constant sobbing she called him endearing names and asked him to say a few words to her. Lincoln never regained consciousness.[109]

When Robert Todd Lincoln arrived and saw his mother's condition, he called for Elizabeth

Dixon, Mary's closest Washington friend, who helped her through the ordeal and convinced her to retire to an anteroom, where she rested and looked in on her husband every hour. Mary wanted twelve-year-old Tad brought to the house to see his father die, but the doctors refused. At one point, when Lincoln's breathing became especially difficult, Mary "fell fainting on the floor." Secretary of War Edwin Stanton, who had taken charge of the proceedings, considered her a liability and ordered, "Take that woman out and do not let her in again."[110]

The room was crowded with statesmen. All of Lincoln's cabinet was there, except for William Seward, who had been attacked and almost killed by Booth's accomplice Lewis Paine. Booth had ordered another co-conspirator, George Atzerodt, to assassinate Vice President Andrew Johnson, but Atzerodt, ignoring the order, had instead wandered "aimlessly about the city." So efficient was Stanton that within a few hours, all of Booth's conspirators were seized. Booth himself would be tracked down and killed on April 26 at a farmhouse in northern Virginia.[111]

Mary saw her husband for the last time just as the light of a rainy dawn appeared from the windows like "dim candles." Hearing his snoring noise that his doctors recognized as the beginning of the end, she again cried out, "Oh, have I given my husband to die?" and then collapsed. Her son Robert dragged her away.[112]

At 7:22 a.m. on the morning of April 15, Lincoln took his last breath. Stanton asked Dr. Phineas Gurley, the Lincoln family minister and pastor of Washington's New York Avenue Presbyterian Church, to say a prayer. Robert Lincoln suddenly broke down and leaned on Charles Sumner for support. When the prayer ended, Stanton, tears streaming down his face, raised his right arm and said, "Now he belongs to the ages."[113]

When Douglass heard the reports of Lincoln's death, he was overcome with grief. He was at home in Rochester, and he felt the news as a "personal as well as national calamity." Later that day on April 15, he gave a short impromptu speech at City Hall, where a number of citizens had gathered to mourn the president's death. It was not a time for speeches but for silence and prayer, Douglass said, an echo of his sentiments about the limitations of oratory on the eve of emancipation. Then once again he gave a brilliant speech.[114]

After quoting from Lincoln's Second Inaugural, Douglass searched for meaning in the tragedy of his death. "Though Abraham Lincoln dies, the Republic lives." The president's death had suddenly united blacks and whites in the North and "made us kin." His martyrdom was a symbol of racial reconciliation and forgiveness, of lasting peace with malice toward none and charity for all. Indeed, Douglass likened Lincoln to America's Christ: "it may be that the blood of our beloved martyred President will be the salvation of our country." People would be united, made kin, by their loyalty to their nation rather than their complexion.[115]

If John Brown's death had started the war that ended slavery, as Douglass believed, then Lincoln's death could begin the process of reconciliation between blacks and whites.

Most whites treated Lincoln's death much differently, however. His martyrdom would redeem the nation and facilitate the process of reunion among Northern and Southern whites. He quickly came to symbolize an American Christ who forgave rebels their sins and allowed them to reenter the Union. "Jesus Christ died for the world, Abraham Lincoln died for his country," said one clergyman on the Sunday after Lincoln's death, and his sentiment became a common refrain. Consequently, John Wilkes

Booth became America's Judas. Some called this second Judas "worse than his namesake" because he committed the murder, whereas the first Judas was only a betrayer who collected gold and let others "do the deed of death."[116]

Northern whites led the way in this process of reconciliation. They granted amnesty to almost all rebels and returned confiscated property to them rather than distribute it to the blacks who had helped them win the war. This policy reflected Lincoln's own message of forgiveness in his two inaugural addresses and indeed his own plan for Reconstruction.

The problem with this gesture of forgiveness was that Southerners didn't think they had sinned. Slavery was not wrong, they believed, and the North had been the aggressor. No wonder that in the war's final year, rebels wanted nothing more than to see Lincoln dead (or out of office). Indeed, Confederates had schemed to blow up the White House. And in the immediate wake of Lincoln's assassination, rebels throughout the unoccupied South rejoiced.[117]

Their public rejoicing soon ceased, however. With the war over and their cause lost, Southerners needed to reenter the Union, and they accepted Lincoln's policy of forgiveness without themselves showing contrition. Thoughtful rebel leaders and their Northern sympathizers began treating Lincoln's death as a *national* tragedy. "In Mr. Lincoln, the Southern people have lost their best friend," proclaimed one Democratic editorial. Rebel general Joseph Johnston echoed this sentiment, saying that Lincoln's death "was the greatest possible calamity to the South," owing to his policy of forgiveness. And Confederate vice president Alexander Stephens said he had "horrid dreams" in the wake of Lincoln's assassination; he observed a day of fasting and mourning to honor his former friend.[118] The tragedy of Lincoln's death soon devolved into the redemption of former rebels.

Epilogue

On April 14, 1876, the eleventh anniversary of Lincoln's assassination, Douglass gave the keynote address to commemorate the unveiling of the Freedmen's Monument in Lincoln Park, Washington, D.C. Behind the speaker's stand sat President U. S. Grant, his cabinet, justices of the Supreme Court, congressmen, clergymen, diplomats, and a few black leaders. To the right was a band, which had opened the ceremonies with "Hail, Columbia." In front was the monument, still shrouded by American flags. Spread out around the monument in a semicircle was a crowd of some twenty-five thousand, mostly black.[1]

The monument had originated with a freedwoman named Charlotte Scott, who had moved to Ohio in 1864. A few weeks after Lincoln's assassination she donated five dollars for a statue to commemorate him. Money trickled in over the years, mostly in small bills from freedmen and black veterans. The $17,000 cost of the bronze statue had been paid for entirely by blacks. Congress appropriated $3,000 for the pedestal.[2]

The statue had been designed by Thomas Ball, a Boston sculptor who moved to Florence, Italy, during the war. News of Lincoln's assassination had inspired him to create a monument to freedom in Italian marble. The committee in charge of selecting the design, all white men, heard of Ball's model and commissioned him to cast one in bronze.[3]

President Grant walked to the front of the speaker's stand to unveil the monument. After a moment of silence he pulled the cord to raise the flags. The band played "Hail to the Chief" and the crowd cheered, but it was unclear whether they cheered for Grant or the monument. The statue depicted Lincoln standing with his right hand at a podium holding the Emancipation Proclamation, while his left hand hovers above a kneeling slave (see figure 18). At the base a single word proclaims the statue's meaning: EMANCIPATION.[4]

The figure of the kneeling slave had been an icon among abolitionists from the beginning of the movement, and by the Civil War it had become one of the most famous (or infamous) images in America. Created by whites, the iconic image depicts the slave kneeling all alone and asking in prayer, "Am I Not a Man and a Brother?" For most whites, the iconic image suggested supplication to God and whites for deliverance. Douglass had hoped to revise this paternalistic image. He had commissioned an engraving that shows Christ standing over the kneeling slave, and he had circulated it as the frontispiece of a popular gift book. In the Freedmen's Monument Lincoln became in effect America's Christ.[5]

As Douglass approached the speaker's stand to deliver his address, some in the crowd looked to see whether he walked with the help of a cane. Shortly after Lincoln's death, Mary had given Douglass her husband's favorite walking stick as a memento of their friendship. Since Douglass considered it "a token of sacred interest," he probably left it at home.[6]

He did not like the monument. "A more manly attitude would have been indicative of freedom," he told a friend later that day. But he avoided criticizing it, and instead referred to it as a "highly interesting object" and "a humble offering." He hoped his speech would offer an antidote to the paternalistic image of a slave kneeling before his white redeemer.[7] He knew it would make some people uncomfortable.

"Truth compels me to admit—even here in the presence of the monument we have erected to his memory—that Abraham Lincoln was not, in the fullest sense of the word, either our man or our model. . . . He was preeminently the white men's President, entirely devoted to the welfare of the white men," and he "shared toward the colored race the prejudices common to his countrymen."[8]

Douglass then addressed the white dignitaries in the stands behind him. "You are the children of Abraham Lincoln. We are at best only his step-children."[9]

No doubt many of the white dignitaries considered Douglass insolent and his speech in bad taste. But those who had followed his career would have recognized his penchant for suddenly reversing course and surprising his audience, a technique he had gleaned long ago from *The Columbian Orator*. He employed it now.

By prioritizing the Union over the plight of blacks, Lincoln succeeded "in organizing the loyal American people for the tremendous conflict before them, and bringing them safely through that conflict," Douglass acknowledged. "Had he put the abolition of slavery before the salvation of the Union," he would have alienated large numbers of people and "rendered resistance to rebellion impossible. Viewed from the genuine abolition ground, Mr. Lincoln seemed tardy, cold, dull, and indifferent; but measuring him by the sentiment of his country, a sentiment he was bound as a statesman to consult, he was swift, zealous, radical, and determined."[10]

The speech stunningly encapsulates Lincoln's presidency. The conservative Republican had steered the nation through a revolution. The white man's president who treated blacks as stepchildren had adopted them as his own children, part of the national family. And so by honoring Lincoln, blacks honored themselves, Douglass said.

The great irony in Douglass's speech was that the monument of the kneeling slave with Lincoln standing over him as the Christ figure was more accurate than Douglass wanted to admit. For in 1876, instead of rising to freedom, the slave was sinking back to his knees after standing "a brief moment in the sun."[11] The symbol of Lincoln as America's Christ had helped redeem the Confederacy. Rebel leaders had regained control of their region and had effectively overturned the recent constitutional amendments that abolished slavery and guaranteed suffrage to black men and citizenship to everyone born in America. Most federal troops had already left the South, and less than a year later, following the disputed election of Rutherford B. Hayes, the remaining troops would be removed, ending Reconstruction and leaving freedmen and -women to the fate of unrepentant rebels. Douglass's worst fears from the Civil War years had been realized, and yet he remained largely silent. Why was this?

Like most other black and white abolitionists, Douglass saw the end of the war as the endpoint of an era and of his life's work.[12] It also marked the end of his continual self-making. After the war "a strange and, perhaps, perverse feeling came over me," he confessed. The great joy he felt in helping end slavery "was slightly tinged with the feeling of sadness. I felt that I had reached the end of the noblest and best part of my life; my school was broken up, my church disbanded, and the beloved congregation dispersed, never to come together again." His life's work was now "among the things of memory."[13]

It is an astonishing confession. In his "What to the Slave is the Fourth of July?" speech of 1852, Douglass had summarized the uses of history by saying: "We have to do with the past only as we can make it useful to the present and to the future."[14] But now the past had become the main theme. His Freedmen's Monument speech totally ignored what was happening to blacks in the present. They were being systematically murdered and terrorized by former Confederates, who sought to reestablish slavery in form if not name. And yet President Grant, the congressmen, and the Supreme Court justices who stood behind Douglass refused to fight this new phase of the Civil War; they had declared victory and now turned a blind eye to what was happening. So too did Douglass; in his speech he ignored the new outrages perpetrated against blacks.[15] In this sense he resembled a retired athlete or political leader, whose life's work and great achievements were behind him, unable to reenter the fray with the same passion and in the same way.

Freedom had represented for Douglass and most other abolitionists a glorious culmination rather than the beginning of new struggles. Emancipation had been "the key to a promised land"; like so many of his peers, Douglass had defined the war in millennialist terms, as an apocalyptic war, with Michael and his angels battling against Satan. But the dream soon turned into a nightmare. The new age was nowhere in sight. In the face of growing doubts and disappointments, Douglass (and most of his fellow abolitionists) turned to the past as a source of solace.[16]

Of course, life went on. Douglass was forty-seven years old when the war ended and physically still strong and healthy. He would live another thirty years, but during this period he changed far less than at any other in his life. From 1870 until his death in 1895, he became a Republican Party insider and elder statesman, as he believed that Republicans offered the last best hope for blacks. His unwavering loyalty to his party stemmed in part from his memories of its former radicalism.[17]

In 1870 he moved to Washington, D.C., and purchased the *New National Era*, a Republican Party paper. He seemed only mildly interested in it, however. He never spent that much time with it, either as publisher or corresponding editor. As a result, it lacked the literary style, passion, and sense of purpose that had defined the *North Star* and its successors. At times, the *New National Era* seemed more concerned with economic matters than black rights, which reflected a shift in the Republican Party away from civil rights and toward the interests of Gilded Age capitalists. Just four years after he purchased the *New National Era*, in the wake of the Panic of 1873, it went under. In its last year, it often "read like a journal issued by lobbyists for big business."[18]

Douglass was more effective stumping for Republican candidates. In 1872 he helped reelect

Figure 18.
Freedmen's
Monument in
Washington,
D.C.
*(National
Portrait
Gallery,
Smithsonian)*

Grant by convincing blacks to remain loyal to the party, despite massive corruption and defections by such leading radicals as Charles Sumner. To Douglass, Grant and the Republicans constituted "the only visible hope of the colored race in the United States. Outside of these we see no power that is likely to stand between the Negro and murder." A year earlier, Grant had sent federal troops into the South to fight the Ku Klux Klan and other white supremacy groups. But as wealthy Republicans sought economic alliances with Southern planters, such activism became increasingly rare.[19]

The party of Lincoln, Grant, and now Douglass, which had long encouraged self-making for white men and had recently granted freedom and citizenship to every American and suffrage to all men, was fast becoming a party of wealthy industrialists who shut the door on those struggling upward.

When Douglass's Rochester home burned down in 1872, he considered it a sign of the times. As soon as he heard the news, he took the next train to Rochester. When he arrived, he went to a hotel but was turned away because he was black. What a change the war had brought! In the 1850s Rochester had been one of the most racially egalitarian cities in the country. Now he could not even rent a room, which prompted fears that someone had deliberately burned his home. "The sentiment which repelled me at [the hotel] burnt my house," he concluded. He moved Anna and the children, who had remained in Rochester and were unhurt, to Washington.[20]

Party loyalty and political life in Washington had their perks. In 1874 Douglass was appointed president of the Freedmen's Bank, even though he had no banking experience. Created by the federal government in 1865, the bank operated as an independent institution to help freedmen save money. But soon after Douglass settled into his plush new office, he discovered that the bank was insolvent. Its white directors were incompetent or corrupt; they had loaned $500,000 to the robber baron Jay Cooke at 5 percent interest (less than half the going rate), amid rumors that Cooke's financial empire was about to crumble (which it did). Such loans destroyed the bank, and Douglass soon realized that its directors had hoped to use his good name to restore public confidence. Initially he tried to save the bank, depositing $10,000 of his own money and sending telegrams to Southern freedmen urging them not to make runs on local branches. But three months into his presidency, the bank closed its doors for good. "It has been the black man's cow, but the white man's milk," he concluded. Although he recouped all but 10 percent of his investment, freedmen lost half of their deposits.[21]

In 1877 Douglass finally received a coveted Republican appointment. He had campaigned the previous year for the presidential candidate Rutherford B. Hayes in what became a disputed election with Democrat Samuel Tilden. An electoral commission awarded Hayes the presidency, contingent upon congressional approval; to placate Southern Democrats, Hayes agreed to remove the last federal troops from the South, thus ending the project of Reconstruction. As if to mask his betrayal of blacks, Hayes appointed Douglass marshal of the District of Columbia. It was the first time a black man received a federal appointment requiring Senate approval, and it was a highly visible position, for the job entailed parading dignitaries around the city. Douglass was slow to speak out against Hayes, prompting critics to say that "a fat office gagged him."[22]

Party loyalty sometimes blinded Douglass to the class struggle fueling the racial divide. Many wealthy Republicans had shown interest in blacks as a means to gain votes and political power. But once they realized that they no longer needed black votes, they abandoned them and forged new alliances with unrepentant Southern elites.[23]

Douglass's own economic status blinded him to the conditions of the mass of blacks. During the Gilded Age he became a rich Republican. He could command as much as five or six hundred dollars for two lectures, and in one three-month period he received $3,700 for lecturing to elite whites on such varied topics as journalism and folklore. In 1877 he purchased an estate in Anacostia known as Cedar Hill, a beautiful brick home with sixteen acres that looked down onto the Capitol. Between speaking fees, investments, and his government income, he soon amassed a small fortune of $300,000.[24]

Given his stature as an elder statesman, perhaps it is understandable that Douglass no longer sought to radically transform his world or continually remake himself. "Government is better than anarchy and patient reform is better than violent revolution," he argued after Reconstruction.[25] It was a profound reversal from his stance as a Radical Abolitionist. In fact he now downplayed aspects of his former radical past. In his third autobiography he republished his editorial on John Brown's raid but deleted the sentence that said he was ever ready to "organize, combine, and even to conspire against slavery" when there was "a reasonable hope of success."[26] Now he resembled Lincoln in his gradual and comparatively conservative approach to reform.

Douglass's turn to the past after the war was not unique. It paralleled the retreat of most other abolitionists from their millennialist ideals. He became more secular in his worldview and no longer believed that God could affect the affairs of the world. As a result, a heaven on earth increasingly seemed to him a dangerous illusion. Material facts, history, and the laws of nature now trumped "all the prayers of Christendom." After witnessing four years of horrific war, he became far more pragmatic, and he understood the costs of trying to realize national ideals.[27]

Douglass's memory of Lincoln and their friendship continued to influence his life and ideals. He increasingly sought to shape himself in Lincoln's image. His loyalty to the Republican Party resembled Lincoln's; and like his former friend, he protested within the limits of the law and his party. Not once in the postwar period did Douglass endorse extralegal means to end oppression.[28]

In his postwar speeches, Douglass frequently referred to Lincoln and their friendship, and by the 1880s he could ignore the fact that he had been one of Lincoln's harshest critics. He now called him "the greatest statesman that ever presided over the destinies of this Republic" and the man most responsible for "American liberty."[29] He even likened Lincoln to a god: "no one had a more godlike nature," he said in 1893.[30]

At times, Douglass tried to channel Lincoln's thoughts, much as he had done with God before and during the war, when he had defined himself as a prophet. Evangelical Christians were now asking "What would Jesus do?"; Douglass occasionally wondered "What would Lincoln do?" He asked this question at an 1883 address on the anniversary of emancipation in the District of Columbia. "Could Abraham Lincoln have foreseen the immense cost, the terrible hardship, the awful waste of blood and treasure involved in the effort to" save the Union; "could he have foreseen the tears of the widows and orphans, and his own warm blood trickling at the bidding of an assassin's bullet, he might have thought the sacrifice too great," Douglass concluded.[31] Were the 620,000 deaths worth the nominal quasi-freedom of four million slaves? The great abolitionist was no longer sure.

Most of the time, however, Douglass did not question the costs of black freedom. Although he was now more pragmatic, able to balance his ideals against the realities of his world, he remained an activist for the rest of his life. "When the slave was a slave I demanded his emancipation, and when he was free, I demanded his perfect freedom—all the safeguards of freedom. In whatever else I may have failed, in this I have not failed." He demanded black freedom in a number of ways: by protesting against lynchings, Ku Klux Klan terrorism, tenant laws, and sharecropping; by urging reform within the Republican Party; and mostly by recalling memories of slavery, abolition, and Lincoln.[32]

Douglass fell in love with his new Cedar

Hill home in Anacostia. He walked five miles every morning, where he would gaze down at the Capitol, and he worked out regularly with dumbbells. His children and grandchildren often visited, sometimes staying for months at a time. He was a benevolent patriarch, spoiling them with money and attention. He joined the Uniontown Shakespeare Club and was appointed recorder of deeds for the District of Columbia, which required even less work than the post of marshal.[33]

Anna died in 1882. She was almost seventy years old, Douglass sixty-four. For years she had been suffering from severe rheumatism, which kept her immobile and at times paralyzed. In her last months, she received "faithful constant care" from nurses, and she died quietly. "Mother," as Douglass now called her, "was the post in the center of my house and held us together."[34]

Eighteen months after Anna died, Douglass married Helen Pitts, a college-educated white woman who was twenty years his junior and worked as his secretary. News of the marriage outraged many whites and blacks, including family members, partly because he did not explain it well. While Anna had been "the color of my mother," Helen was "the color of my father," he said, which suggested to some people that he was now drawn to the white part of his identity. He also insisted that men and women, "no matter of what race or complexion," should "be allowed to enjoy the rights of a common nature." Color "was an artificial issue raised to justify . . . the degradation" of blacks.[35]

They had a wonderful marriage. Whereas he and Anna had little in common after leaving Baltimore, he and Helen shared many common interests, from activism to their love of music, literature, and travel. In 1886 they went on a grand tour of Europe, which was then in vogue among middle-class Americans. In England they stayed with Julia Griffiths Crofts, whom Douglass had not seen in twenty-six years. They visited Paris, Rome, Greece, and Egypt, and sat together for numerous photographs. The trip represented a striking contrast with his former marriage to Anna, who had not liked to travel and never appears with him in a photograph.[36]

Ottilie Assing was living in Paris when she heard about Douglass's marriage to Helen Pitts. Years earlier, when Douglass fled America after John Brown's raid, she had hoped he would meet her in Paris (he didn't). Now the news came like a bolt of lightning: Helen was a much younger woman; and she and Frederick had been married by a minister in a church.[37]

On a sunny August afternoon a few months after Frederick and Helen's marriage, Ottilie

Assing walked to the Bois de Boulogne on the west side of Paris. She sat down on a bench that was somewhat hidden from the park's walking path. She carefully removed a small vial from her purse, uncorked it, perhaps thought of Goethe's Werther, and then swallowed the potassium cyanide. Her body was discovered later that night, and the police, finding the vial, determined the cause of death to be suicide.[38]

For eleven years, until his death in 1895, Frederick and Helen were kindred spirits. They entertained distinguished guests and students from Howard University, recited the verse of Paul Lawrence Dunbar and other poets, and sometimes played duets together, Douglass on violin and Helen at the piano. But mostly they discussed civil rights and attended reform meetings and conventions.[39]

A few weeks before Douglass died of heart failure in February 1895, a young black student traveled to Providence, Rhode Island, where Douglass was visiting. He wanted to know what advice Douglass might have for a man like himself, who was thinking about a career. "What have you to say to a young Negro just starting out? What should he do?" he asked. Douglass rose to his full height, looked at the young man and then up to the heavens, and in his rich baritone voice said, "Agitate! Agitate! Agitate!"[40]

Acknowledgments

THIS BOOK BEGAN as part of a larger project on interracial friendship. In 2005 I published an essay on Douglass and Lincoln in *Time* magazine, and I am grateful to *Time*'s editors Chris Farley, Priscilla Painton, and Andrea Dorfman for helping me sharpen both the essay and my thinking about Douglass and Lincoln.

I have been extremely fortunate to be able to work with Jon Karp at Twelve. A brilliant editor and publisher, he is also a pleasure to work with and an ideal person to have at the helm. He has an exemplary eye and ear for prose; and his insights, whether addressing broad themes or plot, pacing, word choice, and endings, have been dazzling and always on the mark.

Nate Gray at Twelve has also been very helpful and supportive. Five years ago, I had the good fortune to supervise Nate's senior thesis at Harvard on John Brown in the American imagination, and it remains one of the best I've read. His sensitivity to language is extraordinary. I'd also like to thank my copyeditor, Roland Ottewell, another wordsmith who is so careful and detailed that I found myself humbled while reviewing his work. Thanks, too, to my managing editor on the project, Robert Castillo, for his wise suggestions, flexibility, and patience.

A number of scholars read some or all of the manuscript and provided crucial feedback. Zoe Trodd gave the manuscript such a careful reading, and provided such detailed suggestions, that I found myself in awe of her timely reports. Dan Aaron also read the entire manuscript, and his penetrating criticism was invaluable. David Blight offered timely and crucial suggestions, and he helped me clarify my argument. Jamie Jones was another enormously helpful close reader, and her suggestions have been indispensable. Gary Ross shaped my understanding of Lincoln and narrative techniques in ways that go far beyond these two subjects. Sally Jenkins's suggestions, conversation, and her own examples for approaching and interpreting the past have made me a better writer. David Brion Davis continues to raise the bar, inspiring me in all kinds of ways. And Steve Mintz's penetrating questions have forced me to rethink or clarify various aspects of the project.

A number of other people helped me on various parts of the book: Larry Buell, David Donald, Leland de la Durantaye, Stanley Engerman, Jeff Ferguson, Paul Finkelman, Skip Gates, Walter Johnson, Randall Kennedy, Maurice Lee, Robert Levine, Tim McCarthy, Luke Menand, Rich Newman, Peter Nohrnberg, Susan O'Donovan, Charles Ogletree, Robert Paquette, Manisha Sinha, Ben Soskis, James Brewer Stewart, Robert Wallace, and John Wood.

Then there are the scholars with whom I was never able to speak directly, yet their voices have been ever present, as it were, during the research and writing: Robert Abzug, Paul Angle, Jean Baker, Roy Basler, John Blassingame, Gabor Boritt, Michael Burlingame, Richard Carwardine, James Colaiaco, Sally Denton, Maria Diedrich, Eric Foner, Philip Foner, William Freehling, Ernest Furgurson, Doris Kearns Goodwin, John Hay, Harold Holzer, Margaret Leech, William McFeely, James McPherson, John Nicolay, James Oakes, Stephen Oates, Lloyd Ostendorf, Benjamin Quarles, David Reynolds, Carl Sandburg, James Simon, Michael Vorenberg, Ronald White, Douglas Wilson, and Jay Winik.

Since I rely heavily on primary sources, I am

grateful to the following archives, including the people who made the material accessible: Boston Public Library, Library of Congress, National Archives, Syracuse University Library, Historical Society of Pennsylvania, University of Rochester Library, Cornell University libraries, Boston Athenaeum, New York Public Library, New York Historical Society, Filson Historical Society, University of Illinois Library at Urbana-Champaign, Harvard libraries, and Yale libraries.

I'd also like to acknowledge family members who went out of their way in helping me finish this project: Bill and Jean Stauffer; Rachel Stauffer and Jim Lawson; Mark, Becky, and Connor LaFavre; Brian and Jan Cunningham; Dan and Alicia Cunningham; Christine Cunningham; and Jim and Kathryn Hourdequin.

Deborah Cunningham and Erik Isaiah Stauffer, to whom I dedicate the book, made it possible: the former because of her brilliant editing, support, and advice at every level; the latter through his infinite curiosity and wonder; and both for their love.

JOHN STAUFFER
Cambridge, Massachusetts

Notes

Abbreviations

BPL—Boston Public Library.

CW—The Collected Works of Abraham Lincoln, ed. Roy Basler. 9 vols. (New Brunswick: Rutgers University Press, 1953).

DPLC—Frederick Douglass Papers, Library of Congress.

DPUR—Frederick Douglass Papers, University of Rochester.

GSP—Gerrit Smith Papers, Syracuse University.

HSP—Historical Society of Pennsylvania.

LPLC—Abraham Lincoln Papers, Library of Congress.

LWFD—The Life and Writings of Frederick Douglass, ed. Philip S. Foner. 5 vols. (New York: International Publishers, 1950–1975).

OR—The War of the Rebellion: A Compilation of the Official Records of the Union and Confederate Armies. 128 vols. (Washington, D.C.: Government Printing Office, 1880–1901).

TFDP—The Frederick Douglass Papers, ed. John W. Blassingame, series 1, vols. 1–5 (New Haven: Yale University Press, 1979–1992).

Preface

1. On their common reading I have relied on multiple sources, especially Frederick Douglass, *My Bondage and My Freedom*, ed. John Stauffer (New York: Modern Library, 2003), pp. 81–82; Stauffer, *The Black Hearts of Men: Radical Abolitionists and the Transformation of Race* (Cambridge, Mass.: Harvard University Press, 2002), p. 249; David Herbert Donald, *Lincoln* (New York: Simon & Schuster, 1995), pp. 30–31; David W. Blight, *Beyond the Battlefield: Race, Memory, and the American Civil War* (Amherst: University of Massachusetts Press, 2002), p. 77.

2. Lincoln was six foot four, Douglass six foot one. On average heights I use figures from 1860 and rely on Richard H. Steckel, "A History of the Standard of Living in the United States," especially the table, "Average Height of Native-Born American Men and Women by Year of Birth," in EH.Net Encyclopedia, online at http://www.eh.net/encyclopedia/?article=steckel.standard.living.us.

3. Douglass, *My Bondage*, p. 70; Donald, *Lincoln*, p. 15.

4. On history as the activist's muse, see John Stauffer, foreword, *American Protest Literature*, ed. Zoe Trodd (Cambridge, Mass.: Harvard University Press, 2007), pp. xi–xviii.

5. On the invention of self-making, see chapter 2; and Irvin G. Wyllie, *The Self-Made Man in America: The Myth of Rags to Riches* (New York: Free Press, 1954), pp. 9–10.

6. John W. Blassingame, ed., *The Frederick Douglass Papers*, series 1, vols. 1–5 (New Haven: Yale University Press, 1979–92), vol. 3, pp. 289–300 (hereafter *TFDP*). Compare this early self-made-man speech with that in *TFDP* 1:5, pp. 545–574.

7. The quote is from Lincoln, who argued that "there is no such thing as a freeman being fatally fixed for life." Roy Basler, ed., *The Collected Works of Abraham Lincoln* (New Brunswick: Rutgers University Press, 1953), vol. 3, p. 478 (hereafter *CW*).

8. The quote is from Lincoln's 1860 speech at New Haven: "I am not ashamed to confess that twenty-five years ago I was a hired laborer, mauling rails, at work on a flat-boat—just what might happen to any poor man's son! [Applause.] I want every man to have the chance—and I believe a black man is entitled to it." *CW* 4, p. 24.

9. *TFDP* 5, p. 340. See also Stauffer, *Black Hearts of Men*, pp. 6–7.

10. As Eric Foner has summarized, "the foundations of the industrial capitalist state of the late nineteenth century, so similar in individualist rhetoric yet so different in social reality from Lincoln's America, were to a large extent laid during the Civil War. Here, indeed, is the tragic irony of that conflict. Each side fought to defend a distinct vision of the good society, but each vision was destroyed by the very struggle to preserve it." See Foner, *Politics and Ideology in the Age of the Civil War* (New York: Oxford University Press, 1980), pp. 15–33, quotation from p. 33; Alan Trachtenberg, *Reading American Photographs: Images as History from Mathew Brady to Walker Evans* (New York: Hill and Wang, 1989), pp. 71–118, esp. pp. 114–116.

11. In his dazzling, panoramic six-volume biography of Lincoln, Carl Sandburg includes a generous and sympathetic portrait of Douglass and his relationship with Lincoln. See Sandburg, *Abraham Lincoln: The War Years* (New York: Harcourt, Brace & Company, 1939), vol. 2, pp. 164, 181–187, 414–418; vol. 3, pp. 121, 246, 255, 262–264, 395–396; vol. 4, pp. 97–98, 253.

Two recent books focus on Lincoln and Douglass: James Oakes, *The Radical and the Republican: Frederick Douglass, Abraham Lincoln, and the Triumph of Antislavery Politics* (New York: W. W. Norton, 2007); and Paul Kendrick and Stephen Kendrick, *Douglass and Lincoln: How a Revolutionary Black Leader and a Reluctant Liberator Struggled to End Slavery and Save the Union* (New York: Walker & Company, 2008). Neither Oakes nor the Kendricks address Douglass's and Lincoln's self-making. Since their primary concern is Civil War politics, they offer only brief summaries of Douglass's and Lincoln's lives prior to the mid-1850s.

12. I am grateful to Zoe Trodd for help with this paragraph.

Prologue: *Meeting the President*

1. On slavery in Washington, D.C., and Maryland, see Michael Vorenberg, *Final Freedom: The Civil War, the Abolition of Slavery, and the Thirteenth Amendment* (Cambridge, UK: Cambridge University Press, 2001), pp. 25, 172; Barbara Jeanne Fields, *Slavery and Freedom on the Middle Ground: Maryland during the Nineteenth Century* (New Haven: Yale University Press, 1985), pp. 90–130; Benjamin Quarles, *Lincoln and the Negro* (1962; reprint, New York: Da Capo, 1990), pp. 103–108; Margaret Leech, *Reveille in Washington, 1860–1865* (New York: Harper & Brothers, 1941), pp. 245, 250–251; Henry Wilson, *History of the Rise and Fall of the Slave Power in America*, vol. 3 (Boston: James R. Osgood and Company, 1877), pp. 270–284; Ernest B. Furgurson, *Freedom Rising: Washington in the Civil War* (New York: Vintage, 2004), pp. 99–105, 149, 168–171, 327. On the railroad in Baltimore, see Furgurson, *Freedom Rising*, p. 44.

2. Philip S. Foner, ed., *The Life and Writings of Frederick Douglass*, vol. 3: *The Civil War, 1861–1865* (New York: International Publishers, 1952), pp. 317–318 (hereafter *LWFD*). In November 1862, U.S. attorney general Edward Bates gave free blacks citizenship in a legal opinion, thus reversing the decision by Roger Taney in the

Dred Scott decision of 1857. But Bates's decision did not imply equal rights for blacks, which Douglass sought. See Douglass, "Enlistment of Colored Men," *Douglass' Monthly*, August 1863; Douglass, "The Proclamation and a Negro Army," *The Frederick Douglass Papers*, ed. John W. Blassingame, series 1, vol. 3 (New Haven: Yale University Press, 1985), p. 550 (hereafter *TFDP*); Benjamin Quarles, *The Negro in the Civil War* (1953; reprint, New York: Da Capo, 1989), pp. 168–169.

3. Lewis Douglass, "The 54th Massachusetts at Fort Wagner," *Douglass' Monthly*, August 1863; Douglass to Gerrit Smith, March 6, 1863, *LWFD* 3, p. 320; William S. McFeely, *Frederick Douglass* (New York: W. W. Norton, 1991), p. 224; David W. Blight, *Frederick Douglass' Civil War: Keeping Faith in Jubilee* (Baton Rouge: Louisiana State University Press, 1989), pp. 170–171.

4. Douglass to Major G. L. Stearns, August 1, 1863, *LWFD* 3, p. 368.

5. John W. White Jr., *The American Railroad Passenger Car, Part 1* (Baltimore: Johns Hopkins University Press, 1978), pp. 202–235, quotations from pp. 204, 232. Despite the problems with trains, Douglass loved them and published numerous articles on them in his newspaper, including this aphorism: "Life is a vast railway train, in which we are compulsory passengers. On the outside is written—'No stoppage by the way.'" Douglass considered it an apt metaphor, a corollary to his favorite line from *Hamlet* about Providence shaping our ends. See the *North Star*, September 1, 1848; September 22, 1848.

6. Douglass to Major G. L. Stearns, August 1, 1863, in *LWFD* 3, p. 369; "Protection of Colored Troops," *Douglass' Monthly*, August 1863; Roy Basler, ed., *The Collected Works of Abraham Lincoln* (hereafter *CW*), vol. 6 (New Brunswick: Rutgers University Press, 1953), p. 357.

7. On train travel into Washington, see Furgurson, *Freedom Rising*, p. 44; and B&O schedules from Baltimore to Washington, D.C., in Baker Library, Harvard University. Mark Twain, who worked in Washington immediately after the war, described transportation into the city in this way: "You arrive either at night, rather too late to do anything or see anything until morning, or you arrive so early in the morning that you consider it best to go to your hotel and sleep an hour or two while the sun bothers along over the Atlantic. You cannot well arrive at a pleasant intermediate hour, because the railway corporation that keeps the keys of the only door that leads into the town or out of it takes care of that." Mark Twain and Charles Dudley Warner, *The Gilded Age: A Tale of Today* (1873; reprint, New York: New American Library, 1980), pp. 174–175 (the quote is from ch. 24, written by Twain). Douglass arrived early in the morning, as is evident from his letter to George Stearns: Douglass to Maj. George L. Stearns, August 12, 1863, Historical Society of Pennsylvania (hereafter *HSP*).

8. Leech, *Reveille in Washington*, pp. 250–255; Furgurson, *Freedom Rising*, pp. 12–13, 44, 255–259. The term "contrabands of war" originated early in the war, after slaves sought refuge in the Union camp of General

Benjamin Butler, who retained them and put them to work. See Wilson, *Rise and Fall of the Slave Power*, vol. 3, pp. 286–287; Quarles, *The Negro in the Civil War*, pp. 58–60.

9. Elizabeth Cady Stanton, quoted from Frederick S. Voss, *Majestic in His Wrath: A Pictorial Life of Frederick Douglass* (Washington, D.C.: Smithsonian Institution Press, 1995), p. v.

10. Harriet Jacobs, "Life Among the Contrabands," *Liberator*, September 5, 1862; Jean Fagan Yellin, *Harriet Jacobs: A Life* (New York: Basic Civitas Books, 2004), pp. 158–160, quotation from Jacobs on p. 159; Leech, *Reveille in Washington*, pp. 246–255; Furgurson, *Freedom Rising*, pp. 255–256.

11. Leech, *Reveille in Washington*, pp. 204–233, 261–266; Furgurson, *Freedom Rising*, pp. 237–242. It was perhaps fitting that the Patent Office, the place where new inventions were filed, became a site where wounded bodies were reinvented and hopefully restored.

12. John Hay to John Nicolay, August 9, 1863, in *Letters of John Hay and Extracts from Diary*, vol. 1 (1908; reprint, New York: Gordian Press, 1969), p. 91; Furgurson, *Freedom Rising*, p. 12.

13. George Stearns to Frederick Douglass, August 8, 1863, Douglass Papers, Library of Congress (hereafter *DPLC*); Douglass, *Life and Times of Frederick Douglass* (1881, 1892, reprint, New York: Collier, 1962), pp. 346–347. Douglass's memory of his first meeting with

Lincoln is faulty in a number of places, and so I use *Life and Times* sparingly and with caution.

Stearns met Lincoln only once, with a group of abolitionists. A letter from him would not have impressed Lincoln. On Stearns see Frank Preston Stearns, *The Life and Public Services of George Luther Stearns* (Philadelphia: J. B. Lippincott Company, 1907), pp. 278–279, 285–308; Charles E. Heller, *Portrait of an Abolitionist: A Biography of George Luther Stearns, 1809–1867* (Westport, Conn.: Greenwood Press, 1996), pp. 123–174.

Twain noted that the culture of Washington centered around "Political Influence": "Mere merit, fitness and capability, are useless baggage to you without 'influence.'" See Twain and Warner, *The Gilded Age*, p. 178.

14. Twain and Warner, *The Gilded Age*, p. 152.

15. In 1857, while visiting Boston, some Massachusetts abolitionists told John Brown that Pomeroy "seems to be an important man in Kansas" and then asked if he was a good general. Brown replied with a parable: "I wish the ladies of Massachusetts would make a large military cocked hat, about three feet in length, and a foot and a half in height; and put the tail-feathers of three roosters in it, and send it with their compliments to General Pomeroy." Two years later, after Brown's raid on the federal arsenal at Harpers Ferry, in the hopes of arming slaves and inciting a black revolution, Pomeroy visited him in prison. Brown was grateful for the visit, and he greeted Pomeroy by mimicking Christ: "In prison ye came unto me" (Matt. 25:36). Pomeroy asked if he should attempt to rescue Brown, but Brown

responded, "I am worth now infinitely more to die than to live." Pomeroy's unscrupulousness eventually destroyed his career. See Stearns, *George Luther Stearns*, p. 133; Oswald Garrison Villard, *John Brown, 1800–1859: A Biography Fifty Years After* (1910; reprint, New York: Alfred A. Knopf, 1943), p. 546.

On Pomeroy's antislavery work in Kansas, see Edward Langsdorf, "S.C. Pomeroy and the New England Emigrant Aid Company, 1854–1858," *Kansas Historical Quarterly* 7 (1938): 379–398.

16. At one level, there was not much difference between the Confiscation Act of 1862 and Lincoln's Emancipation Proclamation. Technically, the Confiscation Act freed slaves of rebels who were able to escape to Union lines. (Masters were allowed to retrieve their slaves from Union lines by giving an oath that they had neither joined nor aided the Confederacy.) And the Emancipation Proclamation freed slaves in the rebel states, except in Union-occupied Louisiana and the new state of West Virginia, which, like the border states, required the state legislature to abolish slavery. Practically speaking, the Proclamation did nothing for slaves until they escaped to Union lines.

As the historian Benjamin Quarles astutely noted, the Emancipation Proclamation "actually did not go much further than declaring that the President would thenceforth carry out the antislavery measures of Congress, particularly the Confiscation Act of July 17, 1862, which declared free the slaves who escaped from masters who were rebels." It "was little more than an official sanction of a movement that had already gotten under way. The

Proclamation was an accessory after the fact: Negroes had been making themselves free since the beginning of the war." See Quarles, *The Negro in the Civil War*, p. 162; Quarles, *Lincoln and the Negro*, p. 187.

The Confiscation Act and the Emancipation Proclamation opened the way for recruiting black soldiers.

On Pomeroy introducing the bill that became the Confiscation Act of 1862, see Wilson, *Rise and Fall of the Slave Power*, vol. 3, pp. 331–346.

17. During the war, Pomeroy transferred Indian lands to railroads and settlers. As a member of the Senate Committee on Public Lands, he helped pass legislation benefiting Kansas railroads. He was also the president of Atchison, Topeka, and Santa Fe Railroad, ignoring the conflict of interest between his support of the railroad and duties as a senator. In 1862 he allegedly attempted to bribe W. W. Ross, the government agent of the Pottawatomie Indians, to give an exclusive license to a merchant who would share the profits with Pomeroy.

After the war, Pomeroy became an emblem of Gilded Age corruption. He bribed state senators (who elected U.S. senators) during his 1867 reelection, but escaped censure. His public humiliation came in 1872, when a state legislator held up in Congress $7,000 that Pomeroy had tried to bribe him with in exchange for his vote. Although the courts refused to prosecute, Pomeroy's reputation was ruined. In 1873 he appeared, thinly disguised, as the corrupt Senator Abner Dilworthy in Mark Twain and Dudley Warner's novel *The Gilded Age*.

See Martha B. Caldwell, "Pomeroy's 'Ross Letter': Genuine or Forgery?" *Kansas Historical Quarterly* 13:7

(August 1944): 463–472; Albert R. Kitzhaber, "*Gotter-dammerung* in Topeka: The Downfall of Senator Pomeroy," *Kansas Historical Quarterly* 18 (1950): 243–278; Margaret Lynn Strobel, "A Political Biography of Senator Samuel C. Pomeroy of Kansas," Master's Thesis, Pennsylvania State University, 1962; Twain and Warner, *Gilded Age*, pp. 149ff.; Albert. R. Kitzhaber, "Mark Twain's Use of the Pomeroy Case in *The Gilded Age*," *Modern Language Quarterly* 15:1 (March 1954): 42–56; Bryant Morey French, "Mark Twain, Laura D. Fair and the New York Criminal Courts," *American Quarterly* 16:4 (Winter 1964): 545–561.

18. In *Life and Times*, Douglass says erroneously that he first went to see Lincoln, then Stanton. But immediately after the meeting, Douglass says he first went with Pomeroy to see Stanton. See Douglass to Maj. G. L. Stearns, August 12, 1863, HSP.

The other two contemporaneous documents on Douglass's meeting with Lincoln and Stanton are: Douglass, "Our Work is Not Done," Speech at the Annual Meeting of the American Anti-Slavery Society Held at Philadelphia, December 3–4, 1863, in *LWFD* 3, pp. 383–385 (republished with notes in *TFDP* 1:3, pp. 606–608); and "The Black Man at the White House," *Chicago Tribune*, February 29, 1864.

19. John Eaton, *Grant, Lincoln and the Freedmen: Reminiscences of the Civil War* (New York: Longmans, Green, and Co., 1907), p. 179.

20. Douglass to Stearns, August 12, 1863, HSP.

21. Ibid.

22. In describing how blacks were the victims of two extreme opinions, Douglass was vague; he said only that one opinion "claimed for him too much and the other too little." (Douglass to Stearns, August 12, 1863, HSP.) I have elaborated by synthesizing a number of other writings from Douglass that analyze white perceptions of blacks.

23. Douglass to Stearns, August 12, 1863, HSP.

24. Ibid.

25. Ibid.

26. Ibid. Stanton may have been referring to the Militia Act. Then too, Douglass may have misinterpreted the nature of Stanton's "bill."

See Dudley Taylor Cornish, *The Sable Arm: Black Troops in the Union Army, 1861-1865* (1956; reprint, Lawrence, Kan.: 1987), pp. 46-47, 184-195; Wilson, *Rise and Fall of the Slave Power*, vol. 3, p. 346; George P. Sanger, ed., *The Statutes at Large, Treaties, and Proclamations, of the United States of America. From December 5, 1859, to March 3, 1863 ...*, *Vol. XII* (Boston: Little, Brown and Company, 1863), pp. 597-599.

27. Stanton to Saxton, August 25, 1862, *The War of the Rebellion: A Compilation of the Official Records of the Union and Confederate Armies* (hereafter *OR*), series 1, vol. 14 (Washington, D.C.: Government Printing Office, 1900), p. 377 (emphasis added); Sanger, ed., *Statutes at Large*, pp. 589-592, 597-599; Wilson, *Rise*

and Fall of the Slave Power, vol. 3, p. 370; Cornish, *The Sable Arm*, pp. 46–47, 53–55, 79–83, 181–196; Joseph T. Glatthaar, *Forged in Battle: The Civil War Alliance of Black Soldiers and White Officers* (New York: Free Press, 1990), pp. 7, 37; Benjamin P. Thomas and Harold M. Hyman, *Stanton: The Life and Times of Lincoln's Secretary of War* (New York: Alfred A. Knopf, 1962), pp. 263–264; Stanton, quoted from *George Luther Stearns*, p. 304.

The note Stanton attached to his order to Saxton is included in Wilson, *Rise and Fall of the Slave Power*, vol. 3, p. 370, but not in Stanton's letter to Saxton in the *Official Records*.

Stanton could have ended discrimination in soldiers' pay by reversing the opinion of his solicitor-general, William Whiting, who followed the guidelines of the Militia Act and concluded that blacks should receive the pay of laborers rather than of soldiers. Five months after meeting with Douglass, Stanton "urged Congress to correct the inequity of Negro soldier's pay." See Cornish, *The Sable Arm*, pp. 187–189.

28. Douglass to Stearns, August 12, 1863, HSP.

29. Ibid. In his letter to Stearns, Douglass does not specifically refer to Stanton's promise of a commission, but he implies it: he says Stanton has offered him a job and asks him "to report to Gen. Thomas and cooperate with him," adding that Stanton "would send me sufficient papers [presumably a commission] immediately." Eighteen years later, in his third autobiography, Douglass specifically refers to the commission: "On assuring Mr. Stanton of my willingness to take a commission, he said he

would make me assistant adjutant to General Thomas, who was then recruiting and organizing troops in the Mississippi valley." Since the offer of a commission was such a momentous event for a black man at the time, it is unlikely that Douglass's memory failed him on this point, even though his memory erred in other details of the meeting. It is also possible that Douglass understood Stanton to have offered him a commission when Stanton in fact had not, though this too is unlikely given the import of a commission for a black man. Before agreeing to go South, Douglass would have made sure that he had a commission. See Douglass, *Life and Times*, p. 350.

30. Douglass, *Life and Times*, p. 350.

31. Douglass to Stearns, August 12, 1863, HSP.

32. Douglass was not the first black to be offered a commission in the Civil War. Alexander Augusta was the first African American to receive a medical commission in the U.S. Army, one of seven to receive such appointments. Douglass's son Lewis had already been promoted to the noncommissioned officer rank of sergeant. And Douglass's youngest son, Frederick Jr., was in Mississippi recruiting black troops, but not as a commissioned officer. See Dalyce Newby, "Alexander Thomas Augusta," *American National Biography* online; Lewis Douglass, "The 54th Massachusetts at Fort Wagner," *Douglass' Monthly*, August 1863; McFeely, *Frederick Douglass*, p. 224; Blight, *Frederick Douglass' Civil War*, p. 170.

33. The analogy between orators in the Civil War era and athletes today is especially appropriate because, in the twentieth century, the Civil War "came to resemble in many minds the nation's greatest athletic contest, a kind of mid-nineteenth century Super Bowl between All-American heroes." In the cultures of war and athletics, two kinds of heroes are needed: the warrior and the thinker (orator, politician, coach, writer). There is often as much posturing and competition among the "thinkers" as there is among the warriors.

One might go so far as to say that our culture of sports today replaces a culture of war in the eighteenth and nineteenth centuries, when competition was much more about survival than winning. The defeat at Fredericksburg "dominated the mood of" Washington in December in much the same way that a Red Sox defeat "dominates" the mood of Boston in September.

The analogy of the Civil War with the Super Bowl comes from David Brion Davis, *Inhuman Bondage: The Rise and Fall of Slavery in the New World* (New York: Oxford University Press, 2006), p. 305. On the mood in Washington following Fredericksburg, see Furgurson, *Freedom Rising*, pp. 221–222.

34. This note is in Frederick Douglass Papers, LC. Douglass may have run into J. W. Menard, an African American who worked as a clerk in the Emigration Office of the Department of the Interior. Menard had written Lincoln for help in emigrating to Liberia, and Lincoln recommended him for the job in the Emigration Office. See Quarles, *Lincoln and the Negro*, pp. 122, 193.

35. Douglass, "Our Work is Not Done," *LWFD* 3, p. 384. Montgomery Blair's endorsement of Douglass's pass was ironic, because a year earlier Douglass had attacked Blair's endorsement of colonization.

36. Walt Whitman, *Memoranda During the War*, ed. Peter Coviello (1876; reprint, New York: Oxford University Press, 2004), p. 39. On Lincoln going to the Soldiers' Home, see also Furgurson, *Freedom Rising*, pp. 67, 189–190; Elizabeth Smith Brownstein, *Lincoln's Other White House: The Untold Story of the Man and His Presidency* (New York: John Wiley & Sons, 2005).

37. Whitman, *Memoranda During the War*, pp. 39–41, 78; Whitman, *Leaves of Grass: The First (1855) Edition* (New York: Penguin, 1986), p. 48. Whitman retains his self-characterization as "one of the roughs" through the first three editions of "Song of Myself," a poem that was untitled in the 1855 edition. In the fourth (1867) edition, the line was changed from "Walt Whitman, an American, one of the roughs, a kosmos" to "Walt Whitman am I, of mighty Manhattan the son." See also Daniel Mark Epstein, *Lincoln and Whitman: Parallel Lives in Civil War Washington* (New York: Ballantine, 2004); and Roy Morris Jr., *The Better Angel: Walt Whitman in the Civil War* (New York: Oxford University Press, 2000).

38. Epstein, *Lincoln and Whitman*, pp. 3–44.

39. Lincoln told Gardner, "The imperial photograph, in which the head leans upon the hand, I regard as the best that I have yet seen." Lincoln to Alexander Gardner, August 18, 1863, *CW* supplement 1, p. 199; Charles

Hamilton and Lloyd Ostendorf, *Lincoln in Photographs: An Album of Every Known Pose* (Dayton, Oh.: Morningside House, 1985), p. 139.

40. Noah Brooks, quoted from Furgurson, *Freedom Rising*, p. 222.

41. Lincoln to Meade, July 14, 1863, *CW* 6, pp. 328, 329 (see note on Lincoln's remark to his son); Michael Burlingame, ed., *An Oral History of Abraham Lincoln: John G. Nicolay's Interviews and Essays* (Carbondale: Southern Illinois University Press, 1996), pp. 88–89; John Hay's diary, in John G. Nicolay and John Hay, *Abraham Lincoln: A History*, vol. 7 (New York: The Century Co., 1890), p. 278.

42. Lincoln to Grant, July 13, 1863, *CW* 6, p. 326; "Proclamation of Thanksgiving," July 15, 1863, *CW* 6, p. 332; Lincoln, quoted in James M. McPherson, *Ordeal by Fire: The Civil War and Reconstruction*, 2nd ed. (New York: McGraw-Hill, 1992), p. 332. Lincoln inaugurated the national day of Thanksgiving and issued another proclamation of Thanksgiving for October 3, 1863.

43. David Herbert Donald, *Lincoln* (New York: Simon & Schuster, 1995), p. 448; Carl Sandburg, *Abraham Lincoln: The War Years*, vol. 2 (New York: Harcourt, Brace & Company, 1939), p. 359–372; McPherson, *Battle Cry of Freedom: The Civil War Era* (New York: Ballantine, 1988), pp. 608–611; Stearns, *George Luther Stearns*, pp. 297–300, quotations from pp. 297, 298.

44. Douglass, "The Commander-in-Chief and His Black Soldiers," *Douglass' Monthly*, August 1863, reprinted in

LWFD 3, p. 370; Lincoln, quoted in Sandburg, *Lincoln: The War Years*, vol. 2, p. 368; Donald, *Lincoln*, p. 448; Stearns, *George Luther Stearns*, p. 304.

Douglass had penned his essay, which harshly criticizes Lincoln, before meeting the president. Douglass's articles in *Douglass' Monthly* generally appear in the order in which they were written.

45. *Lincoln in the Civil War in the Diary and Letters of John Hay* (New York: Dodd, Mead & Company, 1939), p. 73; *Letters of John Hay and Extracts from Diary*, vol. 1, p. 91; Donald, *Lincoln*, pp. 448-451.

46. *CW* 6, pp. 374-375.

47. Quarles, *Lincoln and the Negro*, pp. 108-123, 191-194. See also James M. McPherson, "Abolitionist and Negro Opposition to Colonization during the Civil War," *Phylon* 26:4 (4th Quarter 1965): 391-399; James D. Lockett, "Abraham Lincoln and Colonization: An Episode That Ends in Tragedy at L'Ile a Vache, Haiti, 1863-1864," *Journal of Black Studies* 21:4 (June 1991): 428-444; Kinley J. Brauer, "The Slavery Problem in the Diplomacy of the American Civil War," *Pacific Historical Review* 46:3 (August 1977): 439-469; Brainerd Dyer, "The Persistence of the Idea of Negro Colonization," *Pacific Historical Review* 12:1 (March 1943): 53-65; Sharon Hartman Strom, "Labor, Race, and Colonization: Imagining a Post-Slavery World in the Americas," in Steven Mintz and John Stauffer, eds., *The Problem of Evil* (Amherst: University of Massachusetts Press, 2007), pp. 260-275.

48. Quarles, *Lincoln and the Negro*, pp. 111–123, 185–194; *CW* 5, pp. 192, 370–371. Pomeroy was chair of the Senate Committee on Public Land, including land used for colonization.

49. *CW* 5, pp. 371–372.

50. Douglass, "The President and His Speeches," *LWFD* 3, pp. 266–270, quotation from pp. 268, 270.

51. *CW* 5, pp. 371; Quarles, *Lincoln and the Negro*, pp. 112–113, 194.

52. Among Haitians, the island was called L'Ile à Vache, which translates as Cow Island.

53. Quarles, *Lincoln and the Negro*, pp. 113–114, 191–194; *CW* 6, pp. 41–42, 178–179; Lockett, "Lincoln and Colonization," pp. 439–443. Donald erroneously states that with the Emancipation Proclamation, Lincoln abandoned his plans to "colonize blacks outside the United States." Donald, *Lincoln*, p. 430. It is one of the only flaws in a brilliant book that has influenced me greatly.

54. Quarles, *Lincoln and the Negro*, pp. 192–194.

55. Eaton, *Grant, Lincoln and the Freedmen*, pp. 87–93, quotation from pp. 91–92; Quarles, *Lincoln and the Negro*, pp. 192–193; Lockett, "Lincoln and Colonization," pp. 440–443; Noah Swayne to Lincoln, July 16, 1863, in Abraham Lincoln Papers, Library of Congress (hereafter *LPLC*); Eaton to Lincoln, July 18, 1863, LPLC; Robert Dale Owen to Lincoln, August 5, 1863, LPLC. Conditions on Cow Island were worse than slavery, partly owing to a white man who presided over the émigrés like

"an absolute monarch." Eighty-five, or 20 percent of the émigrés, died en route or on the island. Lockett, "Lincoln and Colonization," quotation on p. 440.

56. Eaton, *Grant, Lincoln and the Freedmen*, pp. 87–92, quotation from p. 91.

57. Lincoln to Banks, August 5, 1863, *CW* 6, p. 365 (emphasis added); Lincoln to James C. Conkling, August 26, 1863, *CW* 6, p. 409.

58. Douglass, "Our Work is Not Done," *LWFD* 3, p. 384.

59. Douglass, "Our Work is Not Done," *LWFD* 3, p. 384; Douglass, *Life and Times*, p. 347. In 1864 Pomeroy spearheaded the candidacy of Secretary of the Treasury Salmon P. Chase for president. Lincoln, who had probably already lost trust in Pomeroy when he arrived at the White House with Douglass, in one harsh letter of 1864 said that the senator's incessant requests on behalf of friends were "tormenting my life out of me, and nothing else." Lincoln to Pomeroy, March 12, 1864, *CW* 7, p. 338.

60. Douglass, "Our Work is Not Done," *LWFD* 3, p. 384. A variation of the quote is in Lincoln to Stearns, August 12, 1863, HSP.

61. Douglass, "Our Work is Not Done," *LWFD* 3, p. 384. Douglass quotes Lincoln as saying, "I am charged with vacilating; but, Mr. Douglass, I do not think that charge can be sustained; I think it cannot be shown that when I have once taken a position, I have ever retreated from it." I have altered the quote slightly to avoid the

clunky double negative. A variation of this quote is in Douglass's letter to Stearns: "No man can say that having once taken a position, I have contradicted it or retreated from it." Douglass to Stearns, August 12, 1863, HSP.

62. Douglass to Stearns, August 12, 1863, HSP. In his First Inaugural Lincoln reversed his platform seeking an "ultimate extinction" of slavery by endorsing the proposed Thirteenth Amendment, which Congress had just passed, guaranteeing slavery in the slave states. In his virulent critique of this speech, Douglass acknowledges that Lincoln virtually reversed his policy: "No man reading it could say whether Mr. Lincoln was for peace or war, whether he abandons or maintains the principles of the Chicago Convention upon which he was elected." Douglass then explains Lincoln's policy in the Chicago nominating convention: "The South want to extend slavery, and the North want to confine it where it is, 'where the public mind shall rest in the belief of its ultimate extinction.' This was the question which carried the North and defeated the South in the election which made Mr. Abraham Lincoln President. Mr. Lincoln knew this, and the South has known it all along; and yet this subject only gets the faintest allusion." See Douglass, "The Inaugural Address," *Douglass' Monthly*, April 1861, in *LWFD* 3, p. 72. See also chapter 4 below.

63. Douglass, "Our Work is Not Done," *LWFD* 3, p. 385.

64. Douglass to Stearns, August 12, 1863, HSP.

65. Douglass, *Life and Times*, p. 348.

66. Douglass to Stearns, August 12, 1863, HSP.

67. Douglass, *Life and Times*, p. 359.

68. Douglass to Stearns, August 12, 1863, HSP.

69. John Hay, *Lincoln and the Civil War*, p. 79.

70. The pass is in the Frederick Douglass Papers, Library of Congress (FDLC).

71. C. W. Foster to Frederick Douglass, August 13, 1863, FDLC. Foster, Stanton's secretary, wrote the letter under "instructions" from Stanton. Foster sent a copy of this letter to Brigadier General Daniel H. Rucker, August 13, 1863, FDLC. Douglass's response to Stanton on August 14 is summarized in C. W. Foster to Douglass, August 21, 1863, FDLC.

72. Douglass began publishing *Douglass' Monthly* in June 1858 as a supplement to his weekly, *Frederick Douglass' Paper*, which had originally been the *North Star*. In January 1859 *Douglass' Monthly* became a separate publication. In July 1860 he ceased publishing *Frederick Douglass' Paper* owing to lack of funds, and for the next three years published only a monthly.

73. Douglass, "Valedictory," August 16, 1863, *Douglass' Monthly*, August 1863, reprinted in *LWFD* 3, pp. 374–377, quotations from pp. 374, 376.

74. Douglass to Thomas Webster, Esq., August 19, 1863, *LWFD* 3, p. 377.

75. C. W. Foster to Douglass, August 21, 1863, FDLC.

76. Stearns to Douglass, August 29, 1863, FDLC. See also Blight, *Frederick Douglass' Civil War*, pp. 169–174; McFeely, *Frederick Douglass*, pp. 227–229; Quarles, *Frederick Douglass* (1948; reprint, New York: Da Capo, 1997), pp. 212–214.

77. Douglass, *Life and Times*, 350; Stearns, *George Luther Stearns*, p. 297. See also Julia Griffiths Crofts to Douglass, December 10, 1863, FDLC, in which Crofts expresses her thanks that Douglass remained in Rochester, owing to the danger of going south.

78. Douglass, "Our Work is Not Done," *LWFD* 3, pp. 383, 385.

79. Ibid., p. 385. The full quote reads: "We are not to be saved by the captain, at this time, but by the crew. We are not to be saved by Abraham Lincoln, but by that power behind the throne."

80. *TFDP* 5, pp. 540, 566; John Eaton, quoted from *In Memoriam: Frederick Douglass* (1897; reprint, Freeport, N.Y.: Books for Libraries Press, 1971), p. 71.

One: *Privileged Slave and Poor White Trash*

1. Frederick Douglass, *My Bondage and My Freedom* (1855), ed. John Stauffer (New York: Modern Library, 2003), p. 114. For this section, I am especially indebted to Dickson J. Preston, *Young Frederick Douglass: The Maryland Years* (Baltimore: Johns Hopkins University Press, 1980). In recounting Douglass's story, I rely pri-

marily on *My Bondage and My Freedom* because it is the most detailed of his three autobiographies and it better captures Douglass's inner psychological self.

2. Douglass, *My Bondage*, pp. 46–47, 115, quotation from p. 115.

3. Ibid., p. 116.

4. Ibid., pp. 116, 119–120.

5. Ibid., p. 118. "The ox is the poor man's slave" is from Aristotle, who articulated a natural slave ideal that would be endorsed by every subsequent slave society, including the United States. When Douglass recalled this incident, he had read Aristotle. See David Brion Davis, *In the Image of God: Religion, Moral Values, and Our Heritage of Slavery* (New Haven: Yale University Press, 2001), p. 126; John Stauffer, "Frederick Douglass and the Aesthetics of Freedom," *Raritan: A Quarterly Review* 25:1 (Summer 2005): 114–136.

6. Preston, *Young Frederick Douglass*, p. 121.

7. Douglass, *My Bondage*, p. 8; Stauffer, *The Black Hearts of Men: Radical Abolitionists and the Transformation of Race* (Cambridge, Mass.: Harvard University Press, 2002), pp. 83–84. Frederick declared that "the first seven or eight years of [his life were] about as full of sweet content as those of the most favored and petted *white* children of the slaveholder." But he downplays the class advantages wealthy white children had over him.

8. Preston, *Young Frederick Douglass*, pp. 8, 32.

9. Ibid., pp. 22–30, 41–66.

10. Ibid., pp. 110–111.

11. Douglass, *My Bondage*, p. 203; Douglass, *Life and Times of Frederick Douglass* (1892, reprint, New York: Collier, 1962), p. 206.

12. Preston, *Young Frederick Douglass*, pp. 3–10.

13. Douglass, *My Bondage*, pp. 14–16.

14. Douglass, *Life and Times*, pp. 28–29, quotation from p. 29; Douglass, *My Bondage*, pp. 14–15; Stauffer, *Black Hearts of Men*, pp. 188–190; Preston, *Young Frederick Douglass*, pp. 9–10. As an adult, Frederick discovered in a book on anthropology a picture of an Egyptian pharaoh, whose features closely resembled those of his mother. According to the author, James Cowles Prichard, the pharaoh was more Asian than African and in appearance "approached the Hindoo." On Hindus being viewed as close racial kin of Native Americans, see Henry Rowe Schoolcraft, "The Race of American Indians," *United States Magazine and Democratic Review* 28:155 (May 1851): 429–435; William Ragan Stanton, *The Leopard's Spots: Scientific Attitudes Toward Race in America, 1815–1859* (1960; reprint, Chicago: University of Chicago Press, 1972); and Thomas Gossett, *Race: The History of an Idea in America* (1963; reprint, New York: Schocken, 1968).

15. Douglass, *Life and Times*, p. 513 (quoted); Douglass, "Self-Made Men," Address Before the Students of the Indian Industrial School at Carlisle, Pennsylvania, April 6,

1894, Frederick Douglass Papers, Library of Congress (hereafter FDLC) (quoted). See also Preston, *Young Frederick Douglass*, p. 9; Stauffer, *Black Hearts of Men*, pp. 188–190.

16. Stauffer, *Black Hearts of Men*, pp. 188–190; Preston, *Young Frederick Douglass*, pp. xiv, 9–10; Reginald Horsman, *Race and Manifest Destiny: The Origins of American Racial Anglo-Saxonism* (Cambridge, Mass.: Harvard University Press, 1981), ch. 3.

17. Douglass, *My Bondage*, pp. 18, 33–34, quotations from pp. 33–34; Preston, *Young Frederick Douglass*, pp. 22–30.

18. My interpretation has been inspired by the evidence in Preston, *Young Frederick Douglass*, pp. 22–30. See also Peter Walker, *Moral Choices: Memory, Desire, and Imagination in Nineteenth-Century American Abolition* (Baton Rouge: Louisiana State University Press, 1978), pp. 209–261.

It is also possible that Thomas Auld was Douglass's father; in an 1847 speech Douglass says, "I was given away by my father, or the man who was called my father [Thomas Auld], to his own brother [Hugh Auld]....Thus was I transferred by my father to my uncle." See John W. Blassingame, ed., *The Frederick Douglass Papers*, series 1, vol. 2 (New Haven: Yale University Press, 1982), pp. 42–43 (hereafter *TFDP*).

19. Douglass, *Life and Times*, p. 187.

20. Douglass, *My Bondage*, pp. 101, 104–105; Douglass, *Life and Times*, p. 106 (quoted).

21. Douglass, *My Bondage*, pp. 105–112; Preston, *Young Frederick Douglass*, pp. 105–117, quotation from p. 108.

22. Douglass, *Narrative of the Life of Frederick Douglass, An American Slave, Written by Himself*, ed. David W. Blight, 2nd ed. (Boston: Bedford/St. Martin's, 2003), p. 79.

23. Douglass, *My Bondage*, pp. 117, 120, 122; Preston, *Young Frederick Douglass*, pp. 118–119.

24. Douglass, *My Bondage*, p. 112. Douglass never says how much Thomas Auld received for renting him out; my estimate of over $100 is purposefully low, as Covey's reputation as a slave-breaker allowed him to command lower rents, according to Douglass. On slave hirings, see Clement Eaton, "Slave-Hiring in the Upper South: A Step toward Freedom," *Mississippi Valley Historical Review* 46:4 (March 1960): 663–678, esp. p. 663; Keith C. Barton, "'Good Cooks and Washers': Slave Hiring, Domestic Labor, and the Market in Bourbon County, Kentucky," *Journal of American History* 84:2 (September 1997): 436–460; Jonathan D. Martin, *Divided Mastery: Slave Hiring in the American South* (Cambridge, Mass.: Harvard University Press, 2004).

On converting 1830s money into 2008 currency, I multiply antebellum money (1830–1860) by a factor of 75. I arrive at this figure by comparing a skilled laborer's wage of roughly $500 in the 1840s to an average annual family income in 2000 of around $37,500: 37,500 ÷ 500 = 75. See U.S. Bureau of the Census, *Historical Statistics of the United States: Colonial Times*

28. Douglass, *My Bondage*, pp. 123-124; Douglass, *Narrative*, pp. 83-84. See also John Stauffer, "Frederick Douglass' Self Fashioning and the Making of a Representative Man," in Audrey Fish, ed., *Cambridge Companion to the Slave Narrative* (Cambridge: Cambridge University Press, 2007).

29. Threshing is now done with a combine.

30. *My Bondage*, pp. 125-126; Preston, *Young Frederick Douglass*, pp. 123-124.

31. Douglass, *My Bondage*, p. 126.

32. Ibid., p. 127.

33. Ibid., p. 129.

34. Ibid., pp. 129-130.

35. Ibid., p. 130.

36. Ibid.

37. Ibid.

38. Ibid., p. 156.

39. Ibid., p. 133.

40. Ibid.

41. Ibid., p. 134; Preston, *Young Frederick Douglass*, p. 126.

42. Douglass, *My Bondage*, pp. 134-135.

to 1970, Part I (Washington, D.C.: U.S. Departmen
Commerce, Economics and Statistics Administrati
1995), p. 224; idem, *Statistical Abstract of the Uni
States, 1994: The National Data Book* (Washingt
D.C.: U.S. Department of Commerce, Economics a
Statistics Administration, 1995), pp. 487–488. See a
Stauffer, *Black Hearts of Men*, p. 322, n. 84. I am grate
to Stanley Engerman for helping me with this statist

25. Douglass, *My Bondage*, pp. 120, 123, quotation fro
p. 123.

26. Ibid., p. 123.

27. *TFDP* 1:1, pp. 166–167, 170, 206–209, quotatior
from pp. 166, 170, 208. In his autobiographies Dou;
lass does not mention that he drank on Saturday nigh
while working for Edward Covey, though he says tha
he was "induced" to drink during the holiday betweer
Christmas and New Year (*My Bondage*, p. 145). Ac
knowledging drunkenness would have cut against hi
self-image of an earnest and rebellious slave. He's more
open about his drinking in his temperance lectures in
Scotland in 1846. Here Douglass confesses to getting
drunk on Saturday nights and implicates himself as the
person who fell asleep by a pigsty and then crawled
into it: "I used to think I was a president. And this puts
me in mind of a man who once thought himself a president [i.e., himself]. He was coming across a field pretty
tipsy" and "lay himself down near a pigsty, and the pig
being out at the time, he crawled into it" (*TFDP* 1:1, p.
208).

43. Ibid., p. 135. Douglass refers to Sandy as "a genuine African," but as Preston notes, it is unclear whether this means that he had been born in Africa or embraced African beliefs. See Preston, *Young Frederick Douglass*, p. 227, n. 4.

44. Douglass, *My Bondage*, p. 136.

45. Ibid.

46. Ibid., p. 137.

47. Acts 10:34.

48. Douglass, *My Bondage*, pp. 137–138, 140; Preston, *Young Frederick Douglass*, pp. 127–128.

49. Douglass, *My Bondage*, p. 138.

50. Ibid.

51. Ibid.

52. Ibid., pp. 138, 139; Preston, *Young Frederick Douglass*, p. 128. Preston also uses the phrase "proud of his race."

53. Douglass, *My Bondage*, p. 140.

54. Ibid.; Douglass, *Narrative*, p. 89.

55. On "turning points" in a subject's life, see Louis Menand, "Lives of Others," *New Yorker*, August 6, 2007, pp. 65–66; and Menand, *American Studies* (New York: Farrar, Straus and Giroux, 2002), pp. 3–30. On the power of belief, see William James, *The Will to Believe and Other Essays in Popular Philosophy,* and *Talks to*

Teachers on Psychology and to Students on Some of Life's Ideals: Writings, 1878-1899 (New York: Library of America, 1992), pp. 457-479, 841-880.

56. Douglass, *My Bondage*, p. 141.

57. Ibid.

58. Ibid., p. 146.

59. Ibid., p. 150.

60. Ibid., p. 163.

61. Ibid., p. 165.

62. Ibid., p. 164.

63. Frederick suspected Sandy as the informer based on his conversation with Thomas Auld: "From something which dropped, in the course of the talk, it appeared that there was but one witness against us—and that that witness could not be produced. Master Thomas would not tell us *who* his informant was; but we suspected, and suspected *one* person *only*. Several circumstances seemed to point SANDY out, as our betrayer." Though Douglass suspects Sandy, he does not indict him: "His entire knowledge of our plans ... were calculated to turn suspicion toward him; and yet, we could not suspect him. We all loved him too well to think it possible that he could have betrayed us. So we rolled the guilt on other shoulders." *My Bondage*, p. 172.

64. See William Freehling's brilliant analysis of slave informers in *The Road to Disunion: Secessionists at Bay,*

1776–1854 (New York: Oxford University Press, 1990), p. 79.

With his wife already free, Sandy had more incentive than most slaves to seek his freedom. He had "good sense," as Frederick noted, and probably calculated that by turning on his friends, he could at least negotiate work so that he could live with his wife and possibly also gain his freedom.

65. Douglass, *My Bondage*, p. 170.

66. Ibid.

67. Ibid., p. 177.

68. Ibid., p. 175.

69. On Frederick being worth $1,000, see Preston, *Young Frederick Douglass*, p. 135. On conversion to today's dollars, see note 24 above. Auld's comparative kindness is understandable if Frederick was in fact the half brother of his wife, Lucretia—or perhaps his own son.

Thomas Auld's promise to emancipate Frederick at age twenty-five (as opposed to, say, twenty-one) was based on precedent: a number of Northern states had passed gradual emancipation acts which declared slaves free at age twenty-five. See Arthur Zilversmit, *The First Emancipation: The Abolition of Slavery in the North* (Chicago: University of Chicago Press, 1967).

70. Douglass, *My Bondage*, p. 70.

71. Ibid., p. 183; Douglass, *Life and Times*, pp. 76, 183; Preston, *Young Frederick Douglass*, p. 85.

72. Hugh and Sophia's sense of humility stemmed in part from the fact that Hugh's shipbuilding business had failed and he now worked as a foreman in another yard. Their financial loses coincided with the Panic of 1837, one of the worst depressions in American history. See Preston, *Young Frederick Douglass*, pp. 143-147; Stauffer, *Black Hearts of Men*, pp. 95-133.

73. Douglass, *My Bondage*, pp. 185-190, quotation from p. 190; Douglass, *Life and Times*, pp. 185-187.

74. Douglass, *My Bondage*, pp. 190-193; Douglass, *Life and Times*, pp. 187-191, quotations from pp. 188, 190.

75. Some evidence suggests that Frederick worked nights as a butler during these months when he hired himself out, but if so he never admitted as much, for it suggested obsequiousness and flew in the face of his vow to resist all tyrants. See William S. McFeely, *Frederick Douglass* (New York: W. W. Norton, 1991), pp. 65-66.

76. Douglass, *My Bondage*, pp. 86-90, 192-193; Douglass, *Life and Times*, pp. 190-191; Stauffer, *Black Hearts of Men*, pp. 82-86.

77. Douglass, *My Bondage*, pp. 192-193. The same quotes appear in Douglass, *Life and Times*, pp. 190-191.

78. Douglass, *Life and Times*, pp. 188-199, quotation from p. 188; Preston, *Young Frederick Douglass*, p. 152.

79. John H. White Jr., *The American Railroad Passenger Car*, part 1 (Baltimore: Johns Hopkins University Press, 1978), pp. 2–26, 35, 203–205; Charles Dickens, *American Notes* (1842; reprint, New York: Penguin, 2004), pp. 72–73.

80. Douglass, *Life and Times*, pp. 198–199. Douglass first revealed how he escaped from slavery in an 1873 speech. His first published account was in 1880. He waited until after the Civil War because he did not want the "underground railroad" becoming an "upperground railroad," as he said. He criticized such black abolitionist colleagues as Henry "Box" Brown and William and Ellen Crafts, who published accounts of their sensational escapes shortly after obtaining their freedom, thus exposing their means to slaveowners and making it much more difficult for other slaves to succeed by the same route. See Douglass, *My Bondage*, pp. 187–189, quotation from p. 188.

Douglass published accounts of his escape in places other than *Life and Times*: "Frederick Douglass," *New York Times*, December 27, 1880; "My Escape from Slavery," *Century Magazine*, November 1881; the manuscript in FDLC; and Preston, *Young Frederick Douglass*, p. 229, n. 18. These subsequent accounts closely resemble the one in *Life and Times*.

81. Douglass, *Life and Times*, p. 199.

82. Ibid., pp. 199–200.

83. Ibid., pp. 200–201, quotation from p. 201.

84. Ibid., p. 202; *My Bondage*, p. 199; Stauffer, *Black Hearts of Men*, p. 114.

85. In 1857, Douglass wrote Hugh Auld a private letter wanting to know the whereabouts of Auld's children, adding, "I love you but hate slavery." It was his attempt at a private reconciliation with his former master at the same time that he publicly treated Auld as an enemy. Hugh never responded to the letter, however, owing to his bitterness over the way in which Douglass had characterized him in his best-selling autobiographies (the 1845 *Narrative of the Life of Frederick Douglass* and the 1855 *My Bondage and My Freedom*). See Preston, *Young Frederick Douglass*, p. 168; and Douglass to Hugh Auld, October 4, 1857, reprinted in James G. Basker, ed., *Why Documents Matter: American Originals and the Historical Imagination: Selections from the Gilder Lehrman Collection* (New York: Gilder Lehrman Institute of American History, 2005), pp. 20–21.

86. Douglass, *My Bondage*, p. 104; Stauffer, *Black Hearts of Men*, pp. 188–194.

87. Philip S. Foner, ed., *The Life and Writings of Frederick Douglass*, vol. 1, *Early Years* (New York: International Publishers, 1950), pp. 403–406. In this 1849 letter to Auld, Frederick says he is gratified that Auld has emancipated his slaves, but then points out the distance Auld still needs to travel to become an abolitionist and thus Frederick's friend: "I shall no longer regard you as an enemy to freedom, nor to myself—but shall hail you as a friend to both.—*Before* doing so, however, I have one reasonable request to make of you, with which you

will, I hope, comply. It is this: That you make your conversion to anti-slavery known to the world, by precept as well as example" (p. 404). Auld didn't respond to the letter, nor did he publicly affirm an antislavery stance. As Frederick knew, there was a huge distance between a slaveowner who chose to manumit his slave and an abolitionist who believed that slavery was everywhere an evil.

88. Douglass, *Life and Times*, p. 443. See also Stauffer, "Frederick Douglass and the Aesthetics of Freedom," pp. 131–135. At this reunion, Thomas Auld told his former slave, "Frederick, I always knew you were too smart to be a slave, and had I been in your place, I should have done as you did" (*Life and Times*, p. 443). Frederick tried to reconcile with Hugh and Sophia Auld after the war but they were so upset with him for the way he had portrayed them that they refused to see him. Preston, *Young Frederick Douglass*, p. 168.

89. Preston, *Young Frederick Douglass*, p. 129.

90. A. C. C. Thompson, "To the Public—Falsehood Refuted," and Douglass, "Reply to Mr. A.C.C. Thompson," *North Star*, October 13, 1848. Douglass appended these two letters to later editions of his 1845 *Narrative*, using Thompson's letter as further evidence of the evil of slaveowners and the veracity of his life story. At the time, some readers accused him of never having been a slave. Thompson's letter silenced these critics.

91. Christopher Weeks, *Where Land and Water Intertwine: An Architectural History of Talbot County,*

Maryland (Baltimore: Johns Hopkins University Press, 1984), p. 201. Donald Rumsfeld purchased "Mount Misery" in 2003. See Peter T. Kilborn, "Weekends With the President's Men," *New York Times*, June 30, 2006.

92. William H. Herndon and Jesse W. Weik, *Life of Lincoln*, ed. Henry Steele Commager (1888; reprint, New York: Da Capo, 1983), p. 57 [hereafter *Herndon's Lincoln*]; Carl Sandburg, *Abraham Lincoln: The Prairie Years*, vol. 1 (New York: Harcourt, Brace & World, Inc., 1926), p. 104.

93. David Herbert Donald, *Lincoln* (New York: Simon & Schuster, 1995), quotation from Lincoln on p. 36; Sandburg, *Lincoln: The Prairie Years*, vol. 1, p. 104; *Herndon's Lincoln*, p. 58; Gabor S. Boritt, *Lincoln and the Economics of the American Dream* (1978; reprint, Urbana: University of Illinois Press, 1994), pp. 1–2. Herndon and Sandburg say the dog was left behind and stood on the far bank, afraid to cross, at which point Lincoln waded into the icy water to retrieve it. I follow Donald, who quotes Lincoln from a privately held letter.

94. Sandburg, *Lincoln: The Prairie Years*, vol. 1, p. 102. Sandburg says the Indians named the river "Sangamo," now known as "Sangamon."

95. *Herndon's Lincoln*, p. 66; Donald, *Lincoln*, p. 38. Herndon says that Lincoln "assured those with whom he came in contact" in the summer of 1831 "that he was a piece of floating driftwood." I assume that Lincoln felt the same on the trip to Illinois in 1830.

96. Roy P. Basler, ed., *The Collected Works of Abraham Lincoln* (hereafter *CW*), vol. 4 (New Brunswick: Rutgers University Press, 1953), p. 63. On Thomas asking Abraham to lead the wagon train see Michael Burlingame, *The Inner World of Abraham Lincoln* (Urbana: University of Illinois Press, 1994), pp. 38–39.

Lincoln's cousin John Hanks had already settled near the Sangamon River.

97. Donald, *Lincoln*, pp. 26–27; Douglas L. Wilson and Rodney O. Davis, eds., *Herndon's Informants: Letters, Interviews, and Statements about Abraham Lincoln* (Urbana: University of Illinois Press, 1998), p. 503; Sandburg, *Lincoln: The Prairie Years*, vol. 1, 18.

As Sandburg notes, "Linkhorn" sounded a lot like "Linkern." In the local dialect, people added "r" to their vowels: "sawr" for saw; "sartin" for certain; and so on.

98. *CW* 4, p. 63; Donald, *Lincoln*, p. 36; Sandburg, *Lincoln: The Prairie Years*, vol. 1, pp. 103–104.

99. According to Lincoln, his family left Hardin County "chiefly on account of the difficulties in land titles" in Kentucky. The family was also poor, which fueled worries over land titles. At the time, there were numerous conflicts over them, owing to the state's never having had a United States land survey. *CW* 4, pp. 61–62; Burlingame, *Inner World*, pp. 21–22; Donald, *Lincoln*, p. 24.

100. *CW* 3, p. 511; David Herbert Donald, *"We Are Lincoln Men": Abraham Lincoln and His Friends* (New York: Simon & Schuster, 2003), pp. 7–8.

101. *CW* 3, p. 511; *CW* 4, p. 62; *Herndon's Informants*, p. 106; Burlingame, *Inner World*, pp. 39–40; Donald, *Lincoln*, p. 26; Donald, *Lincoln and His Friends*, p. 4. Brucellosis, a bacterial disease somewhat similar to mad cow, is caused by cows eating the poisonous white snakeroot plant. The victim usually dies after a week of nausea, stomach pains, and coma.

Abraham's stepmother noted that Abraham "didn't like physical labor." As Burlingame argues, "When Thomas tried to instruct Abraham in his own trade of carpentry, the boy demonstrated so little interest that the effort was soon abandoned" (p. 40). Abraham himself recalled that at Pigeon Creek, an axe was "almost constantly" in his hands. *CW* 4, p. 62.

102. *CW* 1, pp. 378–379. For a variation on the same poem, not quite so gloomy, see *CW* 1, pp. 367–370. While living at Pigeon Creek, Lincoln copied a stanza from a popular hymn by Isaac Watts, the famous English psalmodist, that highlights a fatalist's sense of time flying by:

> Time, what an empty vapor 'tis,
> And days how swift they are:
> Swift as an Indian arrow—
> Fly on like a shooting star.
> The present moment just is here,
> Then slides away in haste,
> That we can never say they're ours,
> But only say they're past.

See *CW* 1, p. 1; *Herndon's Lincoln*, p. 37; Sandburg, *Lincoln: The Prairie Years*, vol. 1, p. 132.

103. *Herndon's Lincoln*, 41.

104. Donald, *Lincoln*, p. 28.

105. Herndon quoting Lincoln, in Douglas L. Wilson, *Honor's Voice: The Transformation of Abraham Lincoln* (1998; reprint, New York: Vintage, 1999), p. 13. This book and Wilson's edited volume, *Herndon's Informants*, have been indispensable to me.

106. *Herndon's Informants*, p. 57. Lincoln added, "That's my life, and that's all you or any one else can make of it." To another campaign biographer, Lincoln prefaced his brief sketch with the following note: "There is not much of it, for the reason, I suppose, that there is not much of me." *CW* 3, p. 511. Most scholars identify Lincoln as ambitious at an early age. Sandburg quotes him as telling an Indiana neighbor, "I'm going to be president of the United States," but I'm skeptical about this quote. Sandburg, *Lincoln: The Prairie Years*, vol. 1, p. 52.

107. *Herndon's Informants*, pp. 100, 102, 113 (quoted), 134, 145 (quoted), 176, 597 (quoted), 614; Burlingame, *Inner World*, pp. 38–39, quotation from p. 39. Some of Abraham's neighbors at Pigeon Creek also thought him lazy: "Abe was awful lazy: he worked for me—was always reading & thinking—used to get mad at him." Abraham's cousin Dennis Hanks said much the same thing: "Lincoln was lazy—a very lazy man—He was always reading—scribbling—writing—Ciphering—writing Poetry &c. &c." See *Herndon's Informants*, pp. 118, 104; Wilson, *Honor's Voice*, p. 57.

108. *CW* 3, p. 511 (quoted); *CW* 4, p. 61; Donald, *Lincoln*, p. 33; Burlingame, *Inner World*, pp. 37–42.

109. Burlingame, *Inner World*, pp. 36–42, quotation from p. 36. Lincoln said that blacks and whites "were all slaves one time or another." Ibid., p. 36. As Burlingame notes, "Abraham had grown so alienated [from his father] that he seriously considered running away from home, even though the law required him to stay there and obey his father's command until he reached his majority" (p. 40).

110. Sandburg, *Lincoln: The Prairie Years*, vol. 1, p. 106; *Herndon's Lincoln*, p. 57.

111. *Herndon's Lincoln*, p. 57; Donald, *Lincoln*, p. 36. On jokes and stories being a tradition, see *Herndon's Informants*, pp. 37, 173, 145.

112. *Herndon's Informants*, p. 172. The joke *may* point to Lincoln's insecurities about his manhood, since the humor hinges around a man who has been sexually humiliated by a woman. Then again, maybe he just liked the joke. A number of years later, when asked why he didn't "write out [his] stories and put them in a book," Lincoln responded, "Such a book would stink like a thousand privies." See *Herndon's Informants*, p. 442.

113. *Herndon's Informants*, p. 257 (quoted); *Herndon's Lincoln*, p. 59; Donald, *Lincoln*, p. 36.

114. Elliott J. Gorn, "'Gouge and Bite, Pull Hair and Scratch': The Social Significance of Fighting in the Southern Backcountry," *American Historical Review*

90:1 (February 1985):18-43, quotation from p. 20, paraphrases from pp. 22, 28; Wilson, *Honor's Voice*, pp. 25, 276, quotation from p. 276. See also Nicole Etcheson, "Manliness and the Political Culture of the Old Northwest, 1790-1860," *Journal of the Early Republic* 15:1 (Spring 1995): 59-77; Bertram Wyatt-Brown, *Southern Honor: Ethics and Behavior in the Old South* (New York: Oxford University Press, 1982), pp. 34, 138.

115. *Herndon's Informants*, pp. 5, 27, 28 (quoted), 35-36, 37 (quoted), 95, 149, 240-241, 256-258, 439, 639, 651-652, 672-676; Donald, *Lincoln*, p. 21; Sandburg, *Lincoln: The Prairie Years*, vol. 1, p. 7. On Abraham's mother as a fighter, see Wilson, *Honor's Voice*, pp. 27-28. Wilson says that Nancy Hanks "was as much as 130 to 140 pounds" (p. 28). Abraham never mentioned the rumors of his father's castration or sterility; but if this story, and the one of his mother being a bastard, were true, then he would have been a bastard of a bastard.

116. R. J. Rorabaugh, *The Alcoholic Republic: An American Tradition* (New York: Oxford University Press, 1979), pp. ix, 5-11, 149-156; Stauffer, *Black Hearts of Men*, p. 95; *Herndon's Informants*, p. 170; Gorn, "'Gouge and Bite,'" pp. 22, 29.

117. Gorn, "'Gouge and Bite,'" p. 32; Stauffer, *Black Hearts of Men*, p. 95; Rorabaugh, *Alcoholic Republic*, pp. ix, 5-11. See also Constance Rourke, *American Humor: A Study of National Character* (1931; reprint, Tallahassee: Florida State University Press, 1959), pp. 33-76; Etcheson, "Manliness and the Political Culture," pp. 60-77.

118. *Herndon's Informants*, pp. 149, 645; Wilson, *Honor's Voice*, p. 26; Stephen B. Oates, *With Malice Toward None: A Life of Abraham Lincoln* (1977; reprint, New York: Harper Perennial, 1994), p. 19.

119. *CW* 1, p. 275; *Herndon's Informants*, p. 45; Sandburg, *Lincoln: The Prairie Years*, vol. 1, p. 45; Wilson, *Honor's Voice*, p. 305.

120. Wilson, *Honor's Voice*, p. 26; *Herndon's Informants*, pp. 6–7, 386 (quoted).

121. *CW* 4, p. 63; Donald, *Lincoln*, pp. 37, 575 (quoted); Sandburg, *Lincoln: The Prairie Years*, vol. 1, p. 47.

122. *Herndon's Informants*, p. 73. Accounts vary on how much Offutt offered Lincoln: Lincoln's first cousin John Hanks says "$16—or $20 per month" to build the boat and "50 [cents] per day and $60 to make the trip"; Sandburg says "$12 per month"; Howells says "twelve dollars a month for the time they should be occupied" making the boat; Lincoln himself remembered "ten dollars per month"; Herndon says "fifty cents a day and sixty dollars to make the trip." See *Lincoln's Informants*, pp. 44, 456; Sandburg, *Lincoln: The Prairie Years*, vol. 1, p. 108; W. D. Howells, *Life of Abraham Lincoln* (1860; reprint, Bloomington: Indiana University Press, 1960), p. 27; *CW* 1, p. 320; *Herndon's Lincoln*, p. 611.

123. *CW* 4, p. 62; Sandburg, *Lincoln: The Prairie Years*, vol. 1, p. 87.

124. Burlingame, *Inner World*, p. 40.

125. *CW* 1, p. 6; Donald, *Lincoln*, p. 39; Howells, *Life of Lincoln*, p. 27; *Herndon's Informants*, pp. 17, 44.

126. *CW* 4, pp. 63–64; *Herndon's Informants*, pp. 44, 254, 457; *Herndon's Lincoln*, p. 63.

127. Mark Twain, *Life on the Mississippi* (1883; reprint, New York: Penguin, 1984), p. 50 (quoted); Walter Blair and Franklin J. Meine, *Mike Fink: King of Mississippi Keelboatmen* (New York, 1933), pp. 105–106 (quoted); Gorn, "'Gouge and Bite,'" pp. 29, 35; Rourke, *American Humor*, p. 152.

128. According to the United States Census, New Orleans in 1830 had 21,281 free whites, 16,639 slaves, and 11,906 free blacks, for a total of 49,826 people. See Geostat Center, Historical Census Browser, University of Virginia Library, online at http://fisher.lib.virginia.edu/collections/stats/histcensus/.

129. In 1810 Hardin County had a total population of 5,531, of which there were 6,563 whites, 940 slaves, and 28 free blacks. By 1820 the total population had increased to 10,500, while the slave and free black population remained low, at just over 1,000. In Pigeon Creek, Indiana, the entire county of Perry (later Spencer) had only 13 blacks out of a total population of 3,369 in 1830. These census figures on Hardin County, Kentucky, differ from those obtained by Michael Burlingame. His sources show 1,007 slaves living with 1,627 blacks in Hardin County in 1811. Burlingame, *Inner World*, pp. 21–22.

130. In 1829, a year before Abraham moved there, Illinois passed a law requiring incoming blacks to post a bond of $1,000 as a guarantee of their future good behavior and their ability to support themselves. The bond was more than most Americans earned in a year, and it greatly restricted blacks from settling in the state. Two years later Indiana passed a similar black exclusion law, requiring black settlers to post a $500 bond. See Eugene H. Berwanger, *The Frontier Against Slavery: Western Anti-Negro Prejudice and the Slavery Extension Controversy* (1967; reprint, Urbana: University of Illinois Press, 1971), p. 32.

131. *Herndon's Informants*, p. 457; *CW* 4, p. 64; Burlingame, *Inner World*, pp. 22–23, quotation by Lincoln on p. 22. Lincoln's cousin John Hanks, who was with Lincoln on the flatboat, went so far as to say that it was on this trip that Lincoln converted to the antislavery cause: "I can say knowingly that it was on this trip that he formed his opinions of Slavery: it ran its iron in him then & there." Scholars are understandably wary of relying on Hanks's account, since according to Lincoln, Hanks got off the flatboat at St. Louis and was not even in New Orleans with him. There are no eyewitness accounts of what Lincoln saw in New Orleans. Nevertheless, slavery and the slave trade were so much a part of the city in 1831 that someone like Lincoln, who went there to trade goods, could not help but encounter scenes of slavery.

132. Donald, *Lincoln*, pp. 38–39; Sandburg, *Lincoln: The Prairie Years*, vol. 1, p. 133; *Herndon's Lincoln*, pp. 65–67.

133. *Herndon's Informants*, pp. 73 (quoted), 386 (quoted).

My discussion of Lincoln's fight with Armstrong has been influenced by Wilson's brilliant analysis in *Honor's Voice*, pp. 19-51.

134. *Herndon's Informants*, pp. 73-74, 141, 370, 482, 703.

135. Ibid., pp. 109 (quoted), 112; Donald, *Lincoln*, pp. 27, 40.

136. *Herndon's Informants*, p. 369; Wilson, *Honor's Voice*, pp. 26-29, 35-36.

137. *Herndon's Informants*, pp. 73-74, 80, 369, 386, 402. In one account, Offutt bet $5, not $10 (*Herndon's Informants*, p. 73). Part of the reason there have been so many different accounts of the fight is because there was uncertainty about what happened at the time. As Adam Gopnik said about Lincoln in a different context, "The past is so often unknowable not because it is befogged now but because it was befogged then, too, back when it was still the present." See Adam Gopnik, "Angels and Ages," *New Yorker*, May 28, 2007, p. 37. Neither Lincoln nor Armstrong described the fight.

138. *Herndon's Informants*, pp. 73-74, 80, 386, 402; Wilson, *Honor's Voice*, pp. 31-35; Howells, *Life of Lincoln*, pp. 34-35.

139. Wilson, *Honor's Voice*, p. 20; Howells, *Life of Lincoln*, p. 35; *CW* 1, p. 320. I am sensitive to warnings by scholars about biographers imposing "turning points"

on a subject's life when the subject never did. As I emphasize, however, Douglass and Lincoln refer to their respective fights with Covey and Armstrong as "turning points." Believing it was a turning point shaped their self-definition and subsequent behavior. On "turning points" in biography, see Menand, "Lives of Others," pp. 65-66; and Menand, *American Studies*, pp. 3-30.

140. The Black Hawk War broke out when Black Hawk, a leader of the Sauk and Fox Indians, having been forced west of the Mississippi River and out of their Illinois homeland, returned to the state with some five hundred warriors and about fifteen hundred women and children in the hopes of reclaiming their land. On the Black Hawk War see Kerry A. Trask, *Black Hawk: The Battle for the Heart of America* (New York: Henry Holt, 2006); Patrick J. Jung, *The Black Hawk War of 1832* (Norman: University of Oklahoma Press, 2007); and Donald Jackson, ed., *Black Hawk: An Autobiography* (1955; reprint, Urbana: University of Illinois Press, 1964).

141. *CW* 3, p. 512 (quoted, emphasis added); *CW* 4, p. 64; *Herndon's Informants*, pp. 18 (quoted), 386; Wilson's *Honor's Voice*, pp. 31-33; Donald, *Lincoln and His Friends*, pp. 16-17.

Lincoln served one month as captain and reenlisted for another few weeks as a private. He was an admirable captain: when an old Indian and an ally of the U.S. Army entered Lincoln's camp, some of Lincoln's men wanted to kill him: "The Indian is a damned spy," said one soldier, and another stated, "We have come out to fight the Indian and by God we intend to do so." Lincoln protected the Indian and threatened to beat up anyone who sought to hurt him. See Donald, *Lincoln*, p. 45; *Herndon's Informants*, p. 18 (quoted).

142. *CW* 1, pp. 5–9, quotation from p. 8; Donald, *Lincoln*, pp. 40–43; Etcheson, "Manliness," pp. 59–77. According to Donald, in drafting his campaign handbill, Lincoln "probably had some assistance from John McNeil, the storekeeper, and possibly from schoolmaster Mentor Graham, and they may have been responsible for its somewhat orotund quality" (p. 42).

Lincoln later said that his defeat in his first political campaign was the only time he "was ever beaten on a direct vote of the people." See *CW* 4, p. 64; Donald, *Lincoln*, p. 46.

143. *Herndon's Informants*, pp. 316 (quoted), 333; *CW* 1, p. 11; Wilson, *Honor's Voice*, pp. 31–33.

144. *Herndon's Informants*, pp. 22 (quoted), 316 (quoted), 333–334, 337; Brian Dirk, *Lincoln the Lawyer* (Urbana: University of Illinois Press, 2007), pp. 116–119.

145. *CW* 1, p. 273.

146. *CW* 2, p. 97; Burlingame, *Inner World*, p. 41.

147. Caleb Bingham, *The Columbian Orator*, ed. David W. Blight (1797; reprint, New York: New York University Press, 1997), pp. 209–211.

148. Blight, introduction, *Columbian Orator*, pp. xvi–xix, xxviii, n. 9.

149. Douglass, *My Bondage*, p. 74. In Douglass's memory, Hugh Auld had also said in response to Frederick's reading, "if you give a nigger an inch, he'll take an ell [about 45 inches]; he should do nothing but the will of his master, and learn to obey it."

150. Douglass, *My Bondage*, pp. 80–82, quotation from p. 81; Blight, introduction, *Columbian Orator*, pp. xiii–xvi.

151. Douglass, *My Bondage*, pp. 81–82.

152. Bingham, *Columbian Orator*, p. 12.

153. Oates, *With Malice Toward None*, p. 20; Blight, introduction, *Columbian Orator*, p. xviii. Lincoln may also have had access to a copy of *The Columbian Orator* while living at Pigeon Creek, Indiana. His cousin remembered that Lincoln "was so attached to reading" that he "bought him, I think, the Columbian Orator or American Preceptor." *The American Preceptor*, also edited by Caleb Bingham, included lessons on reading and speaking.

154. *Herndon's Informants*, p. 7. When Lincoln's personal plea to the jury saved Duff Armstrong from a murder charge, he may have recalled another story from *The Columbian Orator*: Cicero's eloquent defense of Ligarius, his friend but also a criminal and Caesar's enemy. Caesar was so moved by Cicero's speech that he pardoned Ligarius.

In New Salem, neighbors sometimes saw Lincoln spread out under an oak tree, "shifting his position as the sun rose and sank, so as to keep in the shade, and utterly unconscious of everything but" the book. See Howells, *Life of Lincoln*, p. 31.

155. Some states in the Deep South had laws prohibiting slaves from reading, but there was no such law in Maryland. Preston, *Young Frederick Douglass*, p. 93.

156. *CW* 3, p. 511.

157. Kenneth Cmiel, *Democratic Eloquence: The Fight Over Popular Speech in Nineteenth-Century America* (New York: William Morrow, 1990), p. 59; Cmiel, "'A Broad Fluid Language of Democracy': Discovering the American Idiom," *Journal of American History* 79 (December 1992): 913–936; Blight, introduction, *Columbian Orator*, p. xxii.

158. Bingham, *Columbian Orator*, pp. 5–14, quotation from pp. 10–11.

159. *CW* 1, p. 1; Sandburg, *Lincoln: The Prairie Years*, vol. 1, p. 19. I've altered the spelling in Lincoln's poem to capture dialect. It appeared in his copybook as:

> Abraham Lincoln
> his hand and pen
> he will be good but
> god knows When

See *CW* 1, p. 1.

160. Douglass to Harriet Bailey, May 16, 1846, Frederick Douglass Papers, Library of Congress. See also Stauffer, *Black Hearts of Men*, p. 159; and Benjamin Soskis, "Heroic Exile: The Transatlantic Development of Frederick

Douglass, 1845-1847," Senior Thesis, Yale University, 1998, pp. 37-38.

In his last autobiography Douglass said that he had "little of the slave accent in my speech" owing to his childhood friendship with Daniel Lloyd, the youngest son of Edward Lloyd V. But his account seems far-fetched, for he spent little time around Daniel. The dialect he uses in his letter is not a severe "slave accent." His accent was no doubt less pronounced than that of other slaves, but he did not sound refined. His accent probably resembled those of free blacks and some poor whites on the Eastern Shore, who spoke in the kind of dialect Frederick uses. Bingham would have considered such accents wholly inappropriate to a democratic leader. During this era, accents denoted class as much as race. Douglass, *Life and Times*, p. 44.

In reconstructing Douglass's and Lincoln's dialects I have drawn primarily from their own writings but have also been influenced by studies that deal with American dialect, especially, Rourke, *American Humor*; Dennis Baron, *Grammar and Good Taste: Reforming the American Language* (New Haven: Yale University Press, 1982); Cmiel, *Democratic Eloquence*; Cmiel, "'A Broad Fluid Language of Democracy'"; Christopher Looby, *Voicing America: Language, Literary Form, and the Origins of the United States* (Chicago: University of Chicago Press, 1996); David Simpson, *The Politics of American English, 1776-1850* (New York: Oxford University Press, 1986); Michael Kramer, *Imagining Language in America: From the Revolution to the Civil War* (Princeton: Princeton University Press, 1992); Thomas Gustafson, *Representative Words: Poli-*

*tics, Literature, and the American Language, 1776-
1865* (Cambridge: Cambridge University Press, 1992);
Gavin Jones, *Strange Talk: The Politics of Dialect Lit-
erature in Gilded Age America* (Berkeley: University of
California Press, 1999), pp. 14-36; Richard H. Brodhead,
*Cultures of Letters: Scenes of Reading and Writing in
Nineteenth-Century America* (Chicago: University of
Chicago Press, 1993), pp. 107-141; and Carrie Tirado
Bramen, *The Uses of Variety: Modern Americanism and
the Quest for National Distinctiveness* (Cambridge,
Mass.: Harvard University Press, 2000), pp. 115-200.

161. Bingham, *Columbian Orator*, p. 7.

Two: *Fugitive Orator and Frontier Politician*

1. Frederick Douglass, *My Bondage and My Freedom*,
ed. John Stauffer (1855; reprint, New York: Modern Library, 2003), pp. 199-901, quotations from pp. 200, 201;
Douglass, *Life and Times of Frederick Douglass* (1892;
reprint, New York: Collier, 1962), pp. 202-205.

2. This panorama of New York is drawn from Charles
Dickens, who visited America in 1841, three years after
Douglass arrived there. See *American Notes* (1842; reprint, New York: Penguin, 2000), pp. 90-108, quotation
from p. 97.

3. Douglass, *My Bondage*, p. 201.

4. Ibid., pp. 200-201, quotation from p. 200; Douglass,
Life and Times, p. 203.

5. Abram J. Dittenhoefer, *How We Elected Lincoln: Personal Recollections* (1916; reprint, Philadelphia: University of Pennsylvania Press, 2005), p. 1.

6. Allan Nevins and Milton Halsey Thomas, eds., *The Diary of George Templeton Strong: Young Man in New York, 1835-1849* (New York: Macmillan, 1952), p. 100. More generally see Ira Berlin and Leslie M. Harris, *Slavery in New York* (New York: New Press, 2005), article by David Quigley on pp. 263-288; Leslie M. Harris, *In the Shadow of Slavery: African Americans in New York City, 1626-1863* (Chicago: University of Chicago Press, 2003), ch. 6; and John Stauffer, ed., *The Works of James McCune Smith: Black Intellectual and Abolitionist* (New York: Oxford University Press, 2006), part 4.

7. In some respects the Panic of 1837 resembled the real estate bubble of 2007 that followed years of easy credit, deregulated markets, and speculative buying.

8. John Stauffer, *The Black Hearts of Men: Radical Abolitionists and the Transformation of Race* (Cambridge, Mass.: Harvard University Press, 2002), pp. 114-118; Samuel Rezneck, "The Social History of an American Depression, 1837-1843," *American Historical Review* 40 (October 1934-July 1935): 662-687; Sean Wilentz, *Chants Democratic: New York City and the Rise of the American Working Class, 1788-1850* (New York: Oxford University Press, pp. 299-301; Reginald Charles McGrane, *The Panic of 1837: Some Financial Problems of the Jacksonian Era* (New York: Russell & Russell, 1965), pp. 22-23, 112-113; Douglass C. North, *The

Economic Growth of the United States, 1790-1860 (New York: W. W. Norton, 1966), pp. 195-203.

9. Edwin G. Burrows and Mike Wallace, *Gotham: A History of New York City to 1898* (New York: Oxford University Press, 1999), pp. 603-618, quotation from p. 616; Henry Ward Beecher, quotation from Stauffer, *Black Hearts of Men*, p. 115.

10. Douglass, *My Bondage*, pp. 201-202, quotation from p. 201.

11. Douglass, *Life and Times*, p. 204 (quoted).

12. Douglass, *Narrative of the Life of Frederick Douglass*, second edition, ed. David W. Blight (1845; reprint, Boston: Bedford/St. Martin's, 2003), p. 113; Douglass, *My Bondage*, p. 202.

13. Rosetta Douglass Sprague, *Anna Murray Douglass: My Mother as I Recall Her* . . . (Washington, D.C.: Fredericka Douglass Sprague Perry, 1900), Frederick Douglass Papers, Library of Congress (hereafter DPLC], p. 8; William S. McFeely, *Frederick Douglass* (New York: W. W. Norton, 1991), p. 65; Dickson J. Preston, *Young Frederick Douglass: The Maryland Years* (Baltimore: Johns Hopkins University Press, 1980), p. 149. My visual interpretation of Anna Murray is extrapolated from the portrait of her as an older woman in Sprague, *Anna Murray Douglass*.

14. Preston, *Young Frederick Douglass*, pp. 149, 151-152; McFeely, *Frederick Douglass*, p. 66; Douglass, *Life and Times*, pp. 205-206; R. Shaw, *The Baltimore*

Collection of Church Music; Containing Psalm and Hymn Tunes, Anthems, ... (Baltimore: Cole, c. 1832); D.W. Krummel, "American Music, 1801–1830," in Shaw-Shoemaker (American Music Bibliography, V), *Anuario Interamericano de Investigacion Musical* 11 (1975): 168–189.

15. Sprague, *Anna Murray Douglass*, pp. 9–10; McFeely, *Frederick Douglass*, pp. 68, 70; Preston, *Young Frederick Douglass*, p. 154.

16. Douglass, *Life and Times*, p. 188.

17. Douglass, *My Bondage*, pp. 199–200.

18. Douglass deviates from a self-definition that is closely tied to family and kinship within the black community, a tradition that was common in black letters up to the 1830s. See John Ernest, *Liberation Historiography: African American Writers and the Challenge of History, 1794–1861* (Chapel Hill: University of North Carolina Press, 2004), pp. 155–218; and Ira Berlin and Leslie S. Rowland, eds., *Families and Freedom: A Documentary History of African-American Kinship in the Civil War Era* (New York: New Press, 1997), p. 3.

19. Preston, *Young Frederick Douglass*, pp. 148–149. Part of this segregation stemmed from the desire among free blacks to become respectable in the eyes of whites, which meant acting superior to slaves; but most of it resulted from slaveowners' attempts to keep the two groups separate—they feared that such intermingling would threaten their property. As Anna's daughter Rosetta noted in a short memoir of her mother, "The

free people of Baltimore had their own circles from which the slaves were excluded; the ruling of them out of their society resulted more from the desire of the slaveholder than from any great wish of the free people themselves." Sprague, *Anna Murray Douglass*, p. 8. See also McFeely, *Frederick Douglass*, p. 67.

20. Preston, *Young Frederick Douglass*, pp. 148–149.

21. Sprague, *Anna Murray Douglass*, p. 10.

22. Ibid., pp. 7–8 (quoted), 10, 13, 14. I replace "household management" with "household manager."

23. Douglass, *Life and Times*, p. 204 (quoted); Douglass, *My Bondage*, p. 202. In *My Bondage*, Douglass spells it "Stewart" and evidently corrects his mistake in *Life and Times*.

24. Douglass, *My Bondage*, pp. 202–203; Douglass, *Life and Times*, pp. 204–205. Ruggles would eventually protect more than a thousand blacks, and given his success at disrupting the slave system, he was one of the South's most wanted men. Indeed, Frederick was not safe staying with him. Ruggles had recently helped secure the arrest of Thomas Lewis, a well-known slave trader and backwoods rogue wanted for beheading a man with a bowie knife. Southerners were looking for him, hoping to capture him and send him into slavery. To make matters worse, the New York police department had just issued a warrant for Ruggles's arrest on trumped-up charges of harboring a slave who had robbed his master of $7,000. Had they found Ruggles's hideout, both he and Frederick would almost certainly

have been captured and sent south. See Allan Nevins, ed., *The Diary of Philip Hone, 1828-1851* (New York: Dodd, Mead & Company, 1936), pp. 342-343; "Arrest of Lewis," *The Colored American*, August 18, 1838; "Caution to Our Readers," *The Colored American*, September 15, 1838.

25. Douglass, *My Bondage*, p. 202; Douglass, *Life and Times*, pp. 204, 205-206; McFeely, *Frederick Douglass*, pp. 68-73; Sprague, *Anna Murray Douglass*, pp. 9-10; Preston, *Young Frederick Douglass*, pp. 151-152; Douglass, *Narrative*, p. 114 (quoted); James L. Fisher, "The Roots of Music Education in Baltimore," *Journal of Research in Music Education* 21:3 (Autumn 1973): 214-224.

26. Sprague, *Anna Murray Douglass*, p. 10; McFeely, *Frederick Douglass*, p. 70; Douglass, *My Bondage*, pp. 202-203; Douglass, *Life and Times*, pp. 204-206; Kathryn Grover, *The Fugitive's Gibraltar: Escaping Slaves and Abolitionism in New Bedford, Massachusetts* (Amherst: University of Massachusetts Press, 2001), pp. 144-146, 287-288.

27. Douglass, *My Bondage*, pp. 203-204; Douglass, *Narrative*, pp. 115-116; Douglass, *Life and Times*, p. 206; Edward C. Papenfuse, foreword, *From Slavery to Salvation: The Autobiography of Rev. Thomas W. Henry of the A.M.E. Church*, ed. Jean Libby (Jackson: University of Mississippi Press, 1994), pp. xiii-xiv; Grover, *Fugitive's Gibraltar*, pp. 144-146.

28. Sprague, *Anna Murray Douglass*, pp. 9, 22 (quoted); Stauffer, *Black Hearts of Men*, pp. 228–229.

29. Douglass, *My Bondage*, p. 204 (quoted); Douglass, *Life and Times*, p. 207 (quoted). Douglass felt comparatively safe in New Bedford, for it was one of the most multiracial cities in the nation, containing a large population of Quakers, who opposed slavery for religious reasons, and blacks who protected each other. Soon after arriving at New Bedford, Douglass heard about a fugitive who got into an argument with a free black man. The latter became incensed and threatened to expose the fugitive and send him back into slavery, but his plan was thwarted by the black community. The A.M.E. Zion church held a special service during which the minister encouraged the congregation to kill the villain. The culprit, who had attended the meeting, jumped out the window and was never seen again. New Bedford, Douglass realized, was a much different place than New York. See Douglass, *My Bondage*, pp. 206–207.

30. Douglass, *My Bondage*, p. 207 (quoted); Douglass, *Life and Times*, p. 209. In *Life and Times* Douglass says he found work on his fifth day in New Bedford.

31. Douglass, *My Bondage*, pp. 208–209; Douglass, *Life and Times*, pp. 210–211.

32. Douglass, *My Bondage*, p. 181; Grover, *Fugitive's Gibraltar*, pp. 157–206.

33. Douglass, *My Bondage*, p. 208; Douglass, *Life and Times*, pp. 211–212, quotations from p. 212; Philip S. Foner, ed., *The Life and Writings of Frederick Doug-

lass, vol. 1, *Early Years, 1817–1849* (New York: International Publishers, 1950), p. 24 (hereafter *LWFD*).

34. "Frederick Douglass Meets an Old Protector," *Chicago Press and Tribune*, February 15, 1859.

35. In 1838 there was only one Zion Methodist church on Elm Street in New Bedford; by 1841 another Zion church was on Second Street. See Robert K. Wallace, *Douglass and Melville: Anchored Together in Neighborly Style* (New Bedford, Mass.: Spinner Publications, 2005), pp. 14–21; William L. Andrews, "Frederick Douglass, Preacher," *American Literature* 53 (December 1982): 592–597; Grover, *Fugitive's Gibraltar*, pp. 149, 161.

36. Douglass, *Life and Times*, pp. 212–213; Wallace, *Douglass and Melville*, pp. 18–21; Andrews, "Frederick Douglass, Preacher," pp. 592–597; *LWFD* 1, p. 24.

37. Wallace, *Douglass and Melville*, pp. 14–21; Herman Melville, *Moby-Dick; or, The Whale* (1851; reprint, New York: Penguin, 1992), p. 6 (ch. 1) (quoted).

38. Melville, *Moby-Dick*, p. 11 (ch. 2) (quoted); Wallace, *Douglass and Melville*, pp. 18–21.

39. Wallace, *Douglass and Melville*, pp. 52–118.

40. Lincoln, quotation from Frank B. Carpenter, "Anecdotes and Reminiscences of President Lincoln," in Henry J. Raymond, *Lincoln: His Life and Letters . . .*, vol. 2 (1865; reprint, Chicago: Union School Furnishing Co., c. 1890), p. 690.

41. Melville, *Moby-Dick*, p. 128 (ch. 27).

42. Douglass, *My Bondage*, p. 210; Douglass, *Life and Times*, p. 213; *LWFD* 1, p. 25.

43. Henry Mayer, *All on Fire: William Lloyd Garrison and the Abolition of Slavery* (New York: St. Martin's, 1998), pp. 98–150; William Lloyd Garrison, "To the Public," January 1, 1831, in William E. Cain, ed., *William Lloyd Garrison and the Fight Against Slavery: Selections from* The Liberator (Boston: Bedford Books, 1995), p. 72.

44. Mayer, *All on Fire*, p. 112.

45. David Brion Davis, *Inhuman Bondage: The Rise and Fall of Slavery in the New World* (New York: Oxford University Press, 2006), pp. 1–11, 250–267; Davis, *The Problem of Slavery in the Age of Revolution, 1770–1823* (Ithaca: Cornell University Press, 1975), pp. 523–556; Mayer, *All on Fire*, p. 123; Paul M. Angle, ed., *Created Equal? The Complete Lincoln-Douglass Debates of 1858* (Chicago: University of Chicago Press, 1958), p. 270.

46. Mayer, *All on Fire*, p. 123; Mark A. Noll, *The Civil War as a Theological Crisis* (Chapel Hill: University of North Carolina Press, 2006), pp. 31–50; Mitchell Snay, *Gospel of Disunion: Religion and Separatism in the Antebellum South* (Chapel Hill: University of North Carolina Press, 1993), pp. 53–112; Davis, *Problem of Slavery*, pp. 523–556.

Masters believed that slavery benefited slaves because it brought them from Africa, Christianized and "civilized" them, and (in their minds) provided them with food, clothing, shelter, and protection. They believed that blacks were like children, innately inferior to whites and incapable of self-government.

47. Mayer, *All on Fire*, pp. 122–124, 217–218.

48. The *Liberator* was not the first newspaper to endorse immediate abolitionism; *Freedom's Journal* (1827–1828) preceded it by four years and was the nation's first black newspaper. But owing to its small circulation and short life, *Freedom's Journal* did not have the influence that the *Liberator* did. See Timothy Patrick McCarthy and John Stauffer, introduction, *Prophets of Protest: Reconsidering the History of American Abolitionism* (New York: New Press, 2006), pp. xiii–xxxiii; and Jacqueline Bacon, *Freedom's Journal: The First African-American Newspaper* (Lanham, Md.: Lexington Books, 2007).

49. Mayer, *All on Fire*, pp. 199–208; Leonard L. Richards, *"Gentlemen of Property and Standing": Anti-Abolition Mobs in Jacksonian America* (New York: Oxford University Press, 1970). By 1841, when Douglass subscribed, white readership had grown substantially, which reflected the growth of antislavery among whites.

50. Stauffer, *Black Hearts of Men*, pp. 117–118; *LWFD* 1, pp. 338–354; Richard H. Sewell, *Ballots for Freedom: Antislavery Politics in the United States, 1837–1860* (New York: Oxford University Press, 1976), pp. 101–106; Robert William Fogel, *Without Consent or Contract:*

The Rise and Fall of American Slavery (New York: W. W. Norton, 1989), pp. 338–354.

51. Douglass, *My Bondage*, pp. 210–212, quotation from p. 212; Douglass, *Life and Times*, pp. 212–213.

52. Douglass, *Narrative*, p. 119 (quoted); Mayer, *All on Fire*, p. 120 (quoted).

53. Douglass, *My Bondage*, p. 21; *LWFD* 1, pp. 24–26. Many slaveholders considered free blacks to be the worst danger to the nation, and colonizationists believed that sending free blacks to Liberia would encourage slaveholders to manumit their slaves.

54. "Communications. Great Anti-Colonization Meeting in New-Bedford," *Liberator*, March 29, 1839; *LWFD* 1, p. 25.

55. Douglass, *My Bondage*, p. 211 (quoted); *LWFD* 1, p. 26; Douglass, *Life and Times*, p. 213.

56. Mayer, *All on Fire*, pp. 300–329.

57. *LWFD* 1, p. 26.

58. Ibid.

59. Mayer, *All on Fire*, p. 306; *LWFD* 1, p. 27; McFeely, *Frederick Douglass*, p. 87; Douglass, *My Bondage*, p. 213; Douglass, *Narrative*, p. 119 (quoted). Douglass remained nervous throughout his speech, and despite his great memory, he did not recall "a single connected sentence" of the speech. His nervousness did not go unnoticed; one woman said he seemed "green and awkward" but made such an "earnest and straightforward state-

ment" that the audience was "greatly moved." Mayer, *All on Fire*, p. 306; Douglass, *My Bondage*, p. 213.

60. Mayer, *All on Fire*, p. 306 (quoted); *LWFD* 1, pp. 26–27.

61. Douglass, *My Bondage*, p. 214; *LWFD* 1, p. 27.

62. *LWFD* 1, p. 27. The initial contract was for three months, which was then renewed.

63. Douglass, *Life and Times*, p. 229 (quoted).

64. Douglass, *Life and Times*, p. 229 (quoted); Mayer, *All on Fire*, p. 281 (quoted); *LWFD* 1, p. 45.

65. *LWFD* 1, p. 44; Mayer, *All on Fire*, pp. 261–284.

66. *LWFD* 1, pp. 45–46, quotation from p. 46.

67. Ibid., pp. 35–47, quotation from p. 35.

68. McFeely, *Frederick Douglass*, p. 92; Sprague, *Anna Murray Douglass*, p. 10; *LWFD* 1, pp. 45–47, 112, quotation from p. 112.

69. Douglass, *Life and Times*, p. 224 (quoted); *LWFD* 1, p. 34.

70. The Eastern Railroad went from Boston to Portland.

71. Douglass, *Life and Times*, pp. 224–225; Mayer, *All on Fire*, p. 307 (quoted); *LWFD* 1, pp. 52–53; McFeely, *Frederick Douglass*, pp. 92–93 (quoted); John W. Blassingame, ed., *The Frederick Douglass Papers*, series 1,

vol. 1, *1841-1846* (New Haven: Yale University Press, 1979), p. 10 (hereafter *TFDP*).

72. *TFDP* 1:1, pp. xxi–lxxxv, 3–23, quotation from p. 3; Douglass, *My Bondage*, p. 214.

73. *LWFD* 1, p. 48. Douglass uses the same language in "The Heroic Slave" (1853): "He had the head to conceive, and the hand to execute." See Ronald T. Takaki, ed., *Violence in the Black Imagination: Essays and Documents*, expanded edition (New York: Oxford University Press, 1993), p. 40.

In 1842 another journalist and an enemy of abolitionists wrote that Douglass was one of the best speakers he had ever heard, adding that the white speakers who followed him would do well to emulate him. *LWFD* 1, p. 52.

74. Douglass, *Life and Times*, pp. 220–223, quotation from p. 222.

75. *TFDP* 1:1, p. 4 (quoted); Stauffer, *Black Hearts of Men*, pp. 28–29; McFeely, *Frederick Douglass*, p. 96.

76. Douglass, *Life and Times*, pp. 226–231, quotation from p. 226. I change "hasten to the work of its extinction" to "hastening its extinction."

77. Douglass, *Life and Times*, p. 228 (quoted). A National Black Convention also met in Buffalo in 1843, which might have contributed to Douglass's success there.

78. Douglass, *Life and Times*, p. 230; Robert V. Remini, *Henry Clay: Statesman for the Union* (New York: W. W. Norton, 1991), pp. 617, 763. According to Douglass,

Clay owned "nearly" fifty slaves in 1847. According to his biographer Robert Remini, he owned thirty-three slaves in 1850. I estimate that he owned forty slaves in 1843.

Clay had lectured in Richmond in 1842, about a year before Douglass came. When a local farmer, Hiram Mendenhall, presented Clay with a petition with over two thousand names urging him to free his thirty slaves, ruffians in the crowd yelled, "Mob him!" "Stab him!" "Kill him!" Clay pleaded with the ruffians to spare Mendenhall's life, which restored order.

While Clay opposed slavery in principle, he never freed any of them in his life. In his will he offered future freedom to the children of his female slaves; at age twenty-five (twenty-eight for men) they would be granted their freedom if they emigrated to Africa. His will reflected his belief in gradual abolition and colonization. He hated abolitionists and thought they were destroying the nation. In fact he refused to touch or even look at the petition and lectured for over an hour on the dangers of abolitionism. See Remini, *Clay*, pp. 617–618, 772–773; H. C. Fox, *Memoirs of Wayne County and the City of Richmond, Indiana*, vol. 1 (Madison, Wis.: Western Historical Association, 1912), pp. 495–497.

Douglass says that Richmond was his first stop in Indiana, but in the partial speaking tour of 1843 in *TFDP*, Richmond appears last on his Indiana stop, though he may have lectured twice at Richmond.

79. McFeely, *Frederick Douglass*, pp. 108–112; *LWFD* 1, p. 57; Douglass, *Life and Times*, pp. 230–231.

80. William A. White, "The Hundred Conventions," September 22, 1843, in *Liberator*, October 13, 1843 (quoted); *LWFD* 1, p. 57; McFeely, *Frederick Douglass*, pp. 108–110. Despite his injuries, Douglass lectured the next day.

81. Frederick Douglass to William A. White, July 30, 1846, DP (quoted); McFeely, *Frederick Douglass*, pp. 110–112.

82. Douglass to William A. White, July 30, 1846, DP (quoted); William A. White, *Following Jesus: And Other Poems* (Philadelphia: George & Wayne, 1845); "A Journal of Every Home," *North Star*, April 5, 1850; "Great Meeting in Faneuil Hall," *North Star*, April 5, 1850; "Sons of Temperance—An Outrage," *North Star*, June 27, 1850; "Free Soil State Convention," *Frederick Douglass' Paper*, July 16, 1852; "To the Republicans of the United States," *The National Era*, January 17, 1856.

83. Douglass, *My Bondage*, p. 215 (quoted); Douglass, *Life and Times*, pp. 216–218, 228, quotation from p. 228; *LWFD* 1, pp. 56–57; Stauffer, *Black Hearts of Men*, pp. 158–159.

84. Douglass, *My Bondage*, p. 216 (quoted).

85. Ibid.

86. Edmund Quincy to Caroline Weston, July 2, 1847, Boston Public Library, reprinted in Robert K. Wallace, "Douglass, Melville, Quincy, Shaw: Epistolary Convergences," *Leviathan: A Journal of Melville Studies* 6:2 (October 2004): 64 (quoted). See also Stauffer, *Black*

Hearts of Men, pp. 158–160; Mayer, *All on Fire*, pp. 364–375.

87. Davis, *Inhuman Bondage*, p. 260; Stauffer, *Black Hearts of Men*, ch. 5.

88. *LWFD* 1, p. 59 (quoted); Douglass, *My Bondage*, p. 216.

89. *LWFD* 1, p. 59 (quoted).

90. Douglass, *My Bondage*, p. 217 (quoted); Mayer, *All on Fire*, pp. 310–311, 316–318.

In March 1843 the Massachusetts state legislature violated this Supreme Court ruling when it prohibited state officials from cooperating in the seizure of fugitives. See Stanley W. Campbell, *The Slave Catchers: Enforcement of the Fugitive Slave Law, 1850–1860* (New York: W. W. Norton, 1972), pp. 13–14; Henry Wilson, *History of the Rise and Fall of the Slave Power in America*, vol. 1 (Boston: Houghton, Mifflin and Company, 1872), pp. 477–487.

91. The following sources state the publication date of the *Narrative* as May: *TFDP* 1:1, p. 27; *LWFD* 1, p. 59; Preston, *Young Frederick Douglass*, pp. 170, 201; and Henry Louis Gates Jr., ed., *Frederick Douglass: Autobiographies* (New York: Library of America, 1994), p. 1056. McFeely says the *Liberator* announced publication of the *Narrative* in May but that it was published in June. See McFeely, *Frederick Douglass*, p. 116.

92. *LWFD* 1, pp. 59–60, quotation from p. 60; McFeely, *Douglass*, pp. 116–117; Gates, ed., *Douglass: Autobiographies*, pp. 1078–1079.

93. Preston, *Young Frederick Douglass*, pp. 170–174, 230, quotation from p. 230.

94. Douglass, *My Bondage*, p. 218 (quoted); *LWFD* 1, pp. 61–62. Abolitionists raised $250 to help fund Douglass's trip.

95. *TFDP* 1:2 (1847), p. 69.

96. *TFDP* 1:3 (1857), p. 190. John Stauffer, "Frederick Douglass and the Politics of Slave Redemptions," in Kwame Anthony Appiah and Martin Bunzl, eds., *Buying Freedom: The Ethics and Economics of Slave Redemption* (Princeton: Princeton University Press, 2007), pp. 219–221.

97. *TFDP* 1:2, p. 59. The best account of Douglass's trip is still Benjamin Soskis, "Heroic Exile: The Transatlantic Development of Frederick Douglass, 1845–1847," Senior Thesis, Yale University, 1998. See also Alan J. Rice and Martin Crawford, eds., *Liberating Sojourn: Frederick Douglass and Transatlantic Reform* (Athens: University of Georgia Press, 1999).

98. *LWFD* 1, p. 136; Stauffer, "Douglass and the Politics of Slave Redemptions," p. 219.

99. *TFDP* 1:2, pp. 59 (quoted), 142; *TFDP* 1:1, pp. 134, 165, 344, 442; *LWFD* 1, pp. 70, 167, 439.

100. Douglass, *My Bondage*, pp. 218-235, quotation from p. 234.

101. *TFDP* 1:2, p. 60 (quoted).

102. *LWFD* 1, p. 127.

103. Douglass, *Life and Times*, pp. 232-258, quotation from p. 241; Douglass, *My Bondage*, pp. 224-228; *LWFD* 1, p. 73.

104. Douglass, *My Bondage*, pp. 224-226, 234; Douglass, *Life and Times*, pp. 255-258; Preston, *Young Frederick Douglass*, pp. 173-175; McFeely, *Frederick Douglass*, pp. 144-145.

105. Douglass quoted from Benjamin Quarles, "The Breach Between Douglass and Garrison," *Journal of Negro History* 23:2 (April 1938): 144-154; *LWFD* 1, pp. 76-77.

When Douglass first expressed his interest in starting his own newspaper, there were no black presses in the United States. A few months later four low-budget black papers emerged but quickly died. Before Douglass, the *Colored American* had been the longestrunning black paper, lasting from 1838 to 1841. *LWFD* 1, pp. 252-253.

106. *LWFD* 1, p. 77. The quote is from Thurlow Weed. Greeley echoed Weed's praise; he said there were passages in Douglass's letters "which, for genuine eloquence, would do honor to any write of the English language, however eloquent."

107. McFeely, *Douglass*, p. 145 (quoted); Preston, *Young Frederick Douglass*, p. 201.

108. On Douglass's decision to move to Rochester, see John Stauffer, "Frederick Douglass and the Making of a Representative African American," *Cambridge Companion to the Slave Narrative* (Cambridge: Cambridge University Press, 2007); and John R. McKivigan, "The Frederick Douglass-Gerrit Smith Friendship and Political Abolitionism in the 1850s," in Eric J. Sundquist, ed., *Frederick Douglass: New Literary and Historical Essays* (Cambridge: Cambridge University Press, 1990), pp. 205-232.

109. Mayer, *All on Fire*, pp. 371-374; Quarles, "Breach Between Douglass and Garrison," pp. 144-154; Tyrone Tillery, "The Inevitability of the Douglass-Garrison Conflict," *Phylon* 37:2 (1976): 137-149; and William H. Pease and Jane H. Pease, "Boston Garrisonians and the Problem of Frederick Douglass," *Canadian Journal of History* 2:2 (September 1967): 29-48.

110. *LWFD* 1, p. 72 (quoted); Henry Clark Wright, quoted from Tillery, "Inevitability of the Douglass-Garrison Conflict," p. 142; Quarles, "Breach Between Douglass and Garrison," pp. 144-146.

Garrison stood apart from the rest of the American Anti-Slavery Society leadership by supporting the purchase of Douglass's freedom. See Mayer, *All on Fire*, p. 372.

111. Douglass, *My Bondage*, pp. 236-238, quotation from p. 237; Douglass, *Life and Times*, pp. 259-261, the

same quotation from p. 260; Pease and Pease, "Boston Garrisonians," pp. 40–43.

112. Roy P. Basler, ed., *The Collected Works of Abraham Lincoln* (New Brunswick, N.J.: Rutgers University Press, 1953), (hereafter *CW*), vol. 4, p. 65; William H. Herndon and Jesse W. Weik, *Life of Lincoln* (hereafter *Herndon's Lincoln*), ed. Henry Steele Commager (New York: Da Capo, 1983), pp. 71–80, quotation from Lincoln on p. 71, quotation from Herndon on p. 80 [hereafter *Herndon's Lincoln*]; David Herbert Donald, *Lincoln* (New York: Simon & Schuster, 1994), pp. 44–47.

113. *CW* 1, pp. 15–16; *Herndon's Lincoln*, p. 89 (quoted); Douglas L. Wilson and Rodney O. Davis, eds., *Herndon's Informants: Letters, Interviews, and Statements about Abraham Lincoln* (Urbana: University of Illinois Press, 1998) (hereafter *Herndon's Informants*), pp. 20, 74, 377, 529, 530; Donald, *Lincoln*, p. 47.

Reuben Radford eventually succeeded in business. By 1840 he owned the Morgan Cross Railroad and was a prominent Illinois Democrat and avid opponent of Lincoln. During the 1840 elections, Radford was in charge of his district's polling booth and there were rumors that he excluded Whigs from voting. Lincoln confronted him and they almost came to blows: "Radford, you will spoil and blow if you live much longer," Lincoln reportedly told him. He wanted to hit Radford: "I intended to knock him down and go away and leave him a-kicking." But no blows were exchanged. See *Herndon's Informants*, p. 475.

114. *Herndon's Informants*, pp. 13 (quoted), 20 (quoted), 170, 378 (quoted), 529–530; Stephen Douglas, quoted from Donald, *Lincoln*, pp. 49–50; William H. Townsend, *Lincoln and Liquor* (New York: Press of the Pioneers, 1934). On Lincoln's opposition to alcohol, see especially *CW* 1, pp. 271–279.

Hardin Bale remembered that Lincoln and Berry "bought a kind of grocery store." William Greene recalled that "Lincoln and Berry kept the grocery store, containing dry goods—groceries—liquors—such a one as was kept every where in the Country at that time." And J. Rowan Herndon, who sold the store to Lincoln, recalled that "the goods consisted of a small assortment of Dry Goods & Grcrys [Groceries]." See *Herndon's Informants*, pp. 13, 20, 378. For a more sympathetic interpretation, see Donald, *Lincoln*, pp. 49–50.

115. *CW* 1, p. 20; *CW* 4, p. 65 (quoted); *Herndon's Lincoln*, pp. 89–90; Donald, *Lincoln*, p. 54; *Herndon's Informants*, p. 20.

Lincoln's credit rating remained problematic until the Civil War. An 1858 report on him from the credit agency Dunn and Bradstreet was evidently so embarrassing that someone purged it after his assassination, leaving "only a black cross in the margin," as Scott Sandage revealed. See Scott A. Sandage, *Born Losers: A History of Failure in America* (Cambridge, Mass.: Harvard University Press, 2005), pp. 156–158, quotation from p. 158.

116. The state assembly was also known as the state legislature.

117. Henry Clay, 1832 speech in the United States Senate, reprinted in *Register of Debates in Congress ...* vol. 8, part 1 (Washington: Gales and Seaton, 1833), p. 277 (quoted). On Henry Clay and the Whig Party, see also Remini, *Clay*; Daniel Walker Howe, *The Political Culture of the American Whigs* (Chicago: University of Chicago Press, 1979); Merrill D. Peterson, *The Great Triumvirate: Webster, Clay, and Calhoun* (New York: Oxford University Press, 1987); Michael Holt, *The Rise and Fall of the Whig Party* (New York: Oxford University Press, 1999); and David Herbert Donald, "Abraham Lincoln: A Whig in the White House," in *Lincoln Reconsidered: Essays on the Civil War Era* (New York: Vintage, 1989), pp. 187–208.

118. Clay, 1832 speech, reprinted in *Register of Debates in Congress*, p. 277 (quoted); Irvin G. Wyllie, *The Self-Made Man in America: The Myth of Rags to Riches* (New York: Free Press, 1954), pp. 9–10; *CW* 3, p. 29 (quoted); *Herndon's Informants*, p. 8; David Herbert Donald, "Abraham Lincoln: Whig in the White House," in *Lincoln Reconsidered: Essays on the Civil War Era* (New York: Vintage, 1984), pp. 167–186.

The passage in which Clay coins the term "self-made men" reads: "I allude to the charge brought against the manufacturing system as favoring the growth of aristocracy.... In Kentucky, almost every manufactory known to me is in the hands of enterprising self-made men, who have acquired whatever wealth they possess by patient and diligent labor." *Register of Debates in Congress*, p. 277.

119. *Herndon's Informants*, p. 8 (quoted); Donald, *Lincoln*, p. 52.

120. *Herndon's Informants*, p. 8; Donald, *Lincoln*, pp. 50, 52.

121. *CW* 4, p. 65; *Herndon's Informants*, p. 540. Bowling Green came to admire Lincoln's amateur legal abilities, and the two became friends. According to one account, Green was something of a father to Lincoln. See Douglas L. Wilson, *Honor's Voice: The Transformation of Abraham Lincoln* (New York: Vintage, 1998), p. 101.

122. *CW* 4, p. 65.

123. Carl Sandburg, *Abraham Lincoln: The Prairie Years*, vol. 1 (New York: Harcourt, Brace & World, 1926), pp. 163-164; Brian Dirck, *Lincoln the Lawyer* (Urbana: University of Illinois Press, 2007), pp. 16-19; Mark E. Steiner, *An Honest Calling: The Law Practice of Abraham Lincoln* (DeKalb: Northern Illinois University Press, 2006), pp. 32-37; Wilson, *Honor's Voice*, pp. 104-108; Robert A. Ferguson, *Law and Letters in American Culture* (Cambridge, Mass.: Harvard University Press, 1984), pp. 11-16, quotation from p. 11. As Ferguson notes, "Since providence had provided Americans with a continent unspoiled by human history, they could confidently order their new country through a correct, theoretical application of man-made or positive law in harmony with the natural order around them" (p. 16).

124. William Blackstone, *Commentaries on the Law of England*, 4 vols. (Oxford: Clarendon, 1765-1769); Dirck, *Lincoln the Lawyer*, p. 17.

125. See Ferguson, *Law and Letters*, pp. 11-33, 305-317; Robert M. Cover, *Justice Accused: Antislavery and the Judicial Process* (New Haven: Yale University Press, 1975), pp. 8-41; David Brion Davis, *The Problem of Slavery in the Age of Revolution*, pp. 469-522; William M. Wiecek, *The Sources of Antislavery Constitutionalism in America, 1760-1848* (Ithaca: Cornell University Press, 1977), pp. 29-39; Priscilla Wald, *Constituting Americans: Cultural Anxiety and Narrative Form* (Durham: Duke University Press, 1995), pp. 7-8, 41-105.

126. Wiecek, *Antislavery Constitutionalism*, pp. 27, 38-39, 259, quotation from p. 259; Cover, *Justice Accused*, pp. 25-30.

127. Dirck, *Lincoln the Lawyer*, p. 11; Cover, *Justice Accused*, pp. 6-7.

128. Steiner, *An Honest Calling*, pp. 31-40, quotation from p. 33; Dirck, *Lincoln the Lawyer*, pp. 16-18; Ferguson, *Law and Letters*, pp. 305-317; Wald, *Constituting Americans*, pp. 47-73; Wiecek, *Antislavery Constitutionalism*, pp. 276-287.

129. *CW* 4, p. 65; William Dean Howells, *Life of Abraham Lincoln* (1860; reprint, Bloomington: Indiana University Press, 1960), p. 31; Steiner, *Honest Calling*, p. 33; Wilson, *Honor's Voice*, pp. 102-107.

Lincoln later summarized his preparation for the law in less monomaniacal terms: "The mode is very simple though laborious and tedious. It is only to get the books, and read, and study them carefully.... Work, work, work is the main thing." *CW* 4, p. 121.

130. Godbey, quoted in *Herndon's Informants*, p. 450; Steiner, *An Honest Calling*, p. 33 (quoted); Dirck, *Lincoln the Lawyer*, pp. 9–19; Wilson, *Honor's Voice*, pp. 102–107.

131. *Herndon's Informants*, p. 254 (quoted); Donald, *Lincoln*, p. 53. Daniel Aaron, *The Unwritten War: American Writers and the Civil War* (New York: Alfred A. Knopf, 1973), pp. 349–352; Nevins, ed., *Diary of George Templeton Strong: The Civil War*, pp. 188, 204–205; Richard Wightman Fox, "Lincoln's Death," Harvard University Warren Center Talk, 2006.

132. *CW* 1, p. 55; Donald, *Lincoln*, pp. 53–54; William E. Baringer, *Lincoln's Vandalia: A Pioneer Portrait* (New Brunswick, N.J.: Rutgers University Press, 1949).

133. Aaron, *Unwritten War*, pp. 350–351; Nevins, ed., *Diary of George Templeton Strong: The Civil War*, pp. 188, 204–205.

134. *CW* 1, p. 48. The poker metaphor suggests the nature of backwoods Illinois politics in 1836.

135. *CW* 1, p. 48; Donald, *Lincoln*, p. 59.

136. *CW* 1, pp. 48, 210; Donald, *Lincoln*, p. 59.

137. *CW* 1, p. 48; Donald, *Lincoln*, p. 59.

138. *CW* 1, p. 48. At the time the federal government enjoyed large revenue surpluses from its sale of public lands.

139. Capitalists needed markets in which to sell their wares; hence their desire for canals and roads. Half of Lincoln's platform was adopted: immigrants were denied the vote, but the federal government refused to help build state roads.

140. Donald, *Lincoln*, pp. 58, 60.

141. Ibid., p. 60; Wilson, *Honor's Voice*, p. 30. In Lincoln's first term as an assemblyman, his legal mentor John Todd Stuart, also a House Whig, "quite overshadowed him," as another assemblyman remembered. Stuart "had more experience than Lincoln. But the next session Lincoln was very prominent. He had by that time become the acknowledged leader of the Whigs in the House." In the 1836–37 session, Stuart was no longer a member of the legislature, having failed in his bid for U.S. congressman. He "had gone out and left [Lincoln] a clear field." Wilson, *Honor's Voice*, p. 159; Michael Burlingame, ed., *An Oral History of Abraham Lincoln: John G. Nicolay's Interviews and Essays* (Carbondale: Southern Illinois University Press, 1996), p. 30.

142. Donald, *Lincoln*, pp. 60–62; *Herndon's Lincoln*, ch. 8.

143. Donald, *Lincoln*, pp. 61–62, quotation from p. 61; *Herndon's Lincoln*, ch. 8.

144. *CW* 1, pp. 74–76, quotation from p. 75.

145. *CW* 1, p. 75 (quoted); *CW* 4, p. 65. In his 1837 protest in the state legislature, Lincoln said nothing about slavery in the territories because the territorial question was not yet an issue. The federal government had not acquired any new territories since 1819, and the Missouri Compromise of 1821 determined the status of slavery in the existing territories—those north of 36°30′ entered as free states, south of that latitude entered as slave states. Beginning in the late 1840s, Lincoln sought to prohibit the further spread of slavery, which he thought would lead to its "ultimate extinction," a far less conservative position than he outlined in 1837. *CW* 2, p. 461.

146. Much has been written about Lincoln's courtship with Ann Rutledge, but there is no surviving correspondence between them or writings by Lincoln about the affair. Only secondhand recollections from neighbors and oral histories survive.

147. Donald, *Lincoln*, p. 55 (quoted); Wilson, *Honor's Voice*, p. 115 (quoted); *Herndon's Informants*, p. 73.

148. Donald, *Lincoln*, pp. 56–57, quotation from p. 57; *Herndon's Informants*, p. 403 (quoted); *Honor's Voice*, p. 117. On Lincoln's depression, see Joshua Wolf Shenk, *Lincoln's Melancholy: How Depression Challenged a President and Fueled His Greatness* (Boston: Houghton Mifflin, 2005).

John McNeil was the name he went by in New Salem; his legal name was John McNamar.

149. *Herndon's Informants*, pp. 256, 610, quotation from p. 610. See also *Herndon's Lincoln*, pp. 116–129; and Douglas Wilson's brilliant analysis of the relationship, to which I am indebted, even though I interpret it differently. Wilson, *Honor's Voice*, pp. 129–141.

150. *Herndon's Informants*, pp. 175, 265, 365–366, 374, 530–531, 609–611; Sandburg, *Lincoln: The Prairie Years*, vol. 1, following p. 208, for the portrait of Mary Owens.

151. *Herndon's Informants*, p. 601.

152. Ibid., pp. 610, 256.

153. Ibid., p. 262.

154. Ibid.

155. *CW* 1, pp. 54, 55.

156. Ibid., p. 78.

157. Ibid. Lincoln tried to be gallant even as he got her to break up with him: "Whatever woman may cast her lot with mine, should any ever do so, it is my intention to do all in my power to make her happy and contented; and there is nothing I can imagine that would make me more unhappy than to fail in the effort. I know I should be much happier with you than the way I am, provided I saw no signs of discontent in you" (p. 78). He thought he saw signs of Mary's discontent, however, and so advised her to acknowledge her unhappiness.

158. Ibid., p. 94. Mary understood Lincoln's attempt to preserve his honor yet end the engagement. She met

with him in person, which prompted a final letter from him: "You must know that I can not see you, or think of you, with entire indifference; and yet it may be that you are mistaken in regard to what my real feelings towards you are.... I want in all cases to do right, and most particularly so, in all cases with women.... And for the purpose of making the matter as plain as possible, I now say that you can now drop the subject [of marriage], dismiss your thoughts (if you ever had any) from me forever, and leave this letter unanswered, without calling forth one accusing murmur from me.... What I wish is that our further acquaintance shall depend upon yourself. If such further acquaintance would contribute nothing to your happiness, I am sure it would not to mine. If you feel yourself in any degree bound to me, I am now willing to release you, provided you wish it; while, on the other hand, I am willing, and even anxious to bind you faster, if I can be convinced that it will, in any considerable degree, add to your happiness. This, indeed, is the whole question with me. Nothing would make me more miserable than to believe you miserable—nothing more happy, than to know you were so." Lincoln asked Mary to call off the marriage. She did by never again responding to him.

159. Ibid., pp. 117–118. In this letter to Eliza Browning, Lincoln refers to his effort not to violate "word, honor, or conscience," which led him to try to convince Mary to break off the engagement (p. 119). He also says that when Mary broke off the engagement, his "vanity was deeply wounded by the reflection that I had so long been too stupid to discover her intentions, and at the

same time never doubting that I understood them perfectly; and also that she whom I had taught myself to believe nobody else would have had actually rejected me with all my fancied greatness; and to cap the whole, I then, for the first time began to suspect that I was really a little in love with her." Any rejection, no matter how much he wanted it, was a blow to his vanity. See *CW* 1, p. 119.

160. Ibid., pp. 118–119, quotation from p. 119.

161. Michael Burlingame, *The Inner World of Abraham Lincoln* (Urbana: University of Illinois Press, 1994), pp. 123–146, quotations from p. 124.

162. On Lincoln's relationship with Joshua Speed, I have been influenced by the following sources: Jonathan Ned Katz, *Love Stories: Sex Between Men Before Homosexuality* (Chicago: University of Chicago Press, 2001), pp. 1–25; David Herbert Donald, *"We Are Lincoln Men": Abraham Lincoln and His Friends* (New York: Simon & Schuster, 2003), pp. 29–64; Wilson, *Honor's Voice*, pp. 171–194, 233–264; C. A. Tripp, *The Intimate World of Abraham Lincoln*, ed. Lewis Gannett (New York: Free Press, 2005), pp. 125–152, 225–237.

163. Donald, *Lincoln Men*, pp. 29–31. Joshua Speed loved to tell people the story of how he and Lincoln met, much as married couples sentimentally recount their first meeting or date. See *Herndon's Informants*, pp. 588–591.

164. *Herndon's Informants*, p. 590; Donald, *Lincoln*, p. 66; Donald, *Lincoln Men*, pp. 29–31. Donald calls the

general store "A.Y. Ellis & Company" in *Lincoln*, "Bell & Co." in *Lincoln Men*.

165. Donald, *Lincoln Men*, p. 54; Speed never forgot the first speech he had heard of Lincoln's: it was against George Forquer, a Springfield politician who had defected from the Whig Party to become a Democrat and as a result had received a Democratic position that paid him $3,000 per year. Forquer had just built a big house in Springfield and had erected a lightning rod on top. Lincoln, after defending himself against Forquer's ridicule, ended his speech by saying, "I would rather die now, than, like the gentleman change my politics, and simultaneous with the change, receive an office worth three thousand dollars per year, and then have to erect a lightning-rod over my house, to protect a guilty conscience from an offended God." *Herndon's Informants*, p. 589.

166. *Herndon's Informants*, p. 590.

167. Ibid.

168. Ibid.

169. Ibid.

170. Donald, *Lincoln Men*, p. 38; Douglas L. Wilson, *Lincoln's Sword: The Presidency and the Power of Words* (New York: Alfred A. Knopf, 2007), p. 31; Speed, quoted from Katz, *Love Stories*, p. 5; Speed, quoted from *Herndon's Informants*, p. 430; William Herndon, quoted from Wilson, *Honor's Voice*, p. 245; Robert Todd Lincoln, quoted from Donald, *Lincoln Men*, pp. 226–227, n. 15.

William Herndon also said that Lincoln "poured out his soul" to Speed; and Lincoln's White House secretaries and biographers John Nicolay and John Hay claimed that Speed was "the only—as he was certainly the last—intimate friend that Lincoln ever had." See Wilson, *Honor's Voice*, p. 245; and Nicolay and Hay, *Abraham Lincoln: A History*, vol. 1 (New York: Century Company, 1890), p. 194.

171. Donald, *Lincoln Men*, pp. 32–34, quotation from p. 33.

172. Ibid., pp. 32–34.

173. *Herndon's Informants*, pp. 21, 30, 141, 156, 470; Wilson, *Honor's Voice*, pp. 72–77, 190–198; Donald, *Lincoln Men*, pp. 33–34.

Speed told Herndon, "I do not think [Lincoln] had ever read much of Byron previous to my acquaintance with him," adding that Lincoln became "a great admirer of some of Byron's poetry." In another letter to Herndon, Speed says that Lincoln "forsook Byron," suggesting that over time Lincoln abandoned Byron after having loved him.

Another friend, William Greene, said that "Burns was [Lincoln's] favorite." Greene also said that "Shakespeare, Burns and Byron were his favorite books." And a third observer said that "Lincoln loved Burns generally." See *Herndon's Informants*, pp. 21, 30, 141, 156, 470.

174. *CW* 1, p. 79; Donald, *Lincoln Men*, pp. 33–34, 48; Shenk, *Lincoln's Melancholy*, p. 32.

Speed once marveled at Lincoln's mind, noting that "impressions were easily made ... and never effaced." "No," Lincoln responded; you are mistaken. "I am slow to learn and slow to forget that which I have learned. My mind is like a piece of steel, very hard to scratch anything on it and almost impossible after you get it there to rub it out." *Herndon's Informants*, p. 499.

175. On spiritual or romantic friendship, see Katz, *Love Stories*; David S. Reynolds, *Walt Whitman's America: A Cultural Biography* (New York: Alfred A. Knopf, 1995), pp. 194–234, 390–403; Caleb Crain, *American Sympathy: Men, Friendship, and Literature in the New Nation* (New Haven: Yale University Press, 2001); David Leverenz, *Manhood and the American Renaissance* (Ithaca: Cornell University Press, 1989); E. Anthony Rotundo, *American Manhood: Transformation in Masculinity from the Revolution to the Modern Era* (New York: Basic Books, 1993); Rotundo, "Romantic Friendship: Male Intimacy and Middle Class Youth in the Northern United States, 1800–1900," *Journal of Social History* 25:1–25; Peter Gay, *The Bourgeois Experience: Victoria to Freud*, vol. 2, *The Tender Passion* (New York: Oxford University Press, 1986), pp. 198–254; Leslie A. Fiedler, *Love and Death in the American Novel* (New York: Criterion Books, 1960); Fiedler, "Come Back to the Raft Ag'in, Huck Honey!" in *A New Fiedler Reader* (Amherst, N.Y.: Prometheus Books, 1999); David Deitcher, *Dear Friends: American Photographs of Men Together, 1840–1918* (New York: Harry N. Abrams, 2001); Michael Pakaluk, ed., *Other Selves: Philosophers on Friendship* (Indianapolis: Hackett Publishing Company, 1991);

Ronald A. Sharp, *Friendship and Literature: Spirit and Form* (Durham: Duke University Press, 1986); Gilbert C. Meilaender, *Friendship: A Study in Theological Ethics* (Notre Dame: University of Notre Dame Press, 1981); Leroy S. Rouner, ed., *The Changing Face of Friendship* (Notre Dame: University of Notre Dame Press, 1994); Robert Brain, *Friends and Lovers* (New York: Basic Books, 1976); Alan Bray, *The Friend* (Chicago: University of Chicago Press, 2003); C. Stephen Jaeger, *Ennobling Love: In Search of a Lost Sensibility* (Philadelphia: University of Pennsylvania Press, 1999).

176. Melville, *Moby-Dick*, pp. 21, 28, 57, 58; John Stauffer, "Douglass, Melville, and the Aesthetics of Freedom," in Samuel Otter and Robert S. Levine, eds., *Douglass and Melville* (Chapel Hill: University of North Carolina Press, 2008), p. 146. See also Robert K. Martin, *Hero, Captain, and Stranger: Male Friendship, Social Critique, and Literary Form in the Sea Novels of Herman Melville* (Chapel Hill: University of North Carolina Press, 1986), pp. 67–94; and Elizabeth Hardwick, *Herman Melville* (New York: Penguin, 2000), pp. 68–97.

177. Mark Twain, *The Adventures of Huckleberry Finn*, ed. Thomas Cooley (New York: W. W. Norton, 1999), pp. 136, 223; Fiedler, "Come Back to the Raft Ag'in, Huck Honey!" pp. 3–12; and the important and brilliant corrective to Fiedler's thesis, Christopher Looby, "'Innocent Homosexuality': The Fiedler Thesis in Retrospect," in Gerald Graff and James Phelan, eds., *Mark Twain, Adventures of Huckleberry Finn: A Case Study in Critical Controversy* (Boston: Bedford/St. Martin's, 2004), pp. 526–541.

Other examples of romantic expressions of male-male intimacy are the young Ralph Waldo Emerson, who called Martin Gay the most attractive man at Harvard. And Daniel Webster was so in love with James Hervey Bingham, a Dartmouth classmate, that his salutations to Bingham began "Dearly Beloved," and he ended one letter by saying, "Accept all the tenderness I have." See Donald, *Lincoln Men*, p. 37; Rotundo, *American Manhood*, pp. 78-79 (quoted); Crain, *American Sympathy*; David Deitcher, *Dear Friends*.

178. Katz, *Love Stories*, pp. 8-12; Reynolds, *Walt Whitman's America*, pp. 195-200, 390-400. The terms "homosexuality" and "heterosexuality" did not enter the English language until 1892.

179. Reynolds, *Walt Whitman's America*, pp. 195-200, 390-400, quotation from p. 198; Crain, *American Sympathy*, pp. 1-15; Katz, *Love Stories*, pp. 8-12.

180. Reynolds, *Walt Whitman's America*, pp. 195-200, 390-400; Daniel A. Helminiak, *What the Bible Really Says About Homosexuality* (San Francisco: Alamo Square Press, 1994); Bray, *The Friend*; Jaeger, *Ennobling Love*.

181. Reynolds, *Walt Whitman's America*, pp. 195-196, 391-394, quotation from p. 195; Katz, *Love Stories*, pp. 60-76, 358-359, 402-406.

As Reynolds summarizes, "Not until 1882 would 'consenting to sodomy' be criminalized" (p. 394).

Katz essentially concurs: he compiled a list of appeals cases in federal and state courts for the crimes of "sodomy" and "buggery," and found only 105 cases nationwide from 1810 to 1900. The vast majority of them involve humans having sex with animals, and of these 105 cases, only *one* involves male-male or female-female sex before 1860: it is an attempted "sodomy, buggery," man with male "youth," which probably means that the sex was forced upon the youth. Katz, *Love Stories*, pp. 402–406, quotation from p. 402.

182. Reynolds, *Walt Whitman's America*, p. 198.

183. Looby, "Innocent Homosexuality," p. 533. The same quotes appear in Reynolds, *Walt Whitman's America*, p. 394; Katz, *Love Stories*, pp. 77–78; Martin Bauml Duberman, "'Writhing Bedfellows': Two Young Men from Antebellum South Carolina's Ruling Elite Share 'Extravagant Delight,'" *About Time: Exploring the Gay Past* (New York: Gay Presses of New York, 1986), p. 7.

184. As Orlando Patterson perceptively notes, homoerotic longings were most common in honor-based cultures like the one Lincoln lived in. See Patterson, "The Code of Honor in the Old South," *Reviews in American History* 12:1 (March 1984): 29.

185. On Withers, see C. Vann Woodward, ed., *Mary Chesnut's Civil War* (New Haven: Yale University Press, 1981), p. 8; on Hammond, see Drew Gilpin Faust, *James Henry Hammond and the Old South: A Design for Mastery* (Baton Rouge: Louisiana State University Press, 1982), pp. 18–19. Woodward does not mention Withers and Hammond's erotic friendship; Faust quotes from the same letter I do but argues that it reflects a "vio-

lent expression at mastery" rather than an erotic friendship.

186. Melville, *White-Jacket, or The World in a Man-of-War* (1850; Evanston and Chicago: Northwestern University Press and the Newberry Library, 1970), pp. 170–175 (ch. 42), quotation from p. 171.

187. B. R. Burg, *An American Seafarer in the Age of Sail:The Erotic Diaries of Philip C.Van Buskirk, 1851–1870* (New Haven:Yale University Press, 1994), esp. pp. 24–31, 73–74; *The Diary of Philip C.Van Buskirk*, Manuscripts and University Archives, Allen Library, University of Washington, Seattle. I am deeply grateful to John Wood for introducing me to Philip Van Buskirk's diary and enriching my understanding of romantic friendships more generally.

188. Whitman, "A Woman Waits for Me" (1867, 1871), and "Native Moments" (1860, 1881), in *Leaves of Grass*, ed. Sculley Bradley and Harold W. Blodgett (New York: W. W. Norton, 1973), pp. 101, 109 (quoted); Reynolds, *Walt Whitman's America*, pp. 198–200, quotation from p. 199.

189. Donald, *Lincoln Men*, pp. 34, 53, 227.

190. *CW* 1, p. 283. Speed wrote this letter the day after he married Fanny Henning, and enclosing the violet could also symbolize the consummation of his love for Fanny. In his response, Lincoln implies that Fanny was the one who picked the violet: "I mean to preserve and cherish [it] for the sake of her who procured it to be sent." Still, it is significant that Speed (and possibly Fanny) would

want Lincoln to vicariously participate in their sexual intimacy. As Jonathan Katz brilliantly notes, women facilitated the intimacy between Lincoln and Speed. See *Love Stories*, pp. 3–25, especially pp. 14, 24.

On the violet as a symbol of sexuality, see Kathy J. Phillips, "Billy Budd as Anti-Homophobic Text," *College English* 56:8 (December 1994): 901; Beverly Seaton, "Towards a Historical Semiotics of Literary Flower Personification," *Poetics Today* 10:4 (Winter 1989): 690–691, 694; R. H. Fogle, "A Reading of Keats's 'Eve of St. Agnes,'" *College English* 6:6 (March 1945): 327; Alfred J. Kloeckner, "The Flower and the Fountain: Hawthorne's Chief Symbols in 'Rappaccini's Daughter,'" *American Literature* 38:3 (November 1966): 329.

191. *Herndon's Informants*, p. 499; Wilson, *Lincoln's Sword*, pp. 31–32.

192. Katz makes a similar point in analyzing one of Lincoln's letters. See *Love Stories*, p. 13.

193. Donald, *Lincoln Men*, p. 50.

194. *CW* 1, pp. 259, 266, 267, 269, 281.

195. Tripp, *Intimate World of Abraham Lincoln*, pp. 250–251; Donald, *Lincoln*, p. 35.

196. Allen Thorndike Rice, ed., *Reminiscences of Abraham Lincoln by Distinguished Men of His Time* (New York: North American Review, 1888), p. 241 (quoted); Donald, *Lincoln Men*, p. 38.

197. Herndon, quoted from Burlingame, afterword, *Intimate World of Abraham Lincoln*, p. 230 (quoted); Wil-

son, *Honor's Voice*, p. 127. While Lincoln felt awkward around *eligible* women, he evidently lost his shyness with prostitutes.

198. *Herndon's Informants*, p. 481; Michael Burlingame, afterword, *Intimate Lincoln*, p. 230.

199. *Herndon's Informants*, p. 719; Wilson, *Honor's Voice*, pp. 181–185, quotation from p. 183.

200. My reading of Lincoln and Speed has been greatly informed by David Donald's excellent chapter on their friendship in *Lincoln Men*. I was struck by Donald's use of rhetorical gymnastics to deny the possibility of any homoeroticism in Lincoln and Speed's friendship. He ignores the blurred boundaries between eros and ardor, friendship and sex in American romantic friendships and in the long tradition from the classical era through the twentieth century. And he cites the opinion of Dr. Charles B. Strozier, the psychoanalyst and biographer of Lincoln, who argues that *if* Lincoln and Speed had a sexual friendship, then Lincoln would have been "a bisexual at best, torn between worlds, full of shame, confused, and hardly likely to end up in politics." Yet as Donald himself notes, the binary understanding of sexuality, implicit in Strozier's argument, did not exist in Lincoln's day. The case of James Henry Hammond, one of the most famous politicians in the South and clearly "bisexual" (according to Strozier), explodes Strozier's and Donald's arguments, for Hammond's friendship with Withers neither affected his public or political career nor created shame and confusion. It was Strozier's mentor Freud, the father of psychoanalysis, who

influentially asserted that homosexuality and bisexuality were diseases. Indeed Freud argued that romantic friendship was a mask for homoerotic longings. See Peter Gay, *Freud: A Life for Our Time* (New York: Anchor, 1988).

201. Donald, *Lincoln Men*, pp. 32 (quoted), 45; Fiske Kimball, "Jefferson's Designs for Two Kentucky Houses," *Journal of the Society of Architectural Historians* 9:3 (October 1950): 16; Clay Lancaster, "Jefferson's Architectural Indebtedness to Robert Morris," *Journal of the Society of Architectural Historians* 10:1 (March 1951): 9; Gary Lee Williams, "James and Joshua Speed: Lincoln's Kentucky Friends," Ph.D. Dissertation, Duke University, 1971.

For examples of Speed's style resembling Lincoln's, see Speed to Lincoln, July 13, 1849; September 22, 1859; May 19, 1860; November 14, 1860; October 26, 1863; in Abraham Lincoln Papers, Library of Congress (hereafter LPLC).

202. On the significance of lyceum lecture circuits see Donald M. Scott, "The Popular Lecture and the Creation of a Public in Mid-Nineteenth-Century America," *Journal of American History* 66:4 (March 1980): 791–809, esp. p. 798.

203. *CW* 1, pp. 110, 111, 112, 115.

204. Ibid. pp. 278–279, quotations from p. 279.

205. Ibid., pp. 282–283. In his letter to Speed, Lincoln suggests that few people had read the speech, which had been published in the *Sangamo Journal*.

206. Donald, *Lincoln*, p. 105; Wilson, *Honor's Voice*, pp. 222-225.

207. *Herndon's Informants*, pp. 187-188, quotation from p. 187; *CW* 1, p. 226 (quoted); Wilson, *Honor's Voice*, pp. 223-224.

208. Shenk, *Lincoln's Melancholy*, pp. 55-56; Wilson, *Honor's Voice*, pp. 223-231.

209. Speed, quoted from *Herndon's Informants*, pp. 197, 475; *CW* 1, pp. 229, 282.

210. Donald, *Lincoln Men*, p. 42; Katz, *Love Stories*, p. 18; Shenk, *Lincoln's Melancholy*, pp. 55-56; Wilson, *Honor's Voice*, pp. 224-231.

211. Donald, *Lincoln Men*, p. 43.

212. *CW* 1, p. 281.

213. Donald, *Lincoln Men*, p. 45.

214. Ibid., pp. 45-47, quotations from pp. 46, 47.

215. Donald, *Lincoln Men*, p. 54. Speed, now living at Louisville, advertised "Valuable Slaves for Sale."

216. *CW* 1, p. 260.

217. The Northwest Ordinance would become a crucial foundation for Lincoln's understanding in the 1850s that the federal government had the constitutional right to prohibit the spread of slavery.

218. Richard E. Hart, "Springfield's African Americans as a Part of the Lincoln Community," *Journal of the Abra-*

ham Lincoln Association 20:1 (1999): 35–54; Paul Finkelman, "Slavery and the Northwest Ordinance: A Study in Ambiguity," *Journal of the Early Republic* 6 (Winter 1986): 369; Finkelman, "Evading the Ordinance: The Persistence of Bondage in Indiana and Illinois," *Journal of the Early Republic* 9 (Spring 1989): 21–51; Eugene H. Berwanger, *The Frontier Against Slavery: Western Anti-Negro Prejudice and the Slavery Extension Controversy* (Urbana: University of Illinois Press, 1971), pp. 10–35. The 1818 constitution also stipulated that children of existing slaves would be born free.

219. See The United States Census. A new constitution in 1848 finally abolished the state's remaining slaves, but Lincoln had nothing to do with its passage; he was serving a term as a U.S. congressman in Washington. The state had grown so much in eight years, almost doubling in size, that freeing its few remaining slaves no longer seemed threatening.

220. The Black Codes were rarely enforced, and so in one sense Lincoln's refusal to condemn them was a pragmatic political decision.

221. Billy was born in Haiti and some scholars spell his name "de Fleurville," though in his letter to Lincoln in 1863 (the only extant correspondence between them) he signs his name William Florville. See Florville to Lincoln, December 27, 1863, LPLC; Benjamin Quarles, *Lincoln and the Negro* (1962; reprint, New York: Da Capo, 1990), pp. 26–28; Dirck, *Lincoln the Lawyer*, p. 149.

222. Quarles, *Lincoln and the Negro*, p. 26 (quoted); William Cullen Bryant, quoted from Donald, *Lincoln*, p. 67; *CW* 1, p. 79 (quoted).

223. *Herndon's Lincoln*, p. 531; Donald, *Lincoln*, pp. 55-56; Olive Carruthers, *Lincoln's Other Mary* (Chicago: Ziff-Davis Publishing, 1946).

224. Mary Todd thus contradicted the antebellum ideal of the demure wife and republican mother, whose cultural role was to raise the next generation of virtuous Americans.

225. Wilson, *Honor's Voice*, pp. 215-218, quotations from pp. 215, 216; James A. Brussel, M.C., "Mary Todd Lincoln: A Psychiatric Study," *Psychiatric Quarterly* 15 (Supplement 1/January 1941): 7-8, quotation from p. 8; Jean H. Baker, *Mary Todd Lincoln: A Biography* (New York: W. W. Norton, 1987), pp. 3-98.

226. *Herndon's Informants*, p. 443. See also Wilson, *Honor's Voice*, p. 215-220.

227. *CW* 1, pp. 261, 280, 282. See also Donald, *Lincoln Men*, pp. 48-55; Wilson, *Honor's Voice*, pp. 221-256.
"Your last letter gave me more pleasure than the total sum of all I have enjoyed since that fatal first of Jany. '41," Lincoln wrote Speed on March 27, 1842. See *CW* 1, p. 282. Acquaintances of Mary Todd and Lincoln also worked to bring the couple back together.

228. On Mary's helping Lincoln, see Jean H. Baker, *Mary Todd Lincoln*, pp. 94-97.

Politically, Shields was a sitting duck, for after Democrats killed the state bank, causing its notes to be worthless, Shields had to tell the people of Illinois that they had to pay their taxes in silver or gold rather than the state's banknotes. The state "refused to honor the currency of its own institution." See Wilson, *Honor's Voice*, pp. 265–283, quotation from p. 266; Donald, *Lincoln*, pp. 90–93.

Shields later became a United States senator and Civil War general. *CW* 1, p. 62.

229. On Shields see William H. Condon, *Life of Major-General James Shields: Hero of Three Wars and Senator from Three States* (Chicago: Press of the Blakely Printing Co., 1900).

230. There were a total of four "Rebecca Letters." Mary Todd and her friend Julia Jayne authored one of them. It was Lincoln's "Rebecca Letter" that outraged Shields and prompted the duel. See Roy P. Basler, "The Authorship of the Rebecca Letters," *Abraham Lincoln Quarterly* 2 (June 1942): 80–90; Baker, *Mary Todd Lincoln*, pp. 94–96.

Lincoln's "Rebecca Letter" offers another example of his proclivity for gender-bending: he tells the story as a woman.

231. *CW* 1, pp. 291, 292, 293. Twain's *Huckleberry Finn* is considered one of the first major works of fiction written in first-person dialect.

232. *CW* 1, p. 295.

233. Ibid., p. 296.

234. Ibid., pp. 299–300.

235. Ibid., p. 300.

236. While political attacks were considered fair game, personal attacks became affairs of honor and grounds for dueling. See Wilson, *Honor's Voice*, pp. 276–279.

237. Elliott J. Gorn, "'Gouge and Bite, Pull Hair and Scratch': The Social Significance of Fighting in the Southern Backcountry," *American Historical Review* 90:1 (February 1985): 43.

238. *CW* 1, p. 301.

239. Lincoln, quoted from Wilson, *Honor's Voice*, p. 281.

240. *CW* 1, p. 114.

241. *Illinois State Journal*, April 27, 1860. As a location Lincoln selected an island on the Mississippi River, technically in Missouri, where dueling was still legal. It was just outside of Alton, Illinois, where the abolitionist Elijah Lovejoy had been murdered five years earlier.

242. Baker, *Mary Todd Lincoln*, p. 97. Remini, *Henry Clay*, pp. 41, 53–56. Clay challenged John Marshall, the cousin of the chief justice of the Supreme Court, to a duel in 1807, after the two assemblymen had gotten into a fistfight in the state legislature. They dueled with pistols and Clay was wounded in the right thigh. Marshall was unhurt.

243. *CW* 1, p. 303 (quoted); Donald, *Lincoln Men*, pp. 50–51.

244. Wilson, *Honor's Voice*, pp. 290–291. When a small boy asked Lincoln where he was going on his wedding day, he replied, "To hell, I reckon."

245. Herndon, quoted from Donald, *Lincoln Men*, p. 157.

246. *Herndon's Informants*, p. 431; Donald, *Lincoln*, p. 93.

247. *TFDP* 1:2, p. 148 (quoted). See also *LWFD* 1, pp. 151–153; Stauffer, *Black Hearts of Men*, pp. 150–152.

248. Robert Burns, "Is There for Honest Poverty," in *Robert Burns: Selected Poems*, ed. Carol McGuirk (New York: Penguin, 1993), pp. 181–182. See also Stauffer, *Black Hearts of Men*, pp. 150–152.

249. Stauffer, *Black Hearts of Men*, pp. 60–62.

250. Whitman, *Poetry and Prose* (New York: Library of America, 1982), pp. 1152–1161, quotations from p. 1153.

251. *CW* 1, p. 280 (quoted); Wilson, *Honor's Voice*, p. 256 (quoted). I am indebted to Wilson's interpretation of Lincoln.

Three: *Radical Abolitionist and Republican*

1. John Blassingame, ed., *The Frederick Douglass Papers* (hereafter *TFDP*), series 1, vol. 2 (New Haven: Yale University Press, 1982), p. 138.

2. Philip S. Foner, ed., *The Life and Writings of Frederick Douglass* (hereafter *LWFD*), vol. 1 (New York: International Publishers, 1950), pp. 284–290, quotation from p. 290.

Clay, like Lincoln, called for gradual and "cautious" emancipation accompanied by removal of free blacks to a colony outside the United States. For Clay (and Lincoln), emancipation primarily benefited whites. With emancipation in Kentucky, "we shall elevate the character of white labor, and elevate the social condition of the white laborer; augment the value of our lands, improve the agriculture of the state, attract capital from abroad to all the pursuits of commerce, manufactures and agriculture; [and] redress, as far and as fast as we safely and prudently could, any wrongs which the descendants of Africa have suffered at our hands."

See Robert V. Remini, *Henry Clay: Statesman for the Union* (New York: W. W. Norton, 1991), pp. 718–719.

3. Henry Clay, quoted from Remini, *Henry Clay*, p. 733; David Herbert Donald, *Lincoln* (New York: Simon & Schuster, 1995), p. 135; Wendell Holmes Stephenson, *Isaac Franklin, Slave Trader and Planter of the Old South; with plantation records* (Baton Rouge: Louisiana State University Press, 1938).

4. "Abolition of Slavetrading in the District of Columbia," *North Star*, January 5, 1849; Lincoln, quoted from Donald, *Lincoln*, p. 135.

5. "Abolition of Slavetrading in the District of Columbia," *North Star*, January 5, 1849; Donald, *Lincoln*, p. 136.

6. Douglass, "Gott's Resolution," *North Star*, January 12, 1849.

7. Howell Cobb owned over two hundred slaves and became a major-general of the Confederacy. Alexander Stephens became the vice president of the Confederacy and the post-Reconstruction governor of Georgia. Robert Toombs made a fortune in slaves and became the Confederate secretary of state and then brigadier general. And Albert Gallatin Brown owned about eighty slaves, advocated secession as early as 1850, and became a Confederate captain and senator.

8. *TFDP* 1:2, pp. 151–152, 153. Douglass paraphrases Revelation 13:10.

9. *TFDP* 1:2, p. 153.

10. Ibid., p. 89; *LWFD* 1, p. 315. Lord Byron, "Childe Harold's Pilgrimage," canto II (1812), in *Selected Poems*, ed. Susan J. Wolfson and Peter J. Manning (New York: Penguin, 1996), p. 121.

11. Richard Bradbury, "Frederick Douglass and the Chartists," in Alan J. Rice and Martin Crawford, eds., *Liberating Sojourn: Frederick Douglass and Transatlantic Reform* (Athens: University of Georgia Press, 1999), pp. 169–170. Douglass doubtless was familiar with the line from the song of fugitive slaves: "I kept my eye on the bright north star, / And thought of liberty." See Benjamin Quarles, *Frederick Douglass* (1948; reprint, New York: Da Capo, 1997), p. 81.

12. *North Star*, December 3, 1847; *LWFD* 1, pp. 75–100, 280–290; Quarles, *Frederick Douglass*, pp. 80–98; Shelley Fisher Fishkin and Carla L. Peterson, "'We Hold These Truths to Be Self-Evident': The Rhetoric of Frederick Douglass' Journalism," in Eric J. Sundquist, ed., *Frederick Douglass: New Literary and Historical Essays* (New York: Cambridge University Press, 1990), pp. 189–204; John Stauffer, *The Black Hearts of Men: Radical Abolitionists and the Transformation of Race* (Cambridge, Mass.: Harvard University Press, 2002), pp. 158–168.

13. Frederick Douglass to Amy Post, October 28, 1847, Frederick Douglass Papers, University of Rochester (hereafter DPUR); *LWFD* 1, pp. 75–83; *LWFD* 5, pp. 69–72; Quarles, *Frederick Douglass*, pp. 80–82. Quarles says that the first issue of the *North Star* was published in the basement of Rochester's A.M.E. Zion church. If so, then Douglass rented his office at 25 Buffalo Street shortly thereafter.

14. *LWFD* 1, pp. 306–307, 369–370; Quarles, *Frederick Douglass*, pp. 80–82.

15. Quarles, *Frederick Douglass*, p. 118; Howard W. Coles, *The Cradle of Freedom: A History of the Negro in Rochester, Western New York, and Canada* (Rochester: Oxford Press, 1941), p. 136. Douglass often found fugitives waiting on the steps of his office as he arrived for work in the morning.

Coles's rare and hard-to-find book is invaluable in its oral testimonies that capture details of Douglass's life in Rochester. Since it relies heavily on memory, it needs to be used with care, and I quote from it when there is corroborating evidence of similar sentiments.

16. Quarles, *Frederick Douglass*, p. 119. Douglass estimated that he assisted about eight fugitives a month in the five months per year that he was in Rochester.

17. Douglass, "A Sister Rescued From Slavery," *North Star*, December 3, 1847; "Anecdotes of Douglass," *New York Times*, February 25, 1895.

18. *LWFD* 5, p. 72.

19. *LWFD* 1, pp. 84–88; Coles, *Cradle of Freedom*, pp. 123, 127, 156–159. No. 4 Alexander Street was later changed to no. 297 Alexander Street.

20. Coles, *Cradle of Freedom*, p. 158.

21. Rosetta Douglass Sprague, *My Mother as I Recall Her* (Washington, D.C., 1900), Douglass Papers, Library of Congress (hereafter DPLC), p. 14; Coles, *Cradle of Freedom*, p. 157.

22. Rosetta, who had lived with a Quaker family in Albany, already knew how to read but got help with her writing from the woman.

23. Coles, *Cradle of Freedom*, p. 158.

24. Ibid., pp. 158–159.

25. *LWFD* 1, pp. 336–343, quotation from p. 341.

26. Frederick Douglass, *Narrative of the Life of Frederick Douglass*, ed. David W. Blight (1845; reprint, Boston:

Bedford/St. Martin's, 2003), p. 59; Douglass, *My Bondage and My Freedom*, ed. John Stauffer (New York: Modern Library, 2003), p. 66. For a rich analysis of this anecdote, see Albert E. Stone, "Identity and Art in Frederick Douglass' Narrative," *CLA Journal* 17 (1973): 192–213.

27. On the Burned-Over District, see Whitney R. Cross, *The Burned-Over District: The Social and Intellectual History of Enthusiastic Religion in Western New York, 1800–1850* (Ithaca: Cornell University Press, 1950); and Michael Barkun, *Crucible of the Millennium: The Burned-Over District of New York in the 1840s* (Syracuse: Syracuse University Press, 1986). On Spiritualism and women's rights see Ann Braude, *Radical Spirits: Spiritualism and Women's Rights in Nineteenth-Century America* (Boston: Beacon, 1989). On Douglass attending the Seneca Falls convention and as a women's rights reformer, see *LWFD* 1, pp. 320–321, 352, 354–355; Philip S. Foner, ed., *Frederick Douglass on Women's Rights* (1976; reprint, New York: Da Capo, 1992), pp. 4–24; Stauffer, *Black Hearts of Men*, pp. 224–232.

Late in life, Douglass looked back to his participation in the women's movement as his most satisfying accomplishment. "When I ran away from slavery, it was for my people; but when I stood up for the rights of women, self was out of the question, and I found a little nobility in the act." Foner, *Douglass on Women's Rights*, p. 14.

28. Coles, *Cradle of Freedom*, pp. 127, 160, quotation from Douglass on p. 127. The United States Census lists only 699 blacks living in Monroe County (which includes Rochester) in 1850, out of a total population of

87,650. Many fugitives lived there temporarily before crossing over to freedom in Canada, and they were not listed on the census.

29. "Anecdotes of Douglass," *New York Times*, February 25, 1895 (quoted); Coles, *Cradle of Freedom*, pp. 131, 158; Quarles, *Frederick Douglass*, p. 83; *LWFD* 1, pp. 84–85.

30. William Cooper Nell, *The Colored Patriots of the Revolution* (Boston: Robert F. Wallcut, 1855), pp. 361–362, quotation from p. 362; *LWFD* 1, p. 84; Coles, *Cradle of Freedom*, pp. 133–134.

31. Douglass to Amy Post, April 28, 1846, DPUR; William S. McFeely, *Frederick Douglass* (New York: W. W. Norton, 1991), pp. 148–149.

32. *LWFD* 1, pp. 85–87, 306–307, 369–370; Quarles, *Frederick Douglass*, pp. 88–89; Douglass to Elizabeth Pease, November 8, 1849, Boston Public Library (hereafter BPL).

33. *LWFD* 1, p. 283.

34. *LWFD* 1, pp. 84, 92, 306–307, 369–370; *LWFD* 5, pp. 70–72.

35. *LWFD* 1, pp. 314–320, quotation from p. 315. Of the nation's free blacks, just over half (262,000) lived in the slave states of the upper South.

36. *LWFD* 1, pp. 314–316, quotation from p. 315; Mc-Cune Smith, "The Odd Fellows' Celebration," in John Stauffer, ed., *The Works of James McCune Smith: Black*

Intellectual and Abolitionist (New York: Oxford University Press, 2006), pp. 159-163; Theda Skocpol et al., *What a Mighty Power We Can Be: African American Fraternal Groups and the Struggle for Racial Equality* (Princeton: Princeton University Press, 2006).

37. *LWFD* 1, p. 369.

38. Quarles, *Frederick Douglass*, p. 89; *LWFD* 1, pp. 86-87; *LWFD* 2, p. 210. Garrison called the first issue of the *North Star* "another proof of [Douglass's] genius and is worthy of especial praise." *Liberator*, January 28, 1848; Quarles, *Frederick Douglass*, p. 82.

39. *LWFD* 1, pp. 86-91, 306-307; Quarles, *Frederick Douglass*, pp. 87-88, 91-95, 105-106; McFeely, *Frederick Douglass*, pp. 162-166; Coles, *Cradle of Freedom*, pp. 157-159. See also the correspondence between Julia Griffiths (after she married, Julia Griffiths Crofts) and Douglass in DPLC; and Julia Griffiths to Gerrit Smith in Gerrit Smith Papers, Syracuse University (hereafter GSP).

Julia's sister Eliza may have been the governess who taught Anna and the children to read and write.

40. Jane Marsh Parker, "Reminiscences of Frederick Douglass," *The Outlook* 2 (April 6, 1895): 552 (quoted); Quarles, *Frederick Douglass*, pp. 87-88; *LWFD* 1, pp. 87-89.

41. Coles, *Cradle of Freedom*, p. 158 (quoted); Quarles, *Frederick Douglass*, p. 87.

42. Coles, *Cradle of Freedom*, p. 158.

43. *LWFD* 2, p. 166.

44. *National Anti-Slavery Standard*, September 24, 1853 (quoted); Quarles, *Frederick Douglass*, p. 105.

45. Garrison, editorial, *Liberator*, November 18, 1853 (quoted); William H. Pease and Jane H. Pease, "Boston Garrisonians and the Problem of Frederick Douglass," *Canadian Journal of History* 2:2 (September 1967): 41–42.

46. Susan B. Anthony to Garrison, December 13, 1853, BPL (quoted); *LWFD* 2, pp. 62–66, 548, n. 34, quotation from Foner on p. 64.

47. Stauffer, *Black Hearts of Men*, pp. 15, 60, 128.

48. Ibid., pp. 134–135, 141–142. Normally it is spelled "Timbuctoo" or "Timbuktu," but I am following the spelling of the settlers on Smith's land.

Gerrit Smith's efforts to create a vibrant black community at Timbucto were not successful. By 1848, when Douglass moved to Rochester, only about twenty or thirty families had settled in Timbucto. The major obstacle was start-up costs. Would-be pioneers needed wagons, mules (or oxen), and enough staples to survive the first harsh winter. And since most recipients didn't have the money for these things, they sold their deeds. There were other problems as well. The land was of poor quality and the climate harsh, as Gerrit had acknowledged, and by the mid-1850s, many of the settlers faced foreclosure by the New York State Treasury for failure to pay taxes. Then too, a number of whites living in the region tried to cheat the settlers out of their land. They posed as guides and showed them lots that were not theirs, often a swamp or a mountain peak, to dissuade them from moving. Other settlers sold their land for a song to swindlers or gave it away as remuneration for bogus fees. Understandably, they became disenchanted, and of the hundred or so people who settled at Timbucto, almost all of them left by the Civil War. See Stauffer, *Black Hearts of Men*, p. 157.

49. Stauffer, *Black Hearts of Men*, ch. 5.

50. I alter the sentence slightly for clarity, which reads: "In this, your new home, may you and yours, and your labors of love for your oppressed race, be all greatly blessed of God." See Gerrit Smith to Frederick Douglass, reprinted in the *North Star*, January 8, 1848.

51. Stauffer, *Black Hearts of Men*, pp. 155–158; McFeely, *Frederick Douglass*, p. 151.

52. Stauffer, *Black Hearts of Men*, pp. 160–162; After Gerrit Smith learned that Douglass had gotten punched in the face for walking down Broadway in New York City arm in arm with Julia Griffiths and her sister Eliza, he wrote him to say, "Think not, my dear Douglass, that it is you colored men alone who suffer from this insane and rampant prejudice. The wound it inflicts on you, it inflicts on us who sympathize with you, and who have identified ourselves and made ourselves colored men with you. In your sufferings, we suffer. In your afflictions, we are afflicted." Gerrit Smith to Frederick Douglass, June 1, 1850, reprinted in the *North Star*, June 13, 1850; Stauffer, *Black Hearts of Men*, p. 162.

53. David W. Blight, *Frederick Douglass' Civil War: Keeping Faith in Jubilee* (Baton Rouge: Louisiana State University Press, 1989), p. 30. Douglass described his relationship to Garrison in paternalistic terms. "I stand in relation to him [Garrison] something like that of a child to a parent," he told Charles Sumner. *LWFD* 2, p. 210.

54. Garrison, quoted from William E. Cain, ed., *William Lloyd Garrison and the Fight Against Slavery: Selections from* The Liberator (Boston: Bedford/St. Martin's, 1995), p. 36 (quoted). See also James Brewer Stewart, *Holy Warriors: The Abolitionists and American Slavery* (New York: Hill and Wang, 1976), pp. 98–99; Henry Mayer, *All on Fire: William Lloyd Garrison and the Abolition of Slavery* (New York: St. Martin's, 1998), pp. 443–445.

55. Smith and his fellow legal theorists also borrowed heavily from such international laws as the Somerset decision. See William M. Wiecek, *The Sources of Antislavery Constitutionalism in America, 1760–1848* (Ithaca: Cornell University Press, 1977), pp. 27–39, 205–227, 249–275; *Gerrit Smith's Constitutional Argument* (Peterboro, N.Y.: Jackson and Chaplin, July 18, 1844), pp. 1–16, GSP; *Letter of Gerrit Smith to S.P. Chase, on the Unconstitutionality of Every Part of American Slavery* (Albany: S. W. Green, 1847), GSP; *Substance of the Speech Made by Gerrit Smith in the Capital of the State of New York*, March 11, 12, 1850 (Albany: Jacob T. Hazen, 1850), GSP; William Goodell, *Views of American Constitutional Law, in Its Bearing upon American Slavery* (Utica: Jackson & Chaplin, 1844); Lysander

Spooner, *The Unconstitutionality of Slavery* (1845; reprinted and revised, Boston: Bela Marsh, 1860).

56. Wiecek, *Sources of Antislavery Constitutionalism*, p. 18. I have also been influenced by Robert M. Cover, *Justice Accused: Antislavery and the Judicial Process* (New Haven: Yale University Press, 1975), pp. 1–29, 154–158.

57. The due process clause declares that "no person shall be deprived of life, liberty or property without due process of law."According to Gerrit Smith, the Constitution empowered the federal government to abolish slavery in the states, because it guaranteed to each state a republican form of government and protected against domestic violence.

58. The apportionment clause determined representatives and direct taxes by "adding to the whole number of free persons . . . three fifths of all other persons."

59. *Gerrit Smith's Constitutional Argument*, GSP; *Smith to Chase on the Unconstitutionality of Slavery*, GSP; *Gerrit Smith in the Capital of the State of New York*, GSP; Goodell, *Views of American Constitutional Law*; Spooner, *Unconstitutionality of Slavery*; Wiecek, *Sources of Antislavery Constitutionalism*, pp. 249–275; Stauffer, *Black Hearts of Men*, pp. 22–27.

60. Stauffer, *Black Hearts of Men*, pp. 38–39; Cover, *Justice Accused*, pp. 154–158.

61. This is precisely what Southerners did when they seceded.

62. David Brion Davis, *The Problem of Slavery in the Age of Revolution, 1770-1823* (Ithaca: Cornell University Press, 1975), pp. 255-284, 469-522. Lincoln borrowed the term "ultimate extinction" from Clay. See Henry Clay, quoted from Remini, *Henry Clay*, p. 718.

63. *LWFD* 1, pp. 352, 361.

64. Ibid., pp. 374-379, quotations from pp. 375, 376.

65. On numerous occasions, Frederick and Anna stayed with Gerrit and his wife, Nancy, at the Smith mansion house in Peterboro. Nancy and Anna traded tips about gardening, which they were both passionate about, while Gerrit and Frederick debated law and politics. See Stauffer, *Black Hearts of Men*, p. 162.

66. *LWFD* 2, pp. 149-150; *LWFD* 5, p. 196.

67. *LWFD* 2, pp. 149-150 (quoted). See also *TFDP* 1:2, pp. 462, 477; Stauffer, *Black Hearts of Men*, pp. 162-166; John R. McKivigan, "The Frederick Douglass-Gerrit Smith Friendship and Political Abolitionism in the 1850s," in *Frederick Douglass: New Literary and Historical Essays*, pp. 212-215.

68. Cover, *Justice Accused*, p. 6; *LWFD* 2, pp. 149-157; Gerrit Smith, *To the Members of the Liberty Party*, October 10, 1851 [broadside], GSP; Douglass, "Gerrit Smith's Address," *Frederick Douglass' Paper*, December 25, 1851.

I borrow the phrase "always becoming" from Robert Cover. As he notes, "The flux in law means that the law's content is frequently unclear. We must speak of direction and of weight as well as of position. This frequent lack of clarity makes possible 'ameliorist' solutions. The judge may introduce his own sense of what 'ought to be' interstitially, where no 'hard' law yet exists. And he may do so without committing the law to broad doctrinal advances (or retreats)."

69. Stauffer, *Black Hearts of Men*, pp. 166–168, 174–181, quotation from Douglass on p. 166; Douglass to Gerrit Smith, May 28, 29, 1851, GSP. Douglass insisted that "you make me morally, intellectually, and mechanically responsible for the character of the paper," as he told Gerrit. In 1852, for example, he supported the Free Soil presidential platform while also working tirelessly to elect Gerrit Smith to Congress.

70. *LWFD* 2, pp. 151–152; Coles, *Cradle of Freedom*, p. 141; Stauffer, *Black Hearts of Men*, pp. 166–168.

71. Stauffer, *Black Hearts of Men*, p. 166.

72. *LWFD* 2, p. 158. See also McFeely, *Frederick Douglass*, p. 150; Stauffer, *Black Hearts of Men*, pp. 166–168.

73. *LWFD* 2, p. 205. Their collaboration lasted another nine years.

74. *North Star*, May 15, 1851; *LWFD* 2, p. 54; Douglass to Gerrit Smith, May 21, 1851, GSP.

75. Douglass told Gerrit Smith in March 1852 that Garrisonians "accuse me now, openly, of having sold myself to one Gerrit Smith, Esq., and to have changed my

views more in consequence of your purse than your arguments!" *LWFD* 2, p. 174.

Eight years later in 1860 Garrison declined to attend a convention at Syracuse in part because he knew Douglass would be there. "The fact that Frederick Douglass is to be present at the celebration, and to participate therein, would powerfully repel me from attending. I regard him as thoroughly base and selfish, and I know that his hostility to the American Anti-Slavery Society and its leading advocates is unmitigated and unceasing. . . . In fact, he reveals himself more and more to me as destitute of every principle of honor, ungrateful to the last degree, and malevolent in spirit. He is not worthy of respect, confidence, or countenance." Garrison to Samuel J. May, March 21, September 28, 1860, BPL, reprinted in *LWFD* 2, pp. 64–65.

76. *LWFD* 5, p. 165. See also Hugh C. Humphreys, "'Agitate! Agitate! Agitate!': The Great Fugitive Slave Law Convention and Its Rare Daguerreotype," *Madison County Heritage* 19 (1994): 4–22; and Philip S. Foner and George E. Walker, eds., *Proceedings of the Black State Conventions, 1840–1865*, vol. 1 (Philadelphia: Temple University Press, 1979), pp. 43–53.

77. *LWFD* 5, p. 166.

78. Stauffer, *Black Hearts of Men*, pp. 19–20, 133, 163–168.

79. The Compromise of 1850 included the following provisions: admitting California as a free state; organizing the remaining territories taken from Mexico into

New Mexico and Utah without restrictions on slavery; settling the Texas–New Mexico boundary dispute; compensating Texas for debts assumed as an independent republic; ending the slave trade (but not slavery) in Washington, D.C.; and passing the Fugitive Slave Act, which is discussed below.

80. *LWFD* 2, p. 106. On Clay orchestrating the Compromise of 1850 see Remini, *Henry Clay*, ch. 40.

81. *LWFD* 5, pp. 235, 236.

82. Allan Nevins, *Ordeal of the Union,* vol. 1, *Fruits of Manifest Destiny, 1847-1852* (1947; reprint, New York: Collier, 1992), pp. 380-382, quotation from p. 381; Cover, *Justice Accused*, pp. 175-191. The vast majority of fugitives came from the upper South owing to the difficulty of making it to free soil from the lower South.

83. Nevins, *Ordeal of the Union,* vol. 1, *Fruits*, p. 386.

84. Joan D. Hedrick, *Harriet Beecher Stowe: A Life* (New York: Oxford University Press, 1994), p. vii.

85. Robin W. Winks, *The Blacks in Canada: A History* (New Haven: Yale University Press, 1971).

86. Seward, Chase, and Sumner called the Fugitive Slave Act unconstitutional because it denied suspects the right to a jury trial and due process and gave judicial power to people who were not judges. See Charles Sumner to Frederick Douglass, September 9, 1860, *Douglass' Monthly*, December 1860; John Niven, *Salmon P. Chase: A Biography* (New York: Oxford University Press, 1995);

Glyndon G. Van Deusen, *William Henry Seward* (New York: Oxford University Press, 1967); Richard H. Sewell, *Ballots for Freedom: Antislavery Politics in the United States, 1837–1860* (New York: Oxford University Press, 1976), pp. 237–240.

87. William H. Seward, quoted in his speech in the Senate on March 11, 1850, in *LWFD* 2, 558, n. 4.

88. *LWFD* 2, p. 116.

89. Technically the Free Soil Party in 1852 had become known as the Free Democratic Party. At the convention John P. Hale was nominated for president and received about 150,000 votes, half Martin Van Buren's total as the Free Soil presidential candidate in 1848. See Sewell, *Ballots for Freedom*, p. 249.

90. *TFDP* 2, pp. 389, 390. Douglass used the same line— "the only way to make the Fugitive Slave Law a dead letter is to make half a dozen more dead kidnappers"—in other speeches; see for example *TFDP* 2, p. 277; *TFDP* 3, p. 419.

91. *TFDP* 2, pp. 391, 392. I slightly altered the exact quote, which reads, "I am proud to be one of the disciples of Gerrit Smith, and this is his doctrine."

92. Douglass editorial, *Frederick Douglass' Paper*, August 20, 1852.

93. It was a tradition of New York State blacks to celebrate the Fourth of July on the fifth for two reasons: to avoid confrontations with drunken whites on the fourth, and to distinguish their independence from the

unfulfilled principles of the Declaration of Independence. See Shane White, "'It Was a Proud Day': African Americans, Festivals, and Parades in the North, 1741–1834," *Journal of American History* 81:1 (June 1994): 38–39.

94. *TFDP* 1:2, pp. 360, 367, 387. On the speech see David W. Blight, *Narrative of the Life of Frederick Douglass*, pp. 146–148; and James A. Colaiaco, *Frederick Douglass and the Fourth of July Oration* (New York: Palgrave Macmillan, 2006).

95. Sewell, *Ballots for Freedom*, p. 292. Frederick Douglass noted the Republican Party's debt to the Liberty Party: "Nothing is plainer than that the Republican party has its source in the old Liberty Party," which "in 1848 fused with the Free Soil party.... Out of this Free Soil party has come the Republican party, and it is thus in its origin, history and pretensions, the anti-slavery party of the country, and must live or die as the abolition sentiment of the country flourishes or fades." *LWFD* 2, p. 490.

96. *Proceedings of the Convention of Radical Political Abolitionists* (New York: Central Abolition Board, 1855), pp. 3, 44–45; Stauffer, *Black Hearts of Men*, pp. 8–14, 22–27.

97. In 1848 Brown made a pilgrimage to Gerrit Smith's home at Peterboro, where Brown asked to live in the black community at Timbucto. Gerrit gave him some land, and Brown moved his large family there that year.

98. *North Star*, February 11, 1848; *LWFD* 2, p. 49.

99. Douglass, *Life and Times of Frederick Douglass* (1881, 1892; reprint, New York: Collier, 1961), p. 273. According to Douglass, Brown "denounced slavery in look and language fierce and bitter, thought that slaveholders had forfeited their right to live [and] that the slaves had the right to gain their liberty in any way they could."

100. Ron Brown chaired the Democratic National Convention in 1988. Peter J. Boyer ("Ron Brown's Secrets," *New Yorker*, June 9, 1997, p. 67) mistakenly says that Brown was the first black to chair a national political convention. McCune Smith's appointment as chair of the convention was not the only example of the party's efforts to act on its principle of racial equality. Later that year Radical Abolitionists nominated Douglass for secretary of state of New York, making him the first black man to be nominated for a political office. Two years later they nominated McCune Smith for the same post. See Stauffer, *Black Hearts of Men*, p. 24. On McCune Smith, see John Stauffer, *Works of James McCune Smith*, pp. xiii–xl.

101. Richard J. Hinton, *John Brown and His Men* (New York: Funk and Wagnalls, 1894), p. 19.

102. "Radical Political Convention," *National Anti-Slavery Standard*, July 7, 1855; Stauffer, *Black Hearts of Men*, pp. 13–14.

103. The Twelfth Amendment specifies that when an elector casts his two votes, one for president and the

other for vice president, one vote must be for someone outside the elector's own state.

104. Sewell, *Ballots for Freedom*, p. 287; *LWFD* 2, pp. 396–401.

105. David Herbert Donald, *Charles Sumner*, Part 1 (1960; reprint, New York: Da Capo, 1996), pp. 293–294. Gerrit Smith served a term in the House of Representatives from 1853 to 1854, got to know Preston Brooks, and felt sure that Brooks had been drinking when he assaulted Sumner: "But for liquor [Brooks] would never have committed his enormous crime." See *Mr. Gerrit Smith on the President's Message*, December 21, 1857 (broadside), GSP.

106. Donald, *Sumner*, Part 1, pp. 295–296, quotation from Crittenden on p. 296; *Alleged Assault upon Senator Sumner* (House Report, No. 182, 34th Congress, 1st Session), pp. 23–79. Two House members, Ambrose S. Murray and Edwin B. Morgan, heard the beating from the vestibule and tried to intervene, but Representative Lawrence Keitt, a friend and colleague of Brooks's from South Carolina, threatened them with his cane.

107. *Congressional Globe*, 34th Congress, 1st Session (1856), p. 530; James F. Simon, *Lincoln and Chief Justice Taney: Slavery, Secession, and the President's War Powers* (New York: Simon & Schuster, 2006), p. 108; Donald, *Sumner*, Part 1, p. 293; David S. Reynolds, *John Brown, Abolitionist* (New York: Alfred A. Knopf, 2005), pp. 158–161.

108. Donald, *Sumner*, Part 1, p. 298; Roy P. Basler, ed., *The Collected Works of Abraham Lincoln* (New Brunswick: Rutgers University Press, 1953), vol. 2, p. 514 (hereafter *CW*); Reynolds, *John Brown*, pp. 158–161, quotation from p. 161.

Brooks loved to brag about his deed: "I wore my cane out completely but saved the head, which is gold. The fragments of the cane are begged for as sacred relics. Every Southern man is delighted and the abolitionists are like a hive of disturbed bees. They are making all sorts of threats. It would not take much to have the throats of every Abolitionist cut." Reynolds, *John Brown*, p. 161.

109. Donald, *Sumner*, Part 1, pp. 298, 304, 308, 312–347. In the House, there was a motion to expel Brooks, but it lacked the required two-thirds vote. The Senate made no effort to punish him, although he was fined $300.

110. Reynolds, *John Brown*, p. 149.

111. Ibid., p. 156.

112. William Phillips, *The Conquest of Kansas, by Missouri and Her Allies* (Boston: Phillips, Sampson and Company, 1856), p. 297; Reynolds, *John Brown*, pp. 156, 157.

113. Reynolds, *John Brown*, pp. 154–157, 171–173, quotation from p. 155; *New-York Herald*, June 8, 1856 (quoted); Stauffer, *Black Hearts of Men*, pp. 195–198; Reynolds, *John Brown*, pp. 171–173.

114. Douglass, *Life and Times of Frederick Douglass* (1892, reprint, New York: Collier Books, 1962), p. 303; Stauffer, *Black Hearts of Men*, p. 198.

115. *LWFD* 5, p. 197.

116. Samuel Flagg Bemis, *John Quincy Adams and the Union* (New York: Alfred A. Knopf, 1956), p. 338. See also William Lee Miller, *Arguing About Slavery: The Great Battle in the United States Congress* (New York: Alfred A. Knopf, 1996), pp. 153-193; Sewell, *Ballots for Freedom*, pp. 121-123.

117. Stauffer, *Black Hearts of Men*, p. 26; *LWFD* 5, p. 197; *TFDP* 3, p. 428.

118. Donald, *Lincoln*, p. 388.

119. Lincoln, "Final Emancipation Proclamation," in *Abraham Lincoln: Great Speeches* (New York: Dover, 1991), p. 99 (emphasis added); Stauffer, *Black Hearts of Men*, p. 27.

120. Sewell, *Ballots for Freedom*, p. 301; *LWFD* 2, pp. 363-365. On the history of the Slave Power, see David Brion Davis, *The Slave Power Conspiracy and the Paranoid Style* (Baton Rouge: Louisiana State University Press, 1969); Leonard L. Richards, *The Slave Power: The Free North and Southern Domination, 1780-1860* (Baton Rouge: Louisiana State University Press, 2000).

121. Dred Scott's owner had voluntarily taken him into a free state and a free territory. When Scott returned to Missouri he sued for his freedom. The Supreme Court narrowly determined that he remained a slave. But

James Buchanan asked the Court to establish a broad interpretation on the case, in order to "settle" the slavery issue.

On the *Dred Scott* decision, I have relied on Paul Finkelman, *Dred Scott v. Sandford: A Brief History with Documents* (Boston: Bedford Books, 1997); Don E. Fehrenbacher, *The Dred Scott Case: Its Significance in American Law and Politics* (New York: Oxford University Press, 1978); Mark A. Graber, *Dred Scott and the Problem of Constitutional Evil* (Cambridge: Cambridge University Press, 2006); Simon, *Lincoln and Chief Justice Taney*; *Dred Scott v. Sandford*, 60 U.S. (19 How.) 393 (1857).

122. The quote is from the *Harrisburg Semi-Weekly Telegraph*, March 30, 1857, which summarized Northern antislavery views; reprinted in Sewell, *Ballots for Freedom*, p. 301.

On the *Dred Scott* decision implying that if slaveholders went into a free state, the Constitution would protect their property, Lincoln suggests this in his "second Dred Scott decision" (see below); and Paul Finkelman, *An Imperfect Union: Slavery, Federalism, and Comity* (Chapel Hill: University of North Carolina Press, 1981), pp. 285–338. Chief Justice Taney in his majority decision argues that if slaveholders took their slaves into free states, the Constitution would protect them. See Finkelman, ed., *Dred Scott v. Sandford*, p. 76.

123. Taney, quoted in Finkelman, ed., *Dred Scott v. Sandford*, p. 61.

124. Taney made it clear that blacks were not citizens "within the meaning of the Constitution of the United States." Finkelman, ed., *Dred Scott v. Sandford*, p. 69.

125. Douglass's predictions proved accurate.

126. *TFDP* 1:3, p. 167. Douglass relied on his constitutional understanding to denounce the chief justice of the Supreme Court. The Supreme Court did not have a monopoly on the meaning of the Constitution. Congress and the president had equal authority in defining law. And if they too ignored the antislavery aspects of the Constitution, then it was up to the people themselves to declare by their words and actions that any law upholding slavery was absolutely void because it contradicted "the laws of nature and of nature's God."

127. Douglass commends Lincoln in a speech celebrating British West Indian emancipation. See *TFDP* 1:3, pp. 233–238.

128. In Philip Foner's edition of the speech, Douglass spells Lincoln's name "Abraham." But *TFDP* is generally more accurate in its transcriptions. Compare *LWFD* 5, p. 407; and *TFDP* 1:3, p. 233. It was not uncommon for journalists to confuse "Abraham" for "Abram." See *CW* 2, pp. 333, 366–367.

129. *TFDP* 3, p. 236. I'm quoting from Douglass's speech, where the emphases are slightly different than in Lincoln's printed copy. See *CW* 2, pp. 461–462. Had Douglass given the speech, he would have changed "ultimate extinction" to "immediate extinction."

130. *TFDP* 1:3, p. 237. In this speech commending Lincoln, Douglass spends more time attacking Stephen Douglas, whom he considered "one of the most restless, ambitious, boldest and most unscrupulous enemies with whom the cause of the colored man has to contend." Senator Douglas was fighting Lincoln "at immense disadvantage": as a Democrat he had to defend the *Dred Scott* decision; but as the architect of the Kansas-Nebraska Act, he had to support the doctrine of popular sovereignty, which gave the people of a territory the right to sanction or exclude slavery. The two positions were incompatible. "It seems to me that the white Douglas should occasionally meet his deserts at the hands of a black one." *TFDP* 1:3, pp. 236–237.

131. Stauffer, *Black Hearts of Men*, pp. 170–173; Reynolds, *John Brown*, pp. 248–267. Brown said God had created mountains as "hills to freedom." He had read everything he could find on Toussaint L'Ouverture, the great leader of the Haitian Revolution, and he knew that the success of this massive slave rebellion had hinged on fugitives' using the mountains as a base of operations. Stauffer, *Black Hearts of Men*, pp. 170, 255, quotation from p. 255.

132. Douglass, *Life and Times*, pp. 274–275.

133. Ibid., p. 315.

134. Douglass had moved to a new home at 1023 South Avenue, on the outskirts of Rochester (now the Highland Park section). He had chosen this section "because of its remoteness from the city and the prying eyes of

federal officers and slave catchers." See Coles, *Cradle of Freedom*, p. 144.

135. John Brown, "Provisional Constitution," in Zoe Trodd and John Stauffer, eds., *Meteor of War: The John Brown Story* (New York: Blackwell, 2004), p. 110.

Brown's "Provisional Constitution" resembled Douglass's constitutional beliefs in another way: instead of calling for disunion or the overthrow of the existing government, Brown hoped to realize the full potential of the United States Constitution, through "amendment and repeal" if necessary.

136. Douglass, *Life and Times*, p. 316. Harpers Ferry is now in West Virginia, which seceded from Virginia and became a Northern state during the Civil War.

137. Green was the son of an African king; hence the sobriquet "Emperor." He was sold into slavery in South Carolina during the illegal slave trade, and then later fled to Rochester. As Douglass noted, South Carolina "was no easy matter to run away" from; very few slaves made it to free soil. See Douglass, *Life and Times*, p. 317; Coles, *Cradle of Freedom*, p. 144.

138. Douglass, *Life and Times*, pp. 317–318. The meeting with Brown was delayed because at Chambersburg Douglass was "instantly recognized" and the townspeople wanted a speech. He complied and then he and Green found their way to the quarry (p. 318).

139. Douglass, *Life and Times*, p. 319.

140. Ibid., p. 320.

141. Ibid., p. 319.

142. Ibid.

143. Ibid.

144. Douglass, *Life and Times*, p. 320.

145. The slaves didn't rally to Brown's aid probably because they, like Douglass, understood the risks and were not ready to die. The response of slaves and free blacks in and around Harpers Ferry suggests that they knew of Brown's plan and contemplated helping him. See Stauffer, *Black Hearts of Men*, pp. 256–257.

146. Five of Brown's men escaped and ten were killed in the fight.

147. J. E. B. Stuart was in Washington, D.C., when Brown and his men raided the arsenal. He had fought against Brown in Kansas as a cavalry officer and volunteered as a special assistant in Lee's company.

148. Reynolds, *John Brown*, pp. 363–367, quotations from pp. 364–366.

149. *LWFD* 2, pp. 483–484 (emphasis added). In his speech, Seward declared, "We have never been more patient, and never loved the representatives of other sections more than now." *Congressional Globe*, 36th Congress, 1st Session, p. 913; *LWFD* 2, p. 569, n. 38.

150. The refrain of the John Brown song is "His soul is marching on." According to some accounts, blacks began singing it shortly after his death, setting it to the hymn "Say, Brothers, Will You Meet Us." By the summer

of 1861, the John Brown song had become a Union favorite, an inspiration for troops as they too marched to their death. In 1862 Julia Ward Howe used the same music of the John Brown song to write "The Battle Hymn of the Republic." See Franny Nudelman, *John Brown's Body: Slavery, Violence, and the Culture of War* (Chapel Hill: University of North Carolina Press, 2004); Stauffer, *Problem of Evil*, pp. 287–289; George Kimball, "Origin of the John Brown Song," *New England Magazine* 1:4 (December 1889): 371–376.

151. *LWFD* 2, p. 484.

152. "The Liberty Party Nominations," *Douglass' Monthly*, October 1860; *LWFD* 2, pp. 97–98.

153. William W. Freehling, *The Road to Disunion,* vol. 2, *Secessionists Triumphant, 1854–1861* (New York: Oxford University Press, 2007), pp. 203–268, quotation from p. 246; David Brion Davis, *The Great Republic: A History of the American People* (Lexington, Mass.: D. C. Heath and Company, 1992), p. 579. Freehling's analysis of how and why John Brown's raid contributed to secession is simply brilliant.

154. Davis, *The Great Republic*, p. 582.

155. On the details of the execution, see *The Life, Trial and Execution of Captain John Brown* (1859; New York: Da Capo, 1969), p. 100.

156. John Rhodehamel and Louise Taper, eds., *"Right or Wrong, God Judge Me": The Writings of John Wilkes Booth* (Urbana: University of Illinois Press, 1997), p. 67;

Gene Smith, *American Gothic: The Story of America's Legendary Theatrical Family—Junius, Edwin, and John Wilkes Booth* (New York: Simon & Schuster, 1992), p. 80.

157. Rhodehamel and Taper, eds., *Writings of John Wilkes Booth*, pp. 106–108. Booth was called "the handsomest man in America." Although he had recently moved to the North, he continued to identify himself as a Southerner.

158. Ibid., pp. 53, 60.

159. Ibid., pp. 53, 60, 129–130.

160. Douglass, *Life and Times*, p. 307.

161. Ibid., pp. 309–310, quotation from p. 309; Stauffer, *Black Hearts of Men*, p. 249.

162. Douglass, *Life and Times*, pp. 306–313, 321–324.

163. *LWFD* 5, p. 467.

164. *LWFD* 2, p. 463.

165. Ibid., p. 462 (emphasis added). In *Life and Times*, Douglass reprints this essay but deletes the sentence saying he is ever ready to conspire against slavery. By the 1870s he had become a Republican insider and repudiated extralegal violence; and so he downplayed his militancy in the 1850s in this last autobiography. See Douglass, *Life and Times*, p. 312 and the epilogue.

166. *LWFD* 2, pp. 459–460.

167. James McCune Smith accurately described Douglass's self-transformation by saying that he had changed more in his eight years at Rochester than during his eight-year rise from slavery to internationally acclaimed orator. Stauffer, *Black Hearts of Men*, p. 160; James McCune Smith, "Frederick Douglass in New York," *Frederick Douglass' Paper*, February 2, 1855.

168. *TFDP* 1:3, p. 291. I quote from the self-made-man speech Douglass gave on January 4, 1860, but it is the same speech he gave in October 1859.

169. At the time there was a thirteen-month lapse between being elected to Congress and beginning the congressional term.

170. *CW* 1, p. 421.

171. Ibid., p. 433. Lincoln's actual quote reads, "from beginning to end, the sheerest deception." I altered it for stylistic purposes.

172. Ibid., p. 437.

173. As John Quincy Adams noted, Polk overrode the provision of the Constitution that gave to Congress the "exclusive" power to declare war. See Bemis, *John Quincy Adams and the Union*, p. 496.

174. *CW* 1, p. 439.

175. *Journal of the House of Representatives of the United States (Congressional Globe)*, 30th Congress, 1st Session, January 3, 1848 (Washington: Wendell and

Van Benthuysen, 1847–48), pp. 184–185, quotation from p. 184. The resolution passed the House by one vote.

176. Herndon, who was Frederick Douglass's age, studied law with Lincoln and Lincoln's partner Stephen Logan. He became Lincoln's partner in December 1844, after passing the Illinois bar. Logan and Lincoln amicably dissolved their partnership, and Logan brought his son David into his firm. The Lincoln-Herndon partnership lasted until 1861.

177. *CW* 1, p. 451. See also David Herbert Donald, *Lincoln* (New York: Simon & Schuster, 1995), p. 123.

178. Jean H. Baker, *Mary Todd Lincoln: A Biography* (New York: W. W. Norton, 1987), p. 136.

179. Baker, *Mary Todd Lincoln*, p. 137.

180. The Todd family home "always depended on slave labor" and Mary Todd had "publicly acknowledged black cousins." See Baker, *Mary Todd Lincoln*, pp. 18, 65–70, quotations from pp. 18, 70.

181. Charles Dickens, *American Notes* (1842; reprint, New York: Penguin, 2004), p. 126.

182. Ibid., p. 72.

183. Donald, *Lincoln*, p. 120.

184. Dickens, *American Notes*, pp. 129–130.

185. Carl Sandburg, *Abraham Lincoln: The Prairie Years*, vol. 1 (New York: Harcourt, Brace & World, 1926), p. 352.

186. Baker, *Mary Todd Lincoln*, p. 139; Constance McLaughlin Green, *Washington: Village and Capital, 1800-1878* (Princeton: Princeton University Press, 1962), pp. 147-149, 173.

187. Alexander Mackay, quoted from Margaret C. S. Christman, *1846: Portrait of the Nation* (Washington, D.C.: Smithsonian Institution Press, 1996), p. 30.

188. Dickens, *American Notes*, pp. 125, 135-136; Gerrit Smith, *Speeches of Gerrit Smith in Congress* (New York: Mason Brothers, 1856), p. 411.

189. Baker, *Mary Todd Lincoln*, p. 138; *CW* 1, p. 391.

190. "From Washington," *New York Times*, September 21, 1854.

191. Sarah Meer, "The Ethiopian Serenaders and Ethnic Exhibition," in Alan J. Rice and Martin Crawford, *Liberating Sojourn*, pp. 146, 148.

192. Baker, *Mary Todd Lincoln*, p. 140.

193. *LWFD* 5, p. 142.

194. James Brewer Stewart, *Joshua R. Giddings and the Tactics of Radical Politics* (Cleveland: Press of Case Western Reserve University, 1970), p. 168.

195. Henry Wilson, *History of the Rise and Fall of the Slave Power in America*, vol. 1 (Boston: Houghton, Mifflin & Company, 1872), pp. 429-430, quotation from p. 429.

Henry Wise of Virginia, who later prosecuted John Brown, declared that if Adams succeeded in destroying slavery, "the great democratic principle of equality among men would become obsolete." Adams shot back that Wise had no grounds from which to discuss the meaning of democracy: you are a slaveowner, you help murder a man in a duel, and then you come into Congress with your "hands dripping with human gore," Adams said. Wilson, *History*, vol. 1, p. 430.

196. Wilson, *History of the Rise and Fall of the Slave Power*, vol. 1, p. 430.

197. Ibid., vol. 1, p. 671.

198. Ibid. vol. 2, p. 162.

199. Bemis, *John Quincy Adams and the Union*, pp. 534–537.

200. *CW* 1, p. 448.

201. *Herndon's Informants: Letters, Interviews, and Statements About Abraham Lincoln* (Urbana: University of Illinois Press, 1998), p. 499; Douglas L. Wilson, *Lincoln's Sword: The Presidency and the Power of Words* (New York: Alfred A. Knopf, 2007), p. 31.

202. W. D. Howells, *Life of Abraham Lincoln* (Bloomington: Indiana University Press, 1960), p. 40.

203. *CW* 1, p. 420.

204. Perhaps when Lincoln looked down at the floor and saw the tobacco stains they reminded him of Springfield.

205. For example, when Lincoln employed artifice on behalf of Duff Armstrong, Jack Armstrong's son.

206. *CW* 1, pp. 347–348, quotation from p. 347. A year earlier, in May 1844, Lincoln had expressed a tentative and qualified opposition to the annexation of Texas. At the Illinois statehouse he read letters opposing annexation from Henry Clay, Martin Van Buren, and Thomas Hart Benton; and he concurred with them "in the opinion that annexation *at this time* upon the terms agreed upon by John Tyler was altogether inexpedient." *CW* 1, p. 337 (emphasis added).

207. Donald, *Lincoln*, pp. 122–123, quotation from p. 123. Lincoln's two predecessors in the House, Edward Baker and John Hardin, both became officers in the Mexican War, Hardin becoming one of the war's many casualties.

208. *CW* 1, p. 447. Most Whigs opposed the war but voted for supplies to fight so as not to appear unpatriotic. Significantly Giddings and Adams and other abolitionist congressmen opposed the war and refused to fund it.

209. Donald, *Lincoln*, p. 125.

210. *CW* 2, pp. 20–22.

211. Joshua Giddings, quoted from *Congressional Globe*, 30th Congress, 1st Session, vol. 17, p. 179. I assume that Lincoln thought highly of the waiter because in his testimony Giddings said that the man "had be-

come well and favorably known to members of *this* House" (p. 179).

William Wick, a Democrat from Indiana, said that some of the facts in Giddings's testimony of the waiter being arrested and sold south "were untrue or that facts important to be known were suppressed" (p. 180). But Wick did not elaborate. After some debate, Giddings modified the resolution by deleting the clause "to remove the seat of government to some free state" (pp. 179–180).

See also Stewart, *Joshua Giddings*, p. 147; Donald, *Lincoln*, p. 135.

212. *CW* 2, p. 322. Lincoln tells Joshua Speed, "I confess I hate to see the poor creatures hunted down, and caught, and carried back to their stripes, and unrewarded toils; but I bite my lip and keep quiet."

213. Albert Beveridge, *Abraham Lincoln, 1809–1858*, vol. 1 (Boston: Houghton Mifflin, 1928), p. 482; Donald, *Lincoln*, p. 137.

214. Stewart, *Joshua Giddings*, p. 153.

215. Lincoln considered Clay damaged goods as a presidential candidate, since Clay had been a candidate on numerous occasions but had never been elected. Besides, Lincoln thought him too old and too familiar a face. He loved that Taylor was totally unknown as a politician.

216. Elbert B. Smith, *The Presidencies of Zachary Taylor and Millard Fillmore* (Lawrence: University Press of Kansas, 1988).

217. "Rowdyism in Congress.—Drunkenness," *North Star*, March 23, 1849.

218. Wilson, *The History of the Rise and Fall of the Slave Power*, vol. 2, p. 671; "Rowdyism in Congress.—Drunkenness," *North Star*, March 23, 1849.

219. "Rowdyism in Congress.—Drunkenness," *North Star*, March 23, 1849.

220. Ibid.

221. *CW* 1, p. 431.

222. Baker, *Mary Todd Lincoln*, p. 143. Lincoln's seat had been controlled by Whigs for almost a decade.

223. *CW* 2, p. 7.

224. Baker, *Mary Todd Lincoln*, pp. 144–145. John P. Gaines accepted the Oregon governorship after Lincoln turned it down and was hamstrung by a Democrat-controlled legislature.

225. Lincoln's congressional term ended in March 1849. In November 1854 Lincoln was elected as a state assemblyman while also having his sights on the United States Senate. After realizing that a state legislator was ineligible for the Senate, he resigned his seat. See Baker, *Lincoln*, p. 148.

226. *CW* 3, p. 512. See also *CW* 4, p. 67.

227. Herndon, quoted from Donald, *Lincoln*, p. 157.

228. Burlingame, *The Inner World of Abraham Lincoln*, pp. 271, 273; Jesse W. Weik, *The Real Lincoln: A Portrait* (Boston: Houghton Mifflin, 1922), p. 94; "Reminiscences of 'Mr. Eaton,'" *Belvedere Standard*, April 14, 1868.

229. Burlingame, *Inner World of Abraham Lincoln*, p. 272.

230. Ibid., p. 273; *Herndon's Informants*, p. 597.

231. Burlingame, *Inner World*, p. 275; Justin G. Turner and Linda Levitt Turner, eds., *Mary Todd Lincoln: Her Life and Letters* (New York: Alfred A. Knopf, 1972), p. 46.

232. Weik, *The Real Lincoln*, p. 99; Burlingame, *Inner World*, p. 275.

233. *Herndon's Informants*, p. 445; Burlingame, *Inner World*, pp. 275–276.

234. Burlingame, *Inner World*, p. 276.

235. Henry Haynie, "Success," *Youth's Companion*, September 1, 1898; Burlingame, *Inner World*, p. 276.

236. *CW* 3, p. 29.

237. *CW* 2, p. 122.

238. Ibid., p. 126.

239. Ibid., p. 123. Lincoln quotes from one of the public journals and adopts its language "chiefly because I could not in any language of my own so well express my thoughts" (p. 122).

240. Fillmore became president after Zachary Taylor's death in 1850.

241. Davis, *The Great Republic*, p. 562.

242. *CW* 2, p. 492.

243. *CW* 3, p. 435.

244. *CW* 2, pp. 232–233, 256.

245. *CW* 2, pp. 233, 256. John Quincy Adams, probably the most knowledgeable and respected political and legal scholar of the era, almost certainly would have called the Fugitive Slave Act of 1850 unconstitutional.

246. *CW* 2, p. 255.

247. Ibid., p. 256.

248. *CW* 4, p. 67. See also *CW* 3, p. 512.

249. On Stephen Douglas I have relied especially on Robert W. Johannsen's excellent biography, *Stephen A. Douglas* (1973; reprint, Urbana: University of Illinois Press, 1997). Douglas became a leader in the Senate after the deaths of John C. Calhoun, Henry Clay, and Daniel Webster in the early 1850s.

250. Johannsen, *Stephen Douglas*, p. 25; Allan Nevins, ed., *The Diary of John Quincy Adams, 1794–1845* (New York: Longmans, Green and Co., 1928), p. 566 (February 14, 1844).

251. Johannsen, *Stephen Douglas*, pp. 537, 541, 587.

252. Ibid., p. 4.

253. *Diary of John Quincy Adams*, p. 566 (February 14, 1844); Johannsen, *Stephen Douglas*, p. 132.

254. Johannsen, *Stephen Douglas*, p. 876, n. 7.

255. *CW* 1, p. 450. In 1848 Lincoln wrote an old acquaintance who had moved to Natchez, Mississippi: "Perhaps you have forgotten me. Don't you remember a long black fellow who rode on horseback with you from Tremont to Springfield nearly ten years ago, swimming your horses over the Mackinaw on the trip? Well, I am that same one fellow yet."

256. Johannsen, *Stephen Douglas*, p. 542.

257. Baker, *Mary Todd Lincoln*, pp. 84–85; Johannsen, *Stephen Douglas*, pp. 72–73; Wilson, *Honor's Voice*, pp. 239–240.

258. *CW* 2, p. 136.

259. George Julian to F. W. Bird and others, April 29, 1853, Giddings-Julian Papers; Seward, *Ballots for Freedom*, p. 250.

260. *CW* 2, pp. 382–383.

261. David Bromwich, "How Lincoln Won," *New York Review of Books*, October 19, 2006, p. 46.

262. *CW* 2, p. 492.

263. Paul M. Angle, ed., *Created Equal? The Complete Lincoln-Douglas Debates of 1858* (Chicago: University of Chicago Press, 1958), p. 270.

264. Ibid.

265. *CW* 2, p. 229.

266. As Lincoln noted in 1859, "This chief and real purpose of the Republican party is eminently conservative. It proposes nothing save and except to restore this government to its original tone in regard to this element of slavery, and there to maintain it, looking for no further change, in reference to it, than that which the original framers of the government themselves expected and looked forward to." *CW* 3, p. 404.

267. *CW* 2, pp. 230–231.

268. Ibid., p. 275.

269. *CW* 3, p. 478.

270. Ibid., pp. 471–482; Eric Foner, *Free Labor, Free Soil, Free Men: The Ideology of the Republican Party Before the Civil War* (New York: Oxford University Press, 1970). Johannsen, *Stephen Douglas*, pp. 439–447.

271. *CW* 4, p. 67. The full quote reads, "His speeches at once attracted a more marked attention than they had ever before done."

272. State legislators elected senators until 1913, when the Nineteenth Amendment introduced direct popular election.

273. Johannsen, *Stephen Douglas*, p. 451.

274. Ibid., p. 453; *Chicago Tribune*, September 2, 4, 5, 1854.

275. Johannsen, *Stephen Douglas*, p. 454.

276. *CW* 2, pp. 232–235, 238–247.

277. Ibid., pp. 281–282.

278. Johannsen, *Stephen Douglas*, p. 458; *TFDP* 1:2, pp. 538, 541, n. 4.

279. *TFDP* 1:2, p. 541.

280. Ibid., p. 543.

281. Ibid., p. 544.

282. *CW* 2, p. 318.

283. Ibid., pp. 306–307.

284. Ibid., p. 373.

285. Johannsen, *Stephen Douglas*, pp. 518–519.

286. At the Republican nominating convention, Lincoln had pushed for John McLean of Ohio. An associate Supreme Court justice (and one of the two dissenters in the *Dred Scott* decision), McLean was an old-line Whig and Lincoln considered him more conservative than Frémont and thus a better candidate. But he was also over seventy years old and the *New York Tribune* spoke for most Republicans when it called him "an old foggy" and "a marrowless old lawyer." Frémont was young, he had no political past to haunt him, and his "romantic aura" seemed an ideal fit for the new activist party. William L. Dayton of New Jersey was Frémont's running mate, but Lincoln was a vice presidential contender, a

sign that he was gaining national recognition. See *CW* 2, pp. 342-343; Allan Nevins, *Frémont: Pathmaker of the West* (1939; reprint, Lincoln: University of Nebraska Press, 1992), p. 428; Donald, *Lincoln*, p. 193; Sally Denton, *Passion and Principle*, pp. 222-265.

287. *CW* 4, p. 67; Nevins, *Frémont*, p. 428.

288. *CW* 2, p. 350.

289. *CW* 2, p. 367; Johannsen, *Stephen Douglas*, pp. 522-523, 533-539.

290. Nevins, *Frémont*, pp. 448-449.

291. *New York Herald*, December 11, 1856; Harvey Wish, "The Slave Insurrection Panic of 1856," *Journal of Southern History* 5:2 (May 1939): 206-222; Charles B. Dew, "Black Ironworkers and the Slave Insurrection Panic of 1856," *Journal of Southern History* 41:3 (August 1975): 321-338.

292. A major reason for Buchanan's victory was that the third party candidate, Millard Fillmore, ran on a nativist ticket pandering to anti-Catholic prejudice, and took votes from Frémont.

293. *CW* 2, p. 355 (emphasis added). See also *CW* 2, pp. 387-388.

In an autobiographical statement written in 1860, Lincoln said he did not remember saying "anything about a Supreme court decision. He may have spoken upon that subject; ... but he thinks he could not have expressed himself as represented" at Galena.

In his note Roy Basler argues that Lincoln's "later position on the Dred Scott decision was that Republicans should abide by the decision until they could get a reversal by the court."

I disagree. Lincoln campaigned on a platform that sought to prohibit the extension of slavery, and no one could predict whether *Dred Scott* would be reversed. Thus, he did not abide by the Court's decision. See *CW* 4, p. 67 (quoted).

294. *CW* 2, pp. 273, 288.

295. Tocqueville, *Democracy in America*, vol. 1 (ch. 8), pp. 150, 151.

296. Allan Nevins, *Ordeal of the Union*, vol. 2, *The Emergence of Lincoln: Douglas, Buchanan, and Party Chaos, 1857-1859* (1950; reprint, New York: Collier, 1992), p. 112.

297. Don B. Fehrenbacher, *The Dred Scott Case: Its Significance in American Law and Politics* (New York: Oxford University Press, 1978), p. 222; Nevins, *The Emergence of Lincoln*, p. 112.

298. Nevins, *The Emergence of Lincoln*, p. 117. Chief Justice Taney saw himself as analogous to the pope, who announced and clarified scripture rather than interpreted it.

299. Tocqueville, *Democracy in America*, vol. 1 (ch. 8), p. 152.

300. *CW* 2, p. 323. As Lincoln said in a letter to Joshua Speed, "As a nation, we began by declaring that '*all men*

are created equal.' We now practically read it 'all men are created equal, *except negroes.'* When the Know-Nothings [a nativist party] get control, it will read 'all men are created equal, except negroes, *and foreigners, and catholics.'* When it comes to this I should prefer emigrating to some country where they make no pretence of loving liberty—to Russia, for instance, where despotism can be taken pure, and without the base alloy of hypocracy." Lincoln had a falling out with Speed in the 1850s as they evolved in different directions politically. Speed voted Democratic in 1856 and 1860 and became a wealthy slaveowner. See David Herbert Donald, *"We Are Lincoln Men": Abraham Lincoln and His Friends* (New York: Simon & Schuster, 2003) ch. 2.

301. *CW* 2, pp. 404–408.

302. Ibid., p. 222.

303. Ibid., p. 318.

304. *CW* 4, p. 169. Lincoln alludes to Proverbs 25:11.

305. In his debates with Lincoln, Judge Douglas tried to deny the fact that in *Dred Scott* the Supreme Court declared his own doctrine of popular sovereignty unconstitutional, since popular sovereignty allowed settlers to prohibit slavery from spreading. Douglas tried to get around this by saying that it was up to the settlers to enforce the law and protect slaveowners' property. See Johannsen, *Stephen Douglas*, p. 569.

306. *CW* 2, p. 401.

307. Ibid.

308. Angle, ed., *Created Equal?*, p. 36.

309. Ibid., p. 56.

310. *CW* 3, p. 471.

311. *CW* 2, p. 402.

312. Jackson merely acted on his presidential rights of veto.

313. Johannsen, *Stephen Douglas*, p. 640. See also Don E. Fehrenbacher, "The Origins and Purpose of Lincoln's 'House-Divided' Speech," *Mississippi Valley Historical Review* 46:4 (March 1960): 615–643. Fehrenbacher argues that Lincoln's nomination was a response to eastern Republicans who supported Douglas owing to the senator's refusal to support the admission of Kansas as a slave state (p. 616).

314. Lincoln, "House Divided," in *Great Speeches*, p. 30.

315. Ibid., p. 29.

316. *CW* 3, pp. 404–405, 423.

317. Nevins, *The Emergence of Lincoln*, p. 195; Jenny Wahl, "The Economic Consequences of the Dred Scott decision," 150th Anniversary of *Dred Scott v. Sandford*: Race, Citizenship, and Justice, Harvard Law School, April 6–7, 2007. Many Northerners blamed the Panic of 1857 on the South.

318. Paul Finkelman, ed., *Dred Scott v. Sanford*, p. 76; Finkelman, *Imperfect Union*, pp. 285–338.

319. Lincoln, "House Divided," in *Great Speeches*, pp. 30–31. On the significance of his "House Divided" speech, see Fehrenbacher, "Lincoln's 'House-Divided' Speech," pp. 615–643.

320. A twentieth-century analogy of Lincoln's audaciousness in his "House Divided" speech would be Joseph McCarthy declaring in 1954 that former president Harry Truman, President Dwight Eisenhower, Chief Justice Earl Warren, and Senator Lyndon Johnson were all secret communists, conspiring to overthrow the government.

321. Lincoln, "House Divided," in *Great Speeches*, p. 25.

322. *CW* 3, pp. 548–549; Earl M. Maltz, "Slavery, Federalism, and the Structure of the Constitution," *American Journal of Legal History* 36:4 (October 1992): 488.

323. On this "second Dred Scott" case, *Lemmon v. People*, see especially Paul Finkelman, *An Imperfect Union*, pp. 291–343; Fehrenbacher, *Dred Scott Case*, pp. 60–61, 444–445; and William M. Wiecek, "Slavery and Abolition Before the United States Supreme Court, 1820–1860," *Journal of American History* 65:1 (June 1978): 34–59; Wiecek, *The Sources of Antislavery Constitutionalism in America, 1760–1848* (Ithaca: Cornell University Press, 1977), pp. 286–287; Maltz, "Slavery, Federalism, and the Structure of the Constitution," pp. 466–498; and *Lemmon v. People*, 20 N.Y. 562 (Court of Appeals, 1860).

324. *Lemmon v. People*. The counsel for Lemmon argued that "property in man" was no different from

other forms of property and that "no state could pass laws" that would threaten this property. Slavery "was not morally wrong and not contrary to the self-evident truths of the Declaration," he emphasized. "There was no law of nature or of God against slaveholding." Wilson, *History of the Rise and Fall of the State Power*, vol. 2, p. 642.

325. *New York Tribune*, March 8, 1857; Maltz, "Slavery, Federalism," p. 489. Lincoln read the *New York Tribune* and was familiar with the Lemmon case. See *CW* 4, pp. 548–549.

326. Samuel A. Foot, *Reasons for Joining the Republican Party*.... (New York, 1855).

327. Allan Nevins, ed., *The Diary of George Templeton Strong: The Civil War, 1860–1865* (New York: Macmillan, 1952), p. 57.

328. Wiecek, "Slavery and Abolition," pp. 57–58; Fehrenbacher, *Dred Scott Case*, pp. 444–445.

329. Fehrenbacher, "Lincoln's 'House-Divided' Speech," p. 615.

330. *CW* 2, p. 522; Johannsen, *Stephen Douglas*, p. 663.

331. Johannsen, *Stephen Douglas*, pp. 663–664.

332. Douglas refused to endorse the admission of Kansas as a slave state primarily because the proslavery legislature and its Lecompton Constitution were corrupt. Moreover, Southerners rejected his doctrine of "popular sovereignty" because it allowed settlers to exclude

slavery from a territory. Southerners cited *Dred Scott* and declared that any attempt to exclude slavery from the territories was unconstitutional.

333. Johannsen, "The Lincoln-Douglas Campaign of 1858: Background and Perspective," *Journal of the Illinois State Historical Society* 73 (Winter 1980): 245.

334. *CW* 2, pp. 531–532. Douglas opened for an hour, Lincoln then spoke for an hour and a half, and Douglas concluded for a half hour. Douglas opened four of the debates, Lincoln three.

335. Johannsen, "Lincoln-Douglas Campaign," p. 244.

336. Douglas challenged Lincoln to a fistfight at Havana, a town later made famous by Edgar Lee Masters in his *Spoon River Anthology* (1915).

337. *CW* 2, pp. 541, 542.

338. Nevins, *The Emergence of Lincoln*, pp. 376–386, quotation from p. 385; Donald, *Lincoln*, pp. 214–215; Johannsen, *Stephen Douglas*, p. 541.

339. Donald, *Lincoln*, p. 215 (quoted); Nevins, *The Emergence of Lincoln*, pp. 377–378.

340. Nevins, *The Emergence of Lincoln*, pp. 377–378, quotations from p. 378.

341. Nevins, *The Emergence of Lincoln*, pp. 376–396; Donald, *Lincoln*, pp. 215–227. Jonesboro, a poor town in the southern part of the state, drew only fifteen hundred people, and Alton, their last stop, also drew a much smaller crowd.

342. Nevins, *The Emergence of Lincoln*, pp. 376, 381.

343. Donald, *Lincoln*, p. 227.

344. *LWFD* 5, p. 540, n. 56; *CW* 3, p. 172.

345. *CW* 2, p. 501.

346. It's difficult to determine whether Lincoln would have beaten Judge Douglas in a popular election. Illinois was divided, with the northern half of the state voting Republican and the southern half Democratic.

347. *CW* 3, pp. 377, 395.

348. Frederick J. Blue, *Salmon P. Chase: A Life in Politics* (Kent, Oh.: Kent State University Press, 1987), p. 119 (quoted); John Niven, *Salmon P. Chase: A Biography* (New York: Oxford University Press, 1995), pp. 192, 211, quotation from p. 211.

349. *CW* 3, p. 496. On Lincoln and Brown, see also David Reynolds's excellent discussion in *John Brown, Abolitionist*, pp. 424–430.

350. *CW* 3, p. 502. Lincoln also called Brown insane but acknowledged that he had shown "great courage" and "rare unselfishness." *CW* 3, pp. 496, 503.

351. Fifteen months later Lincoln would evade his duty in dealing with traitors.

352. *CW* 3, p. 541. Booth had performed in New York City and read the New York papers regularly.

353. Donald, *Lincoln*, p. 237.

354. *CW* 4, p. 39; Charles Hamilton and Lloyd Ostendorf, *Lincoln in Photographs: An Album of Every Known Pose* (Dayton, Oh.: Morningside House, 1985), pp. 34–36.

355. Lincoln, "Address at Cooper Institute," in *Great Speeches*, p. 39.

356. Ibid., p. 49. A common meaning of "cool" in the 1850s was "calmly and deliberately audacious or impudent in making a proposal or demand." See the *Oxford English Dictionary*.

357. Donald, *Lincoln*, p. 239; Lincoln, quoted from Reynolds, *John Brown*, p. 427; Harold D. Holzer, *Lincoln at Cooper Union: The Speech That Made Abraham Lincoln President* (New York: Simon & Schuster, 2004), p. 157.

Lincoln and most of his contemporaries referred to his speech and the venue as "Cooper Institute." Officially, however, the school was (and is) Cooper Union. But in 1859 the People's Institute organized public lectures and programs at the school, prompting most people to call the school "Cooper Institute," even though its proper name was still Cooper Union. I use Cooper Union except when quoting Lincoln and his contemporaries. See *CW* 3, p. 522; Holzer, *Lincoln at Cooper Union*, p. 6. Holzer's book is indispensable.

358. *CW* 4, p. 48; Donald, *Lincoln*, pp. 244–245.

359. *CW* 4, p. 24 (quoted); Donald, *Lincoln*, p. 245. See also *CW* 3, pp. 477–479.

360. Michael Tadman, *Speculators and Slaves: Masters, Traders, and Slaves in the Old South* (Madison: University of Wisconsin Press, 1989), pp. 289–290; Stauffer, *Black Hearts of Men*, p. 117; Robert W. Fogel, *Without Consent or Contract: The Rise and Fall of American Slavery* (New York: W. W. Norton, 1989), p. 71.

361. Wilson, *History of the Rise and Fall of the Slave Power*, vol. 2, pp. 515–623.

362. Ibid., vol. 2, pp. 633–642. Wilson gives another example of declension: in the early Republic James Monroe gave a passport to a slave of John Randolph, describing him as "a citizen of the United States." But in the 1850s the black dentist John Rock of Massachusetts wanted to travel to Europe for his health and applied for a passport. Lewis Cass, the secretary of state, replied that "a passport, being a certificate of citizenship, has never, from the foundation of the government, been given to persons of color" (p. 638).

363. Ibid., vol. 2, pp. 655–665.

364. Reynolds, *John Brown*, p. 429; George Fitzhugh, *Cannibals All! or, Slaves Without Masters* (Richmond, Va.: A. Morris, 1857).

365. Donald, *Lincoln*, p. 251. Baker, *Mary Todd Lincoln*, pp. 161–162, places the quote at the election rather than the nomination.

366. *CW* 4, p. 75; Donald, *Lincoln*, pp. 250–251.

367. Speed to Lincoln, Abraham Lincoln Papers, Library of Congress (hereafter LPLC).

368. On Southerners accusing Hannibal Hamlin of being a mulatto, see Christoph Lohmann, ed., *Radical Passion: Ottilie Assing's Reports from America and Letters to Frederick Douglass* (New York: Peter Lang, 1999), p. 205.

Southern newspapers implied that Lincoln would be arrested or killed if he tried to preach his "damnable" doctrines in the South. And in the eleven months between Harpers Ferry and the election, Yankees traveling in the South were run out of town, imprisoned, tarred and feathered, or killed—and they weren't even Republicans.

Judge Douglas campaigned in the South and spent election day in Mobile, Alabama. But he had spent his career courting Southerners. See Johannsen, *Stephen Douglas*, p. 798; *Memphis Avalanche*, quoted in *New York Times*, October 25, 1860; Ollinger Crenshaw, *The Slave States in the Presidential Election of 1860* (Baltimore: Johns Hopkins University Press, 1945), pp. 80–85; McPherson, *Battle Cry of Freedom*, pp. 212–213.

369. *CW* 4, p. 84.

370. Doris Kearns Goodwin, *Team of Rivals: The Political Genius of Abraham Lincoln* (New York: Simon & Schuster, 2005), pp. 277–278.

371. Donald, *Lincoln*, p. 256.

372. Though he became more vocal in his opposition to slavery as he got older, even as president from 1824 to 1828 John Quincy Adams hated it. In 1820, after an argument with John C. Calhoun over the Missouri

Compromise, he wrote in his diary, "Slavery is the great and foul stain among the North American Union, and it is a contemplation worthy of the most exalted soul whether its total abolition is or is not practicable....A dissolution, at least temporary, of the Union, as now constituted, would be certainly necessary, and the dissolution must be upon a point involving the question of slavery, and no other. The Union then might be reorganized upon the fundamental principle of emancipation. This object is vast in its compass, awful in its prospects, sublime and beautiful in its issue. A life devoted to it would be nobly spent or sacrificed." See Samuel Flagg Bemis, *John Quincy Adams and the Foundations of American Foreign Policy* (New York: Alfred A. Knopf, 1969), pp. 409–435, quotation from p. 418.

373. Wilson, *History of the Rise and Fall of the Slave Power*, vol. 2, p. 704; McPherson, *Battle Cry of Freedom*, p. 233.

374. Robert Temple, introduction, *Aesop: The Complete Fables* (New York: Penguin, 1998), pp. ix–xxiii, quotation from p. xvii; *Aesop's Fables* (London, 1818); Keith Hopkins, "Novel Evidence for Roman Slavery," *Past and Present* 138 (February 1993): 3–27.

375. Donald, *Lincoln*, pp. 31–32; *TFDP* 1:4, p. 122; *TFDP* 1:5, p. 414.

376. The content of Aesop's fables was antithetical to self-making. In the fable about the pole-cat and Aphrodite, for instance, the pole-cat falls in love with a handsome young man and asks Aphrodite, goddess of love,

to change her into a human girl. Aphrodite complies but wants to find out whether or not the transformation is authentic. Just before the couple consummate their love in the "nuptial chamber," Aphrodite releases a mouse into the room. The woman suddenly begins acting like a pole-cat, chasing the mouse around the room, and so Aphrodite changes her back to her former condition. *Aesop's Fables*, p. 62.

377. Coles, *Cradle of Freedom*, p. 160.

378. Nevins, ed., *Diary of George Templeton Strong: The Civil War*, pp. 204–205. Strong's dialect is only slightly exaggerated. In praising Lincoln he calls him "the best President we have had since old Jackson's time, at least, as I believe."

379. Temple, ed., *Aesop: The Complete Fables*, p. 47. John Brown would have reduced Lincoln's story to one sentence: "Talk is a national institution."

Four: *Abolitionist Warrior and War President*

1. Philip S. Foner, ed., *The Life and Writings of Frederick Douglass* (hereafter *LWFD*), 5 vols. (New York: International Publishers, 1950–1975), vol. 3, p. 57.

2. Ibid., p. 87.

3. On the significance of Haiti to the nineteenth century see David Brion Davis, *Inhuman Bondage: The Rise and Fall of New World Slavery* (New York: Oxford University Press, 2006), pp. 157–174; C. R. L. James,

Black Jacobins: Toussaint L'Ouverture and the San Domingo Revolution (New York: Vintage, 1963); Laurent Dubois, *Avengers of the New World: The Story of the Haitian Revolution* (Cambridge, Mass.: Harvard University Press, 2004). Though Douglass loved Rochester, he "detest[ed] the climate." See Douglass to Sylvester Rosa Koehler, May 5, 1868, Frederick Douglass Papers, University of Rochester (hereafter DPUR).

4. *LWFD* 3, p. 82.

5. Ibid., p. 83.

6. Frederick Douglass, *My Bondage and My Freedom*, ed. John Stauffer (1855; reprint, New York: Modern Library, 2003), p. 292.

7. "Haytian Emigration," *Douglass' Monthly*, March 1861.

8. *LWFD* 3, p. 72.

9. Ibid., p. 74.

10. Ibid., p. 72 (emphasis added).

11. William M. Wiecek, *The Sources of Antislavery Constitutionalism in America, 1760-1848*, (Ithaca: Cornell University Press, 1977), pp. 276-287. President James Buchanan proposed the amendment; *LWFD* 3, p. 431. See also the excellent discussion by Michael Vorenberg, *Final Freedom: The Civil War, the Abolition of Slavery, and the Thirteenth Amendment* (Cambridge: Cambridge University Press, 2001), pp. 9-22.

12. Lincoln, "First Inaugural," in *Abraham Lincoln: Great Speeches* (New York: Dover, 1991), p. 60 (emphasis added).

13. To Douglass, Lincoln deceived himself in believing that slaveholders themselves would one day emancipate their slaves. After all, they had just seceded from the Union solely because Lincoln would not respect their right to carry slaves into territories, even though he respected their rights in the states.

Douglass knew that slaveholders would never willingly emancipate their slaves, for slaves were more valuable than gold. Collectively they were worth about $2 billion, roughly equal to the value of American manufacturing. Relying on slaveholders to give up their slaves was a bit like asking capitalists to burn their stocks or asking thieves to hand over stolen goods.

See *LWFD* 3, pp. 74, 87. The figure of $2 billion is based on four million slaves multiplied by an average price of $500 per slave. For the value of American manufacturing at the time, see Douglass C. North, *The Economic Growth of the United States* (New York: W. W. Norton, 1966), p. v.

14. *LWFD* 3, pp. 67, 71–80.

15. Lincoln, "First Inaugural," in *Great Speeches*, p. 54. Douglass quotes him in *LWFD* 3, p. 76.

16. *LWFD* 3, p. 76.

17. Ibid.

18. Lincoln, "First Inaugural," in *Great Speeches*, p. 58. Two months after Lincoln's Inaugural Address, in May 1861, Chief Justice Roger Taney ruled that the South "had a constitutional right to secede from the Union." See James F. Simon, *Lincoln and Chief Justice Taney: Slavery, Secession, and the President's War Powers* (New York: Simon & Schuster, 2006), p. 194.

19. Lincoln, "First Inaugural," in *Great Speeches*, p. 61.

20. *LWFD* 3, p. 72.

21. Ibid., pp. 79–80.

22. Lincoln, "First Inaugural," in *Great Speeches*, p. 61.

23. Douglass's shrewd critique of Lincoln's Inaugural wasn't the first time he criticized Lincoln. A month after the election Douglass upbraided him and the Republican Party for pledging to uphold the fugitive slave law. He was so mad at Lincoln that he called him abolitionists' worst enemy. "He and his party will become the best protectors of slavery where it now is," he predicted. He hoped for disunion, believing that it would awaken the nation to "the possibility of a higher destiny than perpetual bondage." Douglass's prediction proved accurate, though through most of the secession crisis he had much higher expectations. See *LWFD* 2, pp. 527, 528.

24. *LWFD* 3, pp. 59–60.

25. Ibid., pp. 66–67.

26. "The President Elect," *Douglass' Monthly*, March 1861; David Herbert Donald, *Lincoln* (New York: Simon & Schuster, 1995), pp. 273–274, quotation from p. 274; John H. White Jr., *The American Railroad Passenger Car*, part 1 (Baltimore: Johns Hopkins University Press, 1978), pp. 314, 346.

During the leg from Buffalo to Albany, Lincoln and his party were served dinner in one of the first railroad dining cars "especially fitted up for that purpose." See the *Cleveland Plain Dealer*, February 18, 1861; White, *American Railroad Passenger Car*, part 1, p. 314.

27. "President Elect," *Douglass' Monthly*, March 1861.

28. *CW* 4, p. 222.

29. *LWFD* 3, pp. 67, 102; William W. Freehling, *Prelude to Civil War: The Nullification Controversy in South Carolina, 1816–1836* (New York: Harper & Row, 1966), pp. 264–292; Davis, *The Great Republic: A History of the American People* (Lexington, Mass.: D.C. Heath and Company, 1992), p. 503. Freehling notes that Jackson did seek to avoid an armed encounter in South Carolina and recommended to Congress a lowering of the tariff.

30. LWFD 3, p. 71; Donald, *Lincoln*, pp. 277–279; Ernest B. Furgurson, *Freedom Rising: Washington in the Civil War* (New York: Vintage Books, 2004), pp. 42–44. Lincoln disguised himself by wearing a soft felt hat instead of his trademark stovepipe hat and draping a coat over his shoulder. A *New York Times* correspondent fictionalized the disguise by claiming that Lincoln wore

a Scotch plaid cap and long military coat. Cartoonists then picked up on the Scotch theme, lampooning Lincoln by depicting him peering out nervously from a freight car in tam and kilts. Lincoln regretted following Pinkerton's advice. As he told one congressman after taking office, "I did not then, nor do I now believe I should have been assassinated had I gone through Baltimore as first contemplated, but I thought it wise to run no risk where no risk was necessary." See Donald, *Lincoln*, p. 279.

31. Lincoln, "First Inaugural," *Great Speeches*, p. 57.

32. As Lincoln said in his Inaugural, "there needs to be no bloodshed or violence; and there shall be none, unless it be forced upon the national authority. The power confided to me will be used to hold, occupy, and possess the property and places belonging to the government, and to collect the duties and imposts [taxes]; but beyond what may be necessary for these objects, there will be no invasion." Lincoln, "First Inaugural," in *Great Speeches*, p. 56.

McPherson argues that Buchanan and Lincoln agreed "on little else" but their refusal to condone disunion. James M. McPherson, *Battle Cry of Freedom: The Civil War Era* (New York: Ballantine Books, 1988), p. 246.

33. On Fort Sumter, one of the most written-about subjects in American history, see James McPherson's brilliantly pithy synthesis in *Battle Cry of Freedom*, pp. 264–275.

34. *LWFD* 3, p. 89.

35. Ibid., p. 91.

36. Ibid.

37. Roy Basler, ed., *The Collected Works of Abraham Lincoln* (hereafter *CW*), 9 vols. (New Brunswick: Rutgers University Press, 1953), vol. 4, pp. 331–332.

38. *LWFD* 3, p. 92.

39. *CW* 4, p. 332.

40. *LWFD* 3, p. 97.

41. Ibid., p. 95.

42. McPherson, *Battle Cry of Freedom*, pp. 250–251.

43. *OR* series 2, vol. 1, p. 750; *LWFD* 3, p. 95.

44. A. J. Slemmer to Lorenzo Thomas, March 18, 1861, *OR* series 2, vol. 1, p. 750.

45. "Ungrateful Proceedings," *Douglass' Monthly*, May 1861; *LWFD* 3, p. 95.

46. Carolyn L. Karcher, *The First Woman in the Republic: A Cultural Biography of Lydia Maria Child* (Durham: Duke University Press, 1994), pp. 446–447; *LWFD* 3, pp. 95–96.

47. Donald, *Lincoln*, pp. 254, 255, 273, 306, quotation from p. 306; John Hay, "Ellsworth," *Atlantic Monthly* 8 (1861): 119–125; Ruth Painter Randall, *Colonel Elmer Ellsworth: A Biography of Lincoln's Friend and First Hero of the Civil War* (1960).

48. *LWFD* 3, p. 108. Northerners began calling Ellsworth the first Union casualty of the war, but in doing so they ignored the existence of blacks.

49. Benjamin Butler to Winfield Scott, May 24, 1861, *OR* series 2, vol. 1, p. 752; Henry Wilson, *History of the Rise and Fall of the Slave Power in America,* vol. 3 (Boston: Houghton, Mifflin, & Company, 1872), pp. 286–287, quotation from p. 286 (emphasis added); Benjamin Quarles, *The Negro in the Civil War* (1953; reprint, New York: Da Capo, 1989), pp. 58–60, quotation from p. 59.

50. Lincoln signed the First Confiscation Act with some ambivalence. "In his opinion Congress had jumped the gun." But he knew that vetoing the bill would make it seem as though he justified the Confederacy's use of slaves for military purposes. See Quarles, *Lincoln and the Negro,* pp. 69–70.

51. *LWFD* 3, pp. 128, 153.

After the first battle of Bull Run, the *New York Tribune* described how "slave-built batteries repulsed the finest army ever organized on the American Continent." Union generals threaded their way through roads obstructed by blacks, plunged into batteries erected by blacks, and as a result "suffered a stunning defeat." According to another article in the *Boston Daily Journal,* a fugitive from Virginia spoke in Boston and said that "there was one regiment of 700 black men from Georgia, 1000 from South Carolina, and about 1000, including his own, in Virginia," which was destined for Manassas when he ran away. See Quarles, *The Negro in the Civil War*, pp. 35–48, quotation from p. 48; *LWFD* 3, p. 433, n. 23.

The Confederacy did not officially sanction the use of black troops, though it did aggressively impress blacks to work as laborers. The above report by the Virginia fugitive describing regiments of black rebel troops probably referred to militia troops organized without the consent of the Confederate government. See Bruce Levine, *Confederate Emancipation: Southern Plans to Free and Arm Slaves During the Civil War* (New York: Oxford University Press, 2006), pp. 1–17; Quarles, *The Negro in the Civil War*, pp. 35–49.

What is significant about these reports is that Douglass believed blacks fought as rebel soldiers because, given the Union's tacit support of slavery, they deemed it more prudent to show loyalty to their state than to an enemy of their state. See Quarles, *The Negro in the Civil War*, pp. 38–39.

52. The Confederate guerrilla commander Meriwether Jeff Thompson, the former mayor of St. Joseph, Missouri, described a raid on a Dutch-German settlement. After stealing some horses and wagons, Thompson ordered his men to retreat from the settlement, "but the temptation to have a brush before leaving was too great." Thompson's men "charged into the town of Hamburg, scattering the Dutch in all directions. My men fired on them as they ran through the fields, although unarmed, and killed 1, mortally wounding 5, . . . and brought away 13 prisoners and 25 horses." See Michael Fellman, *Inside War: The Guerrilla Conflict in Missouri During*

the American Civil War (New York: Oxford University Press, 1989), p. 181.

53. Sally Denton, *Passion and Principle: John and Jessie Frémont, the Couple Whose Power, Politics, and Love Shaped Nineteenth-Century America* (New York: Bloomsbury, 2007), pp. 301–313, quotation from p. 312.

Denton's biography of the Frémonts is convincing, well-researched, and a refreshing revision from the numerous accounts describing Frémont as an inept and arrogant opportunist. The other sympathetic biography of Frémont that I have relied on is Allan Nevins, *Frémont: Pathmarker of the West* (1939; reprint, Lincoln: University of Nebraska Press, 1992), pp. 473–528.

54. Frémont, "Proclamation," August 30, 1861, *OR* series 2, vol. 1, pp. 221–222, quotation on p. 221. The proclamation is also reprinted in Denton, *Passion and Principle*, pp. 419–420.

Three days after Frémont's proclamation the guerrilla rebel commander Meriwether Jeff Thompson issued a retaliatory order declaring that for every member of the Missouri guerrilla rebel forces "put to death ... I will hang, draw, and quarter a minion of said Abraham Lincoln. . . . I intend to exceed General Frémont in his excesses and will make all tories that come in my reach rue the day that a different policy was adopted by their leaders." See M. Jeff Thompson, "Proclamation," September 2, 1861, *OR* series 2, vol. 1, p. 222.

On Meriwether Jeff Thompson, see Doris Land Mueller, *M. Jeff Thompson: Missouri's Swamp Fox of the*

Confederacy (Columbia: University of Missouri Press, 2007).

55. Denton, *Passion and Principle*, p. 313.

56. Richard Hofstadter, *The American Political Tradition and the Men Who Made It* (New York: Vintage, 1989), quotation from T. Harry Williams on p. 165; Denton, *Passion and Principle*, p. 314.

57. Denton, *Passion and Principle*, pp. 312–314, quotation from Harriet Beecher Stowe on p. 312; James M. McPherson, *The Struggle for Equality: Abolitionists and the Negro in the Civil War and Reconstruction* (Princeton: Princeton University Press, 1964), pp. 72–74.

Douglass published a long list of the laudatory responses to Frémont's proclamation from papers around the country. See *Douglass' Monthly*, October 1861.

58. Frémont to Lincoln, September 8, 1861, *OR* series 2, vol. 1, p. 767. On Lincoln's letter to Frémont, see *CW* 4, pp. 506–507.

59. Denton, *Passion and Principle*, pp. 314–323, 326–328; McPherson, *Struggle for Equality*, pp. 72–74. Around the same time that he relieved Frémont of command, Lincoln also fired Benjamin Butler.

60. *LWFD* 3, p. 130.

61. David W. Blight, *Frederick Douglass' Civil War: Keeping Faith in Jubilee* (Baton Rouge: Louisiana State University Press, 1989), p. 151.

62. *LWFD* 3, pp. 183-184.

63. Ibid., p. 119; Stauffer, "Douglass and the Aesthetics of Freedom" *Raritan* 25:1 (Summer 2005): 131.

64. *LWFD* 3, p. 154.

65. Ibid., pp. 47, 151-155, quotations from pp. 151, 155.

66. McPherson, *Battle Cry of Freedom*, p. 9; Peter Kolchin, *American Slavery, 1619-1877* (New York: Hill and Wang, 1993), pp. 241-242.

67. *LWFD* 3, pp. 155-157.

68. On guerrilla warfare in the border states see Fellman, *Inside War*; Robert Mackey, *The Uncivil War: Irregular Warfare in the Upper South, 1861-1865* (Norman: University of Oklahoma Press, 2004); McPherson, *Battle Cry of Freedom*, pp. 284-307; Jean H. Baker, *The Politics of Continuity: Maryland Political Parties from 1858 to 1870* (Baltimore: Johns Hopkins University Press, 1973); Lowell Harrison, *The Civil War and Kentucky* (Lexington: University of Kentucky Press, 1975); Harold Hancock, "Civil War Comes to Deleware," *Civil War History* 2 (1956): 29-56.

69. McPherson, *Battle Cry of Freedom*, pp. 284-289, quotation from p. 289.

70. *CW* 4, pp. 506, 517-518; *LWFD* 3, pp. 161-162.

71. McPherson, *Battle Cry of Freedom*, pp. 284-307. In my efforts to give credence to Douglass's understanding of the border states, I draw a different conclusion

from McPherson even though I have relied on his facts. Most historians have dismissed Douglass's (and other abolitionists') view of the border states, arguing that they did not properly appreciate their importance. Douglass's military strategy was risky, but he had a shrewd understanding of how to control the border states.

72. *Douglass' Monthly*, September–December 1861.

73. *LWFD* 3, pp. 157, 158. See also David P. Crook, *The North, the South, and the Powers, 1861–1865* (1974).

74. *LWFD* 3, pp. 156–157, quotation from p. 156. See also Bruce Levine, *Confederate Emancipation*, pp. 1–17; Quarles, *Negro in the Civil War*, pp. 35–49; and note 51 above.

75. *LWFD* 3, p. 157.

76. Ibid., p. 156.

77. "The Would-Be Mobocrats at Syracuse," *Douglass' Monthly*, December 1861.

78. *LWFD* 3, p. 21; McPherson, *Struggle for Equality*, pp. 81–90.

79. *LWFD* 3, pp. 18–20, 110–111, quotation from p. 110.

80. *TFDP* 1:3, p. 508.

81. Thaddeus Stevens, quoted from McPherson, *Battle Cry of Freedom*, p. 358.

82. Karl Marx and Frederick Engels, *The Civil War in the United States* (New York: International Publishers, 1937), p. 79; *LWFD* 3, p. 18.

83. McPherson, *Struggle for Equality*, pp. 81–82; Seymour Drescher, "Servile Insurrection and John Brown's Body in Europe," in Paul Finkelman, ed., *His Soul Goes Marching On: Responses to John Brown and the Harpers Ferry Raid* (Charlottesville: University Press of Virginia, 1995), pp. 296–334.

84. McPherson, *Struggle for Equality*, pp. 81–82.

85. Herman Melville, "Donelson," *Battle-Pieces and Aspects of the War* (1866; reprint, New York: Da Capo, 1995), p. 52. On the historical bases of Melville's brilliant poem, see Stanton Garner, *The Civil War World of Herman Melville* (Lawrence: University Press of Kansas, 1993), pp. 138–140.

86. Melville, "Donelson," *Battle-Pieces*, p. 52.

87. Howard W. Coles, *The Cradle of Freedom: A History of the Negro in Rochester, Western New York, and Canada* (Rochester: Oxford Press, Publishers, 1941), p. 127. In the twentieth century the Pinnacle Hills section of Rochester became known as Highland Park. Douglass's home burned down in 1872, and for years Keller Florist did business on the site.

88. Christoph Lohmann, ed., *Radical Passion: Ottilie Assing's Reports from America and Letters to Frederick Douglass* (New York: Peter Lang, 1999), pp. 69, 163–164, quotation from p. 163; Maria Diedrich, *Love*

Across Color Lines: Ottilie Assing and Frederick Douglass (New York: Hill and Wang, 1999), p. 133.

89. *TFDP* 1:1, pp. 21–22. Douglass received upwards of $200 per engagement as his lecture fee.

90. John Stauffer, *The Black Hearts of Men: Radical Abolitionists and the Transformation of Race* (Cambridge, Mass.: Harvard University Press, 2002), ch. 2; Stauffer, "Daguerreotyping the National Soul: The Portraits of Southworth and Hawes, 1843–1860," *Prospects* 22 (1997): 69–107; Joan L Severa, *Dressed for the Photographer: Ordinary Americans and Fashion, 1840–1900* (Kent, Oh.: Kent State University Press, 1995).

During the Civil War Gerrit Smith had a footlong beard and John Brown's beard was almost two feet long when he died. The war spawned a new fashion in beards.

91. Philip S. Foner, ed., *Frederick Douglass on Women's Rights* (1976; reprint, New York: Da Capo, 1992), pp. 21–22; Stauffer, *Black Hearts of Men*, p. 229. I altered the quote slightly.

92. On Assing and Douglass, the two excellent works are Diedrich, *Love Across Color Lines*; and Lohmann, ed., *Radical Passion*.

93. Lohmann, ed., *Radical Passion*, p. 330 (quoted); also pp. 39, 56–87, 127–129, 199–203.

94. Diedrich, *Love Across Color Lines*, pp. 54–58.

95. Its title in German was *Morgenblatt für gebildete Leser*.

96. Diedrich, *Love Across Color Lines*, pp. xxi–xxii, 131–167. Diedrich speculates that Assing mistook Ann Douglass for a maid.

97. Since Douglass could not read German, he was probably not aware of the extent to which Assing exoticized him.

98. Lohmann, ed., *Radical Passion*, pp. 68, 69. For other examples of Assing's exoticizing Douglass, see ibid., pp. 94–95, 163–164. Assing's translation of *My Bondage and My Freedom* is *Sclaverei und Freiheit*, 1860.

99. Diedrich, *Love Across Color Lines*, pp. xxii, 84–87, 127–129, 199–203.

100. Clara Mundt's *Aphra Behn* (1849) is loosely based on the seventeenth-century English writer Aphra Behn, and Mundt's black hero is drawn from the title character of Behn's most famous novel, *Oroonoko: or, The Royal Slave*.

101. Lohmann, ed., *Radical Passion*, p. 69.

102. Ibid., pp. 333, 340; Diedrich, *Love Across Color Lines*, p. 186.

103. Diedrich, *Love Across Color Lines*, pp. 216–219.

104. Assing quoted in Henry Louis Gates Jr., "A Dangerous Literacy: The Legacy of Frederick Douglass," *New York Times Book Review*, May 28, 1995, p. 4.

105. Lohmann, ed., *Radical Passion*, p. 341; Diedrich, *Love Across Color Lines*, chs. 4–7.

106. Lohmann, ed., *Radical Passion*, pp. 207, 210. One could speculate that one reason why Douglass wanted to go to Haiti was to leave his family and start over with Assing, but there is simply no evidence for this. Douglass always prioritized his public life over private life. And there is plenty of evidence that his planned trip to Haiti was sparked by his frustration over Lincoln's Inaugural.

107. Only twenty-eight letters between Douglass and Assing survive. Some were destroyed when Douglass's Rochester home burned down in 1872, and later they destroyed most of the remaining letters between them. The extant letters are published in Lohmann, ed., *Radical Passion*, pp. 329–367. See also Diedrich, *Love Across Color Lines*, pp. xviii–xxi; Gates, "Dangerous Literacy," pp. 3–4.

108. Lohmann, ed., *Radical Passion*, pp. 333, 340; Gates, "Dangerous Literacy," p. 4.

109. Diedrich, *Love Across Color Lines*, pp. 311–320.

110. Lohmann, ed., *Radical Passion*, pp. 198, 333.

111. *TFDP* 1:2, p. 438; *TFDP* 1:3, p. 552.

112. Diedrich, *Love Across Color Lines*, p. 227; Stauffer, *Black Hearts of Men*, p. 231.

Assing characterized religion as a disease and likened a religious "awakening," in which large numbers are converted, to an "epidemic" that can "devastate an area." See Lohmann, ed., *Radical Passion*, p. 137.

113. C. Vann Woodward, ed., *Mary Chesnut's Civil War* (New Haven: Yale University Press, 1985), p. 25.

114. Stauffer, *Black Hearts of Men*, p. 25. Radical Abolitionists introduced the idea that "the personal is political." In the twentieth century the slogan was adopted by Italian fascists and then in the 1970s it became a feminist mantra.

115. In 1860 the population of the eleven Confederate states was 9.14 million, of whom 5.5 million were whites, while the population of the North (not including the border states) was 18.9 million.

116. *LWFD* 3, pp. 226–232, quotation from p. 228. In Douglass's tally of Union versus Confederate victories, he drew attention to the surrender of fifteen thousand rebel troops at Fort Donelson, a stockade in northern Tennessee, during Grant's Kentucky and Tennessee campaign, in which Grant also captured Fort Henry and Nashville.

117. Douglass, "The Popular Heart," *LWFD* 3, pp. 232–233, quotation from p. 232.

118. Arthur Zilversmit, *The First Emancipation: The Abolition of Slavery in the North* (Chicago: University of Chicago Press, 1967), pp. 220–222. Zilversmit notes that New Jersey's gradual emancipation law elevated slaves to the status of apprentices or indentured servants. As a result the census continued to define them as slaves.

The abolition of slavery in the District of Columbia compensated masters $300 per slave and it encouraged colonization for freedmen and -women. Douglass ignored these unpleasant features of the abolition bill.

119. *LWFD* 3, pp. 233–234. Sumner's colleague Senator Henry Wilson had introduced the abolition bill for Washington, D.C., but Douglass gave more credit to Sumner because he considered him more influential and more resolute in his abolitionism.

120. *LWFD* 3, pp. 255–256, quotation from p. 256 (emphasis added). Douglass focused on what Lincoln did, not what he said. *LWFD* describes it as Himrod's Corners, *TFDP* as simply Himrod.

121. On the description of the setting, see *TFDP* 1:3, p. 521.

122. *LWFD* 3, p. 256.

123. *CW* 5, pp. 222–224; *LWFD* 3, p. 256.

124. *LWFD* 3, p. 248.

125. Ibid., p. 258.

126. Congress had been debating a confiscation bill since December, but no one could have predicted what its final shape would look like.

127. "An Act to suppress Insurrection, to punish Treason and Rebellion, to seize and confiscate the Property of Rebels, and for other Purposes," *The Statutes at Large, Treaties, and Proclamations of the United States of America, from December 5, 1859, to March 3, 1863....* vol. XII (Boston: Little, Brown and Company, 1863), pp. 589–592, quotation from p. 592.

The act vowed to punish high-ranking rebels with death or prison for their crimes. Rebels forever forfeited the right to hold office; and all their property was subject to confiscation pending the president's order.

For an excellent summary of the bill see Henry Wilson, *The History of the Rise and Fall of the Slave Power*, vol. 3, pp. 331–346.

128. Douglass, "The Confiscation and Emancipation Law," *Douglass' Monthly*, August 1862.

In another article of the same issue, Douglass said that "the legislature has put a sword into the hands of the President, with the general approbation of the country, and everyone is wondering why he delays to strike.... Nobody expects that these laws are to remain a dead letter." See Douglass, "What the People Expect of Mr. Lincoln," *Douglass' Monthly*, 1862.

129. *CW* 5, p. 341. I discuss the first draft of this proclamation below, which is reprinted in *CW* 5, pp. 336–337.

130. "Senator Sumner and the President," *Douglass' Monthly*, July 1862.

131. *LWFD* 3, p. 269. Lincoln's speech appears in *CW* 5, pp. 370–375.

132. *LWFD* 3, p. 268. I slightly revise the quote.

133. *CW* 5, pp. 433–435.

134. *LWFD* 3, p. 274. One thing damping Douglass's joy over Lincoln's preliminary Emancipation Proclamation was news of the death of his abolitionist friend Abram

Pryne by suicide. Pryne, a minister and New York state legislator, had worked closely with Douglass and Gerrit Smith for years and edited Douglass's paper during his absence in the wake of John Brown's raid.

Douglass saw much of himself in Pryne. "Though he was white and we colored, though he was born free and we a slave, there were so many points of resemblance between his early life and our own that we were brought into great nearness to each other." Orphaned at age eleven, Pryne became a boatman on the Erie Canal, a brutal "highway of moral and intellectual ruin as well as commerce." But he experienced a radical conversion, went into the ministry, and became well-known in abolitionist circles. He was a self-made man "in the best sense." His suicide stemmed from a protracted attack of typhus fever, which left him "prey to insanity." See "Rev. Abram Pryne," *Douglass' Monthly*, October 1862.

135. *LWFD* 3, p. 273.

136. Ibid., p. 310.

137. Ibid., pp. 310–311.

138. Ibid., p. 309.

139. Ibid., p. 274.

140. Ibid., p. 310. For a description of the A.M.E. Zion church see Coles, *Cradle of Liberty*, p. 109.

141. Douglas then gave a brilliant speech focusing on the continued duties of the lovers of liberty. "Slavery has existed in this country too long and has stamped its character too deeply and indelibly to be blotted out

in a day or a year or even in a generation. The slave will yet remain in some sense a slave long after the chains are taken from his limbs; and the master will retain much of the pride, arrogance, imperiousness, and love of power, acquired by his former position of master." Although slaves would cease being slaves of individual masters, their enemies would endeavor to make them slaves "of society at large." *LWFD* 3, pp. 310–312.

For an analysis of the speech, see Stauffer, "Frederick Douglass and the Aesthetics of Freedom," *Raritan* 25:1 (Summer 2005): 130–131.

142. *TFDP* 1:3, p. 388.

On Lincoln's speaking at the Tremont Temple, see Reinhard H. Luthin, "Abraham Lincoln and the Massachusetts Whigs in 1848," *New England Quarterly* 14:4 (December 1941): 630–632. On the New Year's Day celebrations see Douglass, "Rejoicing Over the Proclamation," *Douglass' Monthly*, February 1863; *TFDP* 1:3, pp. 567–569; Quarles, *The Negro in the Civil War*, pp. 163–183; Stauffer, "Imagining Emancipation," in Steven Mintz and John Stauffer, eds., *The Problem of Evil* (Amherst: University of Massachusetts Press, 2007), pp. 221–230.

143. Quarles, *The Negro in the Civil War*, p. 171.

144. *TFDP* 1:3, p. 547.

145. *TFDP* 1:3, p. 568; Quarles, *The Negro in the Civil War*, pp. 172–173; Stauffer, "Imagining Emancipation," pp. 226, 229. Charles Wesley, *Hymns for the New Year's Day* (London, 1750).

146. Douglass, *Life and Times of Frederick Douglass* (1892; reprint, New York: Collier, 1962), pp. 354–355 (quoted); *TFDP* 1:3, pp. 551, 552, 563–564; *LWFD* 3, p. 306.

147. Donald, *Lincoln*, p. 271.

148. Ibid., p. 259.

149. Ibid., p. 271.

150. *CW* 4, pp. 129–130. I changed Lincoln's term "affection" to "affectation" for clarity.

151. Donald, *Lincoln*, p. 271.

152. Ibid., p. 259; Robert Temple, ed., *Aesop: The Complete Fables* (New York: Penguin, 1998), p. 147.

In using humor to manage these tense situations, Lincoln anticipated Mark Twain. It was a short step from these stories to Huck Finn's satirical anecdotes about the murderous Grangerford family.

153. The most viable compromise plan was to extend the Missouri Compromise line (36°30′) west through all the national territories, prohibiting slavery north of the line and allowing it south of it. Donald, *Lincoln*, p. 268; Henry Wilson, *History of the Rise and Fall of the Slave Power*, vol. 3, ch. 3.

154. *CW* 4, pp. 149, 150.

155. Ibid., p. 183.

156. Ibid., p. 157.

157. Ibid., p. 183.

158. Ibid.

159. Donald, *Lincoln*, p. 273.

160. Lincoln, quoted from Donald, *Lincoln*, p. 272.

161. *CW* 4, p. 190; Donald, *Lincoln*, pp. 272-273.

162. *CW* 4, pp. 220-221.

163. Ibid., p. 220.

164. White, *The American Railroad Passenger Car*, part 1, p. 346. Adjacent cars housed Lincoln's secretaries John Hay and John Nicolay, who would remain among his closest companions for the next four years, his friend Elmer Ellsworth, and a few Illinois politicians.

165. Donald, *Lincoln*, p. 275.

166. Ibid.

167. *CW* 4, p. 219.

168. Ibid.

169. Allan Pinkerton, *The Spy of the Rebellion* (1883; reprint, Lincoln: University of Nebraska Press, 1989).

170. Donald, *Lincoln*, p. 279.

171. Johannsen, *Stephen Douglas*, p. 840; Donald, *Lincoln*, p. 279.

172. McPherson, *Battle Cry of Freedom*, p. 264.

173. Even in this first draft, Lincoln defended the fugitive slave law.

174. *CW* 4, p. 260.

175. Ibid., p. 261.

176. Ibid., p. 254; Donald, *Lincoln*, p. 283.

177. Donald, *Lincoln*, p. 283.

178. *CW* 4, pp. 317–318. Seward proposed to threaten war with Spain and France, and possibly Great Britain and Russia as well, by announcing a vigorous "*spirit of independence* on this continent against European intervention." Unless European nations quit interfering in the West Indies and Mexico, Lincoln should "convene Congress and declare war against them."

179. *CW* 4, p. 260.

180. Ibid., pp. 261–262.

181. Lincoln, in *Great Speeches*, p. 61.

182. Carl Sandburg, *Abraham Lincoln: The War Years*, vol. 1 (New York: Harcourt, Brace & Company, 1939), p. 120.

183. Ibid., p. 139.

184. In Lincoln's mind, his support for the amendment did not contradict his central pledge to the American people. He believed that the ultimate extinction of slavery would occur in not less than a hundred years, and by then slaveholders would begin to voluntarily emanci-

pate their slaves. The unamendable amendment would remain in the Constitution, full of sound and fury but signifying nothing. See Paul M. Angle, *Created Equal: The Complete Lincoln-Douglas Debates of 1858* (Chicago: University of Chicago Press, 1958), p. 270.

185. Donald, *Lincoln,* p. 284.

186. Lincoln never felt comfortable suspending the writ of habeas corpus. In his July 4, 1861, message to Congress he was defensive about it, asking, "are all laws *but one* [habeas corpus] to go unexecuted, and the government itself go to pieces, lest that one be violated?" The country was in a state of anarchy, as laws were being resisted "in about one-third of the states." *CW* 4, p. 430.

187. Robert W. Johannsen, *Stephen Douglas* (1973; reprint, Urbana: University of Illinois Press, 1997), pp. 842–844, quotations from pp. 843, 844.

188. Ibid., pp. 844–845; Sandburg, *Lincoln: The War Years*, vol. 1, pp. 138–139.

189. Johannsen, *Stephen Douglas*, pp. 858–872, quotations from pp. 859, 860.

190. *CW* 5, p. 49 (emphasis added).

191. Had Frederick Douglass known of Lincoln's reconciliation with Stephen Douglas, he would not have been so surprised when Lincoln revoked Frémont's emancipation proclamation.

192. Browning to Lincoln, September 11, 1861, Lincoln Papers, Library of Congress (hereafter LPLC).

193. Browning to Lincoln, September 30, 1861, LPLC.

194. *CW* 4, pp. 531, 532.

195. *CW* 4, p. 532. Lincon reportedly said that "while he hoped to have God on his side he must have Kentucky." See McPherson, *Battle Cry of Freedom*, p. 284.

196. Speed to Lincoln, September 1, 1861, LPLC.

197. Speed to Lincoln, September 3, 1861, LPLC. Roy Basler says this letter is from James Speed, Joshua's brother, but it is in Joshua's handwriting and signed by him. In this, I agree with David Herbert Donald, *"We Are Lincoln Men": Abraham Lincoln and His Friends* (New York: Simon & Schuster, 2003), p. 60.

198. As Speed put it, "So fixed is public sentiment in this state against freeing negroes and allowing negroes to be emancipated, . . . that you had as well attack the freedom of worship in the North, or the right of a parent to teach his child to read, *as to wage war in a slave state on such a principle.*" Speed to Lincoln, September 3, 1861, LPLC (emphasis added).

199. Denton, *Passion and Principle*, pp. 317–319.

200. Ibid., pp. 319–320.

201. *TFDP* 1:3, p. 508.

202. McPherson, *Battle Cry of Freedom*, p. 356.

203. Donald, *Lincoln*, pp. 335–337, quotations from pp. 336, 337.

204. McPherson, *Battle Cry of Freedom*, pp. 490–510; Donald, *Lincoln*, p. 360.

205. *CW* 5, p. 279.

206. Donald, *Lincoln*, p. 337.

207. *CW* 5, pp. 144, 145.

208. McPherson, *Battle Cry of Freedom*, p. 498.

209. Donald, *Lincoln*, p. 346; Donald, *Charles Sumner*, part 2, p. 51.

210. *CW* 5, p. 192; Wilson, *History of the Rise and Fall of the Slave Power*, vol. 3, pp. 283–284; Donald, *Lincoln*, p. 348; Quarles, *Lincoln and the Negro*, p. 115.

211. *CW* 5, p. 169. Lincoln offered another reason for revoking Hunter's emancipation proclamation to Salmon Chase, who had supported it: "No commanding general shall do such a thing, upon *my* responsibility, without consulting me." *CW* 5, p. 219.

212. *CW* 5, pp. 223, 317–319.

213. In early July 1862 Lincoln met with congressmen from the border states and told them that if the war persisted, slavery "in your states will be extinguished by mere friction and abrasion—by the mere incidents of the war." Slavery would be dead "and you will have nothing valuable in lieu of it." Accept my offer, and "take the step" that will shorten the war and secure compensation for you, he said. "I do not speak of emancipation *at once*, but of a *decision* at once to emancipate *gradually*." *CW* 5, p. 318.

214.The Second Confiscation Act states that "all the estate and property, moneys, stocks, and credits of such person [rebel] shall be liable to seizure as aforesaid, and it shall be the duty of the President to seize and use them for military purposes."

See "An Act to suppress Insurrection, to punish Treason and Rebellion, to seize and conficate the Property of Rebels, and for other Purposes," *The Statutes at Large, Treaties, and Proclamations of the United States of America, from December 5, 1859, to March 3, 1863....* vol. XII (Boston: Little, Brown and Company, 1863), p. 591.

215. "An Act to suppress Insurrection, to punish Treason and Rebellion, to seize and conficate the Property of Rebels, and for other Purposes," *The Statutes at Large, Treaties, and Proclamations of the United States of America, from December 5, 1859, to March 3, 1863....* vol. XII, p. 591.

216. *CW* 5, pp. 328–331; Donald, *Lincoln*, pp. 364–365.

217. *CW* 5, pp. 336–338; Donald, *Lincoln*, pp. 364–365.

218. Donald, *Lincoln*, pp. 364–366.

219. *CW* 5, p. 341. Lincoln's proclamation constituted the first paragraph of the draft of his emancipation proclamation.

220. Ibid., p. 357.

221. In August 1864 Lincoln estimated that there were between 100,000 and 200,000 black men now "in the service of the Union." I use the figure 150,000, which

is common among historians. See *CW* 7, p. 506; Blight, *Frederick Douglass' Civil War*, p. 187.

222. Donald, *Lincoln*, p. 359.

223. Quarles, *Lincoln and the Negro*, pp. 115–117, quotation from p. 115. Quarles's account of this meeting remains the most insightful.

224. Ibid., pp. 115–117.

225. Henry Highland Garnet, quoted from *Pacific Appeal*, October 11, 1862; Donald, *Lincoln*, pp. 367–368.

226. Quarles, *Lincoln and the Negro*, p. 117.

227. Donald, *Lincoln*, p. 368. The standard account of this meeting among sympathetic Lincoln biographers is that Lincoln hoped to make the idea of emancipation more palatable to the border states. They ignore or downplay the fact that Lincon was a devoted champion of colonization.

228. Horace Greeley, "The Prayer of Twenty Millions," *New York Tribune*, August 20, 1862; *CW* 5, p. 389; Quarles, *Lincoln and the Negro*, pp. 128–129, has an excellent discussion.

229. *CW* 5, p. 388.

230. In August 1864 Lincoln quoted from his 1862 letter to Greeley about his chief purpose being to save the Union and then declared, "All this I said in the utmost sincerity; and I am as true to the whole of it now, as when I first said it." *CW* 7, p. 499.

231. Douglass, "Reasons for Issuing the Proclamation of Emancipation," *Douglass' Monthly*, October 1862.

232. *CW* 5, pp. 403–404.

233. Ibid., p. 420.

234. Welles, *Diary*, quoted from Donald, *Lincoln*, p. 374.

235. Donald, *Lincoln*, p. 374.

236. Artemus Ward, "High-Handed Outrage at Utica," *The Complete Works of Artemus Ward* (1862; reprint, New York: G. W. Dillingham Co., 1898), pp. 36–37; Donald, *Lincoln*, pp. 374–375.

237. *CW* 5, p. 434.

238. *CW* 6, pp. 106, 114–115; Richard Carwardine, *Lincoln: A Life of Purpose and Power* (New York: Alfred A. Knopf, 2006), pp. 169–286; Francois Furstenberg, *In the Name of the Father: Washington's Legacy, Slavery, and the Making of a Nation* (New York: Penguin Press, 2006), pp. 193–232.

239. Sandburg, *Lincoln: The War Years*, vol. 2, pp. 8, 9, 10.

240. *CW* 5, p. 503; Quarles, *Lincoln and the Negro*, p. 123.

241. *CW* 6, p. 29.

242. Sandburg, *Lincoln: The War Years*, vol. 2, pp. 16–17.

243. Henry M. Turner, quoted from Dorothy Sterling, ed., *Speak Out in Thunder Tones: Letters and Other Writings by Black Northerners, 1787–1865* (1973; reprint, New York: Da Capo, 1973), pp. 315–317; Stauffer, "Imagining Emancipation," pp. 226–227.

244. *CW* 7, pp. 281–282.

245. Burke, quoted in Sandburg, *Lincoln: The War Years*, vol. 2, p. 10.

246. Karl Marx, quoted in David Brion Davis, "The Emancipation Moment," in Gabor S. Boritt, ed., *Lincoln, the War President* (New York: Oxford University Press, 1992), pp. 87–88.

Five: *Friends*

1. James McPherson, *Battle Cry of Freedom: The Civil War Era* (New York: Ballantine Books, 1988), p. 770; Carl Sandburg, "The Darkest Month of the War," *Abraham Lincoln: The War Years*, vol. 3 (New York: Harcourt, Brace & Company, 1939), pp. 167–225.

2. Grant, quoted from Ernest B. Furgurson, *Freedom Rising: Washington in the Civil War* (New York: Vintage Books, 2004), p. 305; McPherson, *Battle Cry*, p. 732; Margaret Leech, *Reveille in Washington 1860–1865* (New York: Harper & Brothers, 1941), pp. 322, 344–346, quotation from p. 346.

3. Roy Basler, ed., *The Collected Works of Abraham Lincoln* (hereafter *CW*), 9 vols. (New Brunswick: Rutgers University Press, 1953), vol. 7, pp. 394–396, quota-

tion from p. 394; Furgurson, *Freedom Rising*, p. 305. Although there was much laughter and cheers during Lincoln's talk, reporters were effectively barred from covering the event, since no accommodations were made for them.

4. McPherson, *Battle Cry of Freedom*, pp. 756–758, quotation from Holmes on p. 757; Leech, *Reveille in Washington*, pp. 329–346; Furgurson, *Freedom Rising*, p. 317. According to Furgurson, Lincoln was the only president to face enemy fire while in office.

5. Whitman, "Specimen Days," in *The Portable Walt Whitman*, pp. 446–447.

6. Sandburg, *Lincoln: The War Years*, vol. 3, pp. 167–168.

7. Leech, *Reveille in Washington*, p. 346; *CW* 7, pp. 448–449; Nevins, *Frémont*, p. 576; Sandburg, *Lincoln: The War Years*, vol. 3, pp. 167–184. As George Templeton Strong noted in his diary, gold "has run wild," selling for as high as $230 an ounce. Allan Nevins and Milton Halsey Thomas, eds., *The Diary of George Templeton Strong: The Civil War, 1860–1865* (New York: The Macmillan Company, 1852), p. 460.

8. Strong, *Diary: The Civil War*, pp. 467, 474. Strong was the treasurer of the Sanitary Commission, which later became the Red Cross.

9. Nicolay and Hay, *Lincoln: A History*, vol. 9, p. 221; McPherson, *Battle Cry of Freedom*, pp. 760–773.

10. On Copperheads see Jennifer L. Weber, *Copperheads: The Rise and Fall of Lincoln's Opponents in the North* (New York: Oxford University Press, 2007).

11. McPherson, *Battle Cry of Freedom*, pp. 768–769.

12. *Miscegenation or the Millennium of Abolitionism*, quoted from Elise Lemire, *Miscegenation: Making Race in America* (Philadelphia: University of Pennsylvania Press, 2002), p. 119; Sidney Kaplan, *American Studies in Black and White: Selected Essays* (Amherst: University of Massachusetts Press, 1991), pp. 47–100.

13. *LWFD* 3, p. 51.

14. David W. Blight, *Frederick Douglass' Civil War: Keeping Faith in Jubilee* (Baton Rouge: Louisiana State University Press, 1989), pp. 182–184; McPherson, *Battle Cry of Freedom*, pp. 698–717.

15. Peyton McCrary, *Abraham Lincoln and Reconstruction: The Louisiana Experiment* (Princeton: Princeton University Press, 1978); Nathaniel Banks to Lincoln, December 30, 1863, Lincoln Papers, Library of Congress (hereafter *LPLC*); LaWanda Cox, *Lincoln and Black Freedom: A Study in Presidential Leadership* (Columbia, SC: University of South Carolina Press, 1981), pp. 89–97; Ted Tunnell, *Crucible of Reconstruction: War, Radicalism and Race in Louisiana 1862–1877* (Baton Rouge: Louisiana State University Press, 1984), pp. 36–65; Eric Foner, *Reconstruction: America's Unfinished Business* (New York: W. W. Norton, 1992), chs. 1–2; James M. McPherson, *The Struggle for Equality: Abolitionists and the Negro in the Civil War and*

Reconstruction (Princeton: Princeton University Press, 1964), pp. 287–294; McPherson, *Battle Cry of Freedom*, pp. 698–713.

16. *Liberator*, March 11, 1864; McCrary, *Lincoln and Reconstruction*, pp. 271–272; McPherson, *Struggle for Equality*, pp. 288–290.

17. *The War of the Rebellion: A Compilation of the Official Records of the Union and Confederate Armies* (Washington, D.C.: Government Printing Office, 1880–1901), series 1, vol. 15, pp. 666–667; *OR* series 1, vol. 34, part 2, pp. 227–231; McPherson, *Struggle for Equality*, pp. 289–290.

18. McPherson, *Battle Cry of Freedom*, pp. 698–717. Lincoln pocket-vetoed the Wade-Davis bill by not signing it. The bill was named for Benjamin Wade and Henry Davis, both radical Republicans.

19. Wendell Phillips, quoted in *New York Tribune*, June 1, 1864; McPherson, *Struggle for Equality*, pp. 267–278.

20. *LWFD* 3, p. 404.

21. *LWFD* 3, p. 403; Blight, *Frederick Douglass' Civil War*, pp. 182–183.

22. *CW* 6, pp. 408, 409.

23. Lincoln vetoed the Wade-Davis bill partly because he said he was unwilling to be "inflexibly committed to any single plan of restoration." *CW* 7, p. 433.

24. John Eaton, *Grant, Lincoln, and the Freedmen* (New York: Longmans, Green, and Co., 1907), p. 86. For a superb article on the Davis Bend experiment see Steven Joseph Ross, "Freed Soil, Freed Labor, Freed Men: John Eaton and the Davis Bend Experiment," *Journal of Southern History* 44:2 (May 1978): 213–232.

25. Ross, "Freed Soil," pp. 217–219, quotation from Eaton on p. 217.

26. William Wells Brown, *The Negro in the American Rebellion: His Heroism and His Fidelty* (Boston, 1867), p. 299.

27. Lincoln told Eaton to continue his supervision of freedmen at Davis Bend "on the same principles as in the past." Ross, "Freed Soil," p. 222.

28. *CW* 6, p. 409.

29. Eaton, *Grant, Lincoln, and the Freedmen*, p. 173.

30. Ibid., p. 172.

31. Ibid., p. 173.

32. Ibid.

33. Ibid., pp. 168, 174, quotation from p. 174.

34. Ibid., p. 174.

I am not sure which speech of Douglass's Eaton heard, so my account of it stems from Eaton. In the list of Douglass's "partial speaking tour," there is no mention of a Toledo speech in 1864. Douglass possibly gave his "Mission of the War" speech, which he delivered frequently in the spring of 1864, though if he did he added criticism of Lincoln for not retaliating against rebels for murdering captured black soldiers.

In his "Mission of the War" speech Douglass compares Lincoln to Stephen Douglas. The Illinois senator had not cared whether slavery were voted up or down. Back in 1858 Lincoln had denounced Douglas's sentiment "as unworthy of the lips of any American statesman." But now the president uttered "the same heartless sentiments" by saying that he would save the Union with or without slavery. *TFDP* 4, pp. 12-13.

35. Shortly before Douglass met Lincoln on August 10, 1863, Lincoln had signed an order aimed at preventing rebels from murdering blacks, which stipulated that "for every soldier killed in violation of the laws of war a rebel soldier shall be executed." See John David Smith, ed., *Black Soldiers in Blue: African American Troops in the Civil War Era* (Chapel Hill: University of North Carolina Press, 2002), p. 47; McFeely, *Frederick Douglass*, p. 228; Douglass, *Life and Times*, pp. 348-349.

36. Forrest, quoted from Sandburg, *Lincoln: The War Years*, vol. 3, p. 37.

37. Sandburg, *Lincoln: The War Years*, vol. 3, pp. 36-41, quotation from p. 38; Nathan Bedford Forrest, quoted from *OR* series 1, vol. 32, part 1, pp. 610-611; *CW* 7, p. 329; Benjamin Quarles, *The Negro in the Civil War* (1953; reprint, New York: Da Capo, 1989), p. 207; Dudley Taylor Cornish, *The Sable Arm: Black Troops in the Union Army, 1861-1864* (1956; reprint, Lawrence: University Press of Kansas, 1987), pp. 173-180; Benjamin

Quarles, *Lincoln and the Negro* (1962; reprint, New York: Da Capo, 1990), pp. 177–183.

38. *CW* 7, pp. 302, 303. See also ibid., pp. 328–329, 345–346.

39. Eaton, *Grant, Lincoln, and the Freedmen*, p. 174.

40. Ibid. It was a private letter.

41. *CW* 7, p. 243; Eaton, *Grant, Lincoln, and the Freedmen*, pp. 174–175.

42. *CW* 7, p. 101. There are doubts about the authenticity of this letter, and so it needs to be read with care. But the quote is consistent with other statements Lincoln made in the summer and fall of 1864. The entire quote reads, "I cannot see, if universal amnesty is granted, how, under the circumstances, I can avoid exacting in return, universal suffrage, or, at least, suffrage on the basis of intelligence and military service." On questions of authenticity, see Ludwell H. Johnson, "Lincoln and Equal Rights: The Authenticity of the Wadsworth Letter," *Journal of Southern History* 32 (1966): 83–87; and Harold M. Hyman, "Lincoln and Equal Rights for Negroes: The Irrelevancy of the 'Wadsworth Letter,'" *Civil War History* 12 (1966): 258–266.

43. Eaton, *Grant, Lincoln, and the Freedmen*, p. 175.

44. Ibid.

45. Ibid., p. 176.

46. Douglass, *Life and Times of Frederick Douglass, Written by Himself* (1892; reprint, New York: Collier, 1962), p. 359.

47. William P. Dole to Lincoln, August 18, 1864, LPLC.

Every account of this second meeting between Douglass and Lincoln dates it August 19, 1864, based on Joseph T. Mills's diary entry of August 19 of the meeting. But what probably happened was that Douglass met with Lincoln on August 18, and Mills's diary entry of August 19 refers to the previous day. See *CW* 7, pp. 506–508.

Douglass refers to a messenger from the White House arriving for him in William Dole's carriage on another occasion, and so I assume that when he arrived on the train, a messenger and carriage were similarly waiting for him. Douglass, *Life and Times*, p. 359.

48. *LWFD* 3, p. 384.

49. *TFDP* 1:4, p. 12. For an excellent analysis of Douglass's speech "The Mission of the War," see Blight, *Frederick Douglass' Civil War*, pp. 175–178.

50. Douglass refers to Lincoln's December 1863 Message to Congress, in which he said, "for a long time it had been hoped that the rebellion could be suppressed without resorting to [emancipation] as a military measure."

51. *TFDP* 1:4, pp. 12, 13.

52. *CW* 7, p. 508. See also McFeely, *Frederick Douglass*, pp. 232–234; and Blight, *Frederick Douglass' Civil War*, pp. 182–184.

53. *CW* 7, p. 508.

54. In his diary entry Mills does not record any response. He also notes that "the President appeared to be not the pleasant joker I had expected to see, but a man of deep convictions & an unutterable yearning for the success of the Union cause." *CW* 7, p. 507.

55. Charles Hamilton and Lloyd Ostendorf, *Lincoln in Photographs: An Album of Every Known Pose* (Dayton, Oh.: Morningside, 1985), p. 188, compare with p. 138.

56. *CW* 7, p. 451.

57. *LWFD* 3, p. 423.

58. *CW* 7, p. 500. Lincoln clearly believed that without blacks as allies, the Union could not be saved.

59. Lincoln opens the letter by saying, "To me it seems plain that saying reunion and abandonment of slavery would be considered, if offered, is not saying that nothing *else* or *less* would be considered, if offered."

60. *LWFD* 3, p. 423.

61. Douglass, *Life and Times*, pp. 358–359; *LWFD* 3, pp. 423–424.

62. Ibid.

63. *LWFD* 3, p. 424; Douglass, *Life and Times*, pp. 358–359.

64. Douglass, *Life and Times*, p. 358.

65. Ibid., p. 359.

66. Ibid.

67. Quarles, *Lincoln and the Negro*, pp. 202–206; Sandburg, *Lincoln: The War Years*, vol. 3, pp. 402–404.

68. Keckley, *Behind the Scenes*, p. 65; Quarles, *Lincoln and the Negro*, pp. 202–206, quotation on p. 204; Jennifer Fleischner, *Mrs. Lincoln and Mrs. Keckly: The Remarkable Story of the Friendship Between a First Lady and a Former Slave* (New York: Broadway Books, 2003).
    Keckly spelled her name "Keckly" but in other sources it appears as "Keckley."

69. Quarles, *Lincoln and the Negro*, pp. 205–206, quotations from p. 206; Sandburg, *Lincoln: The War Years*, vol. 3, pp. 402–404.

70. *Washington Chronicle*, January 2, 1864, quoted from Sandburg, *Lincoln: The War Years*, vol. 3, p. 403.

71. Lamont D. Thomas, *Rise to Be a People: A Biography of Paul Cuffe* (Urbana: University of Illinois Press, 1986), pp. 72–73; Rosalind Cobb Wiggins, ed., *Captain Paul Cuffe's Logs and Letters, 1808–1817: A Black Quaker's "Voice from Within the Veil"* (Washington, D.C.: Howard University Press, 1996), pp. 59–61, 206–233.

72. Thomas, *Rise to Be a People*, pp. 73-74, quotation from Cuffe on p. 73, quotation from district attorney on p. 74; Wiggins, ed., *Captain Paul Cuffe's Logs*, pp. 211-213; Cuffe, quoted from Cadbury, "Negro Membership in the Society of Friends," p. 199. According to Cadbury, since Madison's wife, Dolley Payne, was raised as a Quaker, he would have been used to Cuffe's plain Quaker speech. But in 1794 the Quakers disowned Dolley after her marriage to Madison, an Episcopalian and slaveholder.

73. Frederick Douglass, *Life and Times*, pp. 346-349, 357-359, 365-567, quotations from pp. 347, 366.

74. Eaton, *Grant, Lincoln, and the Freedmen*, p. 175.

75. Douglass, *Life and Times*, pp. 359-360.

76. *LWFD* 3, pp. 405-406.

77. Strong, *Diary: The Civil War,* p. 478.

78. *LWFD* 3, p. 424.

79. *LWFD* 3, p. 445.

80. *CW* 7, pp. 533-534; Furgurson, *Freedom Rising*, p. 323. According to contemporaries, Lincoln's numerous proclamations of Thanksgiving bolstered Union morale and demoralized the rebels.

81. *CW* 1, p. 273.

82. On the concept of forgiveness I have relied on Charles Griswold, *Forgiveness: A Philosophical Exploration* (Cambridge: Cambridge University Press, 2007);

Jeffrie G. Murphy and Jean Hampton, *Forgiveness and Mercy* (Cambridge: Cambridge University Press, 1988); Trudy Govier, *Forgiveness and Revenge* (New York: Routledge, 2002); Robert D. Enright and Joanna North, eds., *Exploring Forgiveness* (Madison: University of Wisconsin Press, 1998).

83. Douglass, *Life and Times*, pp. 361–363; Blight, *Frederick Douglass' Civil War*, pp. 186–187.

The Thirteenth Amendment abolishing slavery passed by only a few votes. It was ratified on December 6, 1865. For a superb treatment of the subject, see Michael Vorenburg, *Final Freedom*.

84. Ronald C. White Jr., *Lincoln's Greatest Speech: The Second Inaugural* (New York: Simon & Schuster, 2002), pp. 24–32, quotation from Noah Brooks on p. 31.

85. Douglass, *Life and Times*, p. 362.

86. White, *Lincon's Greatest Speech*, pp. 34–35; William C. Allen, *The Dome of the United States Capitol: An Architectural History* (Washington, D.C.: Government Printing Office, 1992), pp. 17–60.

87. Herman Melville, *Battle-Pieces and Aspects of War* (1866; reprint, New York: Da Capo, 1995), p. 17.

88. Allen, *The Dome of the United States Capitol*, pp. 42–57, quotation from Jefferson Davis on p. 42; White, *Lincoln's Greatest Speech*, p. 35.

89. Douglass, *Life and Times*, p. 364. Douglass noted that "Mr. Johnson was drunk," even though it was still early in the morning (p. 365).

90. White, *Lincoln's Greatest Speech*, p. 40; Leech, *Reveille in Washington*, p. 358; "Attempted Assassination of Frederick Douglass," *Chicago Tribune*, February 28, 1866.

The *Chicago Tribune* offers no details about the assassination attempt on Douglass, and I have not been able to locate any from Douglass. After Lincoln's death, many people called assassination a new kind of crime in America; but Douglass suspected that presidents William Henry Harrison and Zachary Taylor, both of whom died shortly after taking office, had been poisoned by agents of the Slave Power. See *TFDP* 1:4, pp. 108–109, 113–115.

91. Douglass, *Life and Times*, pp. 363, 365, 366.

92. Ibid., p. 366.

93. Ibid.

94. *CW* 8, pp. 393–394; Donald, *Lincoln*, pp. 580, 581.

95. Two of Booth's recruits, Samuel Arnold and Michael O'Laughlen, "had served as private soldiers in the Confederate ranks." Lewis Powell (a.k.a. Paine) and John Surratt, later recruits, had also served in the Confederacy. Rhodehamel and Taper, eds., *Writings of John Wilkes Booth*, pp. 12, 13.

96. Ibid., p. 13.

97. Ibid., p. 120.

98. Ibid., pp. 12–15, quotation from Booth on pp. 14–15.

99. Ibid., pp. 147–149, quotation from p. 147.

100. Donald, *Lincoln*, p. 569.

101. Smith, *American Gothic*, p. 105; Gordon Samples, *Lust for Fame*, p. 224.

102. Rhodehamel and Taper, eds., *Writings of John Wilkes Booth*, pp. 149–150.

103. Jean H. Baker, *Mary Todd Lincoln: A Biography* (New York: W. W. Norton, 1987), pp. 242–243, quotation from p. 242; Donald, *Lincoln*, pp. 594–596; Sandburg, *Lincoln: The War Years*, vol. 4, pp. 262, 272–273.

104. Julia Shephard, quoted from Sandburg, *Lincoln: The War Years*, vol. 4, p. 280 (emphasis added).

105. Sandburg, *Lincoln: The War Years*, vol. 4, pp. 272–273, 278–279; Donald, *Lincoln*, p. 597.

106. Sandburg, *Lincoln: The War Years*, vol. 4, pp. 277–281; Baker, *Mary Todd Lincoln*, p. 243; Donald, *Lincoln*, p. 597.

107. Donald, *Lincoln*, p. 597 (quoted); Baker, *Mary Todd Lincoln*, p. 243 (quoted); Sandburg, *Lincoln: The War Years*, vol. 4, pp. 281–283.

108. Baker, *Mary Todd Lincoln*, pp. 244–245; Donald, *Lincoln*, pp. 597–598; Jay Winik, *April 1865: The Month That Saved America* (New York: HarperCollins, 2001), pp. 218–229, 253–258.

109. Baker, *Mary Todd Lincoln*, pp. 244–245; Donald, *Lincoln*, pp. 598–599.

110. Donald, *Lincoln*, p. 598 (quoted); Baker, *Mary Todd Lincoln*, pp. 244–245.

111. Donald, *Lincoln*, p. 599 (quoted); Sandburg, *Lincoln: The War Years*, vol. 4, pp. 286–297; Rhodehamel and Taper, eds., *Writings of John Wilkes Booth*, pp. 16–18.

112. Baker, *Mary Todd Lincoln*, pp. 244–245 (quoted); Sandburg, *Lincoln: The War Years*, vol. 4, pp. 286–297.

113. Donald, *Lincoln*, p. 599 (quoted); Sandburg, *Lincoln: The War Years*, vol. 4, pp. 286–297.

Some scholars, including Jay Winik and James Swanson, interpret Stanton as saying "Now he belongs to the angels." As Adam Gopnik notes in a superb essay, since the room where Lincoln died was so crowded, it was difficult to determine, even at the time, what was said. "The past is so often unknowable not because it is befogged now but because it was befogged then, too, back when it was still the present. If we had been there listening, we still might not have been able to determine exactly what Stanton said." See Adam Gopnik, "Angels and Ages: Lincoln's language and its legacy," *The New Yorker*, May 28, 2007, pp. 30–37, quotation from p. 37; James L. Swanson, *Manhunt; The Twelve-Day Chase for Lincoln's Killer* (New York: William Morrow, 2006), pp. 137–138; Winik, *April 1865*, pp. 258, 428.

114. *TFDP* 1:4, pp. 74–79, quotation from p. 76; Douglass, *Life and Times*, pp. 371–372; Blight, *Frederick Douglass' Civil War*, p. 188.

115. *TFDP* 1:4, pp. 74–79, quotations from pp. 76, 78; Douglass, *Life and Times of Frederick Douglass*, p. 372; Blight, *Frederick Douglass' Civil War*, p. 188. Blight's reading of Douglass's reaction to Lincoln's death is simply brilliant.

116. Sandburg, *Lincoln: The War Years*, vol. 4, p. 361. As Sandburg notes, "Over and again were the parallels drawn of Lincoln and Christ in blood of atonement dying for mankind, and of Lincoln having his Judas no less than Christ" (p. 361).

117. Rhodehamel and Taper, eds., *Writings of John Wilkes Booth*, pp. 13, 21 n. 39.

118. Allan Nevins, *The War for the Union: The Organized War to Victory, 1864–1865* (New York: Charles Scribner's Sons, 1971), pp. 335–336.

These final paragraphs have been inspired by David Blight, *Race and Reunion: The Civil War in American Memory* (Cambridge, Mass.: Harvard University Press, 2002); and Sandburg, *Lincoln: The War Years*, vol. 4, pp. 361ff.

Epilogue

1. On the Freedmen's Monument celebration I have relied on the following sources: "The Lincoln Monument," *New York Times*, April 15, 1876; *Oration by Frederick Douglass Delivered on the Occasion of the Unveiling of the Freedmen's Monument in Memory of Abraham Lincoln, in Lincoln Park, Washington, D.C., April 14th 1876* (Washington, D.C.: Gibson Brothers, 1876),

Douglass Papers, Library of Congress (hereafter *DPLC*); *Inaugural Ceremonies of the Freedmen's Memorial Monument to Abraham Lincoln* (St. Louis, 1876); *TFDP* 1:4, pp. 427–440.

2. *Oration by Frederick Douglass*, pp. 18–19.

3. Ibid., pp. 19–20.

4. Ibid., p. 20.

5. Stauffer, "Creating an Image in Black," in Timothy Patrick McCarthy and John Stauffer, eds., *Prophets of Protest: Reconsidering the History of American Abolitionism* (New York: New Press, 2006), pp. 256–267; Julia Griffiths, ed., *Autographs for Freedom* (1854), frontispiece.

Ball's original design shows the kneeling slave as "perfectly passive, receiving the boon of freedom from the hand of the great liberator," according to the pamphlet published after the ceremony. Ball altered this image to make the emancipated slave "an agent in his own deliverance." As the pamphlet notes, the slave in the Freedmen's Monument is "represented as exerting his own strength with strained muscles in breaking the chain which had bound him." To many blacks, however, the slave looked rather passive. See *Oration by Frederick Douglass*, p. 19.

6. *LWFD* 4, p. 174.

7. *TFDP* 1:4, pp. 428, 432.

8. Ibid., p. 431.

9. Ibid., p. 432.

10. Ibid., p. 436. It's significant that Douglass now considered Lincoln's tardiness about emancipation during the first year of the war to be a shrewd political move. It was part of Douglass's amnesia, which paralleled the nation's collective amnesia.

11. W. E. B. Du Bois, *Black Reconstruction in America* (New York, 1930), p. 30.

12. William Lloyd Garrison quit publishing the *Liberator* and retired from activism after the war. By treating emancipation as an end rather than a commencement, he too ignored the great struggle that lay before the friends of freedom.

13. Douglass, *Life and Times*, p. 373; *LWFD* 4, pp. 99–101.

14. *TFDP* 1:2, p. 366.

15. *LWFD* 4, pp. 98–99; William S. McFeely, *Grant: A Biography* (New York: W. W. Norton, 1982), pp. 416–425. In his Freedmen's Monument speech, Douglass's only allusion to the massive terrorism against blacks is when he refers to "the spirit of barbarism, which still lingers to blight and destroy in some dark and distant parts of the country."

16. W. E. B. Du Bois, *The Souls of Black Folk* (1903; reprint, New York: Penguin Books, 1989), p. 7; John Stauffer, "Imagining Emancipation," in *The Problem of Evil: Slavery, Freedom, and the Ambiguities of American Reform*, eds. Steven Mintz and John Stauffer (Am-

herst, Mass.: University of Massachusetts Press, 2007), pp. 221–230; John Stauffer, "Frederick Douglass and the Aesthetics of Freedom," *Raritan* 25:1 (Summer 2005), pp. 114–136.

17. On the role of memory in Douglass's thought, I am especially influenced by David W. Blight, *Frederick Douglass' Civil War: Keeping Faith in Jubilee* (Baton Rouge: Louisiana State University Press, 1989), pp. 219–245.

18. *LWFD* 4, pp. 56–57, 90 (quoted); William S. McFeely, *Frederick Douglass* (New York: W. W. Norton, 1991), pp. 273, 286, 297.

19. *LWFD* 4, pp. 62, 72 (quoted); *New National Era*, March 31, 1871.

20. *LWFD* 4, p. 80 (quoted); *New National Era*, June 13, 1872; McFeely, *Frederick Douglass*, pp. 274–276.

21. *LWFD* 4, pp. 86–89, quotation by Douglass on p. 89; McFeely, *Frederick Douglass*, pp. 281–286; Matthew Josephson, *The Robber Barons: The Great American Capitalists, 1861–1901* (1934; reprint, New York: Harcourt Brace Jovanovich, 1962), pp. 165–173.

22. *LWFD* 4, pp. 99–102, quotation from p. 101.

23. *LWFD* 4, pp. 104–105.

24. *LWFD* 4, pp. 90–94, 104–105; "Personal," *Harper's Weekly*, June 9, 1888. In 1881 *Harper's Weekly* claimed that Douglass had a fortune worth over $100,000. See "Personal," *Harper's Weekly*, November 26, 1881.

25. Douglass, quoted from McFeely, *Frederick Douglass*, pp. 317, 318; John Stauffer, *Black Hearts of Men: Radical Abolitionists and the Transformation of Race* (Cambridge, Mass.: Harvard University Press, 2002), p. 279.

26. The original editorial is in *LWFD* 2, p. 462 (quoted); the excised editorial is in *The Life and Times of Frederick Douglass* (1881, 1892; reprint, New York: Collier Books, 1962), p. 312.

27. Douglass, *Life and Times*, pp. 479 (quoted), 480; Stauffer, "Frederick Douglass and the Aesthetics of Freedom," pp. 131–136; Stauffer, *Black Hearts of Men*, pp. 278–280.

28. On the role of memory in Douglass's postwar thought, see Blight, *Frederick Douglass' Civil War*, pp. 219–245.

29. *TFDP* 1:5, p. 78.

30. *TFDP* 1:5, p. 536.

31. Douglass, "Address Delivered at the Congregational Church, Washington, D.C., on the 21st Anniversary of Emancipation in the District of Columbia," April 19, 1883, p. 14, *DPLC*.

32. *LWFD* 4, pp. 103–113, quotation from Douglass on p. 113; Blight, *Frederick Douglass' Civil War*, pp. 219–245.

33. *LWFD* 4, pp. 113–114; McFeely, *Frederick Douglass*, pp. 291–304.

34. *LWFD* 4, p. 115.

35. *LWFD* 4, p. 116 (quoted); Stauffer, "Frederick Douglass and the Aesthetics of Freedom," p. 134.

36. *LWFD* 4, pp. 115–118, 120–128; McFeely, *Frederick Douglass*, pp. 320–334.

37. Maria Diedrich, *Love Across Color Lines: Ottilie Assing and Frederick Douglass* (New York: Hill and Wang, 1999), pp. 368–373.

38. Diedrich, *Love Across Color Lines*, pp. 368–373.

39. *LWFD* 4, pp. 116–120. Now that Douglass was no longer continually remaking himself, it was easier for him to find deep and lasting love.

40. Joseph Winthrop Holley, *You Can't Build a Chimney from the Top* (New York: William-Frederick Press, 1948), p. 41; *LWFD* 4, p. 149 (quoted); Roy E. Finkenbine, "Frederick Douglass," *American National Biography Online*.

About Twelve
MISSION STATEMENT

TWELVE was established in August 2005 with the objective of publishing no more than one book per month. We strive to publish the singular book, by authors who have a unique perspective and compelling authority. Works that explain our culture; that illuminate, inspire, provoke, and entertain. We seek to establish communities of conversation surrounding our books. Talented authors deserve attention not only from publishers, but from readers as well. To sell the book is only the beginning of our mission. To build avid audiences of readers who are enriched by these works—that is our ultimate purpose.

For more information about forthcoming TWELVE books, you can visit us at www.twelve books.com.